WORKING-CLASS HOLLYWOOD

D0083740

WORKING-CLASS HOLLYWOOD

SILENT FILM AND THE SHAPING
OF CLASS IN AMERICA

Steven J. Ross

PRINCETON UNIVERSITY PRESS   PRINCETON, NEW JERSEY

Copyright © 1998 by Princeton University Press
Published by Princeton University Press, 41 William Street,
Princeton, New Jersey 08540
In the United Kingdom: Princeton University Press,
Chichester, West Sussex

All Rights Reserved

Third printing, and first paperback printing, 1999

Paperback ISBN 0-691-02464-2

The Library of Congress has cataloged the cloth edition of this book as follows

Ross, Steven J., 1949–
Working-class Hollywood : silent film and the shaping of class
in America / Steven J. Ross.
p. cm.
Includes bibliographical references and index.
ISBN 0-691-03234-3 (alk. paper)
1. Working class in motion pictures. 2. Silent films—History
and criticism. 3. Motion pictures—Political aspects—United States.
4. Working class—United States—History—20th century. I. Title.
PN1995.9.L28R67 1998
791.43'6520623—dc21   97-8462

This book has been composed in Berkeley Book Modified

The paper used in this publication meets the minimum requirements of
ANSI/NISO Z39.48-1992 (R1997) (*Permanence of Paper*)

http://pup.princeton.edu

Printed in the United States of America

10 9 8 7 6 5 4 3

For Linda

Contents

Illustrations

Preface _____

"I ONCE said something about the lower class in the hearing of my mother," biographer Stephen Birmingham recounted several years ago. "She slapped me and said: 'There are no classes in America!' Then she said, 'of course there are, but we *never* talk about it." Americans today do not like talking about "class" and when they do, they like to think of themselves and their nation as "middle class." This became clear to me after several years of teaching social and labor history at the University of Southern California. Most of my undergraduates assumed that the United States had always been a middle-class society and that anyone who considered themselves middle class *was* middle class. I argued that this was not always the case. For much of the nineteenth century, Americans talked about themselves as producers who belonged to a broadly defined working class. Not until the early decades of the twentieth century did large numbers of people talk about themselves as consumers who belonged to a broadly defined middle class.[1]

After years of similar discussions, I began wondering how Americans came to produce this common-sense "truth" about the middle class. Like many other "new" working-class histories of the 1980s, my first book, *Workers On the Edge: Work, Leisure, and Politics in Industrializing Cincinnati, 1788–1890*, ended on the eve of two developments that profoundly altered modern class identities: the rise of mass production and mass consumption. Rather than return to the nineteenth century, I decided to take my research forward and try to understand how twentieth-century Americans came to conceive of themselves and their nation as "middle class." At the same time, I also wanted to understand why so many Americans today seem to hold disparaging views of blue-collar workers and labor unions.[2]

Unsure how to start such a massive undertaking, I began working with fellow historian Michael Kazin on a history of Labor Day parades. I hoped that studying the changing language and cultural imagery of class from 1882 to the present would offer clues for understanding the transition from working-class to middle-class identity. It did, but not in the way I expected. As I read through early twentieth-century labor newspapers, I kept coming across descriptions of feature films and newsreels made by workers, socialists, labor unions, and radical organizations. Curious to know more about these films, I consulted two pioneering works in the social history of American cinema, Robert Sklar's *Movie-Made America* and Lary May's *Screening out the Past*. Although both contained a great deal of information about the economic and cultural contexts in which movies emerged, they said nothing about these early worker filmmakers. I did find a substantial literature about radical filmmakers of the 1930s and 1940s, but there were few references to worker or radical productions of the silent era. Unwittingly, I had uncovered the existence of a previously "unknown" working-class film movement.[3]

I soon set out to learn more about these working-class productions. Since histories of the early movie industry yielded little information, I turned to sources rarely used by cinema scholars: labor and radical periodicals, union records, and union convention proceedings. To my surprise, these seemingly staid documents contained a wealth of information about changing economic and labor conditions within the burgeoning movie industry, astute reviews of the latest movies, and extensive descriptions of films made by labor and the political left. Taken collectively, they revealed how unionists and radicals, upset by the way they were being depicted on the screen, decided to produce films that offered audiences positive portrayals of their organizations and goals. In this country, as well as in England, France, Belgium, Germany, Holland, and the Soviet Union, labor and the left used the newest medium of mass culture, silent movies, as a political weapon in their struggles for greater justice and power.[4]

Reconstructing the history of working-class films and filmmakers was only half the story. To understand the significance of this oppositional film movement, I had to understand what they were opposing. That meant learning about the history of the early film industry and the ways in which filmmakers portrayed the general problems of working-class life. Reading through trade periodicals, censorship records, government documents, and watching nearly two hundred silent movies made by unionists, radicals, reformers, commercial filmmakers, government agencies, and big businesses led me to see the myriad ways in which different groups used film to shape public consciousness about class conflict and class identity. Just as I was preparing to publish my initial findings, Kay Sloan, Peter Stead, and Kevin Brownlow produced excellent books that analyzed silent movies by and about workers. With the appearance of these works and several of my own articles, the worker film movement finally moved out of the realm of the "unknown."[5]

My research eventually revealed six themes that struck me as especially important: first, class was a central theme in silent films, and audiences saw hundreds of movies that dealt with strikes, union organizing, and socialist efforts to overthrow American capitalism; second, workers and radicals made movies that challenged the dominant political ideals of the day and offered alternative visions for achieving a more democratic society; third, frightened that radicalism on the screen might inspire radicalism off the screen, censors and government authorities fought to keep these images out of American theaters; fourth, movies and the movie industry had a rich history well before the emergence of "Hollywood" and its attendant studio system; fifth, working-class people were the industry's main audience before American entry into World War I (April 1917) and it was not until the construction of movie palaces after the war that the bulk of the "middle class" flocked to the movies on a regular basis; and sixth, the changing class composition of audiences in the 1920s was accompanied by a shift from highly polemical films that explored conflict between the classes to far more conservative films that emphasized fantasies of love and harmony among the classes.

By this point, I knew I had found my next book. Here was a medium that turned abstract ideas of "class," "class conflict," and "class identity" into visible images that were seen by millions of Americans. In so doing, movies played an important role in shaping, not just reflecting, popular understandings of these vague and often confusing terms. Class and class consciousness are not static academic concepts but dynamic human relationships forged and expressed in a variety of settings—in the workplace, the neighborhood, the family, the voting booth, and, the movie theater. "Class," as English scholar E. P. Thompson observes, "is a cultural as much as an economic formation." The ways in which people come to perceive their "social class" depend not only on what they do for a living but, as historian Philip Ethington notes, "upon the discourse or language within which individuals understand their position in society."[6]

Movies offered one such language. They taught audiences, especially newly arrived immigrants, what it meant to dress, to think, and to act like a member of a particular class. Emerging at a time when dramatic changes in production and occupations generated great confusion over traditional class identities, movies presented Americans with competing visions of what the working class, middle class, and upper class looked like. Whether the vast numbers of white-collar and service sector employees would think of themselves as working class or middle class (something not clear at the time), and whether they would identify their interests with unions or employers could be strongly influenced by what they saw on the screen. Certainly movies were not the only institution offering such lessons. Yet by attracting 80 to 100 million people a week in the late 1920s, a figure that nearly equaled the entire population, movies were bound to have a profound impact on national consciousness.

Writing a book about how silent filmmakers dealt with class required me to cross disciplinary lines in order to answer a number of perplexing questions: How did filmmakers transfer abstract ideas about class and class conflict into concrete images that moved across a screen? How did films made by workers and radicals differ from other films? Did these movies have any impact outside the movie theater? Why did Hollywood filmmakers of the 1920s shift their focus from the problems of working-class life to the promises of middle-class consumerism? What were the political costs of this shift?

As a labor historian, I knew that movies were not just objects of amusement but products made in workplaces. A thorough analysis of movies also had to include an analysis of the industry that produced them. I was especially interested in seeing how the rise of the large corporate industry that came to be known as Hollywood and ensuing changes in studio labor relations affected the images of unions, strikes, and working-class life seen on the screen. In short, I wanted to analyze the material factors that affected the content and ideology of silent films and see how those ideas spread back through society.

Answering questions about the political and cultural impact of film led me to read works in cultural studies. Movies can change the ways in which people think about themselves and their world, but how they do so is a subject of heated debate among scholars. For many years, writings about film were dominated by scholars who emphasized the allegedly manipulative powers of mass culture. Neo-Marxist theorists (from Frankfurt School writers of the 1930s and 1940s to New Left radicals of the 1960s and 1970s) and conservative "mass society" critics of the Cold War era tended to portray movies, radio, and television as activities imposed from above upon gullible audiences. Working people were seen as passive consumers of culture and rarely as actors capable of producing culture. These scholars presented mass culture, especially film, as a phenomenon that lulled the working classes into believing they were happier than they really were and, in so doing, dissipated energies that might otherwise have gone into constructive political action.[7]

The received wisdom of both schools, however, proved inadequate in explaining the existence of a grass-roots worker film movement dedicated to altering class consciousness and inspiring class action. Recent works in cultural studies proved far more useful in helping me place this movement in a larger political context. During the past decades, a new generation of scholars rejected the idea that people "must be 'cultural dopes,'" and documented the intense interclass struggles over the reception and uses of mass culture. In Europe, Raymond Williams, Richard Hoggart, Stuart Hall, and others portray popular and mass culture as contested terrains of resistance and accommodation to the dominant ideas and values of society. In the United States, Roy Rosenzweig, Frank Couvares, Kathy Peiss, and Lizabeth Cohen reject social-control models and show how working-class audiences often used various forms of mass culture to further specific class, gender, and ethnic needs.[8] Practitioners of the "new" film history also contest simplistic notions of a united bourgeoisie (that is, ruling capitalist class) easily imposing its will on movies and the movie industry. They show how economic, social, political, and technological pressures affected the content of film and the evolution of the film industry. Yet, although these studies have sharpened our understanding of the vibrant cultural struggles between different groups and classes, they still portray mass culture as something produced from above and see the power of the masses as confined largely to the realm of reception.[9]

This book takes these works a step further by telling four interconnected stories: how silent filmmakers portrayed working people and their struggles; the rise and fall of the first worker film movement; the important role silent movies played in shaping modern class identities; and how the changing structure of the film industry, especially the emergence of what came to be known as Hollywood, effected all of the above. The title *Working-Class Hollywood* reflects the tensions within an industry that made working people the frequent subjects of its films but fought to keep worker filmmakers on its outskirts. At the same time, it also reflects the possibilities for creating a different kind of film industry. Hollywood did not have to become the fantasy factory that it is today. Between 1900 and 1930, when the class character of the movies was still being formed, worker filmmakers fought with movie industry personnel, federal agencies, and local and state censors to define the kinds of images and political subjects audiences would be allowed to see. The outcome of these struggles were critical to our own times, for the victors got to set the ideological visions of class relations that would dominate American cinema for the next seventy years.

Silent films offer a window into the problems, politics, and conflicts of the early twentieth century. By placing movies in their larger historical context and analyzing their repeated images and messages, we can begin to see how ideology was visualized, popularized, and sold to mass audiences. In shaping the way earlier generations of Americans looked at workers, unions, radicals, employers, capitalism, and socialism, silent filmmakers also affected the way Americans today think—or fail to think—about questions of class and class identity. Let us open that window and look at a world that is far less distant than many people might believe.

Acknowledgments _____

I THOUGHT I could finish this book in three or four years. Ten years later, I find myself indebted to many friends and institutions. Fellowships from the John and Dora Haynes Foundation, the Arnold and Lois Graves Foundation, and the University of Southern California provided me with time and money for research and writing. I am grateful for the help given to me by archivists at the Academy of Motion Picture Arts and Sciences (especially Sam Gill); the Museum of Modern Art (Charles Silver, Mary Corliss); the George Eastman House (Paolo Cherchi Usai); the Library of Congress (David Parker); the American Museum of the Moving Image (Richard Koszarski); the Cinema/Television Library, U.S.C. (Ned Comstock, David Shepard); the Film and Television Archives (Danny Einstein, Bob Git, Eric Aijala) and University Research Library (Sharon Huling) of U.C.L.A.; the National Archives; the Special Collections Department and Theater Arts Collection, New York Public Library; the Special Collections Department, University of Washington; Special Collections, Hillman Library, University of Pittsburgh; and the Southern California Library for Social Studies and Research (Sara Cooper and Mary Tyler). Thanks to Victoria Watkins for helping with early research and to Dana Frank for sharing her notes on the Seattle labor movement with me.

I was able to give greater life to my understanding of the silent era by interviewing a number of people who either worked in the industry during the silent era or were involved in radical filmmaking during the 1930s and 1940s. I want to thank the following individuals for talking with me: studio workers Roy Brewer, Bill Edwards, Ted Ellsworth, Harry Eston, and Milton Sarati; Seattle unionist and former Teamster's union president Dave Beck; actress Rose Hobart; radical filmmaker Leo Hurwitz, and film critic David Platt.

I also want to acknowledge those who commented on various parts of the manuscript. Thanks go to my graduate students, past and present: Derek Adams, Clark Davis, Jill Fields, John Horn, Karen Ward Mahar, Laurie Pintar, George Potamianos, Emily Rader, and Tom Zakim. Likewise, thanks to my colleagues at U.S.C. for their encouragement over the years. Some went even further and actually read my work: Elinor Accampo, Lois Banner, Margo Bistis, Ron Gottesman, and Mauricio Mazon. Ed Perkins, who teaches business history at U.S.C., has been a special friend and great critic. Convincing Ed that my arguments *might* be right has forced me to become a much tougher thinker. Thanks, too, to Ed Berenson, Kevin Brownlow, Bob Edelman, and Ruth Graham for alternating kind praise with excellent criticism. My most consistent source of intellectual advice has come from the members of the Los Angeles Social History Study Group, folks who know how to combine good food with even better discussions: Hal Barron, Nancy Fitch, Doug Flamming, Jackie Greenberg, Darryl Holter, Sandy Jacoby, Lon Kurashige, John Laslett, Margo McBane, Jan Reiff, Bob Slayton, Frank Stricker, Devra Weber, Henry Yu, and Leila Zenderland. I also want to thank the members of the Working-Class History Seminar of the Pittsburgh Center for Social History and the Shelby Cullom Davis Center at Princeton University who commented on earlier versions of this project.

I am fortunate to have had two editors on this book: Lauren Osborne and Mary Murrell. Lary May and Charles Musser, the manuscript's not so anonymous readers, helped turn this into a far better book. I want to thank Lary for teaching me a great deal about American history over the years; although we disagree on a number of issues, I continue to value his advice, wisdom, and friendship. Likewise, Charlie, a superb scholar of the silent era, offered me meticulously detailed suggestions for improving the manuscript. Phil Ethington, a U.S.C. colleague, study group member, and close friend, gave me the intellectual support and smart advice I needed to finish the project. He constantly pushed me to go farther than I thought I could and even read the manuscript twice to make sure that I followed through on his suggestions.

No one is happier that this book is finally done than my children, Lydia and Gabriel. They have lived with Daddy retreating to his study for far too many weekends. I promise them that now I will practice leisure rather than just write about it. My greatest thanks go to Linda Kent, my wife and best friend. Without her support, insight, and companionship over the years, my life, as well as this book, would have been very dull, indeed. This book is lovingly dedicated to her.

Part I

THE RISE OF THE MOVIES:
POLITICAL FILMMAKING AND THE
WORKING CLASS

Introduction _____

Class conflict is not a subject we usually associate with the movies. However, during the first three decades of the twentieth century, when the movie industry was still in its formative stages, movies and movie theaters were battlegrounds for control of the consciousness and class loyalties of millions of Americans. Going to the movies was more than just an evening's entertainment. It was an experience that could transform lives. This is the story of what movies used to be, of an industry that began long before Hollywood, California, became the nation's filmmaking capital, and of the people who tried to change the world through film. To understand the tremendous power of early movies, we need to go back several decades before motion pictures made their debut in the United States and enter the world of the millions of working-class men, women, and children whose nickels and dimes would build the American film industry.

During the late nineteenth century, class conflict was a burning issue that created deep cleavages in American society. *Progress and Poverty* (1879), as the title of Henry George's best-selling book suggested, were the dual legacies of the industrial revolution: progress for some, poverty for many. Earlier generations of skilled craftsmen who built complete products and were well paid for doing so were slowly replaced by semi- and unskilled factory operatives who performed a series of poorly paid repetitive tasks. If a man lost an arm or a leg on the job, he was let go and forced to fend for himself. This was a world with no health care plans to help with illness or injury, no unemployment insurance for hard times, and no social security for old age. With many fathers unable to feed and house their families, and women paid only a fraction of the wages earned by men, millions of boys and girls were forced to forsake their childhood and go to work in factories, mines, or textile mills, where many were maimed—physically or psychologically—for life.

Life outside the workplace was often bleak, especially for the millions of immigrants who poured into the nation's cities. Coming to what they had hoped would be the land of opportunity, Italians, Russians, Poles, and other émigrés found themselves living in slums where sanitation was minimal and disease rampant; where infants often died before their first birthday; where the smell of streets fouled by horses assaulted the senses; where crowded tenement flats that lacked ventilation, sanitary facilities, hot water, and sunlight provided little haven from the rigors of daily life.

Life on the farm and on the western frontier proved equally difficult. Fluctuating crop prices meant periodic bankruptcy for families that had worked the land for decades. In the South, former slaves and poor whites entered a new kind of quasi slavery working as sharecroppers. Out in the Far West, Chinese, Japanese, and Mexican immigrants met with extreme prejudice at the hands of Anglo residents who resented them, politicians who discriminated against them, and employers who hired them to perform the most dangerous jobs at low wages.

This was only one side of America. The Civil War that ended in 1865 brought peace to the nation and great wealth to the few who became millionaires from lucrative wartime contracts. Those living in mansions along New York's Fifth Avenue, in opulent apartments on San Francisco's Nob Hill, and on estates in Newport, Rhode Island, were interested in the sweet, not the sweat, of life. They did not want to know who made the fabric for their silk gowns or wove the wool for their suits—or who built their homes, their streets, and their city. The "New Rich," as one former newsman dubbed them, were more concerned with throwing extravagant dinner parties designed to impress their peers. At one such party, "cigarettes rolled in hundred-dollar bills were passed around after the coffee and consumed with authentic thrill."[1] Little wonder, then, that millions of ordinary Americans were filled with a sense of hopelessness and despair, a sense that this was the only way the world could be.

Some people, however, believed justice could be achieved, and risked their lives in its pursuit. In the economic realm, workers repeatedly challenged employers by striking for better pay, fewer hours, and safer working conditions. But working-class protests were frequently beaten back by capitalists who relied on private armies, federal troops, and national guardsmen to suppress strikes—often at the cost of hundreds killed and thousands wounded. In the political arena, impassioned citizens challenged Democrats and Republicans by organizing rival United Labor, Populist, and Socialist parties that promoted agendas for change that were often quite radical in their rhetoric. But these challenges were thwarted by the established parties, who coopted third-party candidates and adopted their more reformist demands.[2]

There was one realm in which challenges to authority were not so easily suppressed by employers, troops, or politicians. Beginning at Koster and Bial's Music Hall in 1896 and blossoming after the opening of the first "nickelodeons" (the early name for movie theaters) in 1905, the leisure realm was revolutionized by a new medium that communicated directly with millions of Americans; a realm which, in its early years, expressed political views that were remarkably sympathetic to the plight of the working class.

Movies captured the public imagination like nothing before them. They were markedly different from previous forms of popular culture that were locally created and associated with particular groups or classes. Movies became "mass culture" in two important ways: they were mass-produced commercial products and they reached a mass audience that included all groups, classes, and regions. Although newspapers are generally considered the nation's first medium of mass culture, their readership was divided by sectarian politics and by the language of the paper. Not many conservatives were likely to read the socialist *New York Call*, nor were many unionists likely to look at the anti-labor *Los Angeles Times*. And few native-born Americans were likely to read a foreign-language newspaper. Movies, however, transcended political and language differences and attracted a diverse array of Americans. "Far more people today are reached by the moving picture than by the daily press," one reporter noted in 1908, "and while we read the newspaper only in parts, the moving picture we see complete."[3]

Visual images maintained a strong grip on the mind's eye and treated complex political issues more clearly than most books, newspapers, or speeches. Immigrants who neither read nor spoke English could understand visual messages. When asked why he had offered political cartoonist Thomas Nast the extraordinary sum of $500,000 to stop caricaturing him and his Tammany Hall cronies in *Harper's Weekly*, New York's infamous "Boss" Tweed reportedly responded: "I don't care so much what the papers write about me—my constituents can't read; but they can understand pictures."[4]

Film was even more realistic than newspaper cartoons. Watching early movies in a dimly lit storefront theater was a profound and perhaps life-altering experience for millions of workers and immigrants who believed no one knew or cared about their hardships. Imagine their amazement as they looked up and saw *their* struggles and aspirations on the screen. Surrounded by people who laughed when they laughed and cried when they cried, movie neophytes felt less alone, less alienated than before. Hard-working immigrants who came to the Land of Opportunity only to face poverty and distress might stop blaming themselves for their plight after watching a film like *The Italian* (New York Motion Picture Co., 1915). Like its hero, Beppo Donnetti, they might begin to realize that many of their problems were caused by crooked politicians, avaricious companies, and a judicial system that turned a deaf ear to the sufferings of the poor. And once they realized this, they and millions like them might try to change the world.

Social realism and political commentary are not the hallmarks of the modern movie industry. Yet there was a time when entertainment and political engagement did not seem incompatible, and when movies and Hollywood were not synonymous in the minds of most Americans. The movie industry began as a small-scale business with small, spartan theaters spread throughout the country and production facilities centered largely in New York, Philadelphia, and Chicago. When entrepreneurs saw how wildly popular the new medium had become among the nation's working masses, they quickly opened film companies in Florida, Colorado, Texas, New Jersey, Louisiana, and California. The first movie studio did not reach Hollywood until 1911, and even as late as 1914, recounted one silent filmmaker, "the name Holly-wood meant nothing to the people of this country; even the picture fans hadn't heard of it."[5] Only after the outbreak of World War I that year and the suspension of European filmmaking did the modern entity we call "Holly-wood" begin to take shape.

From their inception, movies were vehicles of propaganda as well as edu-cation and entertainment. They were made by groups that today we would not usually associate with the film industry. Although some middle-class reformers and religious leaders condemned films for their allegedly immoral and corrupting influence, others seized on their potential to sway public opinion and win greater support for their cause. Before expensive multi-reel features severely limited access to the market, the modest costs of making a one- or two-reel film allowed a wide range of reform organizations, labor unions, socialists, communists, politicians, bankers, businesses, woman suffragists, religious associations, and government agencies to produce par-tisan films that addressed national debates over the values and directions of American society.

Silent films quickly became part of an expanding public sphere in which competing political ideas were discussed and public opinion molded. Mo-tion pictures took people out of their neighborhoods and brought the won-ders—and problems—of the age to life in a way that no other medium could rival. In so doing, movies turned local and regional issues into subjects of national concern. What went on in the sweatshops of New York's Lower East Side or in the textile mills of North Carolina could now be seen by distant audiences in Oklahoma and Nebraska. Similarly, the bitter labor conflicts that raged in western coal and copper fields were portrayed and explained to recently arrived immigrants as well as longtime residents of eastern and southern states.

No sector initially responded with more enthusiasm to the early movies than the nation's working class. The black sharecropper in Kentucky, the Hungarian steel worker in Pennsylvania, the Jewish garment worker in New York, and the Mexican cannery worker in California reacted so strongly to the poignant scenes of sadness and joy on the screen that they quickly em-braced the medium as their own. "For a mere nickel," explained one con-temporary writer, "the wasted man, whose life hereto has been toil and sleep is kindled with wonder; he sees alien people and begins to understand how like they are to him; he sees courage and aspirations and agony and begins to understand himself. He begins to feel a brother in a race that is led by many dreams."[6]

For nearly two decades after the first nickelodeon opened in 1905, movies and the working class were intertwined in three important ways: working people were the industry's main audience; they were the frequent subjects of films; and they were makers of movies—both as employees who labored in studio lots and as independent producers who turned out their own pictures. Often referred to as "the poor man's amusement," movie theaters took root in blue-collar and immigrant neighborhoods and slowly spread outward into middle-class areas and small towns throughout the nation. The low cost of moviegoing made films accessible to virtually every man, woman, and child. By 1910, nearly one-third of the population flocked to movie theaters each week; a decade later, nearly half the population did so.[7]

A medium that "started by being entertainment for people of small means" quickly evolved into what filmmaker William de Mille hailed as "the most socially important form of drama in the world." Filmmakers were more concerned with portraying the hardships of working-class life during the silent era than at any subsequent time in the industry's history. Movies turned class struggles previously confined to the hidden, private realm of factories, mines, and fields into highly visible parts of public culture. Displaying a depth of political commitment and range of competing ideologies and passions rarely seen today, silent filmmakers presented conservative, liberal, radical, and populist solutions to the most heated labor problems of the age. And they did so in an entertaining fashion that captured viewers' attention and lingered in their memories far longer than the printed word or spoken phrase. In comparing the film version of Upton Sinclair's *The Jungle* (1914) to the novel, one movie reviewer noted: "It is possible to read the book and then merely register a vow never to eat tinned goods again. But after seeing the picture we begin to have burned into us that Packingtown made enormous profits not simply out of tainted food, but out of the ruined lives of men and women."[8]

The openness of a new industry that included producers such as the American Federation of Labor, the Ford Motor Company, the National Association of Manufacturers, the Women's Political Union, and the National Child Labor Committee allowed a wide range of political points of view to reach the screen. Yet of all these groups, working-class filmmakers were the most ambitious and persistent. As early as 1907, workers, radicals, and labor organizations were making movies that challenged the dominant ideology of individualism and portrayed collective action—whether in the form of unionism or socialist politics—as the most effective way to improve the lives of citizens. Over the next two decades, labor and the left forged an oppositional cinema that used film as a medium of hope to educate, entertain, and mobilize millions of Americans.

The people who led this movement were not filmmakers who happened to be radicals, but members of labor and radical organizations who grasped the manipulative powers of film and used them to reach vast numbers of men and women who never attended union rallies or listened to socialist speakers. These early propagandists of the screen understood film's potential for uniting diverse groups of wage earners whose religion, ethnicity, language, race, and gender differed but whose basic problems were the same. Coming from a variety of backgrounds, worker filmmakers (a term I use to describe workers, labor or radical organizations, or worker-owned production companies who made labor-oriented films) shared one common goal: to make wage earners understand that their collective power was far greater than they realized; that a united working class could solve many of the problems that plagued the nation.

Presenting their political messages in the form of entertaining melodramas and love stories, worker-made movies offered viewers blueprints for change that enabled them to *see* what the future could look like. Movie audiences throughout the country watched fiery New York stenographer Louise Laffayette lead striking factory workers in a successful battle for higher wages and union recognition. They watched working-class voters reject the corrupt politics of the past and elect iron molder Dan Grayson to serve as governor of California on the Socialist ticket. They watched European, Hispanic, black, and female textile workers in Passaic, New Jersey, join together to challenge the combined power of mill owners and local police. They watched working people become the heroes and heroines of their own lives.[9]

It was, however, a strange cast of characters who led the worker film movement. The most prominent participants included a poor boy from Kentucky who began working on a flatboat at the age of fourteen and who thirty years later made a socialist film that featured a cast of 10,000; a pioneering producer who opened Hollywood's first studio in 1911 and then several years later, after his conversion to socialism, sold his business to the Brotherhood of Railway Trainmen; a shady writer-director who was tailed during the first World War by J. Edgar Hoover's secret agents for allegedly smuggling guns across the Mexican border; a writer who thought of himself as the world's greatest radical intellectual; a producer-distributor who ran a labor film company while running for governor of New York on the Socialist ticket; and a former "die-hard Republican" who was sentenced to twenty years in Leavenworth prison by future baseball commissioner Judge Kenesaw Mountain Landis for his anti-war activities. No studio screenwriter could have invented a more eclectic group to challenge the nation's political and economic establishment.[10]

Much to their delight, worker filmmakers discovered that what happened on the screen could affect class relations outside the movie theater. Connecticut mill workers went out on strike in 1916 after watching strike scenes in *The Blacklist* (1916). Recently converted socialists testified that radical films such as *From Dusk to Dawn* (1913) and *The Jungle* (1914) inspired them to join the movement. Seattle labor unions were roused to combat anti-union campaigns after viewing *The New Disciple* (1921). What inspired some, however, frightened others. Unnerved by the frequency with which cinematic radicalism was translated into workplace radicalism, local and state movie censors often banned worker films "calculated to stir up . . . antagonistic relations between labor and capital."[11] Federal authorities also moved to limit the exhibition of radical films. Bureau of Investigation director J. Edgar Hoover considered these class-conscious productions so dangerous that he assigned agents to send him extensive information about the films and their makers. These guardians of law and order feared that labor movies, like Labor Day parades, might pull thousands of workers onto city streets. And what if, instead of peaceful marches, movies sparked violent protests?

This ambitious working-class quest to politicize audiences grew far more difficult in the postwar era. The rapid expansion of American film production signaled the rise of a new type of film industry and the birth of "Hollywood" as a metaphor to describe it. By the early 1920s, Hollywood was less a place than a new way of doing business. It was "invented" by a small group of ambitious entrepreneurs, led by the likes of Adolph Zukor, Jesse Lasky, William Fox, and Carl Laemmle, who transformed the modestly sized, geographically dispersed industry of prewar years into a powerful, well-financed studio system, centered in Los Angeles county, that attempted to dominate all ends of the business and force all rivals off the screen.

Far from being the liberal institution it is depicted as today, Hollywood pushed the politics of American cinema in increasingly noncontroversial and anti-radical directions. Studio moguls realized they could make big money by turning moviegoing into a "respectable" entertainment that catered to the rapidly expanding and amorphous ranks of the middle class. This was a time when class identities were still in flux; it was unclear whether the mushrooming numbers of low-level white collar and service sector employees were working class or middle class. Playing to people's dreams of upward mobility, industry leaders built exotic movie palaces in "safe" neighborhoods and provided luxurious amenities that allowed moviegoers to think they were middle class—at least for a few hours. Hesitant to make controversial films that might alienate newly won audiences, studios abandoned old themes of class conflict in favor of making films that promoted conservative visions of class harmony; films that shifted attention away from the problems of the workplace and toward the pleasures of the new consumer society. At the same time that worker filmmakers were trying to heighten class consciousness, Hollywood producers were suggesting that class no longer mattered.

Could worker filmmakers continue making class-conscious movies in such an environment? Or would they be stopped by those who feared that powerful moving images would move the masses too far? The stakes involved in these battles were high. The winners would shape the ways in which subsequent generations of moviegoers would look at the problems of class and the possible solutions to class conflict.

Silent films played a vital role in molding the political consciousness of millions of Americans. Movie audiences were not just consumers of culture but citizens who voted on election day. Seeing the same problems and the same images over and over again undoubtedly forced many moviegoers to think about contemporary issues in new ways. What people saw on the screen could sway public policy. Films advocating the abolition of child labor, prison reform, and factory safety laws helped raise public awareness and, in so doing, eased passage of laws aimed at correcting these problems. By making class conflict visible, movies played an equally important role in shaping public responses to hotly contested class issues. Whether citizens would demand greater protection for strikers or strikebreakers, for unions or employers, and whether they would consider voting for socialist politicians might well be decided by what they learned in movie theaters. Consequently, what viewers did not see, as movie censors understood, could be as important as what they did see.

Working-Class Hollywood is a story of one of the greatest power struggles in American history—a struggle for the control of American consciousness. During the early decades of the twentieth century, no one knew what form the emerging movie industry would take, either in terms of its structure or the politics of its films. The fantasy industry we now call Hollywood was only one of several possibilities. Hollywood did not just happen. It was shaped by a series of contentious skirmishes among an array of groups with a variety of political visions. None, however, fought harder or longer than the worker filmmakers who battled to create a movie industry in which liberal and radical films about working people and their problems would remain a regular part of American cinema; an industry in which Hollywood and the working class would be synonymous. *Working-Class Hollywood* is both a history of what was and a reminder of what could have been.

1 _____

Going to the Movies: Leisure, Class, and
Danger in the Early Twentieth Century

ON A WARM spring night in 1910, millions of excited Americans set out for
an evening of entertainment. In San Francisco, an elegantly dressed couple
stepped out of their carriage and entered the luxurious lobby of the Columbia Theater, where they had come to hear *Tosca*. In Boston, a middle-aged
merchant and his wife journeyed to the Shubert Theater, bought two orchestra seats for one dollar each, and prepared to be amused by the musical
comedy *The Midnight Sons*. In Kansas City, a group of less well-heeled clerical workers met downtown at the Orpheum Theater, paid their forty-five
cents, and settled in to enjoy ten acts of vaudeville. In New York City, thousands of working people—native born and foreign born, black and white,
young and old—made their way to neighborhood movie theaters where,
after paying five or ten cents, they proceeded to cheer, boo, and sing along
with the images that flickered across the screen.

The desire for fun is timeless, but the ways in which people have amused
themselves are not. The early years of the twentieth century witnessed the
dramatic appearance of a variety of new commercial recreations. As the
average work week decreased and wages rose, Americans looked for new
ways to spend their increased time and money. An emerging generation of
entrepreneurs quickly discovered that a population willing to buy their food
rather than grow it, and buy their clothing rather than make it, would also
buy their entertainment rather than create it. In large cities, small towns,
rural hamlets, and mining camps the thirst for fun sparked the unprecedented proliferation of dance halls, billiard parlors, vaudeville and burlesque houses, amusement parks, and professional sports. Yet none of these
activities was more popular than the movies. By 1910, 26 million people,
nearly 30 percent of the nation's population, flocked to the movies each
week. Ten years later, 50 million Americans, half the population, went
weekly to one of the 15,000 theaters or 22,000 churches, halls, and schools
that screened movies.[1]

Going to the movies is not an activity most Americans today associate
with danger or transgressive behavior. But this was not always the case. No
early amusement created greater fear—and pleasure—than the movies.
From the appearance of the first nickelodeons in 1905 until the early 1920s,

when star-studded features and lavish picture palaces gave the industry a patina of respectability, movies and movie theaters were often arenas of turmoil and contention. The political content of films and the places in which they were shown were far more open and unpredictable during the first two decades of the new century than at any subsequent time. Often located in working-class areas where few "respectable" folks dared enter, movie theaters were fluid social spaces over which audiences exerted considerable control, places where anything might happen and where boisterous patrons frequently transgressed middle-class boundaries of acceptable behavior. Romance, fantasy, sex, adventure, and politics could all be found at the movies.

An activity that most working-class patrons saw as simple fun, others viewed as a dangerous enterprise fraught with untold political consequences. At a time when the country was repeatedly rocked by bitter strikes and deadly incidents of class violence, the growth of a powerful medium that appealed directly and primarily to working-class audiences proved frightening to local and national leaders. Far from being harmless diversions, many early films presented poignant stories of immigrants and workers suffering at the hands of employers, politicians, and hypocritical clergy and civic leaders. More frightening still, the victims of injustice in films often fought back—and won.

By creating a common link between millions of working people who were often divided by ethnicity, religion, race, and gender, movies emerged as a vehicle capable of expressing a new public identity dominated by working-class sensibilities. Reformers such as Frederic C. Howe wrote worriedly about films that "tended to excite class feelings," and warned of the day when movies would become "the daily press of industrial groups, of classes, of Socialism, syndicalism, and radical opinion."[2] Concerned with what they perceived as the multiple political, moral, and physical dangers posed by movies and movie theaters, politicians, clergy, reformers, and civic leaders struggled to alter their forms or shut them down completely.

The years between 1905 and April 1917, between the rise of nickelodeons and American entry into World War I, mark a critical era in the evolution of the movie industry and the class character of its films and audience. This was a time when Hollywood was simply a place and not yet a powerful institution; when audiences, critics, and industry leaders fought over the political direction the fledgling industry would take. To understand why movies could fire the imagination of millions of people and cause consternation among so many others, we need to understand the myriad ways in which they were experienced and the class dangers they appeared to pose. This chapter tells the story of what it was like to go to the movies in the years before the first World War: who went, what they saw, and what they did at this most favored of all amusements.[3]

Working-Class Leisure and the Rise
of Commercial Recreation

"Living for the weekend," a concept so ingrained in modern times, was foreign to the world of the 1800s. Work, not leisure, dominated the daily lives of ordinary Americans. For much of the nineteenth century, wage earners labored ten, twelve, or fourteen hours a day, six days a week. Opportunities for enjoying oneself on Sunday, the one day most workers had off, were often restricted by local blue laws that prohibited commercial amusements from operating on the Sabbath. Consequently, in large cities like New York and small towns like Winona, Minnesota, picnics, sports, church activities, and family outings were among the main forms of popular entertainment.[4]

The leisure revolution of the twentieth century was built upon the industrial revolution of the nineteenth century. The rise of large impersonal factories, the greater reliance on machinery, and the ever-accelerating pace of production created unprecedented increases in output. But they came at the cost of making work more tedious and unsatisfying for the worker. Walter Wyckoff, who left the Princeton Theological Seminary in 1891 and tramped across the country working as an unskilled laborer, spoke sadly about the changing character of work: "There is for us in our work none of the joy of responsibility, none of the sense of achievement, only the dull monotony of grinding toil, with the longing for the signal to quit work, and for our wages at the end of the week."[5]

As work grew less creative and fulfilling, people looked to leisure to provide their lives with new meaning. Rallying around the cry of "Eight Hours for Work, Eight Hours for Rest, and Eight Hours for What We Will," the nation's wage earners succeeded in reducing their labor—largely through strikes and union bargaining—from a seventy-two-hour, six-day work week common before 1860 to a sixty-hour, five-and-a-half-day work week in 1890 (with Saturday afternoons off) and a fifty-one-hour week in 1920. Men and women not only went home earlier, but they also went home with increasingly fatter pay checks. Real wages for nonfarm employees rose by 35 percent between 1890 and 1920.[6]

With more money in their pockets and more time to spend it, working people sought new outlets for amusement in order to gain a sense that work, however oppressive, was at least buying them some measure of life. Enterprising businessmen, "cultural entrepreneurs," as they were often called, were only too happy to satisfy their yearnings—for a modest price. The rapid growth of cities between 1870 and 1920, a remarkable 447 percent increase, created vast new markets for commercial recreations. Massive waves of immigrants, whose numbers rose from 5.6 million in 1870 to

13.9 million in 1920, accounted for much of this dramatic urban growth.[7] With so many potential customers living in such close proximity, it was no surprise that business people—many of them immigrants themselves— rushed in to sell cheap amusements to the masses.

Selling entertainment, however, proved far more complicated than most entrepreneurs imagined. The rise of new commercial recreations in the late nineteenth century was paralleled by the reshaping of class identities and by the growing separation of leisure into "respectable" high culture and "suspect" low culture. When French writer Alexis de Tocqueville traveled through America in 1831–1832, he was struck by the absence of a conspicuous elite culture. "Inequality both of wealth and education is certainly found in private life," he observed. "But for the outsider these inequalities are not noticeable." During the 1870s and 1880s, however, a new generation of wealthy citizens began forging a highly visible American elite. They did so by erecting mansions in exclusive areas like Newport, Rhode Island, and along elegant streets like New York's Fifth Avenue and Chicago's Lake Shore Drive; by publishing "blue books" that listed a city's elite families; and by building exclusive cultural institutions for the rich and respectable.[8]

As the upper ranks of American society grew more visible, the composition of the middle class grew more ambiguous. During the early decades of the nineteenth century, workers, manufacturers, farmers, and merchants spoke of themselves as belonging to a common "producing class"—people who, whether employer or employee, performed productive labors that contributed to the nation's wealth. The growth of industrial capitalism and the rapid expansion of corporations in the latter part of the century precipitated dramatic changes in occupational structures and perceptions of class identity. By 1910, several groups were laying claim to the title "middle class." Farmers, manufacturers, and small businessmen comprised what scholars call the "old middle class," a group generally "committed to prudence and self-restraint." Their numbers and power were rivaled by the rise of a "new middle class" of professionals and salaried corporate managers who "tended to have a less than total allegiance to traditional moralism."[9]

The boundaries between working class and middle class also grew more problematic. Rising alongside the "old" and "new" middle class was a third group of low-level white-collar and service-sector employees whose class status remained unclear. Although today white-collar workers are assumed to be middle class, that was not the case during the early decades of the new century. Many of these young clerks, office workers, and salespeople were the gum-chewing offspring of blue-collar parents who had pushed them to take safer, more secure white-collar jobs. Working among the self-professed middle class but often living in working-class households and neighborhoods, these young men and women moved between two worlds. Whether they thought of themselves as middle class or working class was crucial to capitalists and labor leaders alike. Both understood that a united, self-conscious working class composed of blue and white-collar employees could use their numerical superiority as voters to dominate American political life. Consequently, as leisure joined work as an arena in which different classes came to define themselves and each other, controlling the class character of amusements became an important element in controlling the class consciousness of American society.[10]

Although the barriers between classes or between high and low culture were never completely impenetrable, leisure at this time was often stratified by class, ethnicity, race, gender, age, and physical space. Historian Lawrence Levine observes how, under the control of wealthy patrons, cultural activities once widely attended by all classes—opera, theater, symphony—were increasingly "performed in isolation from other forms of entertainment to an audience that was far more homogeneous than those which had gathered earlier." The "prohibitive price" of "our best theatres," Indianapolis social surveyor James Sizer explained in 1917, "practically excludes all except the wealthy and those who are willing to brave public opinion by taking a cheap seat." Moreover, added Sizer, "if you wish to be respectable, you must take a taxicab and wear a dress suit." Opera- and theater-loving immigrants and workers continued attending performances, but they generally did so in less costly and spatially removed neighborhood venues—which were often segregated and patronized by specific ethnic groups.[11]

With millions of people effectively excluded from expensive entertainments, cultural entrepreneurs created an alternative world of cheaper amusements aimed largely at blue-collar audiences and the rapidly expanding ranks of low-level white-collar workers. Although vaudeville, burlesque, dance halls, amusement parks, and professional sports teams all attracted devoted groups of revelers, none were as cheap or as popular as the movies. People in Cincinnati, San Francisco, Detroit, and Waltham (Mass.) went to the movies so often that weekly attendance in 1913 equaled, respectively, 193 percent, 90 percent, 86 percent, and 72 percent of the city's total population.[12]

Statistics alone cannot reveal the excitement that movies generated among countless men, women, and children. Cultural conservatives spoke of movie theaters as places "of darkness, physical and moral," but for working-class audiences they were exhilarating spaces where fantasies could be lived out and where anything could happen.[13] It was the unpredictability of these experiences that made moviegoing so appealing to the masses and so frightening to elites. Although the nation's elite was composed of a variety of groups (businessmen, financial magnates, major land owners, politicians, and civic leaders), many shared a common dread of what might happen if an untamed working class was exposed to the same kinds of entertainments at roughly the same time. To understand the joy and fear elicited by this new form of mass culture we need to enter the world of its participants and reconstruct what going to the movies was like from the point of view of the moviegoer.

Early Movie Theaters

The era of commercial moving pictures began in New York City on Saturday, April 14, 1894, when the Holland brothers opened the nation's first kinetoscope parlor. Excited customers bent over a kinetoscope (what we might call today a peep show), placed their eye on a small viewing port, and saw one of ten brief action scenes produced by at Thomas Edison's laboratory in West Orange, New Jersey. New Yorkers were given an even bigger thrill on April 23, 1896, when Koster and Bial's Music Hall offered the debut of the country's first successful large-screen motion pictures. Audiences gazed in awe at scenes of waves breaking against a Dover pier, a burlesque boxing bout, a group of soldiers marching to the strains of a military band, and a serpentine dancer who undulated across the screen. Most of these films were no more than 150 feet long, and in the course of fifteen minutes vaudeville patrons might see ten or twelve of them. Nevertheless, moving pictures proved so popular that over the next decade they became fixtures in the nation's better vaudeville houses and among traveling shows, which exhibited them at fairgrounds, churches, and local opera houses.[14]

The age of the modern movie theater began in Pittsburgh on June 19, 1905, when vaudeville magnate Harry Davis and his brother-in-law John P. Harris opened the first site devoted exclusively to showing moving pictures. The Nickelodeon, whose name combined the slang word for the cost of admission (nickel) with the Greek word for theater (odeon), was little more than a remodeled storeroom fitted up with a "white linen sheet, some [ninety-six] opera chairs, a crude phonograph, a lot of stucco, burlap and paint, and a myriad of incandescent light." The opening performance, which consisted of fifteen minutes of film, was greeted with such enthusiasm that it ran from eight in the morning until midnight and purportedly attracted over six thousand customers.[15]

The success of this initial venture led Davis and other entrepreneurs to open nickelodeons in cities and villages across the country. By 1913, every community with a population of five thousand had at least one movie theater and most averaged four. Running a nickelodeon proved especially appealing to immigrants with lots of ambition but little cash. Greeks, Hungarians, Italians, Norwegians, Germans, Irishmen, and especially Jews

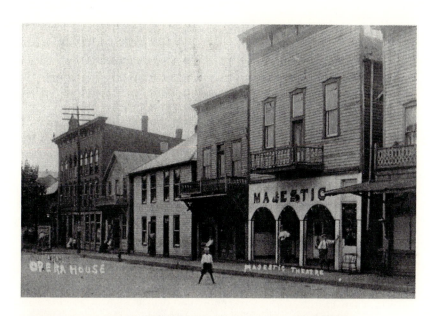

Early films were shown in a wide variety of settings, from the modest Majestic Theatre in Corning, Ohio (top) to the enticing Comet Theatre in New York City (bottom).

were attracted to a venture with low start-up costs and high customer demand. Modest capital requirements and lack of an established male hierarchy in the new business also enabled many women to open their own movie houses. For $200, one could convert a plain storefront into a magical Bijou Dream or Good Time Theater. Future movie industry moguls Adolph Zukor and Marcus Loew (both furriers), William Fox and Harry Warner (clothiers), and Lewis Selznick (a jeweler) all began their ascent to power by switching into the nickelodeon business. When asked what prompted his decision to change trades, Harry Warner, who sold clothing in a store near Davis' Nickelodeon, replied: "I looked across the street and saw the nickels rolling in."[16]

During the next several years, the variety movie theaters expanded to include small storefronts (often known as "nickel dumps") that seated one hundred people; large legitimate theaters or vaudeville houses that were converted into movie theaters; neighborhood theaters built especially to show movies; and, after 1914, opulent movie palaces. Of all these early venues, the nickelodeon was the first to capture the public's imagination. Initially clustered in downtown commercial districts and soon after along densely populated streets in immigrant and working-class neighborhoods, the nickelodeon was designed to attract the eye of the casual passerby. The front of the building was covered in pressed tin or stamped metal that made it shimmer during the day, and bright neon lights spelled out the theater's alluring name—Idle Hours, Dreamland, Happy Times—and lit its exterior at night. Flashy banners and gaudy color posters were plastered across the wall, while barkers or musicians stood next to the box office making loud noises that promised excitement inside. For the ordinary passerby, reminisced one hyperbolic old-timer, these "twinkling, tungsten facades, the apotheosis of pressed tin and light bulb," were "effulgent, wild, and imaginative."[17]

Although contemporary commentators often cringed at the ostentatious exteriors of nickelodeons, they also marveled at their "democratic" interiors. Unlike legitimate theaters or vaudeville houses, where audiences were separated according to their ability to pay, the nickelodeon admitted all customers for a single price and allowed them to sit wherever they wished. Recreational democracy was not, however, desired by all. "In many neighborhoods," *Variety* reported in 1913, "the better class of citizens kept away from the movies because of the strange seat fellows that a nickel made possible." Nickelodeons were, however, warmly embraced by workers and immigrants. Why spend a dime at a "fancy" theater, they reasoned, when you could see a movie for five cents? One Chicago theater lured cost-conscious patrons by charging only two or three cents a show, and exhibitors in Harrison, Arkansas, accepted payment in eggs: two eggs for adults, one for children.[18]

Movie theaters were not the only places people went to see movies. Thousands of churches, schools, unions, factories, settlement houses, and numerous voluntary associations screened carefully selected movies as a means of bolstering attendance. Showing films in church, one Congregational minister discovered, proved an effective way of "reaching out to interest those who remain away from religious service and attend the movies on Sunday."[19]

Avid moviegoers discovered they did not need four walls and a roof to see their favorite films. Bill Edwards, a Los Angeles native and member of Hollywood's first costumers' union, remembers spending evenings with dozens of area residents seated in an open field on Vermont and Jefferson Avenues. The impromptu "theater" was surrounded by a ten-foot high canvas fence and featured a pianist who accompanied the images that flashed on the huge sheet that served as a screen. New Yorker Peggy Nolan recounts a similar experience of packing crackers and dill pickles on Friday nights and going to Chelsea Park to watch movies under the stars. Outdoor screenings in public parks and in open-air theaters called "airdromes" became a regular part of summer life in many of the nation's cities.[20]

Early Audiences

Movie theaters attracted a wide range of patrons. Young and old, black and white, native-born and foreign-born, men and women, poor and well-to-do, Protestants, Catholics, and Jews could all be found at the cinema. Yet few were so passionately devoted to picture shows as the nation's blue-collar workers. Contemporary writers repeatedly referred to movies as the "academy of the working man," the "poor man's amusement," the "Workingman's Theater," and a medium supported by "the nickels of the working class."[21] It was in the "densely populated foreign and labor quarters of the industrial cities," observed film publicist-turned-historian Terry Ramsaye, that movies found their greatest audience. In Manhattan, where Jews, Italians, Poles, and other immigrant wage earners religiously flocked to the movies, a survey conducted in 1910 found that 72 percent of audiences came from the blue-collar sector, 25 percent from the clerical workforce, and 3 percent from what surveyors called the "leisure class." Even in small towns such as Winona, Minnesota, where entrepreneurs hoped to build a middle-class following, movies drew a largely "working-class audience."[22]

Film scholars have debated when middle-class people first started going to the movies, but it is clear that workers and their families composed the bulk of the moviegoing population before World War I. Certainly, some adventurous members of the "old" and "new" middle class attended movies before the war, and especially after the appearance of the first movie palaces in 1914. Confusion over how many went stems from the flawed assumption held by many social surveyors of the time (and by some scholars today) that white-collar workers could be unproblematically classified as middle class. This is a premise that not all white-collar workers shared. We must not read back into the past current assumptions about class identity. It was not until the early 1920s, as we shall see in Chapter 7, when hundreds of luxurious movie palaces were built and when many white-collar and some blue-collar workers came to see themselves as "middle class" that moviegoing became a *regular* activity for all sectors of the middle class.[23]

The appeal of movies was simple: they were cheap, convenient, easily understood, and, most important, fun. For five cents, any man, woman, or child could escape the crowded slums or dismal tenement flats by walking into a nearby theater and find themselves magically transported to another place and time. "If I ever go to Berlin or Paris I will know what the places look like," a Harlem cigar-store clerk gushed in 1907. "I have seen runaways in the Boys de Boulong [sic] and a kidnapping in the Unter der Linden. I know what a fight in an alley in Stamboul looks like. . . . I know a lot of the pictures are fakes, but what of it? It costs only five cents."[24]

Movies offered millions of hard-working men and women a quick fix of pleasure to ease the pain and tedium of the daily work grind. Audiences could forget their problems and allow fantasy to take over—so much so that they occasionally forgot where they were. Film director King Vidor tells of visiting a theater in Texas where a cowboy (and obvious movie neophyte), seeing that his hero "was about to be hung unjustly for cattle rustling," pulled out his "six-shooter and put several shots in the screen." Even more experienced patrons could momentarily lose touch with reality. Such was apparently the case at one Pittsburgh theater in 1914 when a house fly inadvertently flew into the projector lens and was magnified several hundred times. The audience, engrossed in a "thriller," panicked when on the screen there suddenly appeared "a monster with legs like the limbs of a big tree, eyes as big as saucers, and a huge body covered with hair that looked like standing wheat."[25]

Watching movies was easily integrated into the rhythms of a worker's day. Since most neighborhood and downtown theaters had continuous performances that played the same brief films over and over, customers could drop in at any time and stay for several minutes or several hours. White-collar workers were particularly fond of frequenting movies during lunchtime breaks—"nooning" as the practice was popularly known. Likewise, harried wage earners who found themselves "still nervously rushing" at the end of the day could stop at a theater for twenty minutes before heading home and, as one contemporary observer noted, "thus feel that they are getting something out of life."[26]

Immigrants were especially drawn to an entertainment that required little knowledge of English. "The Russian Jew, the German, the Austrian, or the Italian who has not been in this country a week and cannot understand English," explained one socialist daily, "goes to the motion picture theaters because what he sees on the screen is very real to him, and he understands as well as the American." The widespread popularity of movies also helped break down long-standing patterns of ethnic isolation among immigrant groups. Walking into a nickelodeon along the Bowery in New York City, one was likely to see a diverse audience of "Chinamen, Italians, and Yiddish people, the young and old, often entire families, crowded side by side." At the Alhambra Theater in Lowell, Massachusetts, you could find "a dozen different nationalities being represented in the audience."[27]

Movies could educate as well as entertain. It is doubtful, as some contemporary observers feared, that immigrants believed everything they saw on the screen. Traveling across the ocean did not cause people to lose all common sense. Yet by watching movies, recently arrived men, women, and children did get a vision of the kinds of fashions, values, and politics that producers portrayed as typifying American life. The desire to read intertitles (dialogue cards that were flashed on the screen), which were often translated by a *spieler* hired by the exhibitor, may have encouraged many immigrants to achieve English-language skills and prepare them to participate in political life. Indeed, movies could teach immigrants what it meant to belong to a particular class, and whether strikes, labor unions, and radical organizations were needed in their new land. For this reason, movies were both embraced and feared by reformers, radicals, and conservatives.[28]

Although movie audiences were predominantly working class, they did not all attend theaters in the same ways or for the same reasons. Children were among the medium's most ardent devotees. Movies offered boys and girls a chance to see many of the "naughty" things in life that their parents warned them against. Chicago police reported that children comprised 75 percent of the nickel movie audience in 1912, and authorities in one Connecticut mill town discovered that 90 percent of the youngsters surveyed in 1910 went at least once a week. Moviegoing was perhaps more class-specific among children than in any other group. Offspring of wealthy and cultured families, such as Rose Hobart, whose father played cello for the New York Symphony and whose mother sang opera, were often forbidden to enter the workingman's theater. It was simply not a place for "respectable" girls.[29]

Movies were especially important in transforming the gendered uses of public space and expanding the limited range of public amusements available to women. Throughout the nineteenth century, men were free to spend their evenings roaming the streets and participating in any entertainment they desired. Women, however, were expected to remain at home or, if they did venture out, to do so in the company of a proper escort. Single women who walked the city streets at night were often taken for prostitutes, and going to saloons, burlesque houses, or dance halls unchaperoned was unthinkable for "respectable" women of any class.[30]

The explosion of movie theaters after 1905 helped redefine public space by transforming city streets into bustling recreational thoroughfares that were open to everyone, day and night. Working-class women were greatly heartened by these changes. "Tied to her home, with infrequent opportunities after marriage for the balls and dances she loves," settlement house director Mary Simkhovitch observed in 1917, "what social life she has is within a short radius of her home." Neighborhood nickelodeons expanded social possibilities by offering nearby places where mothers and older sisters entrusted with the care of their siblings could go to escape from the drudgery of domestic chores and daily routines. The casual nature of moviegoing fit well into the natural rhythm of their work day. "Mothers do not have to 'dress' to attend them," noted one reporter, "and they take the children and spend many restful hours in them at very small expense." Movie theaters also served as female enclaves where, as the *Jewish Daily Forward* explained in 1908, large crowds of women "gossip, eat fruit and nuts, and have a good time."[31]

Local exhibitors aggressively wooed female patrons by advertising their theaters as day-care centers where busy mothers might leave their youngsters. Pittsburgh's movie houses were often used as a "convenience nursery for children" where, for the "small outlay of the admission price, parents may be free from the responsibility of supervising and taking care of noisy infants." Exhibitors in other cities encouraged harried mothers to "Bring the Children" and assured them that boys and girls in their theaters "are just as safe as they would be in their own homes."[32]

For young single males and females, movie theaters were places to have fun and enjoy romance away from the scrutiny of bosses, parents, and nosy siblings. Workingwomen who lived at home and gave most of their earnings to their parents claimed that movies were among the few affordable entertainments that provided the "stimulus of exciting pleasures" and the possibility of social freedom. For daughters raised in strict immigrant households, movies were one of the rare amusements they could attend without a chaperone. "My parents wouldn't let me go out anywhere else," recounted Italian garment worker Filomena Ognibene, "even when I was twenty-four." Movies were particularly popular with young couples. Men could treat their dates to a night at the cinema for considerably less than it cost to attend a dance hall or vaudeville show. The dark, close quarters of theaters pleased young couples who lacked private space for courting, but worried parents and reformers. "These young people," warned one midwestern investigator, "begin by slight familiarities and are soon embracing each other in the dark during the progress of the entertainment." Insisting that "promiscuous contact of the lips is especially dangerous," authorities in Camden, New Jersey, then in the midst of a flu epidemic, passed an ordinance in 1915 banning kissing in movie theaters.[33]

Come weekends, theater owners usually drew their greatest business from families. "Where a family had only from 15 cents to 25 cents a week for recreation," the *Saturday Evening Post* noted in 1917, "it went into motion pictures." Reformers who were critical of so many aspects of movie culture praised its ability to strengthen family life by luring men away from the saloon and adolescents from disreputable dance halls. "The workingman can afford to take his family to the picture show," observed the Reverend Charles Stelze, "because it usually costs no more than if he spent the evening in a saloon. And he feels a lot better for it the morning after." Neighborhood houses cultivated family trade by providing bargain weekend rates for children and offering special promotional evenings. "You can pay a nickel or a dime," recounted one jubilant Lower East Side resident, "and go home with a whole chicken."[34]

Movies crossed racial lines as easily as they did state lines. The "moving picture theater craze has developed a wonderful stampede among the Negro," the *Chicago Defender* reported in 1910. Yet the "democratic" nature of movie theaters praised in so many newspapers and magazines did not extend to most black audiences. Large theaters in northern cities often forced African-Americans to sit in segregated balconies, while many smaller houses in the North and South excluded them entirely. At Hurtig and Seamon's in New York, which later became the Apollo Theater, Francis "Doll" Thomas, one of the city's first black movie operators, remembered how "you had to go 'round 126th Street and go up the back stairway. They tried to get fancy with it and call it the upper mezzanine, but everybody knew it as 'nigger heaven,' and it was built for that." Some angry patrons protested against such blatant discrimination. When a Bayshore, Long Island, exhibitor refused to allow George Queen to sit in the theater's reserved section, Queen took him to court in 1915 and won $200 in damages.[35]

Excluded from white theaters, black movie fans spent their time and money at one of the nation's "colored" neighborhood houses, many of which were owned by black businessmen. In Lexington, Kentucky, the owners of the Frolic Theater (1907) invited the city's African Americans to watch movies where "they are welcome and can mingle with their fellows unhampered." People patronizing the black entertainment area on Chicago's South Side, known as The Stroll, could drop in at one of twelve movie theaters clustered along the four-block stretch. By 1913, over 200 "colored" houses were catering to the entertainment needs of the nation's black citizenry.[36]

Asian and Mexican immigrants also encountered racism in many local theaters. At Los Angeles' popular Hippodrome Theater, Japanese patrons were forced to sit in undesirable balcony areas, even if seats were available downstairs. "In those days," recounted shoe merchant Mitsuhiko Shimizu, "they insulted us at will. The best thing was not to go outside Little Tokyo at all." Consequently, Shimizu and his friends watched movies at the Japanese-owned Bankoku-za and Toyo-za theaters. In Chicago, Mexican movie fans who were unwelcome in most white and ethnic theaters tended to patronize the friendly confines of the Olympia Theater.[37]

Regardless of the problem, be it encountering racist theater owners or sitting in crowded, uncomfortable nickelodeons, the desire to see moving pictures and the pleasure experienced inside the movie theater succeeded in drawing millions of people to the movies week after week. The twenty or thirty minutes spent at the movies made the fifty or sixty hours spent at work seem almost worthwhile. And yet, once inside the movie theater, audiences did not always try to escape from their problems or indulge in harmless fantasies. Gathered among their own kind, workers and immigrants often talked and fantasized about challenging the dominant political order and creating a very different kind of America. Movies had the power to move the masses—a prospect that did not sit well with the bastions of law and order.

At the Movies: What Audiences Saw, Heard, and Did

Early reformers and social surveyors generally characterized moviegoing as a passive, homogeneous experience in which people plopped themselves down in front of the screen and spent their time in what was at best mindless entertainment and at worst a perversion that fostered crime, sexual profligacy, and class conflict. Social worker Mary Simkhovitch echoed this point of view in 1917 when she insisted that movies were simply "fed out to the auditors, whose reaction is but slight." These critics were wrong. Had they attended shows in immigrant and working-class neighborhoods (which many were afraid to do), they would have discovered that life inside these theaters was filled with talking, yelling, fighting, singing, and lots of laughter. Movie theaters were places where people could recapture the sense of aliveness that had been lost in the regimented factories of the era. As Olga Marx's Uncle Igel told her: "When you go to a movie, you get so exhausted that when you get home you fall asleep like a breeze."[38]

Early movie theaters were fluid social spaces in which working people were able to shape moviegoing experiences to serve their own ethnic, class, gender, racial, and political needs. Neighborhood theaters were not like churches or museums where people spoke in hushed whispers. They were boisterous social centers in which multiple messages could be heard. Audience interaction was as much a part of the moviegoing experience as the movies themselves. As historian Roy Rosenzweig observes: "Whatever the degree of control of the middle and upper classes over movie content, the working class was likely to determine the nature of behavior and interaction within the movie theater."[39]

The first "movies" were little more than a series of several short subjects that lasted a total of twenty or thirty minutes. The standard show at Chicago's Family Electric Theater, and most other early nickelodeons, was "three reels of film and an 'illustrated song' [slides featuring the lyrics to popular tunes] for a nickel." Each of these reels included two or more dramas, comedies, or travelogues, and news films. As the novelty of watching moving pictures wore off, producers began turning out longer, more complex narrative films. By 1910, many theater owners ran programs that might include a two-reel drama or adventure film, a one-reel western, a Keystone Kops comedy, and several reels of "historical and geographical subjects, current events, scenes of commercial and industrial life, and occasionally literary subjects."[40]

Films of this era were silent, but the movie theaters were not. Moviegoing was as much an aural experience as a visual one. Actions on the screen were accompanied by a variety of sounds, some produced by theater personnel and some by audiences. Nickelodeon owners often played phonographs during performances or purchased special sound effects equipment that, for a modest $30, allowed them to enhance visual images with an array of sounds that featured lion roars, car crashes, howling winds, horse trots, steam whistles, and ocean noises. More prosperous exhibitors hired piano players, organists, drummers, and occasionally small orchestras to play during the film and between reel changes. Music-loving wage earners who could not afford local operas or symphonies might hear good music at the movies. Boston theater orchestras, for example, entertained audiences with excerpts from *La Boheme, Tosca, Madame Butterfly*, and other "songs of popular and musical appeal."[41]

Moviegoing was a participatory experience in which audiences became an important part of the show. Drawing upon old music hall and vaudeville traditions, exhibitors hired comics or crooners who urged patrons to join in as "illustrated songs" were flashed on the screen. Local theaters also sponsored amateur nights in which those eliciting popular approval received cheers and prizes, while less talented performers met "with jeers and a long hook" that pulled them off stage.[42]

Phonographs, pianos, orchestras, sing-alongs, and amateur acts all contributed to the melodious and cacophonous sounds that characterized a typical visit to the movies. But the loudest noises came from the audience itself. Unlike today's theaters, where patrons are urged not to talk during the film, silent theaters maintained a communal atmosphere in which audiences regularly booed, cheered, or applauded scenes that reflected harshly or kindly on their lives and politics. The New York League of Motion Picture Exhibitors complained in 1913 of "losing its most desirable element because of the continuous talkfests of certain classes of movie fans," and suggested that managers hand out slips asking patrons to refrain from loud conversations. Yet any neighborhood exhibitor who dared do this would undoubtedly lose his patrons. The working-class movie fan, explained one Los Angeles labor daily, enjoys putting "into the mouths of the silent actors the exclamations, words and lines that he himself would use under the circumstances." Although audiences in upscale movie palaces might do this in silence, neighborhood fans preferred to share their thoughts with everyone around them.[43]

Local theaters also doubled as neighborhood social centers where people went to meet their friends, gossip, flirt, vent frustrations, and discuss politics. They served as living rooms for tens of thousands of wage earners who dwelled in dark, vermin-infested tenements. They were places where men and women might entertain and be entertained. One New York reporter described the casual atmosphere of local houses where "regulars stroll up and down the aisles between acts and visit friends." Although large theaters in downtown commercial districts drew diverse crowds, local houses were frequently dominated by a specific ethnic or racial group. A stranger could determine the ethnic composition of a neighborhood by listening to the languages spoken in its local theaters.[44]

Like other social centers, the character of the movie theater was shaped by the class, ethnicity, race, gender, and politics of the community surrounding it. There was a reciprocal process at work in these neighborhood houses: different groups wanted different kinds of entertainment and exhibitors anxious to build a regular clientele gave them what they wanted. Theaters in African-American neighborhoods of Chicago, Atlanta, Memphis, and Lexington, Kentucky offered customers black vaudeville acts and, after 1913, movies with all-black casts ("race films" as they were called) made specifically for black audiences. Ethnic exhibitors on New York's Lower East Side screened Yiddish films and Yiddish acts for Jewish audiences, and select Kalem comedies for Irish patrons. Theater owners in the Little Tokyo sections of Los Angeles and Sacramento showed features produced for Japanese moviegoers, while their Chicago counterparts often supplemented their programs with Polish playlets.[45]

Movie theaters also maintained an active political life rarely seen in today's entertainment world. Neighborhood houses served as political centers that existed outside the control and norms of middle-class life and, unlike other contemporary political institutions, included women as well as men. Local exhibitors catered to the political tastes of their patrons, even when those tastes ran counter to the dominant values of society. Although women did not win a constitutional amendment granting full suffrage until

1920, New York exhibitor Perry Williams made "voting by women in his [seven theater] lobbies a permanent feature of election day performances" beginning in 1908. Women's rights advocates frequently persuaded theater managers to run suffragist films, such as *Votes For Women* (1912) or *Eighty Million Women Want—?* (1913), and to permit one of their members to speak to audiences during reel changes. Socialists in large cities like New York and Chicago and small towns like Aurora, Illinois, and Yolo, California, were equally successful in bringing radical speakers and films such as *From Dusk to Dawn* (1913) and *The Jungle* (1914) to their local houses.[46]

Public space was transformed into political space as activities previously confined to union halls and street demonstrations became a regular part of neighborhood theater life. Exhibitors allowed unions to show slides publicizing some particular cause or to use theaters to raise funds for needy strikers. Socialist party candidates gave speeches and showed campaign films at neighborhood theaters prior to election day. Indeed, certain houses developed reputations based largely on the political character of their patrons. Theater owners in heavily unionized areas of Long Beach, Los Angeles, and Cleveland encouraged this process by hanging signs in box offices that proclaimed "Concerns Friendly to Organized Wage Earners," and placing newspaper advertisements that read "a staunch friend and in sympathy with the cause of Labor." In Brooklyn, socialists enjoyed gathering with like-minded friends at the Gotham Theater, a house known to welcome radicals.[47]

Not everyone loved the movies, however. As working-class passions for film heated up, so too did the fears of conservative civic leaders. They were concerned that oppositional movements seen on the screen or discussed in the theater might inspire similar working-class movements outside the theater, and felt they had to take action against this "dangerous" mix of politics and pleasure.

Movies under Attack

"Crusades have been organized against these low-priced moving-picture theatres," *Harper's Weekly* reported in August 1907, "and many conservators of the public morals have denounced them as vicious and demoralizing." These crusades continued for several decades as reformers, clergy, politicians, and concerned parents questioned a wide range of real and perceived dangers posed by the new medium. Congress considered the possibility of regulating the movie industry; municipal authorities investigated the types of films being shown and the theaters that showed them; and civic leaders called for censorship boards that would expunge the deleterious content of films. These early critics were not a single elite speaking with a single voice. Rather, they were a diverse group of citizens who tended to divide into two camps. There were those who saw movies as politically dangerous and morally degraded, and fought to exert tighter control over what one group referred to as the "pernicious moving picture abomination." There were also "uplifters," as they were popularly known, who strived to improve a medium they saw as holding great potential for good or evil.[48]

Most of these critics feared that impressionable children, the nation's future leaders, would absorb and mimic the incessant examples of crime, violence, and indecent sexuality that appeared on the screen. Children went to the movies "hoping to find a clue to life's perplexities," social worker Jane Addams asserted in 1909, and what they saw, "flimsy and poor as it often is, easily becomes their actual moral guide." Genuinely concerned about the welfare of minors, critics such as Addams rarely credited children with the ability to separate right from wrong, fantasy from reality. Instead, police reports, newspaper articles, and sermons were filled with accounts of wayward youths whose passion for movies led them to steal money in order to raise the price of admission. The propensity to commit crimes was further hastened by the allegedly immoral films shown inside the theater. "Amateur burglars have robbed houses exactly as portrayed by the pictures," insisted the Society for Prevention of Cruelty to Children in November 1911.[49]

Sexuality on the screen and in the theater were equally troublesome to cultural conservatives. Films that revealed women's undergarments, featured scenes of partially nude women, or told stories of premarital sex were deemed scandalous by more prudish men and women of the time. In Lowell, Massachusetts, citizens voiced fears that movies "teach false ideas of love and tend to destroy the sacredness of marriage." Dimly lit movie theaters were criticized as breeding grounds for sexual delinquency. Countless reports warned of darkened theaters where "boys and men slyly embrace the girls and offer cheap indignities"; where girls "who had always been known as decent" started on a "downward path." Sexual dangers also lurked outside the movie theater where, as a Brooklyn judge warned a grand jury, "young girls are seized by young ghouls and vultures" and sold into "white slavery."[50]

But even more frightening to many critics were the class dangers posed by movies. The politicization of neighborhood houses, the frequent appearance of oppositional values on the screen and in the theater, and the markedly working-class composition of movie audiences raised fears that the new medium would intensify class divisions. In a 1915 article entitled "Class-Consciousness and the 'Movies,'" drama critic Walter Eaton wrote of the dire consequences that might arise from the continued fragmentation of leisure along class lines. "Already the spoken drama and the silent drama are far apart. Each is the amusement, the pastime, of a separate and antagonistic class. . . . From the Syndicalist's point of view, then, surely, the movies should be regarded as a blessing, as an aid in the growth of class consciousness." Although such class divisions were confined to large cities, Eaton warned of the day when movies would reach into smaller towns and foster similar cleavages between "the proletariat . . . and capitalist class."[51]

Class fears were further exacerbated by the decidedly foreign-born character of early audiences and movie producers. Rather than see class violence as rooted in the inequalities bred by industrial capitalism, conservative politicians, manufacturers, and civic leaders repeatedly portrayed strikes and labor conflicts as the work of foreign-born agitators who imported European "isms"—socialism, communism, anarchism—to our shores. The massive influx of millions of eastern, central, and southern Europeans at the turn of the century intensified these xenophobic fears. By 1910, immigrants and their American-born children composed more than 70 percent of the population of New York, Chicago, Boston, Cleveland, Detroit, Buffalo, and Milwaukee, and more than 50 percent in six other cities. The presence of so many foreigners sparked frenzied Americanization campaigns aimed at teaching these "gross aliens," as Henry James called them, traditional "American" values and absorbing them into the mainstream of American life.[52] In this climate of anxiety, it is understandable why a medium that attracted the devoted support of so many immigrants engendered such great suspicion among the nation's largely Protestant cultural and political elite. Here was a business in which foreign-born exhibitors, many of them Jews, showed films made in Catholic countries like France to foreign audiences in foreign-dominated American cities.

Such concerns about the consequences of unregulated working-class leisure activities were certainly not new. Well before the nickelodeon, many of the nation's leaders spoke worriedly about what they perceived as the steady erosion of their public authority and the decline of traditional values of hard work, thrift, and self-restraint. Whether or not this was true, the "guardians of public morality," as one historian called them, acted as if it was, and sought to preserve these values wherever possible. The rapid growth of a powerful new medium that bypassed "the traditional, accepted socializing institutions such as the family, the school, and the church," and spoke directly to millions of immigrants and laborers presented them with a grave new threat. Revolution, explained novelist and radical Jack London, was unlikely so long as a fragmented working class "groped for ways to express the dim and formless thoughts against oppression that grew in their consciousness." Movies hastened that possibility by distributing "knowledge in a language that all may understand." Conservative fears concerning the radical potential of film were raised to new levels in December 1909 and again in September 1911, when socialists in Chicago and Los Angeles, respectively, announced their plans to open movie theaters that would be used to introduce "Socialist propaganda . . . [to] the thousands of people who attend 5 and 10c theaters."[53]

Middle-class anxieties were further heightened by the fact that many early films undermined the power of the dominant culture by mocking strict Victorian sexual codes and attacking the traditional authority of police, employers, clergy, and politicians. Although some reformers responded to these perceived threats by trying to improve the moral character of movies and movie theaters, others reacted by censoring films, raising license fees for exhibitors, enforcing Sunday closing laws, and tightening theater safety standards. Both groups, however, undoubtedly agreed with Cincinnati civic leaders that "healthy recreation in individual and community life" demanded that movies and the movie industry "must submit to social control."[54]

Making Movies Respectable

Film producers and exhibitors responded to their critics by attempting to transform movies from a cheap amusement for the masses into a respectable entertainment for all classes. Although they would not fully succeed until the early 1920s, industry personnel began the process by making quality films and building elegant theaters. Farsighted showmen such as Adolph Zukor, George Kleine, and Vitagraph's James Stuart Blackton believed they could keep censors at bay and attract a more prosperous clientele (and thereby charge higher admission) by producing longer films of more artistic merit. The success of imported "photoplays" such as the four-reel *Queen Elizabeth* (1912) and the eight-reel, two-hour Italian spectacle *Quo Vadis* (1912), which Kleine showed on Broadway, led American producers to adapt popular novels, plays, biblical stories, and narrative poems to the screen. By 1914, the one-reel "short" of earlier years was increasingly replaced by three- or four-reel "features" and even longer "photoplays" that included the first generation of movie stars. The financial and critical success of D. W. Griffith's *The Birth of a Nation* in 1915, a two-and-a-half-hour epic film that was often shown at the astounding price of two dollars ($26 in 1990 dollars), brought national respectability to the medium (except among those offended by the film's blatant racism), and ensured the preeminence of the feature-length film.[55]

The creation of a better class of films that would, in Zukor's words, "kill the [movies'] slum tradition" was paralleled by the construction of a better class of theaters for a better class of patrons. Early movie theaters failed to attract large numbers of "old" and "new" middle-class audiences in part because they were often plagued by poor ventilation, inadequate lighting, filthy interiors, and unsafe facilities. The greatest danger, however, came from the threat of fire. Early films were made on highly flammable nitrate stock and, unless carefully tended to by a skilled operator, could easily catch on fire—especially since patrons and operators smoked in theaters. But owners of nickelodeons and converted theaters frequently showed little regard for fire safety. Their houses lacked adequate fire escapes, fire extinguishers, and metal projection booths that would help contain conflagrations. In New York, one socialist daily worried about the nine hundred "'nicolettes' existing in stores beneath the tenement houses, where . . . if a fire should start, the loss of life would be appalling." By 1910 municipal governments, often with widespread neighborhood support, began passing bills tightening fire safety standards and requiring licenses for all motion picture projector operators.[56]

Innovative exhibitors such as Samuel "Roxy" Rothapfel, a former Marine who began his movie career by running a nickel theater in the back room of a Pennsylvania saloon, succeeded in luring a more prosperous clientele by showing films in safe and comfortable surroundings. In 1911, he converted Minneapolis' Lyric Theater into an elegant movie house that featured the latest releases, an array of singers, and an orchestra whose members were drawn from the city's symphony. In Los Angeles, Thomas Clune opened an equally stylish structure that seated nine hundred and featured an eight-piece orchestra plus an hour and a half of first-class entertainment. Over the next few years, similarly impressive theaters appeared in cities and small towns across the nation.[57]

The transition from elegant movie theaters to opulent movie palaces began on April 11, 1914, when the Strand Theater opened on Broadway and 47th Street. Broadway, capital of the legitimate stage, had been invaded several months earlier when Vitagraph studios converted the Criterion Theater into a movie palace. But the Strand was designed and built exclusively to show movies, and it offered audiences the kind of surroundings most had seen only in films. The socialist *New York Call* declared the 3,500-seat theater the "most imposing and impressive institution of its kind in existence," and marveled at how every "modern device for public comfort and safety has been incorporated and the promoters have sought in every way possible to avoid the beaten tracks everywhere providing novelty." "Roxy" Rothapfel, who was lured to New York to run the Regent Theater and then the Strand, adopted as his motto: "Don't 'give the people what they want'— give them something better." And he did. For 10, 15, 25, or 50 cents for box seats, patrons could enjoy ornate lobbies, opulent interiors, royal-sized restrooms, and uniformed ushers who escorted them to plush seats. The opening program was equally elaborate: an overture played by a fifty-piece orchestra, a quartet singing parts of *Rigoletto*, a Pathé newsreel, a Keystone comedy, and finally, a photoplay, *The Spoilers*.[58]

The Strand was an immediate success. "Great crowds have taxed the capacity of the large auditorium at every performance since the opening of the house last week," observed one reporter. And great crowds continued to pour into the movie palaces that soon opened in Pittsburgh, Seattle, Boston, and other major cities.[59]

By offering the public better films and theaters, industry leaders began attracting greater numbers of white-collar and middle-class patrons. "In Atlanta, Georgia," the *Atlantic Monthly* observed in 1915, "you may often see automobiles packed two deep along the curb in front of a motion-picture theater, which hardly suggests an exclusively proletarian patronage." Even the usually staid theater critics of the *New York Times* were impressed by the changing composition of movie audiences. "If anyone had told me two years ago that the time would come when the finest looking people in town would be going to the biggest and newest theater on Broadway for the purpose of seeing motion pictures," wrote Victor Watson, "I would have sent them down to my friend, Dr. Minas Gregory, at Bellevue Hospital. The doctor runs the city's bughouse, you know."[60]

The opening of elegant theaters and movie palaces did not signal the demise of neighborhood theaters, nor did the middle class suddenly supplant the working class as the medium's dominant audience. Movie palaces accounted for only 1 percent of the nation's theaters in 1915, and New York City, the country's exhibition capital, had only ten luxury houses in 1916. Nickelodeons and small storefront theaters slowly disappeared, but moderately sized neighborhood houses continued to do well. The average theater in 1916 contained 502 seats—larger than the first nickelodeons but considerably smaller than luxury houses. And workers and immigrants continued to fill the bulk of those seats. Even as late as 1924, the Motion Picture Theater Owners' Association insisted that "80 percent of the movie patrons were either poor or only moderately well off."[61]

Luxury theaters and feature films did, however, change the ways in which people went to the movies. The casual and often raucous atmosphere that characterized many neighborhood theaters was missing from the more highly regulated movie palace. It was the palace manager, not the audience, who set the social and political tone of the theater. People now rarely just dropped into a movie palace on the way home from work, for most folks wanted to watch lengthy feature films and the various entertainments that accompanied them from the beginning—especially if they were paying movie palace prices. Many large theaters abandoned the practice of continuous performances and instituted set times for their shows. Audiences were now expected to adjust to the theater's time and not vice versa. The emphasis on time discipline that characterized so much of work life, and which wage earners bitterly protested against, slowly came to dominate the movies.

By April 1917, on the eve of American entry into a war that would change world history and reshape the movie business, industry leaders had achieved a partial victory in their efforts to uplift the movies. Exhibitors worked hard to make theaters safe and respectable. They succeeded in luring all classes to their most luxurious houses. Making the movies themselves safe and respectable, however, proved a far more difficult task. At the same time that exhibitors were downplaying class differences, producers were turning out politically contentious films that dealt with highly divisive themes of class conflict. The diversity of producers and easy access to the screen during the prewar years meant that anyone, from socialists to capitalists, could reach mass audiences with their interpretation of contemporary problems. For many critics, the greatest danger posed by the new medium lay not with what went on in the theater, but with what appeared on the screen. What dangers, then, did audiences see when they looked up at the screen? Could cinematic fantasies actually affect life outside the theater? Answering these questions demands that we shift our attention from movie theaters and their audiences to films and their politics.

2

Visualizing the Working Class: Cinema and Politics before Hollywood

IN THE BRIEF span of thirty-seven months, Americans were indelibly scarred by two devastating tragedies. The first occurred in New York City on March 25, 1911. On the top floors of the ten-story building that housed the Triangle Waist Company, 146 female garment workers were laboring on an insurmountable load of sewing in a dark sweatshop when a fire broke out. As the flames quickly spread, the women, running for their lives, headed for the doors only to discover they were locked. While some met a horrifying death by jumping from the burning building, others were consumed by fire. Standing amid the "heap of dead bodies" that lay broken on the blood-stained streets, reporter William Shepherd remembered the "great strike of last year in which these same girls demanded more sanitary conditions and more safety precautions in the shops. These dead bodies were the answer."[1]

The second infamous event happened on April 20, 1914. When the employees of John D. Rockefeller's Colorado Fuel and Iron Company were evicted from company-owned houses after going on strike in September 1913, they responded by erecting a "village" of tents. Tired of the prolonged walkout and the unbearable eyesore of the workers' shanty town, company leaders decided to end the strike at Ludlow and called in National Guardsmen and company gunmen to help them. The result was a massacre that left a black mark in American history. Twenty-four men, women, and children were gunned down and their tents were set on fire. Two women and eleven children, noted one observer, tried to escape the gunfire by hiding in a hole dug under their tent but "died like trapped rats when the flames swept over them."[2]

Before the invention of film, these deaths and injustices might have been quickly forgotten. But the rise of the movies changed the nation's political consciousness forever. Within a few months of each event, garment workers, coal miners, manufacturers, and government authorities clashed once again, but this time their battles were fought on the nation's movie screens as four movies presented markedly differing views of the conditions that caused these disasters. *The Crime of Carelessness* (Edison 1912), a film financed by the rabidly anti-union National Association of Manufacturers, tried to reshape public memory by shifting attention away from employer neglect of factory safety laws and showing how a sweatshop blaze similar to the Triangle Fire was caused by a careless, cigarette-smoking employee. *The High Road*, produced by the Rolfe Photoplay Company in 1915, presented working-class audiences with a far different vision of events. This time, a money-hungry sweatshop owner and his callous manager, who violate safety codes by locking the workshop doors, are clearly blamed when a fire subsequently takes the lives of several women.

Shifting to the nation's coal fields, *The Miner's Lesson*, made in 1914 by the United States Bureau of Mines in cooperation with the Anthracite Coal Operators, attributed the accidents that played an important role in the Ludlow strike to worker stupidity and not mine-owner treachery. In contrast, *What Is to Be Done?*, produced that same year by socialist Joseph Weiss, revealed how capitalist exploitation prompted the strike at Ludlow and graphically portrayed employers and government authorities conspiring to murder innocent men, women, and children.[3]

Socialists, manufacturers, and government agencies are not the kinds of producers, nor are movies with such overt class politics the kinds of films we usually associate with Hollywood. Indeed, it was precisely because there was no "Hollywood" as such, that these kinds of producers and films could reach the screen on a regular basis. In the years before American entry into World War I, the minimal demands of technological expertise, the constant need for more films, and the relatively modest costs of making movies ($400 to $1,000 a reel in most instances) allowed a wide variety of groups to participate in this still emerging industry. Although commercial companies like Edison, Biograph, and Vitagraph were among the nation's most prominent filmmakers, early producers also included organizations such as the Women's Political Union, the U. S. Department of the Interior, the American Bankers' Association, and the American Federation of Labor.

Movies were far more political and varied in their ideological perspectives during the silent era than at any subsequent time. If we understand politics and power as the ability to influence or gain control over others—family, employees, community, or nation—then mass culture, and movies in particular, constituted an important realm of politics and power in Progressive-era America. Yet, mass culture was not a monolithic entity imposed from above to keep the masses quiet but an arena of struggle between different groups and classes who used film to win greater public support for their cause. Film, as the National Board of Review of Motion Pictures insisted in 1913, was a powerful vehicle "for political, social, religious propaganda, for muckraking . . . [and] for revolutionary ideas."[4]

Movies emerged as class weapons from the start and not in the late 1920s and 1930s, as some cinema scholars have argued. Commercial filmmakers and groups outside the industry recognized the power of this new medium and turned out polemical films that addressed national debates over the dominant values and future direction of American society. The struggles waged between employers and employees in the workplace, in the streets, and in legislatures were recreated and fought out on the nation's movie screens. The stakes involved in these cinematic depictions were often higher than their real-life counterparts. For while workplace conflicts usually involved only hundreds or thousands of people, their filmed recreations reached millions.[5]

Over the next three chapters I will examine, successively, how commercial film companies portrayed the general problems of working-class life; how they, and groups outside the industry, depicted more specific labor-capital conflicts; and, how labor and radical organizations made films that presented their own distinct visions of past and present class struggles. Whenever possible, my examples come from surviving movies that readers can view on their own. Films that I have seen are designated by the inclusion of the production company and the release date in the parentheses following the film's title; films whose information comes largely from reviews and stills only include the release date. I generally use the present tense to discuss films that I have viewed and the past tense for analyses drawn from sources other than the films themselves.[6] Let us begin, then, by exploring the many ways in which filmmakers looked at the people who not only composed their largest audience, but who also made up the largest segment of the population: the working classes. Although many producers simply wanted to entertain, others set out to depict and solve the problems facing wage earners. These politically engaged filmmakers not only looked at the world, they tried to change it. And, to the joy of some and consternation of others, they often succeeded.

Social Problems, Progressivism, and the Movies

Few early filmmakers dramatized the problems of working-class life with greater passion than a slaveholder's son who made his directorial debut in June 1908. David Wark Griffith, known as D. W. Griffith, entered the movie business at a critical moment when industry leaders were trying to silence their critics by producing narrative films with moral lessons that would instruct as well as entertain. But the form that instruction would take was anyone's guess. While companies like Vitagraph tried to build a middle-class audience with "quality films" inspired by Shakespeare, the Bible, and the lives of famous historical figures, the American Mutuoscope and Biograph Company (renamed American Biograph Company in 1910) and its new director preferred melodramas inspired by the lives of their main patrons, immigrants and workers. Although he is usually remembered today as the man who made the brilliant but racist *The Birth of a Nation* (Epoch 1915), D. W. Griffith was, during his Biograph years, one of the most powerful critics of class injustice that the movie industry ever produced. He repeatedly championed the "dangerous classes" and exposed the world to the prejudices of their self-styled "betters." Between 1908 and 1913, his films offered scathing commentaries on the evils of monopolies, the exploitation of farmers and sweatshop workers, the hypocrisy of reformers, and the degeneracy of the idle rich. A brief look at Griffith's Biograph years offers a glimpse into the highly politicized nature of early American film and the role that working people played not only as audiences but as the subjects of their own entertainment.[7]

In visualizing the hardships and injustices of modern society, Griffith drew heavily on events from his own life. Born in Crestwood, Kentucky, on January 23, 1875, David was the fourth son of a devout Methodist mother who came from a well-to-do southern family and a father who had owned slaves and fought in the Civil War. "Roaring Jake," as the former colonel was known, regaled his sons with tales of the Old South, the virtues of Southern femininity, and a wide range of Victorian sentiments. A born storyteller, Jake proved less successful as a planter. After returning from war, the senior Griffith was constantly on the edge of bankruptcy, and when he died in 1885 creditors seized the family farm. Moving to Louisville with his mother and siblings, David quit school and helped make ends meet by working as an errand boy, clerk, and factory laborer. In 1896, the twenty-one-year-old aspiring actor left home and joined a traveling theater company. A nationwide depression caused the company to fall on hard times and David was often left stranded in some unfamiliar city. The tall, lean youth spent the next ten years acting whenever he could and, when he could not, toiling on a lumber schooner along the west coast, picking hops in California, and doing "real muscle-stretching, bone-bending work" as a puddler in an upstate New York foundry. Despite his hard labors, Griffith frequently found himself broke, forced to live in flop houses and to sneak rides on railroad freight cars.[8]

Returning to New York City, Griffith's big break came in June 1908, when he was hired to direct Biograph's *The Adventures of Dollie*. Pleased with his work, Biograph signed the thirty-three-year-old Kentuckian to direct or supervise all its films. With exhibitors clamoring for new products, Griffith was expected to turn out two one-reel films a week and an additional one-half reel comedy or melodrama, a schedule he maintained for nearly a year and a half. By 1913 he had produced nearly 500 films for Biograph. Faced with tremendous pressure to generate new ideas on an almost daily basis, the lanky southerner drew stories from his own experiences and from the problems he found in New York. Although Griffith turned out many films that offered nostalgic and racist visions of the Old South, he also produced some of the most starkly compelling depictions of working-class life ever made by an American filmmaker. His many years of near poverty, recalled actress Lillian Gish, left him "deeply sympathetic to the sufferings of the poor, to the injustices inflicted on them." Griffith used the camera as a weapon to remedy those injustices. "I believe in the motion picture not only as a means of amusement," he wrote in 1915, "but as a moral and educational force."[9]

Griffith's films did indeed present a vision of a morally ordered world, but it was an order highly critical of many of society's dominant authorities. Part autobiographer, part social critic, Griffith depicted the ruinous effects of urbanization and industrial capitalism, and how hard-working families were often torn apart by the greed and heartlessness of landlords, capitalists, reformers, and government officials. *A Corner in Wheat* (Biograph 1909) showed farm communities where families worked together in harmony (perhaps like Griffith's idealized vision of his own family) destroyed by grain monopolists who drove up wheat prices, causing bankruptcy in the countryside and bread riots in the cities. Movies about sweatshop life, such as *The Song of the Shirt* (Biograph 1910) and *The Lily of the Tenements* (Biograph 1911) dramatized the troubles seamstresses faced at the hands of avaricious employers who paid them a pittance for their labors and, along with landlords, sexually harassed them. *A Child of the Ghetto* (Biograph 1910) and *Simple Charity* (Biograph 1910) denounced police and charity workers who treated the poor with suspicion and contempt. Likewise, *One Is Business, the Other Crime* (Biograph 1912) exposed the injustices of a legal system that practiced one law for the rich and another for the poor. Griffith also took his camera into the teeming streets of the Lower East Side to offer Americans stark depictions of the violence, death, and crime that plagued ghetto life.[10]

Not everyone was pleased by Griffith's continuous assault on modern authority figures or his unrestrained sympathy for the working poor. Commenting on *A Child of the Ghetto*, one reviewer warned, "Subjects of this character are calculated to arouse class prejudice unless treated in the most delicate manner." Many of his critics were undoubtedly disturbed by Griffith's vision of a poor but independent proletariat able to help one another survive without the aid of their so-called betters. Immigrants and workers, however, loved seeing him lambaste the people who treated them so badly. The director was especially admired by Los Angeles unionists who printed his articles in their newspaper and made him an honorary member of Local 33 of the International Alliance of Theatrical and Stage Employees Union.[11]

D. W. Griffith helped turn Biograph into one of the most successful companies of its time. However, in October 1913, when the studio refused his request to produce longer films that would allow him to make fuller social statements, Griffith left the company and went on to produce such epic and racist productions as *The Birth of a Nation* (Epoch 1915) and *Intolerance* (Wark 1916). His years at Biograph, brief as they were, proved critical to shaping the politics and subject matter of American cinema. Before Griffith, observes one film scholar, few films "stressed ethnic ties, few chronicled adventures of immigrants—their arrival in the New World, life in tenements, or . . . working conditions in shops or factories."[12] Although he was hostile to blacks and sometimes romanticized the poor, Griffith offered white workers a measure of hope and succeeded in making movies about their problems an integral part of American political culture.

In politicizing the content of his movies, Griffith was the forerunner of what many in power saw as a new and dangerous new kind of entertainer— a progressive filmmaker. Movies arose in the midst of the Progressive era, a period of optimism and activism that began in the 1890s and ended with American entry into World War I in 1917. Progressivism was less a singular movement than a multitude of reform movements that operated at the local, state, and national levels, and involved academics, journalists, politicians, social workers, business leaders, trade unionists, and members of women's clubs. These diverse groups shared a common rhetoric that denounced the laissez-faire policies of the nineteenth century and called for an active government that would promote the welfare of all citizens, especially women and children. Though advocating different means for achieving their goals, Progressives believed that truly dedicated people could solve or, at the very least, ameliorate the many problems caused by industrialization and urbanization.[13]

Condemning extremes of great wealth and dire poverty, Progressives saw themselves as defending the middle ground of American society, and fought to restore equality of opportunity at a time when powerful economic forces prevented its realization. Muckraking journalists exposed the greed and misdeeds of financial giants such as John Rockefeller and J. P. Morgan, while Congress and state legislatures passed laws aimed at curbing the power of trusts and monopolies and protecting Americans against those whom President Theodore Roosevelt called the "malefactors of great wealth." Working at the other end of the spectrum, Jane Addams, Florence Kelley, Lillian Wald, and a new generation of settlement house workers called attention to the suffering of the nation's poor and pursued the cause of social and economic justice for millions of impoverished immigrants and wage earners.

Troubled by the deleterious effects of large-scale capital, Progressives were equally concerned with threats from below posed by militant labor and radical organizations. Many saw the growth of socialism and frequent outbreak of violent strikes as endangering the cause of liberal democracy. Reform, not radicalism, was the Progressive ethos. When workers rose up to fight their oppressors, liberals often found themselves siding with conservative business leaders and politicians. A "powerful irony lay at the heart of progressivism," observes historian Richard McCormick, "reforms that gained vitality from a people angry with industrialism ended up by assisting them to accommodate to it."[14]

Outcries against the injustices of the age also permeated literary and artistic life. The paintings of the "Ash Can" School, the photography of Jacob Riis and Lewis Hine, the poetry of Carl Sandburg and Amy Lowell, the novels of Theodore Dreiser, Upton Sinclair, Frank Norris, and Jack London, and the plays of Austin Adams and Joseph Medill Patterson offered emotional portraits of the widespread poverty and miserable living conditions caused by rapid urbanization and industrialization. The era of the "empty, vapid, meaningless, purposeless drama without thought, without idea, without purpose, is passing," playwright Arthur Hopkins declared in 1913. "We have so many vitally important themes in this country . . . that a translation of these themes to the stage is inevitable."[15]

It was a short leap from the social realism of page and stage to the social-problem film. No less affected by the crusading spirit of the age than their literary counterparts, filmmakers such as D. W. Griffith, Lois Weber, Oscar Apfel, George Nichols, and Barry O'Neil turned out emotionally compelling works that visualized a broad range of controversial issues. Like Griffith, many socially conscious filmmakers spoke from firsthand experience. Lois Weber, who suffered hunger and poverty in her early years and toiled as a social worker and street-corner evangelist before entering the movie business, devoted her career to turning out what she called "missionary pictures." Among other issues, Weber's movies promoted birth control, decried capital punishment, called for stricter child-labor laws, and attacked the hypocrisy of well-to-do churchgoers. Texas-born director King Vidor was inspired by a similar mixture of politics and missionary zeal. "I see the Hand of Fate calling me to reform the world," he wrote in his diary in 1914. "I will start with the Movies."[16]

Idealism was not, however, the only driving force behind the social-problem film. Studios and producers who may not have shared in the reformist spirit of the age nevertheless believed that serious films would enhance the industry's respectability and attract a more prosperous clientele. "Improve your pictures," the *Nickelodeon* advised exhibitors, "and you will improve the class of patrons who come to your theater." Not everyone, however, was committed to making or watching this kind of film. "If you want to send a message," remarked the ever-blunt Samuel Goldwyn, "send it Western Union."[17]

The largest number of social-problem films and, indeed, a significant number of all prewar films, focused on the lives of the industry's main audience: workers and immigrants. In the "period from 1909 to 1914," writes film distributor Tom Brandon, "far more movies were produced about ordinary people—men, women, and children—as people who engage in work and participate in the productive process of society, than at any comparable

length of time since." Despite Brandon's assertion, there is considerable dis-
agreement among film scholars over the political character of Progressive-
era cinema and the prominence of movies dealing with working-class life.
Kevin Brownlow insists the "nickelodeon was not a forum for politics,
and films on working-class themes were rare." Movie producers, adds
Peter Stead, "were as opposed to Socialism and labor unions as their
fellow businessmen." Of the 4,249 films reviewed in the trade press in
1914, only nineteen, claims Brandon, were "directly political."[18] These
views are challenged by Lewis Jacobs and Eileen Bowser, who argue that
prewar films "dealt mostly with the working man and his world," were
highly political, and confronted the "subject of organized labor and labor
unrest" on a regular basis.[19]

Much of the debate and seeming confusion over the political character
and number of films dealing with working-class themes lies in differing
definitions of what constitutes "politics" and what constitutes a "labor"
film. By drawing on recent themes in social and working-class history, we
can resolve these disagreements and look at movies of this era in a new light.
Politics is about more than just politicians, political parties, and organized
political activity. Its fundamental concern is power, and power, as Eugene
Genovese and Elizabeth Fox Genovese so evocatively suggest, is about "who
rides whom and how." Films do not have to offer solutions to problems
in order to be political, nor do they have to devote their entire story to
exploring political issues. Some of the most political films of the era never
referred to political movements. They simply showed ordinary men and
women standing up for themselves. A film is "political" if it depicts the uses
and abuses of power by one individual, group, or class against another.
Adopting this broader view greatly expands the number of movies that can
rightly be called political. Exercises of power, while not always central to
the plot, were seen in thousands of silent films that featured conflicts between landlords and tenants, employers and employees, strikers and militia,
radicals and police, immigrants and government officials, and reformers
and the reformed.[20]

Film scholars also underestimate the prominence of "labor" films because
they employ a narrow interpretation that conceives such films as primarily
about labor unions or labor strikes. Such a restricted view of labor, however,
ignores the vast majority of wage earners who did not belong to unions or
go out on strike: most women, children, immigrants, blacks, and unskilled
male workers. In 1910, for example, less than 6 percent of the total labor
force belonged to unions, and probably a smaller percentage participated in
strikes.[21] Yet not only were these people concerned with the difficulties of
earning a living, they—and their union counterparts—were also concerned
with problems relating to their family, religion, politics, leisure, and community. Borrowing concepts used by working-class historians, I suggest

that we think in terms of a more expansive category of working-class films rather than labor films, and see them as exploring the lives of *all* workers (organized and unorganized) and the problems they faced outside, as well as inside, the workplace.

Film scholars generally classify movies in terms of genres—comedies, melodramas, westerns, science fiction, and the like. However, by adopting a different approach and classifying films in terms of their subjects, we can open up new ways of looking at the political meanings of movies. What scholars refer to as social-problem films are part of a larger body of works that, taken collectively, I would call working-class films. Simply put, working-class films are an expansive category that includes any movie whose plot revolves around working-class protagonists. It is a movie's characters and settings (workplaces, tenements, ghettos, etc.), not its genre, that makes it a working-class film. Indeed, these films often involve stock situations and plot lines that could have used people from any class. But since workers and immigrants formed the core of the industry's early market, producers frequently made them the main protagonists of their movies. Blue-collar, white-collar, and service employees all played starring roles in working-class films.

At no time in the industry's history would filmmakers be more concerned with the lives and hardships of working people than during the Progressive era. Yet there was no single cinematic vision of workers or their struggles. The diversity of producers during this period encouraged a contest of ideas over the ways in which filmmakers would entertain, educate, and politicize their audiences. But first, they had to decide upon the topics they would address and the degree to which they were willing to be explicitly political.

The Rise of Working-Class Films

It is not surprising that so many early films were about working-class life. Given the composition of movie audiences, it would be surprising if that were not the case. It is impossible, however, to provide accurate figures for the exact number of working-class films. In order to judge a film's subject matter and political content we need actually to see it, but since most early movies were shot on nitrate stock and have long since disintegrated or disappeared, it is difficult to talk authoritatively about the number of silent films in any particular genre or category. Contemporaneous film reviews are certainly helpful, yet reviewers were usually more concerned with describing a movie's plot than discussing the class background or politics of its characters. Nevertheless, in looking solely for films explicitly about labor and capital conflicts, I identified at least 605 movies made between 1905 (when nickelodeons appeared) and April 1917 (when the United States entered World War I) that could be classified as working-class films. Had I extended my search to include films that merely featured working-class characters the total number would have reached into the thousands.[22]

Silent filmmakers made so many movies about working-class life, not because they were inherently more political or class conscious than their modern counterparts, but because of the material demands created by the rapid expansion of the movie industry and the changing desires of its patrons. Until 1905, producers and distributors were mainly concerned with supplying vaudeville houses and traveling road shows with a modest number of films—the majority of which were made in Europe. The nickelodeon boom triggered a tremendous expansion of exhibition outlets and created a vast new demand for movies. Although American filmmaking was initially dominated by the Motion Picture Patents Company—a monopolistic group (known as the "Trust") that tried to limit film production to its ten members—the constant shortage of films and the difficulty of enforcing patent laws created opportunities for dozens of ambitious independent companies. By 1911, Trust giants like Vitagraph and Biograph were each turning out more than two hundred films a year, and smaller independents, such as Solax, nearly a hundred. Yet this was still not enough to satisfy the public's insatiable hunger for movies.[23]

Production demands were further complicated by changing audience tastes. As the novelty of watching moving images wore off, patrons asked exhibitors for new and different kinds of films. Hoping to fulfill audience demand and attract new customers, exhibitors began changing their programs daily, and sometimes twice on weekends. This, in turn, created even greater demand for new products. Quantity quickly superseded quality as the central concern of exhibitors, distributors, and producers. With the industry churning out an annual average of four thousand films between 1911 and 1915, the greatest danger companies faced was running out of ideas for new projects.[24]

Producers may well have wanted to make "better" films that would attract prosperous folks and please their critics, but unless they made movies that appealed to their main patrons their businesses were likely to suffer. Unlike today's leading Hollywood studios, which target their big-budget movies at a heterogeneous mass market that includes all classes, races, and ethnic groups, early film companies often geared their products to particular ethnic and working-class audiences. "Instead of brains catering to brains," Moving Picture World critic H. F. Hoffman complained in 1910, "it was a case of class catering to class." Indeed, many early filmmakers came from backgrounds similar to those of their clients. Siegmund Lubin, a Prussian-born Jew who entered the movie business after years of working as an itinerant peddler, and Carl Laemmle, a German-born Jew who sold clothing in the Midwest before opening a nickelodeon and later Universal Film Manufacturing Company, made dozens of movies that catered to Jewish audiences. Kalem's frequent production of films about Irish life, many directed by Sidney Olcott (of Irish descent), earned the company the nickname of "The O'Kalems." Smaller independent companies such as Yankee, Thanhouser, and Reliance also carved out a successful niche by producing films for proletarian moviegoers. Likewise, many of the first "movie stars"—Charlie Chaplin, Mary Pickford, Mack Sennett, and Buster Keaton—came from working-class backgrounds and began their careers by making films that related to the lives and fantasies of working-class audiences.[25]

In addition to featuring working-class protagonists, working-class films also focused on the problems and pleasures of urban life. In the era before large studio lots and elaborate indoor stages, before the "star" system seized the public's imagination, the setting was frequently the star of the show. Most pioneering film companies were located in cities—Biograph, Edison, and Vitagraph in New York, Lubin in Philadelphia, and Essanay and Selig in Chicago—and producers made extensive use of city thoroughfares, buildings, skylines, alleyways, and crowds. *The Skyscrapers* (Biograph 1906) and *The Tunnel Workers* (Biograph 1906) presented extraordinary scenes shot, respectively, atop the city's massive skyscrapers and inside its mammoth underground tunnels. The Lower East Side and its residents were the stars of *A Child of the Ghetto* (Biograph 1910), *The Lily of the Tenements* (Biograph 1911), *The Musketeers of Pig Alley* (Biograph 1912), and dozens of similar films that offered viewers extensive footage of actual street life in this colorful and densely populated area of New York. Scenes of bustling thoroughfares packed with food and clothing stalls, of immigrant women busily bargaining with vendors, of children sitting on fire escapes or hanging out of tenement windows, of Jews, Italians, Irish, and various Eastern Europeans all coexisting within the same cramped space were familiar aspects of everyday life to local residents. But to audiences in small, ethnically homogeneous southern, midwestern, and western towns, they must have seemed like pictures of exotic foreign lands.[26]

In their never-ending search for new ideas, filmmakers frequently adapted famous plays and novels to the screen. The social realism so prominent in contemporary literature was especially favored by producers. Novels by Jack London, Theodore Dreiser, Upton Sinclair, and Frank Norris, plays by David Belasco, Clyde Fitch, and short stories and articles from *McClure's*, *Cosmopolitan*, and the *Saturday Evening Post* were all turned into films. When producers and screenwriters ran out of literary sources they turned to newspapers. "Half-remembered anecdotes, newspaper headlines, cartoons, jokes, domestic affairs, social issues, economic tribulations—all sorts of everyday American ideas and activities," observes Lewis Jacobs, "found their way to the screen."[27]

This diverse array of filmmakers and ideas led to movies about all aspects of working-class life. Working-class films generally fell into one of three categories: one, a vast number of innocuous romances, melodramas, comedies, and adventures that used workers and immigrants as their protagonists, but could just as easily have used middle-class or elite characters; two, a more modest number of social-problem films that depicted the general hardships of working-class life; and three, a smaller group of highly politicized labor-capital films (the subject of the next chapter) that focused on the often violent confrontations between employers and employees. Protagonists in these three categories spanned the entire working class and included factory workers, clerks, miners, saleswomen, shopkeepers, secretaries, farmers, sweatshop workers, policemen, prostitutes, laundresses, and a wide range of other blue- and white-collar employees.

Not all working-class films tried to uplift audiences or solve social problems. Nickelodeon patrons, the *Baltimore Sun* observed in 1907, loved a "broad comedy, broad pathos, melodrama, anything in which there is a hearty, healthy laugh or where the heart thrills and the breath catches."[28] Although social meaning can be found in almost any movie, most comedies were aimed simply at making audiences laugh. A number of early satires brought the sexual titillation and bawdy spirit of burlesque to the screen. Films that revealed women's legs or undergarments, such as *The Dressmakers Accident* (Biograph 1903) and *The Physical Culture Lesson* (Biograph 1906), evoked loud guffaws from filmgoers and angry grumbles from more staid reformers. Ben Turpin, John Bunny, and Al Christie also turned familiar vaudeville sketches and comic-strip characters into wildly amusing films.

Comedy could also be a very political genre. Many forms of laughter came at the expense of characters whom working-class filmgoers undoubtedly enjoyed seeing lampooned. *How Hubby Got a Raise* (Biograph 1910), for example, mocks the pretensions of upwardly mobile white-collar workers, their often ambitious wives, and their prurient bosses. In this film, the aggressive wife of a timid office worker tries to impress his boss, whom she has invited over to dinner, by decorating their modest apartment with lavish furnishings that she borrows from friends and neighbors—including a maid. Of course, the scheme backfires. The boss is appalled that his employee should possess such luxuries and fires him for living beyond his means. Comedians such as Mack Sennett, Mabel Normand, Charlie Chaplin, and the Keystone Kops turned out slapstick farces that featured working-class characters and humorous situations immediately familiar

Comedies such as *Work* (Essanay 1915), starring Charlie Chaplin, mocked the foibles of the "respectable" middle class.

to wage-earning audiences. These films ridiculed virtually every aspect of daily life: work, authority figures, middle-class standards of behavior, and the working class itself. Charlie Chaplin, the master comic of his age, delighted in eliciting laughs by poking fun at the "better" classes. *Work* (Essanay 1915), is a comic nightmare of what happens when an incompetent worker comes to wallpaper the house of a "respectable" middle-class family more concerned that Charlie will steal something than about the lousy job he is doing.[29]

When filmmakers wanted to explore the problems of society in a more serious manner, they turned to drama and its hyperbolic sibling, melodrama. Comedies composed upwards of 70 percent of all fiction films made before 1908. Yet as the locus of demand shifted from vaudeville houses to movie theaters, so too did the form and content of film. Filmmakers responded to audience desires and industrywide pressure to attract a better clientele by turning out more one- and two-reel dramas. When the *New York Dramatic Mirror* analyzed the 242 films produced in July 1910, they found that 53 percent were dramas and melodramas, 35 percent comedies, 9 percent educational, and 3 percent trick and novelty films. During the next two decades, drama and melodrama continued to reign as the dominant cinematic style.[30]

Melodramas were especially successful vehicles for exploring the multi-faceted problems of working-class life because they contained elements that appealed to audiences and reformers alike. Early moviegoers found many of the first narrative dramas hard to follow, especially those based on sources unfamiliar to workers and immigrants. People often stayed to see the "same picture two and even three times," one film critic remarked in 1908, "because they do not understand it the first time." Melodramas offered film-makers plots and characters that were readily accessible to most wage earners. Although the medium of film was new, the melodrama was not. Popular dime novels and theaters specializing in melodramatic plays were well-established parts of nineteenth-century working-class culture. Filmmakers built on this tradition by producing movies with themes that were, as Pennsylvania censors reported in 1915, "well explored by the writer of the old dime novel and the melodrama." Blue-collar audiences found the standard plots, heroes, villains, emotional extremes, and dramatic resolutions of movie melodramas predictable and easy to understand.[31]

Snobbish movie critics occasionally scoffed at the "cheap" melodrama "as a passé genre utterly rejected by society's best element." But for more broad-minded writers and reformers, the social problem melodrama fulfilled long-standing middle-class hopes of making leisure a culturally elevating experience that could teach as well as amuse. The "melodrama does not simply stage a battle between good and evil (with good triumphing)," explains film scholar Robert Lang, "but rather tries to establish that clear notions of good and evil do prevail, and that there *are* moral imperatives." By "preaching a moral," adds Eileen Bowser, the "popular melodrama . . . became the most successful genre of film for satisfying the needs of uplift."[32]

From 1905 to 1917 the movies preached—and the subjects of their sermons were ordinary working people and those who exploited them. Working people, however, were not presented as a homogeneous class but rather as a heterogeneous group of people who encountered a wide range of problems. Producers of working-class films were generally more concerned with dramatizing these problems than with offering specific solutions. Only a small percentage of movies focused on workers as members of organized oppositional groups (that was the task of the labor-capital films discussed in the next chapter). Although some working-class films concentrated on the misfortunes faced by specific ethnic or racial groups, others portrayed difficulties experienced by a wide range of native and foreign-born wage earners. Other scholars have done a meticulous job of analyzing films that depicted the many obstacles facing women, African-Americans, Italians, Jews, Russians, Chinese, Japanese, and other immigrant groups. Rather than duplicate these efforts, let us look at films that explored the more general travails of working-class life.[33]

The Hardships of Daily Life

The social-problem films that formed the core of working-class melodramas were almost always sympathetic to the plight of their subjects. Certainly it would be hard to insult the people who composed the backbone of your audience. Yet these films were also very much a part of the Progressive era, and although specific messages varied with the subject of the film and the perspective of the filmmaker, collectively their political sensibilities reflected the basic reformist tenets—and limitations—of Progressive thought and its largely middle-class, male view of the world. They deplored extremes in class conditions and denounced both excessive wealth and abject poverty. They endeavored to define proper class roles by prescribing acceptable forms of behavior from above and below. They condemned individual capitalists, but never capitalism. They called for reform, but denounced violence or radical solutions. They were sympathetic to the hardships honest working people suffered at the hands of rapacious businessmen, exploitative employers, heartless landlords, greedy money lenders, and the idle rich. But they rarely endorsed collective action by the exploited as a means of solving those ills.

In visualizing their ideological messages, filmmakers were deeply influenced by the gender, age, and occupation of their subjects. Like most Progressive reformers, filmmakers found the exploitation of women, children, and elderly workers far more troubling than conflicts between male employers and employees who, according to dominant notions of masculinity, were expected to fend for themselves. The predominantly liberal sympathies of these more general social-problem films stood in sharp contrast to the varied ideological positions seen in labor-capital films (both were subsets of working-class films). The labor-capital films focused primarily on contentious conflicts involving male workers in heavily organized industries (whom filmmakers assumed were the more important part of the working class), while the former concentrated on women and children who toiled in occupations that were less prone—on the screen at least—to labor organizing or class violence.

Female sweatshop workers, outworkers (those who took work back to their homes), mill workers, and sales clerks were the favorite subjects of social-problem filmmakers. Workers in these films rarely belonged to unions, nor were unions even mentioned. One would never realize from these films that garment trades' workers, women as well as men, engaged in intensive organizing efforts and repeated strikes during the early decades of the century. Social-problem films also reinforced dominant ideals of patriarchy and paternalism. Working women were portrayed less as workers than as women in need of constant protection by well-intentioned males; rarely were they shown as powerful actors capable of solving problems on their own. Labor activism and femininity were assumed to be antithetical. Film-makers repeatedly manipulated the sympathies of their audience by focus-ing on the seemingly most "helpless" members of the working class: women, children, the elderly, and the unemployed. Indeed, it was the very helplessness of these people that attracted filmmakers and added poignancy and pathos to their plots.

Poverty and the daily battle for survival were central themes in numerous working-class films of the era. During the late nineteenth century, the harsh ideology of Social Darwinism led many prosperous Americans to blame the poor for their poverty. These movies, however, depicted the impoverished as hard-working people who either could not find work or were paid starva-tion wages by bosses and charged exorbitant rents by slumlords. Poverty was not a matter of individual failings but was caused by circumstances beyond the control of individuals. Filmmakers delivered their political commentaries through the repeated use of standard story lines, poignant images, editing techniques, and a host of other cinematic devices. In *The Kleptomaniac* (Edison 1905), director Edwin Porter, who maintained a strong "distaste for the workings of large-scale, impersonal capitalistic en-terprises," shows audiences how hunger forces honest but impoverished young women to steal bread in order to feed their families. *From the Sub-merged* (Essanay 1912), one of the most moving films of its time, offers staggering scenes of homelessness, despair, hunger, and downtrodden men forced to sleep on park benches and stand on bread lines in order to get their daily sustenance. The film also offers a blistering indictment of "slumming parties" by wealthy young men and women who journey into the ghettos dressed in tuxedos and gowns in pursuit of novel adventures.[34]

No one was better at visualizing the injustices suffered by the poor and the great disparities of wealth that plagued society than D. W. Griffith. He visualized his politics through the powerful editing technique then called "alternate scenes" and now referred to as crosscutting, parallel editing, or ideological editing.[35] Although these techniques were used by such talented directors as Edwin Porter, Thomas Ince, and Sidney Olcott, Griffith was the undoubted master. He portrayed class differences (and, by extension, differ-ences between good and evil, moral and immoral) by repeatedly contrasting scenes of extravagant consumption by the idle rich with scenes showing the destitution and hardships suffered by the industrious poor.

The Song of the Shirt (Biograph 1908), one of his most powerful and radical films, offers an example of how Griffith uses visual technique to build audience sympathy for the poor and hatred of the rich. The film opens in the tattered but tidy tenement flat of a young seamstress (Florence Law-rence) and her deathly ill sister—a flat in which a sewing machine occupies a dominant position in the middle of the room. Desperate for money,

Florence goes to the Acme Waist Company and begs the foreman for a job. Although suffering rude and abusive treatment, the hard-working woman is overjoyed when she is finally given a small bundle of cloth to sew at home. The camera then cuts to a fancy restaurant where we see the stout company owner and his girlfriend laughing, drinking, and gorging themselves. Having established his basic contrast, Griffith moves back to the tenement flat where we see the company agent inspecting and then refusing to accept the seamstress' work. She points to her obviously dying sister and pleads for another chance, but he callously picks up the clothing and walks out—without paying her a cent. The audience is immediately taken back to the restaurant and we now see the idle boss drinking champagne and cavorting with *two* loose women (virtuous women did not sit on men's laps or kiss them in public). The final scene cuts to the tenement flat where the sickly sister, unable to obtain the medical care she desperately needs (which would undoubtedly cost less than a bottle of champagne), goes into her death throes and dies. Her grief-stricken sibling tears at her hair and the movie ends with her collapsing over the body of her beloved sister.

The basic themes played out in *Song of the Shirt* could be seen in many of Griffith's early films. He delighted in offering viewers scenes contrasting the conspicuous overconsumption of the idle rich with the dignified destitution of the working poor, and showing how employers often treated workers as disposable human machines who, if they broke down or died, could be easily replaced. Audiences loved these themes as much as Griffith. His movies were so popular that Biograph asked its writers in 1912 for more "plots contrasting the rich and poor."[36]

Despite their obvious sympathies, these films also revealed the middle-class fantasies and prejudices of their makers. The poor are portrayed as middle-class people without money. They are respectable folks who have simply fallen on hard times. Scenes of tenement flats, especially in Griffith's movies, reveal clean apartments that usually contain one or two pieces of tasteful, albeit frayed furniture, some china, a few framed photographs, a painting, and perhaps several settings of silverware.[37] Images of unsanitary, crumbling, rat-infested tenement flats that appeared in the photographs of Jacob Riis and his contemporaries were rarely seen on the screen. The compassion of filmmakers was genuine, but it was also contingent upon the poor acting in certain ways: they should be clean, respectable, hard working, virtuous, kind, and supportive of their families. Working people could certainly be all these things, but they could also be mean, dirty, loud, and ill-mannered. Yet rarely do we ever see a sympathetic central protagonist displaying these latter traits. The cinematic poor are in fact idealized versions of how the middle class ought to behave.

The plots of working-class films also revolved around problems faced in the workplace. Hundreds of films featured scenes exposing the horrid conditions of sweatshops, cotton mills, canneries, laundries, factories, and tenement flats used to perform outwork. Audiences repeatedly saw how poor but honest (and unorganized) working men, women, and children—though usually the latter two—were badly treated by employers. Films like *The Ghetto Seamstress* (1910) succeeded in evoking sympathy and outrage among viewers. By exposing the evils of a piecework system "that forces poor immigrant women into virtual slavery," explained one notably impressed movie critic, the film gave native-born citizens a "new impression with respect to the downtrodden and cruelly treated people who came to America."[38]

Movie companies were undoubtedly aware of the large numbers of women attending theaters, and perhaps this was another reason why female wage earners figured so prominently in social-problem films. Working women, whose ranks more than doubled between 1890 and 1910, suffered far more in these films than their male counterparts, for they experienced the dual indignities of economic exploitation and sexual harassment.[39] *The Paymaster* (Biograph 1906), *The Mill Girl* (Vitagraph 1907), and *The Saleslady* (1916) revealed the general hardships of work life as well as the unwanted sexual advances that young working women received from foremen, bosses, and landlords. In *The Octoroon* (1909), nonwhite women laboring in southern turpentine forests were portrayed as the victims of racial, as well as sexual, abuse.[40]

In most instances, heroines were able to fend off lechers—usually with the aid of a friendly male. However, in *Shoes* (Bluebird 1916), director Lois Weber shows how a virtuous young working girl, who supports her elderly parents and shares a bed with her two sisters, ultimately sleeps with "Cabaret" Charlie in exchange for a pair of much-needed shoes. The convergence of economic and sexual exploitation was also portrayed in a number of sympathetic films dealing with prostitution. *Traffic in Souls* (Universal 1913) and *The Wages of Sin* (Klaw and Erlanger 1914) reveal how unemployed factory hands and newly arrived immigrants and country girls, unable to find work in the city, are forced to sell their bodies in order to survive.

The exploitation of child labor was a favorite topic of journalists, photographers, politicians, and filmmakers. Producers such as Carl Laemmle joined the Progressive campaign "to improve labour conditions and forbid the employment of children in sweating shops" by preaching "unashamedly through the medium of his studios."[41] *Children Who Labor* (Edison 1912) and *The Cry of the Children* (Thanhouser 1912) show how manufacturers use child laborers to displace adult workers who, in turn, are forced to send even more of their children to work in order to make ends meet. In some films, such as *A Child of the Ghetto* (Biograph 1910), child or female laborers are able to escape their oppressors by leaving the city for a more idyllic life

Working-class films like *The Ragamuffin* (Lasky 1916) depicted the hardships suffered by female wage earners.

in the countryside. Other films, however, punctured the myth of rural happiness by offering harsh appraisals of life outside the city. *The Spirit Awakened* (Biograph 1912) portrays farmers and rural laborers as hard-working people plagued by many of the same problems as their urban counterparts: greedy money lenders and bullying foremen who threaten to take away their homes and loved ones.

Filmmakers tackled the issue of discrimination against the elderly by dramatizing the plight of aging workers. *Simple Charity* (Biograph 1910) and *What Shall We Do with Our Old?* (Biograph 1911) told sad stories familiar to many working-class viewers—especially those who suffered encounters with much-hated efficiency experts and "scientific" managers. In both films, elderly workers (a cigar maker and carpenter, respectively) are discharged by ruthless foremen bent on weeding out men who cannot work fast enough. Lacking sufficient savings to retire and unable to find an employer who will hire an older worker, their lives come to disastrous ends. In the first instance the starving cigar maker falls ill and dies, and in the second film the carpenter's sick wife needlessly perishes because he is unable to provide the food or medical care that would save her.

The limitations of Progressive ideology that permeated cinematic treatments of poverty are also evident in films about the work world. These movies saw the world in terms of good and bad individuals and rarely in terms of classes. Inequality and injustice are caused by the greed of corrupt men rather than a corrupt economic system. Moreover, the individuals censured in these films rarely seem realistic. In keeping with the exaggerated nature of melodramatic conventions, employers are presented as caricatured figures who are either sex maniacs, the dissipated idle rich, the insatiably greedy, or foreigners who did not go by "American" rules. By employing such highly stereotypical figures, these films suggested that the problems of exploitation were not rooted in the capitalist system, but in the peculiar behavior of wayward individuals. Justice, then, could be achieved by reforming or controlling the behavior of these deviants. It did not necessitate the radical restructuring of business or government.

The prejudices and contradictory feelings filmmakers held toward wage earners were also visible in many of these films. Compassion toward working people was often dependent upon their displaying the seemingly middle-class virtues of industriousness and self-discipline. Dual messages were occasionally delivered within the same film. Sympathetic portrayals of mistreated workers were offset by scenes depicting wage earners as lazy people who would not work hard unless closely supervised. In *The Plain Song* (Biograph 1910), a film showing the commendable efforts of a young working woman to support her elderly parents, Griffith also includes several shots of salesgirls flirting with customers rather than tending to their work, and a janitor who dozes on the job when nobody is around.

Despite their general sympathy for the travails of workers, these films rarely offered solutions to their problems. Workers are portrayed as victims who do not or cannot fight back. Individual protest or collective action is rarely presented as a viable response to exploitation. Instead, workers are advised to keep at their labors and patiently await outside intervention by clergy, reformers, government officials, or repentant capitalists. The call for caution advanced in these films was rooted both in the Progressives' general fears of a working class out of control and in a more specific set of gender prejudices. When it came to women, many filmmakers shared a number of restrictive Victorian attitudes and simply could not, or would not, imagine a world in which powerful women (acting independently or collectively) remedied the problems confronting their lives without male assistance. Working women were sympathetic only so long as they remained pretty, vulnerable, sexually pure, and in need of patriarchal protection.[42]

Children Who Labor, which appeared in the middle of a national debate over child-labor legislation in 1912, provides an excellent example of the ideological perspectives and limitations of one widely distributed reform film. Produced by the Edison Company in cooperation with the National Child Labor Committee, this engaging melodrama opens with a depressing scene of downtrodden children shuffling into a factory to begin their day's labor. Just before entering this hellhole, they lift their arms and implore Uncle Sam, who appears godlike in the clouds, to help them. But Sam ignores their pleas, and the skies over the factory cloud up with the word GREED. Subsequent scenes show how childhood and family life are shattered as callous factory owner Mr. Hanscomb ignores the pleas of reformers and continues to hire cheap child labor instead of more expensive able-bodied men. Conditions at the factory are only changed through a series of bizarre circumstances: Hanscomb's beloved daughter accidentally falls off of a train, is taken in by a poor immigrant family, and is unknowingly sent to work in her father's factory, where she eventually collapses from exhaustion. Only after the inevitable reunion of father and daughter does the former come to realize and remedy his mistakes. The penultimate scene shows happy children passing the factory gate with school books in hand, while fathers and elder sons proudly enter the workplace. The movie ends on a more somber note. An intertitle flashes the message, "Lest We Forget," and the camera cuts to a scene of children vainly imploring Uncle Sam for help as dollar signs flash across the skies.

Children Who Labor was well received by audiences and reviewers. One industry critic claimed he had "never heard the applause that this picture got." And yet, despite its clearly reformist aims, the movie offers little insight into why this situation arose. The evils of child labor and factory exploitation are simply reduced to the greed of individuals. By opening and closing with appeals for government intervention, the film rejects older laissez-faire values in favor of an activist state that would protect the rights of children. But the state is ultimately seen as unwilling or unable to act. The only solution offered comes through the personal conversion of the factory owner and not through action by workers themselves. Neither this nor other films dealing with factory exploitation or the horrors of tenement life ever ask why these conditions arose or challenge the capitalist system that created them or the government that sustained them. Instead they accepted the evils of industrial and urban life as givens and simply went about trying to reform them. Taken collectively, these films, as Kay Sloan so aptly puts it, reflected the "process of ideological containment through romance, redemption, and privatization."[43]

In visualizing the working class, especially its women and children, early filmmakers presented audiences with movies that were sympathetic and safe. Social-problem films dramatized the problems of society in a manner that pleased working-class patrons without alienating the industry's more conservative critics. While empathizing with their plight, these films consistently portrayed workers as relatively powerless and suggested that the real power to change their lives lay outside their world. Patience and paternalism were the watchwords of these productions. Yet, although some film-makers were content with simply exposing the problems of working-class life, others were determined to play an active role in shaping class consciousness and class relations. In few areas of American life were entertainment and ideology more deeply intertwined than in the highly politicized labor-capital films that offered competing solutions to the most contentious class conflicts of the age.

3

The Good, the Bad, and the Violent:
Class Conflict and
the Labor-Capital Genre

SILENT FILMMAKERS were not afraid to confront the most controversial issues of the day. Conflict and tension, they understood, were necessary elements in sustaining the attention of audiences. And no area of national life offered them as many examples of conflict and tension as the tumultuous battles between employers and employees. Despite rhetoric about America's "classless" society, few countries experienced more labor violence in the late nineteenth and early twentieth centuries than the United States. America's second Civil War began in July 1877, when more than a hundred people were killed as federal troops, national guardsmen, and local police brutally crushed a general strike by the nation's railroad workers. Over the next half century, striking working men and women in a wide variety of industries repeatedly clashed with government troops and employer-hired armies equipped with rifles, machine guns, and cannons. Death was often the end result: sixteen deaths during the Homestead Steel Strike of 1892, thirty deaths during the Cripple Creek (Colorado) strike of 1903, and hundreds of deaths during the bloody war that raged in the nation's coal fields during the first three decades of the new century.[1]

The pioneers of American cinema did not avoid these contentious class battles. They tackled them head-on and proposed solutions to the most pressing problems of the day. Politically engaged directors and screenwriters such as D. W. Griffith, Augustus Thomas, Julian Lamothe, and William C. de Mille moved beyond the general depictions of everyday life that characterized most working-class films and offered highly charged explorations of strikes, lockouts, union organizing, and socialist and anarchist efforts to overthrow the capitalist system. Filmmakers knew that movies about strikes or labor unions did not have to be boring. They filled their productions with the same kinds of dramatic elements that are found in today's most successful films: action, violence, romance, and tension.

Class-conscious productions grew so popular by 1910 that movie reviewers began writing about the emergence of a new genre of "labor-capital" films. When critics or scholars speak of genres, they mean a body of similar films in which easily recognizable characters act out "a predictable story pattern within a familiar setting." Genres represent a standardized product. "The audience has some idea of what to expect from a comedy or a Western," explains Eileen Bowser, "just as consumers know what to expect when they order a specific kind of sausage." Like other genres, labor-capital films followed a standard narrative form and utilized stock images, plots, and characters to tell their story. Going beyond entertainment, they also tried to make sense of labor disputes by offering audiences visions of the principal protagonists, their grievances, and the possible solutions to their problems.[2]

Labor-capital films, which were a subset of working-class films, differed from the more general array of working-class productions, and from each other, in the types of workers they examined and the ideological positions they adopted. Unlike most working-class films, labor-capital productions were highly polemical pictures that explored struggles among unions, strikers, capitalists, police, and government troops. They also concentrated on a more controversial sector of the working class. Instead of focusing on unorganized women, children, and elderly wage earners, their plots dealt with adult male workers who labored in the nation's most contentious and highly organized industries: miners, steel workers, railroad workers, and skilled industrial workers. These movies also explored the activities of socialists, anarchists, nihilists, and communists.

In telling their stories, labor-capital films advanced a range of ideological perspectives unequaled in the history of American cinema. Political life at the turn of the century was far more varied and oppositional in nature than today. Americans voted in large numbers for candidates from the United Labor, Populist, Progressive, Socialist, and Prohibition parties. Labor-capital films reflected the political diversity of their times and fell into one of five ideological categories: conservative, radical, liberal, populist, or anti-authoritarian. Between the rise of nickelodeons in 1905 and April 1917, when American entry into World War I altered the politics of films in dramatic ways, producers released at least 274 labor-capital productions. Of the 244 films whose political perspective could be accurately determined, 46 percent (112) were liberal, 34 percent (82) conservative, 9 percent (22) anti-authoritarian, 7 percent (17) populist, and 4 percent (11) radical.[3]

To provide some common understanding, I see conservative films as those that presented worker, union, or radical activity in the worst possible light and rarely explained the causes of strikes or employee discontent. Radical films offered unabashedly positive depictions of socialists, radicals, and their struggles, and equally scathing critiques of capitalists and capitalism. Liberal films decried the exploitation of innocent workers, condemned irresponsible capitalists, called for cooperation between labor and capital, and advocated reform—not radicalism—as the best method for solving the nation's industrial ills. Populist films preached a gut-level hatred of monop-olists and showed how they repeatedly undermined the well-being of ordi-nary citizens. Anti-authoritarian movies, though not directly challenging capitalism, mocked the authority of those who gave working people the hardest time: foremen, police, judges, and employers.[4]

Placing movies into particular ideological categories has arbitrary ele-ments to it and another scholar might well put the same film into a different category. Moreover, 274 films may seem rather scant when compared to the 4,000 to 5,000 films released each year during this period. Yet the pre-cise category of any one film or the relative percentage of labor-capital films compared to all movies is less important than their cumulative impact on audiences. Certainly no one movie was likely to alter a viewer's vision of the world. But seeing the same images and political messages over and over again in hundreds of films dealing with similar problems could change the ways people understood daily events—especially events about which they had little first-hand knowledge. It was by watching labor-capital films that many Americans got their first glimpse of what a socialist, anarchist, strike, lockout, or union organizer looked like—and whether these were people who should be admired or reviled. Indeed, labor-capital films mat-tered the most for people who had the least contact with unions, radicals, or mass movements.

Movies were also attracting and shaping the consciousness of a class in flux. Although movies were initially a working-class medium, not all work-ers saw themselves as part of a single, united working class. The uneven development of industrial capitalism created a variety of workers (skilled and unskilled, blue collar and white collar) and a variety of working-class experiences and needs. Rarely did blue-collar workers in one industry join in common action with blue-collar workers in another industry, let alone with white-collar workers. Class identity was not a fixed economic or social reality but an ambiguous set of relations. Movies gave life to these relations by showing audiences what different classes looked like, the problems they faced, and how they might solve those problems. In so doing, they helped shape, not just reflect, the ways in which millions of blue- and white-collar workers understood the meaning of class. What audiences see, observed a New York Times reporter, "is partly a reflection of what they are. And what they are is no less influenced by what they see."[5]

The battle among filmmakers to create and perpetuate a dominant set of class images was nothing less than a battle to control the mind's eye of millions of citizens. Whether the public would embrace unions or big busi-ness, whether government would use its considerable power on behalf of labor or capital, and whether working people would deal with their employ-ers on an individual basis or through mass organizations like labor unions were matters that might well be decided by what people saw on the screen.

Although some citizens hoped that movies with conciliatory messages would have "a salutary influence" in resolving class conflict, others worried that radical productions would exacerbate tensions by exciting "class feelings" and bringing "discredit upon the agencies of government." Indeed, the greatest fear of labor's enemies was that working-class viewers would find a collective voice while watching silent films.[6]

The Material Roots of Cinematic Ideology

Early filmmakers offered their patrons a wide array of ideological visions of class conflict, but why did their films take on the ideologies they did? Why did an industry that grew hostile to organized labor after World War I start out by making films that expressed strong liberal sympathies toward the struggles of workers, unions, and radicals? For years, scholars posed these questions in terms of whether films shape or reflect society. I would suggest that we can approach this issue more fruitfully by first asking how movies reflected the industry that produced them. To understand the changing ideology of film, we need to examine the material conditions under which they were made and the variety of people who made them. Films are not just cultural artifacts but products made in workplaces by employers and employees. The images of strikes, unions, radicals, and capitalists that appeared on the screen did not simply represent some general trend in society but were closely tied to the changing economic structure of the film industry, the backgrounds of individual filmmakers, and the state of labor relations within the studios. Certainly, it would be hard to imagine an industry perpetually ravaged by strikes and labor problems producing films with a pro-union orientation. We begin our analysis of labor-capital films by venturing beyond the screen to survey the circumstances under which men and women made these movies.

Contrary to the claims of Frankfurt School theorists and a number of neo-Marxian film scholars, there was no single bourgeoisie imposing a single "capitalist" vision upon the public. The film industry was certainly a capitalist business, but not all capitalists were alike. The oppositional character of many labor-capital films was undoubtedly influenced by the oppositional battles fought within the industry itself.[7]

In drawing ideas for tirades against trusts and monopolies, filmmakers had only to look in their own backyards. Many producers entered the business by challenging the monopolistic Motion Picture Patents Company (MPPC). The MPPC, popularly known as the Trust, was formed in December 1908, when famed inventor Thomas Edison convinced eight other production companies, one importer of films (George Kleine), and Eastman Kodak (the sole American manufacturer of raw film) to join together in

limiting the sale of film stock and the production, distribution, and exhibition of movies solely to Trust members. By early 1909, the Trust controlled
virtually all domestic production and by April 1911 its offshoot, the General Film Company, owned 75 percent of the nation's film exchanges. Outsiders such as Carl Laemmle denounced the film monopoly as "an evil
thing" and fought to end its "merciless abuse of privilege" by turning out
their own films. It took until 1915 for a federal court to declare the Trust
an illegal conspiracy in restraint of trade and order it dissolved, but feisty
independent producers and distributors effectively ended its rule several
years earlier.[8]

Many of the early mavericks who succeeded in destroying the Trust were
Eastern European Jews who had suffered hardship in their lives and could
never completely shake the anti-authoritarian sentiments of their youth or
the anti-Semitism they encountered among industry critics who, like one
clergyman, characterized the film business as "a Jewish syndicate furnishing
indecencies for the city." Immigrant producers such as Laemmle, William
Fox, Adolph Zukor, Lewis Selznick, and Samuel Goldwyn played an important role in shaping the subject matter and politics of early films. Fox, who
grew up in the tenements of New York's Lower East Side, considered himself as a youth "a talking Socialist" and insisted that he never forgot the
lessons he learned from radical leaders. As a young man, he reflected, "I was
satisfied that the system then in operation was wrong, and that the proper
social system of the world should be socialistic. I despised both capital and
capitalism." Though not a Jew, Pat Powers, a tough Irishman and cofounder
of Universal Film Manufacturing Company, spent his early years working as
a blacksmith and union organizer. Laemmle, Zukor, Selznick, and Goldwyn
may not have identified with socialists or labor unions, but neither did they
embrace the white Anglo-Saxon Protestant establishment that ran the nation's big businesses, as well as a majority of Trust studios. Although Trust
companies turned out both liberal and conservative movies, small independent firms produced the vast majority of radical films.[9]

The liberal sympathies of working-class and labor-capital films were also
influenced by the large number of women employed in the creative end of
the business. Various studies have shown that women maintained more
positions of power in the prewar era (as producers, directors, writers, script
editors, and heads of script divisions) than at any other time in the industry's history. Although only a few of these women were feminists or radicals,
many could not help but recognize the hardships that plagued working
people. Anita Loos, Lois Weber, Cleo Madison, and others used their positions to make films about problems of particular concern to many female
moviegoers: marriage, sexual equality, birth control, earning a living,
women's suffrage, and labor-capital conflicts. Indeed, fourteen different

women worked as directors, producers, or writers on nearly two dozen pre-war labor-capital films and on dozens of working-class movies.[10]

The relatively inexpensive costs of production and the constant demand for films allowed producers to indulge their political sentiments, or those of their directors and writers. "When film companies turned out several short films a month," explains Kay Sloan, "the production of a potentially controversial film was far less of an economic risk than it would be in the later age of the blockbuster."[11] Exhibitor demand was based on the overall box-office appeal of a company's products rather than on any one film. Moreover, since distributors usually supplied theaters with a block of short films from a particular company, possible financial losses from one weak or controversial film would be offset by the rest.

Filmmakers could also assume liberal attitudes toward strikes and unions because producers faced few major labor problems before 1916. Militant movie operators' unions were well established by 1910 and engaged in numerous disputes with exhibitors across the country. On the nation's movie lots, however, unions were slow to organize, and when they did they remained bitterly divided by jurisdictional disputes over who should control production within the industry. Although there were occasional walkouts and threats of more serious actions, studio unions did not launch a single industrywide strike before the First World War. Organizational efforts by movie actors and actresses were equally ineffective. Unionization campaigns, which began as early as 1910, remained sporadic and largely unsuccessful until the creation of Actors' Equity and the more radical Photoplayers' Union in 1916. Thus, it was easy for film companies to be tolerant of unions on the screen when they did not have to battle them off the screen.[12]

Concentrated efforts to organize the movie industry began in 1916, when AFL president Samuel Gompers sent Jim Gray to Los Angeles, the nation's most anti-union city and the production center for a growing number of studios. Gray attempted to stop the bitter infighting and join the studio crafts (stage hands, electricians, cameramen, and laboratory workers) into a single union. Twenty-five of the largest film companies responded to organizing efforts in Los Angeles and New York by creating the Motion Picture Producers' Association in 1916, the industry's first open-shop organization. The bitterness engendered by increasingly heated battles between unions and studios did not, however, make its way onto the screen until several years later.[13]

There was one significant exception to this relatively harmonious era of labor-capital peace. The radical Industrial Workers of the World (IWW) began stirring up trouble for industry personnel in March 1911, when it chartered Industrial Union Local #442, Motion Picture Theater Workers of New York City. Two years later, Maude Thompson organized five hundred workers at the Edison Company in Orange, New Jersey, into an IWW local that promptly protested poor wages and working conditions. The so-called Wobblies made it to Los Angeles in 1914, when they organized movie extras at the Universal Film Company and demanded that their wages be raised from $1 to $2 or $3 a day. When the company refused, the IWW led the extras out on strike and were reported by *Variety* "to have made threats to demolish the studios and camps." It was probably no coincidence that Edison, a leader of the Trust as well as a target of the IWW, was also one of the most prolific producers of anti-union films before the war.[14]

Ideology and Discourse on the Screen

Material circumstances influenced the political perspectives of many film-makers, but how did they go about translating their politics on to the screen, especially in an era when cinematic ideas had to be conveyed without the use of sound? What did a political film look like?

Although individual labor-capital films offered specific ideological messages, taken collectively films within each of the genre's five categories presented viewers with a powerful discourse that showed them how to think about the totality of class conflict. The distinction between ideology and discourse is subtle. I use the term "ideology" when talking about individual films and the term "discourse" when describing the composite thought of a large group of similar films. Ideology is generally defined as a systematic body of ideas about the way the world is or ought to be. As Raymond Williams explains, ideology is more about conjecture than truth and the term is often used pejoratively to indicate "illusion, false consciousness, unreality, upside-down reality." Discourse, on the other hand, is a self-contained system of logic that constructs and legitimizes its own notions of truth. Whether a particular discourse is true or false is far less important than its ability to create a dominant sense of reality that works, as Michel Foucault notes, "to the exclusion of all other forms of discourse." That is, it did not matter whether a conservative or radical discourse about the motivations of socialists or labor unions was ultimately true; what mattered is that viewers would believe one discourse more than any other and use it as a way to understand class conflict.[15]

For Americans caught up in the maelstrom of social and economic transformations that went beyond their conscious understanding, labor-capital films helped translate abstract ideas about class and class conflict into something they could see and understand. These films are also important to our own times, for they created visual stereotypes of workers, unions, radicals, and capitalists that persist to this day. Through a careful reading of surviving movies, stills, scenarios, and reviews we can see how filmmakers used story lines, stock images, editing techniques, casting, costuming, and chore-ography of crowd scenes to impart a wide variety of images and fantasies about class relations. Although it is important not to ascribe too much im-portance to any one film plot, when read as part of the collective discourse of a political category, plots and other cinematic devices reveal a great deal about the ways in which audiences were taught to know the "normal" pro-gression of reality. Whether millions of wage earners, especially newly ar-rived immigrants, would try to resolve their problems on their own or turn to labor unions and socialist parties for help might well be decided by what they saw on the screen.

Conservative Films

The anti-union campaign inaugurated by employers' associations early in the century was accompanied by scores of conservative films that presented positive images of capitalists and negative depictions of unions, radicals, and their struggles. Although the ideologies and goals of the American Fed-eration of Labor, the Industrial Workers of the World, and the Socialist party were all distinct, conservative films rarely distinguished among differ-ent types of mass movements. The small and often violent IWW, not the larger AFL, was portrayed as the typical labor body. Whether done con-sciously or not, this conflation of groups was bound to prejudice viewers against organized labor. By 1900, AFL leaders such as Samuel Gompers had abandoned their radical dreams in favor of reformist campaigns for higher wages, fewer hours, better working conditions, and closed (all-union) shops. While the AFL called for peaceful class cooperation, the militant IWW declared that the "working class and the employing class have nothing in common" and that "a struggle must go on until the workers of the world organize as a class, take possession of the earth and the machinery of pro-duction, and abolish the wage system." These preachings assumed ominous proportions in 1906 when IWW leader "Big Bill" Haywood and Western Federation of Miners president Charles Moyer were indicted for the bomb-ing murder of former Idaho Governor Frank Steunenberg.[16] Imagine, then, how movies featuring violent IWW-like workers must have frightened film-goers unfamiliar with the divisions within organized labor.

Producers had to be careful in telling their stories, for they did not want to offend working-class audiences. Although only a minority of the popula-tion belonged to unions or radical associations, a majority of Americans were employees and not employers. Conservative filmmakers avoided potential problems by adopting a discourse that was sympathetic to individ-ual laborers but scathing in its denunciations of labor leaders and mass movements; a discourse structured, as one labor periodical observed,

"to show the benevolence of capital and the greed and treachery of [orga-
nized] labor."[17]

Plot lines in these films followed a fairly standard story: a union leader,
outside agitator, or radical troublemaker stirs up previously content workers into a frenzy and turns them into an uncontrollable mob. Strikes are
ordered "on the slightest excuse," noted one reviewer, by leaders who use
them to serve "their own selfish ends." These films rarely explored the
causes of worker protests or efforts by union leaders to negotiate peaceful
settlements. Indeed, strikes invariably turn violent as labor leaders transform law-abiding individuals into lawless mobs that blow up factories or set
fire to the boss's home. Major disaster is ultimately averted through the
calming words of the employer, or the sudden discovery of the agitator's
ulterior motives (which have little to do with the workers' welfare), or the
use of outside force (militia or private police) to restore order, or a combination of these elements.[18]

In keeping with the moralizing tradition of melodrama, most conservative films end by urging workers to trust their employers rather than "outside agitators." Alice Guy Blaché, who was a factory owner as well as head
of Solax studios, closed *A Million Dollars* (1913) with an intertitle that declared: "Our employers are often far better than we give them credit for
being." Some filmmakers preferred a more forceful conclusion. When ungrateful employees in the once happy village of Peacedale decide to follow
an incendiary IWW-type leader who eventually blows up their factory, the
milling manufacturer in *The Strike* (1914) teaches his "workers a lesson
never to listen to agitators" by rebuilding his plant in another town.[19]

Cinematic images of violent strikes and bomb-throwing labor leaders
were not simply products of conservative imaginations. Directors and
screen writers on the right and the left who had never participated in a labor
conflict or met an anarchist or IWW organizer drew their visual inspiration
from a variety of graphic images (photographs, paintings, lithographs),
written materials (newspapers, magazines, novels, government reports),
and popular plays that were familiar to most citizens. Filmmakers turned
these frozen images into moving pictures and dramatized their political
ideas through the use of stereotypes. The Chicago Haymarket Riots of 1886,
for example, generated a wellspring of images that associated anarchists
with labor leaders, and large crowds of workers with unruly mobs. One
frequently reproduced lithograph that initially appeared in the May 15,
1886, issue of *Harper's Weekly* showed a foreign looking, bushy-bearded
orator, with fist raised high, exhorting demonstrators to action as strikers
fired pistols at police.[20]

Drawing on stereotypes created in the wake of the Chicago riots, conservative filmmakers repeatedly portrayed strikes and radical movements as
led by a handful of foreign-born agitators who relied upon violence and

Conservative films such as *The Nihilists* (AM & B 1905) ignored the political roots of radicalism and focused instead on the bizarre initiation rituals performed by nihilists and anarchists.

duped good but naive workers into serving their own corrupt needs. Intertitles were not needed to convey these messages, for, to paraphrase movie critic and former baseball star Yogi Berra, audiences could see a lot just by looking. In *The Nihilists* (AM & B 1905), *The Voice of the Violin* (AM & B 1909), and *The Dynamiters* (IMP 1911), socialist and anarchist men are depicted as Eastern European foreigners with disheveled hair, wild beards, and bulging eyes that shine with madness. Their female counterparts dress in male clothes and look like "modern" women but are decidedly unfeminine. When radicals speak to crowds or to each other they do so in a frenzied fashion full of wild gesticulations and fists punching the air. Scenes of meetings offer no insights into radical politics but focus on bizarre initiation rituals and the inevitable throwing of a bomb. By portraying radicalism as the work of immigrants who brought inappropriate European ideas with them, conservative films were able to ascribe labor troubles to a few foreign-born malcontents and not to any systematic flaw in American capitalism.

Conservative films offered equally derogatory portraits of native-born American socialists. These radicals were depicted either as lazy men who lived off the hard work of others, or as wealthy wastrels who, like the smarmy protagonist in *Playing Dead* (Vitagraph 1915), spouted anti-capitalist rhetoric but led lives far more decadent and morally corrupt than those of the people whom they condemned.[21]

This photograph of orderly Industrial Workers of the World members marching in the Los Angeles May Day parade of 1913 offers a stark contrast to
the violent, moblike men and women portrayed in most conservative labor-
capital films.

Not all films that offered stock images of radicals were conservative. Anarchists and nihilists in *The Girl Nihilist* (1908), *Escape From Siberia* (1914)
and *The Cossack Whip* (Edison 1916) have the same long beards, disheveled
hair, and obsession with bombs as their conservative film counterparts, but
to use a phrase favored by former President Ronald Reagan, they are portrayed as "freedom fighters" seeking to liberate their land from tyranny. So
long as these "freedom fighters" operated in Europe, they received favorable
depictions. Yet the moment they were put into an American context they
were portrayed as terrorists who blew up bridges, buildings, and factories,
and resorted to violence for violence's sake.[22]

Organized labor was the most frequent target of conservative diatribes. In
The Iconoclast (Biograph 1910) and *Bill Joins the WWWs* (Komic 1915),
union leaders are unshaven, slovenly men who look more like immigrants
than "real" Americans. Collective action is condemned or ridiculed through
the costuming and placement of actors. Rank-and-file workers are always
dressed in similar dark outfits and move as a single sheeplike body, while
their leader is a Svengali figure who stands apart from the crowd and mes-
merizes them into blind obedience. Neither film provides any explanation
of the grievances that led men and women to strike or join unions. Strikers

were simply shown "blowing-up bridges, and committing other depreda-
tions," as one group of trade unionists complained in 1910. Likewise,
unionists are depicted as greedy and selfish men who, like the sign-carrying
picketers in *Bill Joins the WWWs*—a parody of the IWW—champion the
cause: "Not Work but Money We Want."[23]

A Poor Relation (Klaw and Erlanger 1914) is an excellent example of a
film whose initial plotting appears sympathetic to workers, but whose overall visual imagery is markedly hostile to strikes and labor unions. The movie
opens with poverty-stricken James Sterrett abandoning his wife and two
small children. The film quickly cuts to several years later and we see Mrs.
Sterrett toiling in a horrible factory that, unbeknownst to her, is partially
owned by James. The camera emphasizes the differences between employer
and employee by cutting between scenes of smartly attired James sitting in
his opulent office and two dozen haggard women working under oppressive
conditions. But the empathetic tone and imagery of the film take an abrupt
turn when workers try to remedy their squalid conditions through collective action. Three nasty and shabbily dressed union leaders barge into
Sterrett's office and present their demands in a rude and aggressive fashion.
Not surprisingly, Sterrett "refuses to deal with the labor union committee."
A strike is called and the initially sympathetic factory workers suddenly
turn into an unruly union mob that unleashes violence with no purpose
other than wanton destruction. When strikers are beaten and clubbed by
mounted police, the dominant impression conveyed is that they deserve
their fate. The camera shows us that the forces of the state never initiate
violence; they only respond to it.

Conservative movies also denigrated unions through plot devices that
pitted labor organizations against family interests. Male unionists were repeatedly shown abrogating the most basic obligation of traditionally defined
gender roles: to feed, clothe, and house their family. Strikebreakers, not
strikers, are the heroic figures in these films. It is only through the efforts of
anti-union women that failed union men become manly again. In *Tim Mahoney, The Scab* (1911) viewers see how strike leader Tim Mahoney's obsti-
nate support of a union struggle causes "his little family to suffer." After his
wife pawns all her possessions—including her beloved wedding ring—and
his children are still hungry, Tim breaks the strike and returns to work,
having finally learned the lesson that "Family union should not be sacrificed
for labor union." The fact that 51 percent of all recorded strikes between
1890 and 1916 were fought to improve wages and allow workers more time
at home with their families is overlooked in conservative discourse.[24]

Although most anti-union films focused on urban industrial unrest, a few
ventured West and involved the prototypical American movie hero, the
cowboy, in the labor conflicts of the age. The ranch foreman in *The Agitator*
(1912) returns from an eastern vacation with "his head full of crazy ideas"

In *Courage of the Commonplace* (Edison 1917), union miners are portrayed as disheveled foreigners who hold their meetings in saloons (top), while good non-union workers are depicted as clean-cut Americans who spend their free time drinking lemonade and singing songs with mine Superintendent John McLean (bottom).

and urges his fellow cattle punchers to demand an equitable division of their employer's wealth. Instead of showing the foreman persuading the men through the justice of his ideas, the film ridicules this long-standing labor goal by having him ply the cowboys with whiskey and then incite them to riot. "Broncho Billy" Anderson, the nation's most popular cowboy and part owner of Essanay, also cast his lot against strikers in *The Strike at the 'Little Jonny' Mine* (1911). When a western mine superintendent refuses to grant higher wages, the miners throw down their tools and adjourn to a nearby saloon to plan their violent revenge. "Broncho Billy" is cast as a "good" miner who refuses to sanction violence and, with the help of his invalid wife and the local sheriff, stops the crazed mob from destroying the mines and lynching the superintendent. In this film, as in so many other conservative movies, it is the virtuous individual, not the collective mob, who eventually persuades the employer to increase wages.[25]

Radical Films

Conservative films did not go unopposed. A small number of filmmakers countered these negative images of radicals by advancing positive depictions of socialists, their struggles, and their goals. Some early movie personnel included directors (Ashley Miller, Augustus Thomas), writers (Julian Lamothe), actors and actresses (Francis X. Conlan, Frank Keenan, Charlie Chaplin, Viola Barry) who considered themselves socialists or were openly sympathetic to the cause. As Conlan, a popular star of stage and screen, told one reporter: "I am an actor and a Socialist and naturally interested in Socialist plays." Director Ashley Miller, another outspoken radical, created quite a sensation in 1915 when he refused to direct, at double his salary, a militarist film (*The Fall of a Nation*) written by archconservative Reverend Thomas Dixon, author of the racist novel *The Clansman* (which was made into *The Birth of a Nation*).[26] The constant search for new material also led less political producers to adapt radical novels, plays, and short stories to the screen, though not always with their original edge. This relative openness toward radicals and radicalism would greatly decline during the repressive Red Scare era of 1919–1921. But in the prewar years, if leftist works or personnel could please audiences and make money for producers, then companies were willing to chance their oppositional politics.

Radical films were not all alike. They often differed as much from each other as they did from their conservative counterparts. In general, a radical film was one that either proposed socialism or some other radical variant as a solution to the ills of capitalist society, or offered an unmitigated critique of capitalism—not just individual capitalists. Although there were differences in the political shadings of individual films, radical discourse followed a fairly standard form. Unlike conservative productions that continually associated radicalism with violence, leftist movies such as *Why?* (1913), *The Jungle* (1914), *Money* (1914), *The Lost Paradise* (1914), *The Eternal City* (1914), *The Rights of Man* (1915), and *Dust* (1916) focused on the brutal working conditions and oppressive exploitation that forced wage earners into action. Socialism was portrayed as a peaceful alternative to violence. Although none of these films has survived, contemporary reviews, photographs, and a press book from *The Jungle* (a film one critic labeled as pure "Socialism, from beginning to end") allow us to piece together the ways in which these political messages were delivered to movie audiences.[27]

In adapting Upton Sinclair's famous novel to the screen, the All Star Feature Corporation employed well-known actors in lead roles (George Nash and Gail Kane) and a distinguished playwright (Augustus Thomas) as its director. Thomas was an especially appropriate choice, for he had begun his working life as a railroad brakeman and served as a leader of the Knights of Labor, a radical organization that called for the abolition of wage labor and establishment of industrial cooperatives, before embarking on a literary career. The story line of this five-reel feature follows Jurgis Rudkus and his family as they journey from Lithuania to the packinghouses of Chicago in search of a better life. The movie tries to show audiences that people are not born socialists; they turn to radicalism when there is no other way to end their suffering. During the course of the film we see the devastation that industrial capitalism inflicts upon workers, bringing "poverty, want, prostitution for women, death, and nameless sorrows" to honest, hard-working immigrants.[28]

In *The Jungle* strikes are not caused by outside agitators or corrupt union leaders, but by the packinghouse owner who orders a 20 percent wage reduction so that he can pay off his family's extravagant bills. Jurgis and his mates are depicted as reasonable men who offer to accept a 10 percent wage cut; but they are brusquely turned down by their employer. Lacking any other recourse, they reluctantly go on strike. The subsequent violence is not precipitated by workers but by police who attack peaceful meetings of strikers, and by a callous foreman who forces Jurgis' wife to sleep with him. Jurgis revenges himself, but in so doing he accidentally kills the foreman, an act for which he is sent to jail. Several months later, Jurgis is released. But he is a crushed man, for his wife and child have died in the interval. The despondent Jurgis finally finds the message of hope when he wanders into a socialist meeting and is enraptured by the powerful words of the main speaker (played by Sinclair and modeled after Eugene V. Debs). Jurgis suddenly discovers that socialism offers "enlightenment as to the way out of the long-hours and short-pay and strike problems." The closing scene shows a

Upton Sinclair, who played the role of a radical orator (modeled after Eugene V. Debs) in *The Jungle* (1914), helps convert Jurgis to the socialist cause.

happy Jurgis working in a rural community that has made the socialist vision of a "Co-operative Commonwealth"—a place where all men and women are equal—a living reality.[29]

A close examination of responses to *The Jungle* reveals how the political perspectives of individual movie critics produced multiple and often contradictory readings of a film's content, quality, and reception. Socialist and labor dailies, not surprisingly, praised the movie for its aesthetic and political qualities. Clement Wood, writing in the socialist *Appeal to Reason*, told how the film brought "tears to the eyes of women and men," and drove the "lesson of Socialism home with a point and a snap that it has never before possessed." *The Moving Picture World*, though somewhat less effusive in its praise, complimented the production's photography, direction, and acting, and noted that it was playing to packed houses in Brooklyn and Manhattan. *Variety* founder Sime Silverman hated the film and told his readers that it was playing to more empty seats than usual in Manhattan. Despite director Thomas' determined efforts to portray socialists as peaceful, law-abiding men, Silverman reported seeing a very different set of images: "This is not a feature picture of wild animals, just about wild socialists, that's all—and Lord knows, that's enough, the way they have done it before the camera." The movie critic from the *Kinematograph and Lantern Weekly*, however, called *The Jungle* "impartial" and insisted it made no

Radical films like *Why?* (1913) dramatized the exploitation children suffered
at the hands of rapacious capitalists.

effort at "influencing the patrons of the picture house in the direction of
Socialism."[30]

Not all radical films were as measured in their tone as *The Jungle*, nor
did they all advance the same solutions. *Why?*, made in 1913 by the
French company Éclair, offered a more anarchistic vision. It portrayed the
hardships of working-class life through a dream sequence showing children
toiling in factories, underpaid seamstresses being forced to use their own
blood to make red thread for the rich, and needless deaths and injuries
caused by railroad monopolies. The penultimate scene featured frightened
capitalists shooting angry workers who, in turn, achieve their revenge by
burning down the Woolworth building and setting fire to most of lower
Manhattan.[31]

Money, a film that espoused "the frankest kind of socialism," revealed the
bitter contempt many socialists held for anarchists. The prime villains in
this film, set in the year 1921, were an insatiably greedy steel magnate and
his partner who acquire control of the world's public utilities, wheat interests, and money markets, and an anarchist who aids them in exploiting their
workers. *The Eternal City* (1914) and *The Rights of Man* (1915), the only two
radical films produced by major American studios (Famous Players and

Lubin, respectively) featured socialist leaders as their central heroes and were clearly sympathetic to their cause. But both films were set in Europe rather than the United States. A number of movies, such as *Martin Eden* (Bosworth 1915), offered favorable portraits of socialist characters but never really explained what socialism was about.[32]

Liberal Films

The greatest number of labor-capital films adopted a liberal discourse that criticized irresponsible capitalists, decried the exploitation of innocent workers, called for cooperation between employers and employees, and advocated reform (not radicalism) as the best method of solving the industrial ills that beset the nation. Yet liberal films, like their radical counterparts, were not all alike. Reform-oriented filmmakers approached their subject in either of two basic ways. Some made movies that were staunchly pro-union, while others were sympathetic to the collective plight of workers but not to collective action.

Advancing the former point of view, William de Mille, son-in-law of famed radical activist Henry George, the author of *Progress and Poverty* (1879), presented viewers with a moving explanation for the causes of labor violence. His five-reel film, *The Blacklist* (1916), was based on the Ludlow massacre of 1914, and revealed how coal mine owners created "a state of practical slavery" by paying employees starvation wages, blacklisting anyone who complained, and enforcing their rule through the use of armed guards. De Mille, who wrote and directed the movie, delivered these messages with scenes of company thugs murdering innocent strikers and burning down their tent colonies. It is only after these horrifying deaths that the miners and the anarchist Red Brotherhood consider resorting to violence.[33]

Like de Mille, other liberal filmmakers defended labor unions (of the AFL rather than the IWW variety) as reasonable and legitimate responses to the unwarranted abuses suffered by workers. Union leaders were regularly portrayed as honest men who battled against injustice and tried to solve their problems in peaceful ways. *The Bruiser* (1916) showed how a longshoreman who was elected head of a strike committee resisted bribes and, through his fierce honesty and nonviolent ways, persuaded his boss to sign a fair agreement with his workers. When class violence occurred in these films, it was usually instigated by corrupt capitalists who employed scabs, police, militia, company spies, or private armies in their battles against employees. In *The Valley of the Moon* (1914), an adaptation of Jack London's novel, viewers watched police mercilessly club striking teamsters, while patrol wagons cruelly trampled over fallen men who "lay with broken heads

Liberal films like *The Blacklist* (1916) recreated events that occurred at the
Ludlow Massacre with powerful scenes of militia and employer-hired thugs
shooting at striking workers and then setting fire to their tent colonies.

and bleeding freely in the open." Strikebreakers, not strikers, were the villains in these films.[34]

Although most liberal films reflected the gender prejudices of filmmakers
(and of most labor unions) and focused on men as the agents of justice, a
small number of productions offered progressive depictions of female activists. *The Girl Strike Leader* (1910), *The Long Strike* (1911), *The High Road*
(1915), and *Her Bitter Cup* (1916) painted compelling portraits of women
labor leaders who led their comrades, male and female, on strike. In *The
Long Strike*, a strike leader courts a Chicago factory owner's son in order to
win higher wages for women strikers. Unlike conservative films in which
the poor heroine marries the wealthy guy, the strike leader here remains
true to her class and rejects the capitalist in favor of a working-class suitor.[35]
The Struggle and *The Blacklist* countered conservative visions of strikes as
antithetical to the interests of women and families by portraying workers'
wives and girlfriends as active supporters of strike actions.

The more numerous and dominant mode of liberal films, one that set an
ideological tone that survives to the present, acknowledged the genuine
economic and physical suffering experienced by wage earners, but condemned violence—by employers or employees—as the answer to their

problems. In D. W. Griffith's *Intolerance*, a cruel millionaire (modeled after John D. Rockefeller) enacts a 10 percent wage cut at his mills in order to raise money for his sister's charities. When workers protest and go on strike, he quickly sends for armed guards and state militia. They arrive with guns and cannons and, without any provocation, open fire on peaceful protesters. The camera cuts to the horrified faces of nearby wives and children who, like the audience, cannot believe what they see. The scene "was not merely violent," recounts cameraman Karl Brown, "it was a brutal massacre, naked and unashamed." Yet unlike the protesting miners in *The Blacklist*, workers in this film deal with the tragedy by quietly leaving the area and moving to the city.[36]

Unstinting in their condemnation of employer uses of violence against workers, these softer liberal films were equally critical and often quite patronizing toward working-class collective action. Unions, strikes, and their leaders were not inherently bad, as was the case in conservative films. They were simply incapable of offering measured responses to their grievances. Three surviving films, *The Girl at the Cupola* (Selig 1913), *Toil and Tyranny* [episode 12 of the Pathé Frères serial *Who Pays?* (1915)], and *The Royal Pauper* (Edison 1917), offer excellent examples of how these attitudes were visualized on the screen. Each begins by dramatizing the causes of worker distress: a foundry owner employs an efficiency expert who fires most of the longtime employees; a bullying foreman forces his men to work extra hours without additional pay; a textile mill owner, known as "The Ogre," fires a delegation of polite, well-dressed workers who ask him for "a square deal."[37]

Each of these actions leads inevitably to a strike. Although strikers are portrayed as having just cause for their protests, they are unable to channel their frustrations in a peaceful direction. Strike leaders are shown as essentially peaceful men who are unable to control their undisciplined comrades. The sympathetic foundry workers of *Girl at the Cupola* become less sympathetic when they refuse the union leader's counsel and beat up the scabs sent to replace them. In *Toil and Tyranny*, peaceful workers (dressed in clean white shirts rather than the more sinister dark costumes used in conservative films) are transformed into a bloodthirsty mob when, after being attacked by police and evicted from company homes, they follow the violent exhortations of a man dressed in black. Once violence begins, the choreography of crowd scenes suddenly becomes similar to conservative films: workers are bunched together and when they speak they do so with arms wildly flailing in the air. In none of these films, or others like them, do we ever see a leader emerge from within the working class who is able to resolve the situation in a peaceful manner.

The general message of these films is that labor and capital need each other to prosper; violence and mutual suspicion must be replaced by co-

Though sympathetic to labor's plight, a majority of liberal films, such as *Who Pays?* (Balboa Amusement Co. 1915), consistently depicted union leaders as unable to control their men.

operation and mutual respect. The epilogue in *The Better Man* (1914) shows blindfolded Justice telling fat Capital and burly Labor "Why quarrel? You are worthless without each other." In the closing scene of *The Right to Labor* (1909), we see "Capital and Labor grasp hands and the angel of prosperity waves the olive branch above them."[38]

Although some liberal films defended collective action by workers, a far greater number saw the solutions to labor-capital conflicts coming from forces outside the working class. Clergy, politicians, reformers, children, suddenly enlightened bosses, the wives, sons, daughters, and girlfriends of owners, or mysterious strangers are the ones who inevitably save the day. Only these outsiders are able to transcend the anger of the moment and think about the long-term welfare of both sides. In *The Dawn of Freedom* (1916), my favorite labor-capital fantasy, a Revolutionary War hero emerges from one hundred and fifty years of suspended animation to lead disgruntled coal miners in a successful quest for justice; in *Spirit of the Conqueror* (1914), my second favorite, Napoleon returns to earth as the reincarnated son of a financier who rejects his capitalist legacy and brings justice to the working classes by heading up the world's most powerful international union.[39]

Populist Films

A fourth category of films reflected a populist sensibility that did not always fit into standard categories of conservative, radical, or liberal. Rather, they examined issues of class and exploitation in terms of an older nineteenth-century producer ideology favored by members of the Populist party and the Knights of Labor, an ideology that saw the world in terms of two classes: producers and nonproducers. The former included people who worked for a living (and that meant the laboring rich as well as the laboring poor), whereas the latter included those who lived off the wealth created by others. For Populists and their cinematic counterparts, the enemy of the wage-earner and small farmer was not the working employer but the monopolist who spent all his time accumulating more wealth, the absentee owner who had little or no contact with the workplace, the banker, lawyer, or real-estate speculator who made money at the expense of others, or the idle rich who lived off what they had accumulated without adding new jobs or wealth to society.[40]

Populist films succeeded in adapting this ideology to the screen with provocative images of monopolists and other nonproducers thwarting the will and undermining the wellbeing of the nation's ordinary citizens. These movies made little effort to be dispassionate or measured in their tone, but appealed directly to the collective anger of audiences. They were the Yellow Press of the screen and, like the popular Hearst newspapers, they gave their patrons what they wanted, regardless of whether their desires were realistic or not. There was little gray area in these films, for they always had clear villains and heroes. They adopted a tone that preached a gut-level class hatred designed to enrage audiences against those Theodore Roosevelt called the "malefactors of wealth." Whereas radicals founded newspapers with calming names like the *Appeal to Reason*, the films of populist directors might be dubbed the *Appeal to Passion*.[41]

No one was more masterful at the populist form than D. W. Griffith. There was a sense of urgency in his films that was rarely equaled. He told workers that they really were being exploited, and that greedy capitalists were the ones exploiting them. The monopolist was exactly what people feared: an unredeemable blood sucker. Worse yet, capitalists committed crimes and unspeakable acts that drove honest working people to ruin and suicide but went unpunished by authorities. Griffith embodied these fears by casting overweight men as his monopolists, dressing them in tuxedos and top hats (or some other form of fancy clothing), and having them puff away on big cigars. In *The Mother and the Law* (Wark 1914), which was later used as the modern story in *Intolerance* (Wark 1916), he featured a heinous

In *A Corner in Wheat* (Biograph 1909), D. W. Griffith raised audience emotions by contrasting the hardships of the working poor with the decadent lives of the monopolists who caused so many of their problems.

character unmistakably modeled after John D. Rockefeller. Like other populist films, Griffith's movies did not offer solutions, nor did they present
sophisticated critiques of capitalism. But he offered audiences something far
more immediate and gratifying: revenge. Catharsis, not change—class hatred, not heightened class consciousness—were the guiding principles of
these films. Like Populists of the political arena, they were scathing in their
attacks of the very rich. But in the film world, unlike the real world, the rich
often got it in the end.

Although workers could not always best the villains who plagued them in
life, populist films allowed viewers to see their enemies suffer on the screen.
Griffith's *The Usurer* (Biograph 1910) tells the story of a rapacious money
lender who never labors, but sends out debt collectors to harass those who
do. Griffith works his audience's emotions to a fever pitch by cutting back
and forth between scenes of the tuxedoed usurer enjoying himself at a lavish
party, and a poor mother and daughter who are being evicted from one of
his tenement flats. Revenge and catharsis come when the mother, who jour-
neys to his office to plead for mercy, unwittingly locks the usurer inside his
vault. We see the villain panic when he realizes what has happened and he
bangs at the door screaming to be let out. But no one hears him. The next
morning, he is found dead, having suffocated alongside his ill-gotten gains.
Similarly, in *A Corner in Wheat* (Biograph 1909), a food monopolist who
causes hunger and riots by driving up wheat prices to exorbitant levels, falls
into a grain elevator and is slowly smothered to death as tons of golden grain
fall on top of him. There were no blueprints for change in any of these films,
but moviegoers undoubtedly left the theater with a sense of satisfaction.[42]

Anti-Authoritarian Films

Audiences also saw a number of anti-authoritarian films that, although they
did not directly challenge capitalism, mocked the authority of those who
often gave workers the hardest time: foremen, judges, police, and employers. *The Coal Heavers* (AM & B 1904), *The Eviction* (Gaumont 1904), and
The Coal Strike (AM & B 1905), are films that poke fun at and show the
ways in which workers get the better of, respectively, foremen, landlords,
and police. Monopolies and monopolists are also mocked in animated
shorts such as *The Coal Trust and the Winter Sun* (Inkwell n.d.), *Witness
Mockefeller* (Inkwell n.d.), and *The Egg Trust* (1910). Although anti-authoritarian and populist films often expressed similar sentiments, the former usually delivered its message in the form of comedy, while the latter
employed melodrama. Anti-authoritarian filmmakers found laughter an especially potent way to score political points. "Humor," observes historian
Joseph Boskin, "is one of the most effective and vicious weapons in the

Anti-authoritarian films such as *The Eviction* (Gaumont 1904) mocked the
authority of landlords, police, employers, and other people who gave workers
a hard time.

repertory of the human mind," one that often "has as its purpose the con-
cealment of malevolent feelings through the verbal expression of belliger-
ency 'without the consequence of other overt behavior.'"[43]

The two most popular comedians of the day, Mack Sennett and Charlie
Chaplin, rejected refined humor for the middle classes in favor of broad
slapstick that appealed to immigrants and wage earners. Sennett, a blacksmith's son and former plumber's assistant, and Chaplin, whose impoverished mother was forced to send him and his brother to the Hanwell School
for Orphans and Destitute Children, drew upon their own working-class
experiences to skewer symbols of authority. Sennett's Keystone Kops delighted audiences with hilarious portraits of police, the representatives of
state authority most frequently encountered by working people, as bumbling incompetents incapable of protecting anyone—including themselves.
Explaining the appeal of his films, the filmmaker told one trade periodical:
"Nearly everyone of us lives in the secret hope that someday before he dies
he will be able to swat a policeman's hat down around his ears." Fantasies
that might not happen in life did happen on the screen. "In any other medium but comedy," Sennett confessed, these devastating caricatures of the
bastions of law and order "would have been stopped."[44]

Whatever Sennett's success, Chaplin reigned as the greatest anti-authoritarian comic of his age. Chaplin's movies, like their more flamboyant
populist counterparts, rarely offered solutions; they stuck to dilemmas and

individual responses to them. His sympathetic working-class protagonists never resort to collective action, but they know how to outwit bosses, foremen, police, government officials, and other agents of authority. *Making a Living* (Keystone 1914), *Work* (Essanay 1915), *The Pawnshop* (Mutual 1916), and *The Floorwalker* (Mutual 1916) offer hilarious send-ups of the work world and middle-class ethos of industriousness. In *The Pawnshop*, Chaplin delights blue-collar audiences by systematically destroying an alarm clock, the symbol of time discipline so hated by workers. In *The Floorwalker*, a foppish department store manager disgusted by customer Charlie's shabby appearance and fearing his potentially larcenous motives tries to throw him out of the store. Middle-class assumptions about respectability are skillfully mocked as Chaplin, who wrote and directed the film, keeps cutting away to scenes of elegantly dressed men and women robbing the store blind while the manager continues to harangue the poor but honest Charlie. *The Count* (Mutual 1916) and *The Rink* (Mutual 1916) offer equally devastating caricatures of upper-class society and its fawning obsession with European aristocracy.

Despite their comic tone, there was always a serious political edge not far from the surface of the comedian's works. "The Chaplin films of 1915–1917," suggests James Combs, "captured something of the contempt for authority and wealth the 'lower orders' of the new cities felt, the irony of America as a 'land of opportunity' when they lived in slums, yet desired to achieve some of the wealth and position from which they are excluded." Indeed, Chaplin's art and politics were deeply intertwined. "Chaplin loves to talk about government and economics and religion," movie producer Samuel Goldwyn recounted. "Mention of a new 'ism' or 'ology' brings him loping from the farthest corner of a room." Chaplin's interest in radical causes also brought him under the scrutiny of J. Edgar Hoover's Bureau of Investigation in the early 1920s and earned him a place on the Bureau's very long list of Communist sympathizers.[45]

Movies as Political Weapons

Audiences were undoubtedly entertained by what they saw on the screen. But what happened when the movie ended and the lights went on? Did these films have any lasting impact on patrons? Although there is some information about audience responses to particular films (which I will explore in the next chapter), we cannot definitively say whether the lives or ideas of large numbers of people were permanently altered by repeated viewings of labor-capital movies. We do know, however, that people in positions of power believed that what happened on the screen did matter. Capitalists, unionists, radicals, reformers, politicians, censors, and government officials argued that movies did indeed play an important role in shaping public consciousness.

The motion picture industry emerged at a time when various businesses and academics were busily developing new techniques of mass persuasion. Advertising agencies, attitudinal studies, marketing techniques, and public relations were being used by a wide variety of groups to measure and shape public consciousness. Movies were a logical extension of these developments and quickly became part of an expanding public arena in which political ideas were discussed and public opinion molded. The National Child Labor Committee, the National Committee on Prison Labor, the East Side Protective Association, the New York Association for Improving the Condition of the Poor, the National American Woman Suffrage Association, and numerous other reform organizations tried to change public policy by making movies that presented their cause to a mass public.[46]

Capitalists and corporations were equally quick to realize the importance of utilizing new methods of propaganda to promote their class interests. Speaking before the Motion Picture Exhibitors' League in 1911, Cleveland Employer Association attorney Edward Hobday explained how "laws and institutions change as public sentiment is moulded and changed. But public sentiment is open to argument, persuasion, and conviction." As big business came under scathing attack from muckraking journalists and labor unions, the National Association of Manufacturers, the American Bankers' Association, the New York Central Railroad, the Ford Motor Company, and many other business entities made movies aimed at improving their public images, disparaging the claims of their critics, and projecting capitalist ideology in a more favorable light. Their success prompted socialist S. E. Beardsly to complain that capitalists were using movies "in moulding and shaping the minds of the people through this medium more than any other agency in the country."[47]

Of all these organizations, the National Association of Manufacturers (NAM) was the most aggressive in employing films as weapons of corporate propaganda. Whereas the Ludlow tragedy prompted John D. Rockefeller to hire public relations mogul Ivy Lee, the tremendous outcry generated by the Triangle fire led NAM to produce two films in 1912 that portrayed employers' heightened concern for workplace safety. The Workman's Lesson and The Crime of Carelessness, both made in cooperation with the Edison Company, are excellent examples of the subtle ways capitalists used movies to promote their interests. Film reviewers accepted both works at face value and praised their producers for attributing equal blame for unsafe working conditions to employers and employees and calling upon both sides to work together to ensure future safety. A close reading of the latter movie, however, reveals a very different set of political messages.[48]

The film opens with a textile mill owner promising a fire inspector to clear all materials blocking his fire exits. The narrative quickly shifts to a love story between two mill workers, Tom and Hilda. When Hilda catches Tom smoking a cigarette near highly flammable materials, she makes him put it out. Several days later, Tom, reprobate that he is, commits the "crime of carelessness" by casually tossing a match into a trashbin. The factory is quickly consumed by fire and when the workers try to escape they find the fire exits blocked or locked. Certain death is avoided when Tom grabs an ax and chops through a wooden wall. Tom's moment of heroism is quickly forgotten as he confesses his role in starting the blaze. Instead of upbraiding the mill owner for locking the fire exits, the workers all turn on Tom. When the mill owner refuses Hilda's plea to rehire Tom, she blames him for the life-threatening conditions in the mills. The boss is dumbstruck. It is clearly the first time he has considered the possibility that he might share in the blame. Instantly realizing the wrongs of his ways, he rehires Tom and insists "We are both to blame; I for not making the factory safe, you for smoking."[49]

It is important to bear in mind that the film was made in the aftermath of the Triangle fire and trial of the factory owners, for it clearly attempts to shift responsibility away from bosses and onto the shoulders of workers. The employer's failure to provide fire escapes, his illegal locking of all fire exits, and his broken promise to the fire inspector are never seriously questioned. The film clearly shows that the fire was Tom's fault and raises the possibility that the Triangle fire was caused by some equally careless seamstress. Even when the boss benevolently admits his mistakes, they are mistakes of carelessness not of greed, of neglect not exploitation. The fact that real garment factory owners repeatedly rebuffed union demands for improved safety conditions is totally ignored. In the movie, it is the employer, not the workers, who leads the movement to make the factory safe.[50]

The success of this and similar films, which, as one historian notes, "circulated through the nation's movie houses as if they were no different from slapstick comedies, westerns, and historical dramas," led other big businesses to take to the screen. Railroad companies parried union attacks on the industry's deplorable safety record—180,000 injuries and 10,000 fatalities in 1912 alone—by producing movies that ascribed workplace accidents to the carelessness and drunkenness of company employees. The American Bankers' Association rebutted organized labor's complaints about low wages by making *The Rewards of Thrift* (1914), a film that showed how conscientious workmen who saved their money rather than spend it on alcohol were able to purchase homes. The Ford Motor Company took these cinematic endeavors a step further by producing *The Ford Educational Weekly*, a regular series of newsreels that, among other things, depicted the safety advances made by assembly-line production and the paternalistic policies of enlightened companies like Ford.[51]

The power and appeal of movies among workers was apparently so great that many employers used films, as Diane Waldman argues, as "part of an overall strategy to diffuse worker discontent, to discourage union activity, and to exert corporate influence over areas of employees' lives outside the workplace itself." Large manufacturers like John Rockefeller and ketchup magnate H. J. Heinz built movie theaters on their factory grounds, and other employers incorporated film into company-sponsored industrial recreation programs. The owners of Atlanta's Exposition Cotton Mills responded to a union organizing drive in 1917 by converting a boarding house into a theater and showing free movies on union meeting nights. "A fellow come here and he just about had them all joining the union," recounted mill worker Alec Dennis. "But at that time, they put that moving picture show there in that boarding house. . . . Well, it would keep people from going to the union meetings at night."[52]

Federal and state agencies joined reformers and capitalists in using films for propaganda purposes. The U.S. Postal Service and the Department of the Interior began producing nontheatrical films in 1903 to publicize their activities and educate their constituencies. Although most early productions focused on seemingly apolitical areas of public service, those touching on labor-capital relations revealed a more class-biased orientation. The state was no more neutral in its filmmaking activities than it was in its frequent use of troops to settle strikes. Movies made by the Bureau of Mines (part of the Department of the Interior), often in cooperation with powerful antiunion corporations, offered the same visual messages as did conservative labor-capital films. *The Miner's Lesson* (BM 1914) and *Sanitation in Mining Villages* (BM c. 1915) showed how industry and state officials sought to ensure the safety and health of ordinary workers. Both films depicted workers as either too stubborn or too stupid to follow the rules and guidelines set by paternalistic bosses and government officials. That fact that miners' unions had *forced* coal operators and state officials to adopt health and safety reforms was never mentioned.[53]

Themes of government and business joining together to protect and promote the interests of working people are dramatically illustrated in *An American in the Making* (BM 1913). Made by the Bureau of Mines under the direction of U.S. Steel's Committee of Safety, this well-made melodrama follows the adventures of Bela Tokaji as he leaves his poor Eastern European home to join his prosperous steel-worker brother in Gary, Indiana, "the Workingman's Model City." Upon arriving in Gary, Bela wants to celebrate in a saloon, but his brother takes him to "a better place than the saloons for his leisure hours," the YMCA (an institution derogatorily referred to by many unionists as the Young Men's Capitalist Association).[54] When Bela shows up for work the next day, he, and the viewer, discover how the company vigilantly safeguards the lives of its employees. In each of the dozen scenes of steel-making activities, workers never use safety equipment until foremen demand that they do. The film cuts to six years later; Bela has been transformed into a real American. He marries the teacher at the company-run English school he faithfully attends, starts a family, and moves into a beautiful home.

The film's message is clear: the company protects those who cannot protect themselves and offers prosperity to those who follow its guidelines. Employers and state authorities are constantly concerned with the welfare of workers, both in and outside the workplace. Workers, on the other hand, are childlike and dependent and show no initiative. Only through faithful obedience to external authority, rather than internally generated organizations like unions, can success—shown here as a good job, pretty wife, large home, and happy family—be achieved. A U.S. Steel publication described the film as the story of an "ignorant Hungarian peasant . . . stupid and uneducated," who ultimately thrives because of the company's safety and welfare programs.[55]

By the second decade of the new century, movies were entrenched as the nation's most popular form of commercial entertainment and one of the most powerful weapons of mass ideology. Reformers, big business, and government agencies understood this and used the new medium to promote their interests. But so, too, did working people. Anxious to capitalize on the tremendous power and appeal of film, workers, unions, and radicals produced films that offered *their* solutions to the labor-capital conflicts of the age; films that called upon millions of working-class moviegoers to rise up and challenge their oppressors through economic and political action. Within a few years of the nickelodeon's appearance, labor filmmakers battled their conservative counterparts for control of the screen and of American consciousness.

4

Making a Pleasure of Agitation: The Rise of the Worker Film Movement

IN MAY 1911, moviegoers at the Folly Theater in Brooklyn, a cinema "mostly patronized by working men and women," took their seats and eagerly awaited the start of the new Edison production, *The Strike at the Mines*. The film, or so they had been led to believe, offered an account of a bitter coal strike that had raged in Westmoreland County, Pennsylvania, for nearly a year and involved over 10,000 men, women, and children. When the lights went off and the film flickered across the screen, the audience was shocked by what they saw. Instead of depicting company guards and state police attacking workers, as was the case in Westmoreland, the film showed vicious union miners beating up innocent scabs and needlessly destroying the kind-hearted mine owner's property. Subsequent scenes of repentant strikers turning against their leaders and humbly begging their employer to reinstate them proved too much for the Brooklyn patrons. Infuriated by "such lying pictures," many "workers in the audience got up . . . [and] left the house in protest."[1]

They were not alone in their anger. Four months later, unionists and radicals in Los Angeles, upset by the many "Trust pictures, which usually put the laboring man in an unenviable light," registered their displeasure by opening the Socialist Movie Theater. The new owners promised to screen only those films that "portray working class life without insulting us." The next month, the American Federation of Labor took an even more dramatic step by making and distributing the first worker-produced feature in American history, *A Martyr to His Cause*, a movie that portrayed John McNamara, then on trial for allegedly blowing up the *Los Angeles Times*, as the innocent victim of anti-union crusaders.[2]

As these three episodes indicate, working-class audiences and activists responded to anti-labor, anti-union films in a number of ways. Some expressed their discontent by walking out of theaters; others endeavored to control what was shown on the screen by opening their own movie houses. Yet the most ambitious reply came in the form of the slow but steady rise of a grass-roots working-class film movement—a term I use to describe films produced by individual workers, labor unions, worker-owned companies, or members of radical, worker-oriented organizations like the Socialist party. The worker film movement of the prewar years was not a well-coordinated, well-funded national campaign that turned out dozens of feature films, but a fragmented quest that reached the screen on a sporadic basis. It was only after the war that a national movement began to blossom. The people who spearheaded these efforts were not filmmakers who happened to be radicals, but workers, unionists, and radicals who used film to bring their message to millions of people not reached by more traditional methods of propaganda. Coming from a variety of backgrounds, they parried the cinematic assaults of capitalists, government agencies, and conservative labor-capital films by making movies that showed unionists and radicals defeating employers, solving the problems of the day, and helping wage earners realize their long-held dreams.

Worker filmmakers understood that there was no one radical or working-class consciousness, but a number of perspectives on the problems of working-class life and their possible solutions. They exploited the new medium to create strong visual images of what it meant to be part of the working class in America. Although advancing different political agendas, their films exposed hundreds of thousands of people in all industries and in all parts of the nation to the same set of images and messages at roughly the same time, and showed a working class that was often divided by ethnicity, religion, gender, race, and skill that their common interests were far greater than their differences. Indeed, film allowed them to do things that no other medium could do. Audiences could actually see what victory over capitalists and politicians looked like, what collective efforts by unionists and socialist legislators could achieve, and how a unified working class could transform a nation.

During the early decades of twentieth century, working people were being shaped and were shaping themselves and others through the medium of film. Beginning in 1907, when a Cleveland union man shot and exhibited films of the strike-ravaged Cripple Creek (Colorado) area to enthusiastic audiences, worker filmmakers produced feature films, newsreels, and short movies designed to amuse, educate, and politicize the great mass of American moviegoers. They knew that Samuel Goldwyn was wrong: message films could be entertaining as well as instructive. Setting their features within the popular form of melodramas and love stories, worker filmmakers turned out liberal and radical labor-capital movies that played to mass audiences, not just unionists, in movie theaters throughout the country.[3]

One class's fantasies were another's nightmares. Although relatively few in number, worker films precipitated bitter struggles over the political content and direction of American cinema. Most histories of censorship focus on battles over the moral and sexual content of film. Censors, however, found films dealing with class struggle even more threatening than cinematic displays of sex and violence. They were afraid that worker-made films and radical pictures such as *The Jungle* would inspire wage earners to challenge the dominant political and economic structures of American society. In their efforts to create an oppositional cinema, worker filmmakers often found themselves battling with local and state censors who were determined to keep these class-conscious films from reaching the screen.

"Use Your Nickel as Your Weapon"

For Frank E. Wolfe, becoming a filmmaker was not the result of chance, as it was for D. W. Griffith, nor was he driven by the same sense of calling that gripped Lois Weber and King Vidor. Making movies was a purely political decision born out of his frustration with the limitations of traditional methods of labor and socialist propaganda. Merging a lifetime of experience as a union organizer and Socialist party activist with cinematic techniques borrowed from Griffith, Wolfe produced the most successful worker film of the prewar era. *From Dusk to Dawn* (1913) joined politics and entertainment in a manner so compelling that more than half a million people gladly paid to see messages they would never go to hear for free. A brief look at Wolfe's journey from riverboat laborer to movie producer helps us understand why people with little or no prior background in film seized upon the new medium to bring their message to the masses.

Born in May 1869, near Princeton, Illinois, Frank Wolfe's early life bore many similarities to that of David Wark Griffith. Like the master filmmaker, Wolfe's father died when he was a young boy and the family moved to Kentucky, Griffith's home state. Forced to leave school to support his family, fourteen-year-old Frank first worked on a flatboat and then in a variety of jobs for the railroad, rising from engine watchman to assistant chief dispatcher in 1889. Appalled by the horrid working conditions he observed, the charismatic dispatcher proceeded to organize railroad telegraph operators and station agents "so thoroughly that not a man at the key at any point on the line was a non-union man." After being fired and blacklisted from all railroad work for his union activities, Wolfe subsequently worked as a telegrapher for the Western Union Telegraph Company, as a reporter and editor for The Associated Press, and as a freelance reporter for a number of newspapers—organizing telegraph workers wherever he went.[4]

Several more years of union work and writing about factory exploitation convinced Wolfe that trade unionism alone would not solve all the problems caused by capitalism. Socialism, he decided, was the best method of achieving a more just world. When the wandering newsman was named managing editor of the *Los Angeles Daily Herald* in 1909, he quickly turned it into "a school for Socialism." Under his tutelage, noted one labor weekly, "hundreds of men" employed on the paper "became Socialists and went on their way to spread the propaganda wherever they might find themselves." Wolfe's politics, however, earned him the enmity of the city's most prominent anti-union spokesman, *Los Angeles Times's* owner Harrison Gray Otis, who used his considerable power to get the crusading editor fired.[5]

Forced to leave the *Herald* in early 1911, Wolfe traveled to the state capital in Sacramento, where he set up the Socialist party's first Legislative Publicity Bureau and earned a reputation as "one of labor's staunchest defenders." Frank returned to Los Angeles that fall to run for city council on the Socialist ticket and to become editor of the newly founded *California Social Democrat*. The forty-two-year-old's extraordinary skill as a writer and publicist also earned him a place on the legal team, led by famed attorney Clarence Darrow, hired by the AFL to defend union leaders John and James McNamara on the charges of blowing up the *Los Angeles Times*.[6]

For a while, it looked as if the Socialist ticket, led by mayoral candidate Job Harriman, would be swept into office. But James McNamara's confession on the eve of the election proved disastrous and the entire Socialist slate was soundly defeated. Losing the trial and the election marked a turning point in Wolfe's life and convinced him that new methods of propaganda were needed if labor and radical organizations were to win nonbelievers over to their cause. The solution, he discovered, was right in front of his eyes. "Socialist propagandists who have seen the maze of people flocking to the nickel pantomime shows and who have later gone into sparsely peopled halls to deliver the message of Socialism have asked me for the answer to the situation," he wrote in July 1913. "I think I have found it." Wolfe proposed to "take Socialism before the people of the world on the rising tide of movie popularity. We are going to make the projecting lens of a weapon for labor. We are going to paint the movie red."[7]

Although not a trained cinematographer, Wolfe was an expert photographer and one of the first reporters to illustrate his stories with photographs. He now planned to use a different kind of camera to tell the "never ending story of the class struggle." And he intended to do so in a manner that would amuse as well as instruct. People who would never go to hear a union or socialist speaker would go "watch the message eagerly" if it was presented in an entertaining form. In September 1913, after several months of work at the Occidental Film studio, writer-director-producer Wolfe completed his five-reel epic, *From Dusk to Dawn*. Delivering the lessons he learned as a unionist and socialist in the form of a love story between two attractive wage earners, Wolfe offered viewers a blueprint for transforming their world that began with workplace militancy and ended with Socialists triumphing at the polls. The movie opened to critical acclaim and crowded theaters. As one enthusiastic patron remarked: "It is clear-cut, revolutionary, and sure to be a great factor in drawing the workers to the Socialist movement."[8] Buoyed by his success, Wolfe began developing plans to open a studio that would entertain and inspire wage earners with a steady diet of socialist films.

Using movies as vehicles of mass propaganda was unique to the twentieth century, but using leisure for political ends was not. During the nineteenth and early twentieth centuries, unions and radical organizations sponsored concerts, theatricals, dances, picnics, opera recitals, and sporting events designed to amuse members and to heighten their commitment to each other and their movement. When it came to movies, however, union and radical leaders were slower to embrace the new medium than rank-and-file members. For people schooled in the old forms of class struggle, like AFL president Samuel Gompers, motion pictures seemed peripheral to the "real" work of unions: workplace organizing and political lobbying. Labor and radical newspapers were equally unimpressed with the new medium, and urged wage earners to spend their money on more uplifting types of entertainment. Pressure from readers eventually forced editors to offer regular movie reviews and gossip columns that featured profiles of movie stars as well as the latest industry intrigues.[9]

The steady appearance of anti-labor movies after 1907 led national leaders to change their staid attitudes toward the political importance of film. The dynamiting of eighty-seven structures between 1906 and 1911 (actions widely believed to be directed by International Association of Bridge and Structural Iron Workers' Union secretary-treasurer John McNamara), precipitated an outpouring of movies that portrayed American unionists as bomb-throwing nihilists. Striking workers in these conservative films, observed the one radical newspaper, were "pictured as brutal monsters, constantly attacking, beating, abusing or robbing the good, angelic, heroic strikebreakers who are always wronged and abused persons. . . . These anti-trades union pictures have been used so frequently and hatred against the organized working class is so carefully cultivated by them, there can be no doubt but it is part of a deliberate campaign to discredit and injure the unions."[10]

Trade unionists and radicals grew increasingly worried about the negative public impact of these films, for they appeared at a critical period in their organizing activities. The AFL, whose ranks nearly tripled between 1900 and 1910, was fighting to increase its national power and legitimacy, while the more radical Industrial Workers of the World was gaining strength on the western frontier. Similarly, Socialist party candidates were capturing local offices around the country, and, after garnering nearly 1 million votes in the 1912 presidential election, the party seemed on the verge of becoming a major national power. The repeated appearance of anti-union, anti-radical films deeply concerned these organizations because the people they were trying to recruit composed the majority of the movie-going public.[11]

We do not know how anti-labor films affected the great masses of movie-goers, but we do know that what was seen in the theater was discussed in the neighborhood. "The crowds not only throng to the shows," *The Nation's* editors observed in 1913, "they talk about them, on the street corners, in the cars, and over the hoods of baby carriages." Working-class patrons at a Lower East Side theater in New York responded to the anti-union film *Tim Mahoney, The Scab* (1911) with remarks such as "Gee, I'd hate to have a scab for a father," and "I would sooner pawn my soul . . . than be a scab." Labor activists feared that such sympathetic comments would be reversed if the flow of anti-labor films remained unchecked.[12]

Beginning in 1910, labor and radical organizations around the country launched aggressive campaigns to stop these visual assaults. In August, Chicago socialists and Washington, D.C., trade unionists called for a national boycott of movie houses "that display lurid scenes of strikers destroying property and committing crimes." Two months later, AFL convention delegates passed a resolution condemning films that "prejudice the minds of the general public against our movement by falsely and maliciously misrepresenting it." Unionists were urged to pressure local theater managers and boycott houses that ran anti-labor films.[13] During the next several years, AFL officials, local trade unionists, and labor newspapers wrote letters to studios, producers, and anti-censorship officials calling for more honest depictions of the struggles fought by union men and women.[14]

Defensive denunciations of anti-labor films did not go far enough for more determined activists. A small but vocal cadre of socialists and militant trade unionists exhorted their organizations to use movies on their own behalf. Their cries met with mixed reactions. Labor and radical leaders, like their business counterparts, knew they had to sway public opinion through new forms of mass persuasion. Yet AFL officials were slow to give up long-standing forms of publicity—speeches, lectures, and periodicals—that, while popular with members, held little appeal for the general public. Socialists, however, were quick to see that a mass movement needed a mass medium. Unlike the AFL, which concentrated on organizing skilled, white male craftsmen, socialists recruited all Americans regardless of skill, race, ethnicity, or gender. Activists such as John Collier urged his comrades to capitalize on the public's craving for film by employing this "most potent form of art, the great unused method of propaganda and publicity" to reach millions of men, women, and children.[15]

Such calls for politicizing popular culture were not unprecedented, for various workers and radicals were already using the stage to convey their ideas to local audiences. Playwright Julius Hopp, who organized New York's Socialist Theater Company in 1908 and the Wage-Earners' Theater League in 1910, found the theatrical world an effective way "to extend the influence of the Socialist movement." Gertrude Caldwell was equally entranced by the

power of the stage and founded Los Angeles' first permanent socialist theater company in November 1910. Union and radical thespians in other cities
mounted occasional performances aimed at "rousing public conscience to
provide better conditions for the working class." The most famous of these
productions, the "Paterson Pageant of 1913," cowritten by John Reed and
staged at New York's Madison Square Garden, dramatized the events of the
New Jersey silk strike to an audience of 15,000 people. Creative radicals,
especially within the IWW and the socialist movement, also utilized songs,
poetry, and art to publicize their cause among the unconverted.[16]

However successful these cultural forays may have proved, others believed that film offered a more powerful means of reaching a large and diverse population. Millions of potential union members, many of whom were
immigrants who could neither read nor speak English, could be reached
through the visual language of the silent screen. No other medium, Bronx
socialist John Black declared in 1912, "could drive home to the wage earners
so effectively the insanity of capitalism and all that it entails as an exhibition
in life-like pictures of the horrible, the unspeakable, misery that results
from the perpetuation of these conditions . . . [and] there is no question but
that when these scenes are portrayed on a screen in all their agony and
suffering their silence will be louder and more impressive than the most
eloquent orator." For this reason, concurred the editors of the *New York
Call*, movies could be used as "a mighty agency for the working class," more
powerful than the spoken word, for "we *see* the message to be conveyed. It
is there, where the eyes cannot miss it."[17]

Rallying audiences to the cry of "use your nickel as your weapon," workers made films that spoke to the lives, experiences, and fantasies of working-
class patrons. There was, however, no single type of worker film or filmmaker. Worker films were made in a number of cities by a variety of people.
Some produced feature films for general audiences, whereas others turned
out short movies and newsreels aimed largely at unions and radicals. Movies
made by trade unionists reflected the reformist perspectives of their producers, whereas those made by socialists adopted a more radical discourse.[18]

Although these first cinematic efforts were sporadic and reflected a number of ideologies and purposes, they shared one common goal: to challenge
the ways in which conservative and many liberal labor-capital films depicted
the goals and activities of labor and radical organizations. The most ambitious filmmakers were determined to reach a mass audience, not just the
already converted; to produce commercially viable theatrical films that
would entertain, not merely preach. "We can make a pleasure of agitation if
we choose," explained one of Frank Wolfe's Los Angeles comrades in 1911,
"and enjoy it as we go along."[19] They did this by giving the dominant film
conventions of the time a radical twist. Wrapping explicit political messages
in the popular garb of narrative melodramas filled with romance and action,

their films focused on stories and laments familiar to generations of workers: poor wages, unsafe working and living conditions, and the repression of wage earners by capitalists, police, politicians, and government troops. The heroes and heroines of these films were not benevolent employers or concerned outsiders, but unionists or socialists who offered solutions to the problems vexing wage earners. Although particular solutions varied according to the ideology of the filmmaker, these movies all advocated collective action—whether in the form of workplace militancy, trade unionism, or socialist politics—as the answer to capitalist exploitation.

Worker films did more than simply reverse the formulas of anti-labor movies in predictable ways. While adopting popular melodramatic styles, they transformed its discourse from one that generally supported individualism into one that promoted the ethos of mutualism. A brief examination of several prominent films allows us to see how unionists and radicals wished to portray themselves, their goals, and their enemies.[20]

Workers Take to the Screen

At 1:07 A.M. on October 1, 1910, an explosion rang out that shook downtown Los Angeles and, within a matter of days, the entire nation. A dynamite blast that destroyed much of the *Los Angeles Times* and claimed the lives of twenty employees provided labor's enemies with new opportunities to associate trade unionism with anarchism. The *Times* was, after all, the nation's leading anti-union newspaper and its owner, Harrison Gray Otis, the city's leading open-shop advocate. Vowing revenge, Otis hired the nation's most famous detective, William J. Burns, to track down the fiends who murdered his employees. The following April, Burns's men burst into a meeting of the International Association of Bridge and Structural Iron Workers in Indianapolis, seized secretary-treasurer John McNamara, and, employing dubious methods, brought him and his brother James back to Los Angeles to stand trial. The AFL, convinced the young Irish brothers had been framed, hired attorney Clarence Darrow and launched a vigorous publicity campaign to free the McNamaras and save the reputation of organized labor.[21]

The arrest of the McNamaras inspired the production of the nation's first worker-made feature film. In the summer of 1911, the AFL's McNamara Legal Defense Committee set out to offer the public "a true and correct representation of the incident that stirred the country" by paying the W. H. Seely Company of Dayton, Ohio, $2,577 to make and distribute *A Martyr to His Cause*. AFL leaders hoped to alter popular opinion about the case and the general nature of unionism by producing a film that would "prove interesting and instructive" to "the general public throughout the country."

Subsequent advertisements boldly hailed the two-reel, twenty-scene picture as the "Greatest Moving Picture Film of the 20th Century."[22]

Merging traditional melodramatic narrative with pointed political messages, *Martyr* uses events in John's life and career to reverse the negative images of anti-labor films and present trade unionists as the true upholders of democratic institutions. John McNamara is depicted as a hard-working citizen who loves his family, his country, and his craft. In offering such a portrait, it might appear as if the AFL was trying to win mass approval by pandering to conservative values. Yet although these values *were* used to support the dominant capitalist culture, *Martyr*'s producers understood that they were not inherently conservative; they were values that formed an important core of American culture and resonated throughout the population. Appeals to God, country, family, and citizenship, as political economist Henry George had shown in the 1880s, could also be used by radicals to defend a vision of American society that attracted conservatives, liberals, and socialists alike. The AFL simply tried to do on film what George had accomplished in his writings and political campaigns. *Martyr* took ideals that employers used to attack unions and instead used them to defend labor organizations and disparage their enemies.[23]

Martyr opens with seventeen-year-old John leaving home and promising his parents to "be a good boy and to play fair in all that he does." The movie quickly cuts to actual scenes of structural iron workers perched high atop a skyscraper passing red hot rivets to one another, and we see the difficult and dangerous life they lead. "Through his industry and sobriety," an intertitle tells us, John is promoted to foreman and then elected secretary of his union. Having established its hero as an industrious, family-loving American, *Martyr* answers conservative portrayals of unionists as lawless and violent men with scenes exposing manufacturers and corrupt courts as co-conspirators who try to crush the spirit of democracy by acting "contrary to the laws and traditions of our republic." Violence is presented not in terms of strikes against employers, but employer assaults against the law. The film shifts attention away from the *Times'* bombing and focuses instead on the illegal search and seizure of union property by police, the kidnapping of John by private detectives, his illegal extradition to Los Angeles, and the repeated violation of his constitutional rights. The movie closes with an emotional scene of John's mother sitting alone, weeping over a letter from her son in which he assures her he is "innocent of any infraction of the law" and that the public will not judge him "until a fair and full defense has been afforded."[24]

More reformist in tone than radical films, *Martyr* was nevertheless more radical than most liberal labor-capital movies. It rejected liberal faith in the ability of outside intervention to solve labor's problems and showed audiences that wage earners could not rely on the benevolence of capitalists, politicians, or courts for justice. Whatever sentiments employers might express in public, in private they break laws and violate the obligations of citizenship in order to get their way. Workers could only achieve justice through collective action, and the best way to do that, the film implies, is through the united power of labor unions.

Martyr opened in Cincinnati in September 1911, where it was seen by an estimated 50,000 people, and played to crowded houses in "leading theaters and moving picture houses" throughout the country. One enthusiastic labor official predicted that the film would earn as much as $100,000. Unfortunately for its producers, its run came to an abrupt halt just after Thanksgiving when brother James McNamara confessed to the bombing.[25]

During the next several years, workers made movies that offered distinctly different views of contemporary society from those produced by most filmmakers. Just as D. W. Griffith used film to rewrite the history of Reconstruction, so too did Frank E. Wolfe use film to rewrite the history of class struggle. Unlike the more reformist AFL, Wolfe set out to tell a story about men and women "whose aim it is to overthrow an entire social system." Yet he was equally adamant about making a film that would "appeal to the masses" and not just socialists and unionists.[26]

Made in 1913 with professional actors and production personnel at the Occidental Studio in Hollywood, *From Dusk to Dawn* was a five-reel epic filled with love, violence, politics, class conflict, and a spectacular cast of over 10,000. Wolfe's story line revolved around the budding romance between iron molder Dan Grayson and laundress Carlena Wayne. Over the course of an hour and a half, audiences saw the pair embark upon a successful struggle against factory exploitation that ended with Dan's election as governor on the Socialist ticket and the couple finding true happiness in each other's arms. More than just another love story, the film provided viewers with a blueprint for change and demonstrated how, by abandoning individualism in favor of collective action, wage earners could succeed in transforming production and politics. The movie, explained one enthusiastic fan, took audiences "from the dusk or darkness of riots and fights, with sticks and stones between unions and capitalists, to the dawn of a new day, where people would have some sense and do things a better way."[27]

Dusk's power lay as much in its creative use of visual imagery as in its narrative guide to action. The film opens with scenes of the poverty-stricken slums inhabited by Carlena and her family, and of the dangerous working conditions endured by Dan and his coworkers. Documentary footage of actual slums and workplaces provide graphic visual insights into the causes of strikes and wage protests. Employing techniques perfected by D. W. Griffith, Wolfe cuts back and forth between shots of the misery endured in working-class slums and the easy lives enjoyed in the mansions of millionaires. But unlike Griffith's poor but clean movie-set tenements, these actual apartments are depressingly dismal hovels. Wolfe also challenges images of worker carelessness and employer benevolence seen in conservative business- and government-made films with scenes showing Dan and Carlena preaching workplace safety to their bosses. Their pleas are ignored and several apprentices, including Fred Wayne (Carlena's brother and Dan's friend), are killed in an explosion that could easily have been avoided.[28]

When Dan and Carlena lead their coworkers in a quest for better wages and working conditions they are discharged. Yet instead of acting like the passive sheep or uncontrollable masses depicted in conservative labor-capital films, rank-and-file workers in the laundry and iron foundry initiate nonviolent strikes in defense of their fired comrades. Wolfe reverses conservative cinematic depictions of law and order by revealing the many methods capitalists used to intimidate and discredit strikers. Strike scenes show peaceful workers marching three abreast, hands clasped, and lips sealed. Only one man advocates violence, but we quickly learn he is a company spy hired to stir up trouble. When picketing proves successful, frustrated employers resort to violence. The camera offers powerful close-ups of hired thugs and police beating up strikers. When this fails to stop them, manufacturers persuade the city council to pass an anti-picketing ordinance prohibiting anyone from speaking with strikebreakers—a measure actually passed by the Los Angeles city council. Dan and Carlena are arrested under the new law, but once again the workers remain committed to their cause; they are strong individuals who do not need leaders to tell them what to do. Unable to intimidate their employees, employers are finally forced to grant the workers' demands.

Workplace victories inspire political action as Dan's friends persuade him to run for governor on the Socialist ticket. Wolfe uses costuming and careful choreography of crowd scenes to depict socialists as respectable, law-abiding citizens who freely choose to join in peaceful collective actions. At a political rally on Dan's behalf, the camera pans over thousands of well-dressed men and women. Neither the speakers nor the audience exhibit any of the frantic physical gestures seen in anti-socialist films. *Dusk* also liberates women from the restricted roles assigned to them in conservative and liberal movies and portrays them as equal partners in the struggle for justice. In this, and many other scenes, Wolfe drew on first-hand experience. His wife, Emma, was a prominent party activist who campaigned to secure protective legislation for women and children. In Wolfe's film, women are seen giving speeches, planning Dan's campaign, and running for office.[29]

Frightened at the prospect of a Socialist victory, capitalists and politicians once again try to subvert the principles of law and order by framing Dan on conspiracy charges. Dan fights back by hiring Clarence Darrow to defend him. Darrow, who reenacts the speech from his own conspiracy trial

Parrying conservative films that repeatedly portrayed working-class crowds as
lawless mobs, Frank Wolfe's *From Dusk to Dawn* (1913) showed viewers that
Socialist politics could be orderly and successful.

(brought about after his defense of the McNamaras), wins the case and
Dan goes on to lead his party to a sweeping victory. The closing scenes take
great pains to depict Socialist politics as offering peaceful solutions to
contemporary problems. The Socialist-controlled Senate, whose chambers
are bedecked in American flags and include several female senators, carefully considers and then passes a "right to work" bill that guarantees jobs for
all wage earners. But Governor Dan believes he has a responsibility to conservative constituents who oppose the bill, and he wavers until Carlena
rushes into his office with a petition bearing the signatures of 250,000 citizens. Convinced that the people have spoken, he signs the bill and the camera fades out on Dan and Carlena holding hands and agreeing to "become
Comrades for life."

From Dusk to Dawn was innovative in its cinematic form as well as its
politics. Wolfe employed techniques that placed him in the vanguard of
contemporary filmmakers. One of the first multireel docudramas ever made,
Dusk used documentary footage as integral parts of its plot and not simply
as colorful background. He mixed studio-produced scenes with shots of
actual strikes, picketing, Labor Day parades, and speeches by prominent
labor leaders. He also capitalized on the emerging popularity of the star
system by featuring well-known labor and political "stars" in his film. Audiences loved this interplay of melodrama and real people and events. Workers and radicals cheered the appearance of their favorite socialist or union

"movie stars"—Clarence Darrow, Job Harriman, and others—or their own faces in one of the crowd scenes.[30]

Wolfe's strategy of mixing entertainment and radical politics succeeded. Audience demand was so great that theater magnate Marcus Loew booked *Dusk* into his entire New York chain, where it was viewed by an estimated one-half million people. In Chicago and nearby towns, where "great crowds" thronged to see it, *Dusk* set new attendance records and played in forty-five theaters in two weeks. Major exhibitors in other cities soon followed suit and the film was shown in first-run houses and neighborhood theaters throughout the country. *Dusk* was also widely praised by socialist and union newspapers. It "will reach thousands who are hard to reach through speeches or printed words," predicted one New York radical paper, and "will drive home the argument of Socialism and the rights of laboring men as nothing else ever has."[31]

From Dusk to Dawn was followed by a film that presented the "true" story of the greatest labor tragedy of the day. *What Is to Be Done?* (1914), a five-reel melodrama made in New York by socialist actor Joseph Leon Weiss, used the setting of a factory strike to dramatize the history and lessons of the Ludlow (Colorado) Massacre. Though this was apparently Weiss' first effort as a writer-director of movies, he was no stranger to the worlds of mass media and popular culture. The forty-two year old Brooklyn resident was an active stage performer, a member of the Hebrew Actors' Union, and a cofounder of the socialist *Jewish Daily Forward*, the nation's largest foreign-language newspaper. Like Frank Wolfe, Weiss understood that to attract a paying audience movies had to entertain, not merely preach. Consequently, he delivered his political messages in the form of a love story between Henry Dryer, a factory owner's liberal son, and Louise Laffayette, a stenographer who organizes workers in his father's factory.[32]

Although less overt in its socialist politics than *Dusk*, Weiss's film is equally adept at using social realism to reveal the hardships of working-class life. Unlike most labor-capital films, which presented myopic visions of labor struggles, *What Is to Be Done?* provides viewers with a broad context for understanding the class conflicts of the age. The film is also remarkably progressive in its portrayal of women educating and politicizing men. Weiss's movie opens with the fiery Louise leading workers in a protest against a 10 percent wage cut. In order to explain to audiences why workers are so upset by such wage reductions, Weiss has Louise deliver a speech to employer representatives depicting the "life, work, and struggle of the working class." As she begins talking, the camera cuts away to a series of brief vignettes that bring her words to life. We see a working-class family whose son dies because they are too poor to buy medicine; a lecherous sweatshop foreman who accidentally starts a fire (similar to the Triangle blaze) while harassing seamstresses; hungry men and women who are forced to stand on bread lines; and distraught wives and children crying over the dead bodies of men killed in a mine explosion. "This is the fate that awaits the producing class," Louise tells the employers' agents. But they ignore her pleas to rescind the wage cut and a general strike is called.[33]

The rest of the film alternates between Louise's growing love affair with Henry, whom she wins over to the workers' cause, and the strikers' struggles for justice. Like the AFL and Wolfe, Weiss was determined to reverse negative images of unionists and mass movements by contrasting the lawless actions of capitalists with the peaceful conduct of striking wage earners. His film was one of the first to acquaint audiences with the employers' practice of using special "employment" agencies to provide them with strikebreakers. When the villainous Mr. Marlowe, owner of one such agency, tells a group of manufacturers: "Our strong arm men must beat up the leaders of the strike else we will never get our men back to work," they readily agree. During the next several scenes audiences see Marlowe's gangsters killing a union leader, using their "implements of Thugdom (guns, black jacks, knives, and clubs)" to beat up strikers, and persuading police to aid them in their crimes. The film's dramatic high point comes during an arbitration hearing when Louise, upset by the violence used against her comrades, asks the negotiators: "Do you know what happened in Colorado?" When they say no, the film quickly dissolves to a scene of the tent colony at Ludlow, and the audience is taken, step by step, through the gruesome story of how gunmen in the employ of John D. Rockefeller's Colorado Fuel and Iron Company set fire to the strikers' tent colony and then shot women and children as they attempted to flee from the blaze. By placing these heart-wrenching scenes after the beating and murder of Dryer's workers, Weiss tried to show viewers that the repression at Ludlow was a regular occurrence and not simply an isolated affair.

Chastened by this horrifying event and fearing public disapproval of his own sullied activities, Henry's father agrees to the workers' terms. Yet the movie ends on a bittersweet note: Dryer grants the wage increase, but he and his Wall Street allies agree to make up their losses by raising prices on all the necessities of life. The camera cuts from a secret Wall Street meeting to a union celebration that comes to an abrupt halt when word of the capitalists' decision reaches them. The closing shot shows the workers raising their hands to heaven and crying out, "Oh God! What is to be done?" To achieve real justice, Weiss implies, wage earners would have to take their battles into the realm of consumption as well as production. *What Is to Be Done?* opened at Manhattan's Grand Street Theater in November 1914, and proved popular enough to be shown again at Brooklyn's Miller Theater the following January.

Taken collectively, these three films helped audiences envision the possibilities of a more just nation, perhaps even a socialist nation. Despite differences in political shading, *Martyr to His Cause, From Dusk to Dawn,* and *What Is to Be Done?* used and transformed traditional melodramatic conventions to address one of the most persistent dilemmas of American ideology: the tensions between individualism and collective action. Literary and cinematic melodramas generally focused on an individual hero or heroine who, through personal initiative, overcame the villain and found love, success, and true happiness. In so doing, these works tended to reinforce the dominant capitalist ethos of individualism. But the AFL, Wolfe, and Weiss realized that melodrama was not inherently bourgeois or individualist. It was, as film scholar Robert Lang observes, "a drama of identity, of protest, of wish-fulfillment," that contained "both progressive and reactionary impulses."[34] Working out of a tradition developed in the radical dime novels of the nineteenth century, worker filmmakers showed audiences that individual desires could best be fulfilled through cooperation and collective activity. Mass movements in these films arise out of individual needs; they are not simply the products of abstract ideologies or manipulative agitators.

Like other labor-capital melodramas, all three films begin by trying to get viewers to identify with key individuals, their loves, their lives, and their plights. Audiences quickly discover that the hero and heroine are unable to achieve success or solve their problems on their own. Love and resolution only come through mutual support and mass action. *Martyr* shows how unions allow hard-working individuals like John McNamara to advance through the ranks, while at the same time protecting the rights of all workers. In *From Dusk to Dawn*, Dan and Carlena need to enlist the support of wage earners to achieve justice in the workplace and the support of voters to purify the political arena. Yet individuals are the ultimate beneficiaries of these group endeavors. Only Dan's Socialist government is able to guarantee every wage earner a job. As for our hero and heroine, their love only comes to fruition after these cooperative efforts have succeeded. *What Is to Be Done?* also links romance to collective action. Louise wins the love and admiration of her capitalist boyfriend not because of her looks, but because of her fervid activities on behalf of other factory employees.

Villains in these films differ from those in most labor-capital movies. They are portrayed as a united class and not merely as a few aberrant figures. Individual initiative, the cornerstone of the Horatio Alger mythology, is not enough to insure upward mobility, for wage earners face the powerful opposition of capitalists and their allies. *What Is to Be Done?* reveals how manufacturers and financiers often meet in secret to plot against working people. *They* know the importance of uniting to defeat their enemy. Workers only stand a chance against such powerful forces by joining together in unions; even the fiery Louise is not strong enough to defeat these foes on her own.

Middle-class assumptions about gender roles and misogynist cinematic depictions of radical women also come under assault in these worker films. Weiss and Wolfe promote visions of working-class womanhood that challenge middle-class notions of domesticated ladies and conservative images of socialist women as unattractive and unfeminine. Louise Laffayette and Carlena Wayne are powerful figures able to lead mass movements without losing their femininity or romantic appeal. Neither are mere adornments of men, but equal partners in the struggle for justice. Middle-class notions of "manliness" are similarly recast in these movies. Being a man means not simply standing on one's own, but knowing when to enlist the support of others, be they women, unions, or radical parties. Manliness also means responding to threats by employers, politicians, or police without resorting to violence.[35]

Though their strengths were many, *Martyr*, *Dusk*, and *What Is to Be Done?* also reflected the prejudices and limitations of their makers. These early films did not represent the struggles of the entire working class but only a segment of it: organized labor, which was predominantly white, male, skilled, and West European. Although white women frequently played prominent roles in cinematic versions of the class struggle, blacks, Hispanics, Asians, and East and Central European immigrants were rarely seen in worker-made features.[36]

While some unions and radicals produced feature films for first-run theaters, others turned out shorter, less costly one- to three-reel movies, newsreels, and nontheatricals (films not necessarily intended for commercial distribution) for neighborhood theaters, union halls, and socialist gatherings. "Labor unions," the *Film Index* informed its readers in 1911, "are not slow to appreciate the advantages of the motion pictures as a means of advancing their cause and special films are being used to drive home the arguments in favor of united action." The first cinematic efforts of workers featured documentary footage of strike sites (1907) and slide shows (1908) shown in local theaters in Cleveland, Ohio, and Independence, Kansas, respectively. The Boot and Shoe Workers' Union went a step further and produced a brief film in 1908 "depicting industrial scenes," which it used in unionization drives.[37]

During the next several years, the increased accessibility and affordability of movie equipment prompted a growing number of groups and individuals to shoot films of strikes, May Day parades, Labor Day parades, and political campaigns. Socialists in Los Angeles and New York publicized their struggles and entertained citizens by making and distributing newsreels between 1911 and 1913 that featured ongoing union struggles, suffragist campaigns, and "all phases of Socialist work." Though produced on a sporadic basis, these news films were quite innovative. The first regular commercial newsreels, the Pathé Weekly, did not appear until 1911, and not until 1913–1914 did news weeklies reach American screens on a regular basis. Worker-produced newsreels were "a decided hit with the large audiences that filled the theater at each of the several performances" in Los Angeles and paid five cents to see them. In New York, word-of-mouth information about the newsreels spread quickly and filmmakers soon received requests from party branches and labor unions in New Jersey, Connecticut, and Massachusetts. These cinematic efforts proved so popular that New York leftists voted "to utilize moving pictures as a permanent feature of Socialist propaganda."[38]

Filmmaking activities also extended to areas outside the nation's major cities. In 1916, the Western Federation of Miners shot scenes of the Calumet (Michigan) copper strikes, where seventy-two men, women, and children were killed at a Christmas Eve disaster, and sent them to union halls and theaters across the nation. These "strikingly Russian-like" films were so provocative that Baldwin-Felts detectives in the employ of the Calumet and Hecla Mining Company stole them when they arrived in New York. Two years earlier, company spy Harry Preston reported how striking workers in Atlanta's Fulton Bag and Cotton Mills made and exhibited movies as part of their strategy "to keep up agitation . . . to gain sympathy of general public . . . [and] to get support of City Officials by picturing filthy and unhealthy conditions of mills."[39]

These shorter productions proved just as important as more ambitious feature films. By projecting scenes of labor parades, strikes, and gatherings on to the screen, worker filmmakers transformed the activities of everyday life into extraordinary cinematic events. For a few brief moments, ordinary workers could enjoy seeing themselves as movie stars and bask in the satisfaction that their lives and struggles were worthy of being seen by thousands of people. Far from being dull, news films could be as emotional as melodramas and more informative than the newspapers. Worker-made newsreels, declared the *New York Call*, were especially important in "breaking the boycott on news relating to capitalist brutality and oppression" and "making known the facts of the class struggle in this country."[40] Indeed, many citizens remained skeptical about labor's repeated claims of capitalist and governmental repression in factories, mining camps, and steel mills. Now there was visual evidence.

Worker-made productions also took on a lighter, more comic tone. Los Angeles unionists enlivened their Labor Day celebration in 1916 by making *General Garrison Bray Who-Tis, The Hero of the Battle of Caloocan*, a "moving picture burlesque" that parodied the career of *Times'* owner Harrison Gray Otis. While proving great fun to make, one participant noted how the film "impressed upon the thousands who were present the fact that the trade unionists of Los Angeles not only do not fear him, but look upon him with good-natured contempt." The public's passion for movies led Socialist politicians in New York and Chicago to turn out films intended to "astonish the natives, please the women and children, and start everybody thinking about Socialism and the Socialist candidates." During the presidential campaign of 1916, the Socialist party, which four years earlier had produced a rather serious newsreel on behalf of Eugene V. Debs, took a more humorous approach and made a short animated cartoon with dancing letters that spelled out the names of its candidates, Allan Benson and George Kirkpatrick. The cartoon "wins applause from the audience," reported one bemused resident of Washington, Pennsylvania, and defines "its message in a way that could not be surpassed."[41]

Movies proved such popular vehicles of propaganda and entertainment that enterprising radicals, such as the Chicago-based Socialist Film Attractions, organized commercial movie companies and offered their services to comrades interested in producing short films. Advertisements in radical periodicals appealed to readers' fantasies by urging them to consider careers as filmmakers. "You can make good wages and make Socialists at the same time by procuring a picture machine outfit," promised one notice.[42]

Local success inspired some radicals to extend their filmmaking efforts across the Atlantic Ocean. After switching from writing plays to shooting newsreels, Julius Hopp grew intrigued with the possibilities of using film "as a new weapon and a new means of propaganda." In July 1913, the thirty-five-year-old Hopp, acting in concert with the New York Socialist party, entered into an agreement "with one of the largest motion picture concerns of the world, with branches in Europe, Asia, Australia, and America to manufacture on a permanent basis such films as will convey most effectively the aims, purposes, methods, and arguments of Socialism." These productions, he told reporters, would feature pictures of "Socialists at work in this country and in Europe and incidents in public life showing Socialist ideas and arguments."[43]

It is unclear whether Hopp's plans were ever realized, for two years later he was busily trying to convert Madison Square Garden into an 8,000-seat movie theater. Nevertheless, we know that socialists throughout Europe were using movies "as a means of educating the working class." As early as January 1911, Parisian workers, convinced that many strikes failed "by reason of the women demanding their men to go back to work," announced their plans to screen class-conscious films that would attract "the laborers' wives and sweethearts." Two years later, socialists and unionists in Leeds, England, opened their own movie theater and set out to spread the "principles of solidarity among the masses" by showing only pro-labor films. By the end of 1914, trade unionists and radicals in England, Holland, France, Germany, and Belgium had organized cooperatives that produced, distributed, and exhibited films and newsreels within and between different nations.[44]

Exhibition and "The Rebellion of the Audiences"

Whereas Frank Wolfe and Joseph Weiss fought to carve out a niche for themselves as independent producers, others waged a parallel campaign to politicize exhibition by controlling the types of films that were seen and the environment in which they were shown. There is an old movie industry cliché that audiences get the films they want. Yet during the prewar era, working-class audiences frequently complained they were getting films they did not want. The structure of the early film distribution system made it difficult for patrons and theater owners to exert much control over the selection of films. Between 1908 and 1912, exhibitors who wanted a guaranteed supply of movies signed contracts with local film exchanges stipulating the number of reels and reel changes they wanted each week; the selection of specific films, however, was usually made by the distributor. As Jonas Rinas explained to his angry union patrons in 1911, small theater owners had "little to say about what attractions shall appear on their curtain."[45] They simply had to take, sight unseen, whatever was sent to them by the distributor. The steady increase of independent producers after 1911 and the formation of independent exchange networks to handle their products gave exhibitors more leeway in choosing films. Yet it was not until the appearance of new distribution-production companies like Paramount in 1914 and the collapse of the Movie Trust in 1915 that exhibitors would exert much greater control over what appeared in their theaters.

Producing movies, worker filmmakers quickly discovered, was only half the battle. To stand any chance of commercial success, they had to get their films into theaters. Yet restrictive distribution policies made it difficult for any filmmaker operating outside the Trust or one of the rival independent distribution organizations to reach a national audience. Small producers who made only one or two films a year either sold them to states rights exchanges (which agreed to distribute a film in specified geographical area) or marketed them on their own. Although the AFL was able to rely on its extensive national network of unions to make arrangements with local theaters, others had to go it alone. Frank Wolfe's success in distributing *From Dusk to Dawn* came as a result of opening sales offices in Los Angeles, Chicago, and New York, and spending months on the road trying to line up exhibitors. Similarly, Upton Sinclair, who bought the rights to *The Jungle* following the bankruptcy of the All Star Film Company, spent several years marketing the film on a state-by-state basis—a task he accomplished by placing advertisements in radical periodicals asking for help in handling local distribution. Building a worker film movement that could reach the screen on a regular basis, then, depended on the ability of people like Wolfe and Weiss to get their products shown and the willingness of audiences to help them.[46]

"FROM DUSK TO DAWN"

IN FOUR PARTS

M'f'd by
The Occidental
M. P. Co. of
California

———

A Story of the
Class Struggle

———

CLARENCE DARROW

Shown in Great Trial Scene
The Famous Plea to the Jury

A Wonderful Feature of Intense Human Interest

Opera House
Managers :—

85 Per Cent. of
Your Theatre-
goers — the
Numberless
Working Class—
Will Want to See
This Picture.

Wolfe promoted his film by placing advertisements in important industry periodicals such as the *Moving Picture World.*

Determined to overcome these obstacles, a number of resolute wage earners opened their own movie theaters. In December 1909, Chicago radicals launched a cinema aimed at spreading "Socialist propaganda . . . [to] the thousands of people who attend five and ten cent theaters." Two years later, twelve union musicians, tired of fighting with theater owners, established their own cooperative movie house in Springfield, Missouri.[47]

Nowhere was the attempt to provide a favorable environment for showing pro-labor and radical films more pronounced than in Los Angeles. In September 1911, socialists and militant trade unionists opened the Socialist Movie Theater in the downtown area on Fifth Street between Los Angeles and Main Street. The owners pledged to exhibit films in which the "toiler will be shown in his true light and not as the menial or the subordinate." "Our theater," they explained, "is the result of the rebellion of the audiences against what was given them. . . . We are weary to the soul of films that always represent us looking up, to the magnate as the star of hope. . . . We propose to reply to such pictures as that by running films showing the truth of labor disputes." Within a short time, the theater's daily program consisted of pro-labor features and locally produced newsreels (probably shot by Frank Wolfe) of strikes, labor parades, socialist political campaigns, and women's suffrage rallies. The movie house proved an immediate success and quickly evolved into a multipurpose political space where labor, socialist, and suffragist organizations showed films and gave talks to enthusiastic audiences.[48]

Unionists and radicals also engaged in more modest forays into exhibition. Bronx socialists believed they could reach a diverse audience by putting together a complete evening of entertainment similar to that offered in better movie houses. On August 26, 1912, they rented the Rose Theater on 169th street and presented a show consisting of *The Cry of the Children, The Merchant of Venice*, several reels of short comedies, and a series of sing-a-longs. But moviegoers that night were also exposed to several brief lectures and socialist-produced newsreels of the Lawrence, Massachusetts, textile strike, recent May Day parades, and other short "pictures portraying the class struggle and working-class life." The evening proved a tremendous success, as over 1,000 men, women, and children crowded into the Rose. Impressed with the results, Socialist party locals in the metropolitan area announced their intention to "avail themselves of this novel means of propaganda."[49]

Workers did not have to make movies or open theaters to use the medium to further their political work. In the years before World War I, unions and radicals employed film in a variety of ways. In Pittsburgh, showing movies at Sunday meetings in 1914 helped the Socialist party increase average attendance from 100 to 3,000. "We make them take their Socialist medicine first," explained C. K. Harvey, "and then give them the movies, but nothing trashy." New York trade unionists employed a "moving picture show" to promote the union label in 1913, and, two years later, screened anti-war films to build up opposition to militarism and pending state constabulary bills.[50] Unions and socialists in California, Georgia, New Jersey, New York, Pennsylvania, Illinois, Wisconsin, and Oklahoma also used films to publicize strikes, raise funds, and attract large crowds to rallies and gatherings. Few of these organizations would have disputed the claim made by one radical periodical that "pictures draw a crowd where other means fail."[51]

Reception, Action, and Conflict

By making movies and controlling movie theaters, workers and radicals brought their messages to diverse audiences across the nation. Although worker movies and newsreels often excluded large portions of the working class, they nevertheless focused on problems that transcended differences in ethnicity, race, gender, and skill: poor housing, unsafe working conditions, mistreatment by bosses, and the desire for a better life. The heroes and heroines of these films may not have been Slovakians, Hispanics, or African-Americans, but they were workers. Wage-earning audiences, whatever their background, saw their lives portrayed on the screen in a favorable way. They might watch these films and think to themselves, "My God, somebody understands my troubles. Somebody understands that my kids are hungry, my job stinks, and my boss is an SOB." It was precisely the prospect that class action on the screen might inspire class action off the screen that so excited worker filmmakers and so frightened their opponents.

Film scholars usually analyze reception in terms of movie patrons' reactions to a particular film. This approach to reception is too narrow, for the impact of film often extended far beyond the movie theater and affected more than just the immediate audience. To assess the political power of any film, we need to expand our notion of the "audience" and the arenas in which reception occurs. In the case of labor-capital films, audiences included not just ticketholders sitting in movie houses, but people outside the theater who reacted strongly to what was shown on the screen: capitalists, censors, police, government officials, union and radical leaders, and the rank-and-file members of their organizations. Likewise, examples of reception should be extended to include censoring films, boycotting theaters, writing angry letters to local authorities, or putting into action lessons learned from watching films.

Worker films elicited a broad range of responses from different groups and classes. Union and radical viewers praised them, capitalists denounced them, and censors banned them. Socialist party leader Eugene V. Debs, who watched *From Dusk to Dawn* at a local Terre Haute theater, marveled at how the "entire audience was gripped and held at truest interest . . . [by] stirring scenes and harrowing exhibitions which can never be forgotten." In Springfield, Massachusetts, one exhibitor reported that worker films proved especially popular "with unionists, union sympathizers, and Socialists." Radical productions also attracted attention outside urban and industrial centers. Frank Wolfe received enthusiastic letters from exhibitors and filmgoers "from Alaska to Mexico, from Maine to Florida," and Upton Sinclair reported that two years after its debut, demand for *The Jungle* remained strong in a number of southern areas.[52]

Boisterous reactions inside the movie theater also testified to audience fondness for militant labor-capital films. Screenings of *A Martyr to His Cause, From Dusk to Dawn, The Jungle*, and various socialist newsreels were punctuated with frequent cheers, enthusiastic applause, and loud comments from politically sympathetic moviegoers. When the orchestra at a Lower East Side theater began playing *La Marseillaise* during a particularly poignant scene in *The Jungle*, the largely immigrant audience spontaneously broke out in song. The same scene produced a similar reaction in Los Angeles. "During the final stirring scene, when Upton Sinclair is telling the story of brotherly love and comradeship," recounted one reporter, "the audience seemed to rise enmasse and the big Auditorium resounded with their cheers."[53] Working-class reception of films was also influenced by the material circumstances surrounding their production. D. W. Griffith's insistence on using union crews to film *Intolerance* (Wark 1916) led Los Angeles carpenters to circulate a letter urging organized labor throughout the country to support the picture.[54]

Worker responses to these films also reflected the hostilities and internal jealousies that plagued labor and radical movements. In the case of the AFL, political rivalries with socialists proved more important than vague notions of cinematic class solidarity. Despite the organization's frequent denunciations of conservative labor-capital pictures, its periodicals paid no attention to any worker-made film other than its own. Similarly, Upton Sinclair's desire to preserve his self-appointed status as the Socialist party's preeminent cultural figure prompted his brusque dismissal of other radical productions. "There have been one or two films which pretended to be Socialist films," he wrote in 1916, "but they are fakes. 'The Jungle' was not advertised as a Socialist film, but it really is one."[55]

Whatever the disagreements among leaders and their organizations, worker films wielded an impact far beyond their modest numbers. Images of resistance to capitalist domination on the screen occasionally incited action outside the movie theater. After seeing *The Jungle*, P. H. Reesburg, a tailor from Toluca, Illinois, wrote Upton Sinclair: "It made Socialists of many . . . and sausage haters of others." Movie projectionist Walter Millsap recounted how watching *From Dusk to Dawn* inspired him to leave his job in the small town of Yolo, California, and join Frank Wolfe at Llano del Rio, a socialist cooperative colony some seventy miles north of Los Angeles. Representatives of the Boot and Shoe Workers' Union insisted that labor films helped spur members to fight for higher wages.[56]

Actions inspired by these films did not delight everyone. In 1916, an angry Connecticut mill owner complained to authorities that viewing *The Blacklist*, a movie "in which the events of a strike were depicted, one being the burning of the superintendent's house by strikers," led his workers to launch a strike at his factory. Other employers, reformers, and government officials were similarly frightened by the prospects of an unregulated medium that could transcend internal class differences and precipitate common class struggles.[57]

The power, or feared power, of these films was evinced by the concerted efforts of local and state censors to keep them off the screen. Beginning in 1907, when Chicago's city council passed the nation's first movie censorship law, many municipal and state governments enacted statutes enabling censors to cut or ban films they considered "immoral or obscene." Scholars of censorship have generally stressed local fears of screen sex, crime, and violence. But films dealing with class struggle proved even more worrisome and were banned in their entirety, not simply cut in a few morally offending places. This was especially true in cities like Chicago, Detroit, Boston, and Springfield, Massachusetts, where censorship was controlled by the police, or in Ohio, where it was controlled by the Industrial Commission.[58]

Film was not a "democratic art," as the *Nation* insisted in 1913, but was subject to the class dictates and prejudices of censors who used their power "to oppose the legitimate activities of the labor union men." The "dominant classes," the National Board of Review of Motion Pictures (NBRMP) went on to explain, were frightened at the prospect of films being used "by the classes out of power in their struggle for power." W. D. McGuire, head of the NBRMP, frequently wrote to Samuel Gompers and liberal producers such as Thomas Ince, alerting them to instances where films were "condemned by state censorship boards because they presented arguments favorable to labor." These revelations came as little surprise to socialist movie critic Louis Gardy, who explained that censors tended to "uphold things as they are, and, being appointed by the system will voice the opinions and demands of reaction . . . and stifle any movement which may bring a better day."[59]

Fearing that actions on the screen might translate into political or workplace radicalism, local authorities moved to stop the exhibition of films they believed encouraged class protest or offered graphic displays of state brutality. Los Angeles' Board of Motion Pictures came within one vote of banning *From Dusk to Dawn* "because of its criticism of the established order of things in Los Angeles" and its blatant efforts at "furthering the 'socialistic' cause." City officials in Minot, North Dakota, banned the film without offering any explanation. The chief of police in Springfield, Massachusetts, ordered exhibitors to remove all posters that "showed policemen with drawn clubs in the act of arresting striking workmen." Even more moderate films such as *A Martyr to His Cause* were subjected to close scrutiny. AFL delegates had to make several visits to NBRMP offices in New York, followed by a telegram from Samuel Gompers—who served on the Board's Advisory Committee—before they finally secured the approval of the influential organization.[60]

Censors did not just discriminate against worker filmmakers; they moved against any production that depicted workers winning strikes or challenging employers. A wave of miners' strikes that swept eastern and midwestern states in 1916 led the members of the Ohio Industrial Commission to suppress *The Strike at Coaldale*, a film "in which the miners of Ohio were shown winning a strike." Chicago meatpackers, upset by the blistering portrayals of squalor and exploitation within their industry, tried to halt production of *The Jungle*; when that failed, they succeeded in pressuring Windy City censors to ban the film.[61] *By Man's Law* (Biograph 1913), which critiqued Rockefeller's greed and manipulation of the police, and *The Mirror of Death* (1914), which showed Mexican workers attacking a mine owner, also fell victim to local authorities. Mrs. Maude Miller, head of the Ohio commission, blocked the former film because "she didn't believe that the rich should be satirized." Efforts to limit displays of class conflict and state violence also extended to newsreels. During a bitter Chicago newspaper lockout in 1912, police censors prohibited exhibitors from screening pictures showing the "wholesale arrest and slugging of union newsboys [by police]."[62]

Struggles waged against capitalists and state authorities on the screen were carried into the halls of government as labor and radical organizations fought to stop class-based censorship. The AFL, though no ally of the Socialist party, joined the leftists in condemning mandatory censorship and opposing Congressional efforts to establish a federal censorship board. Gompers was especially incensed by the hypocrisy of state officials who banned pro-labor films but gave quick approval to features that placed the "wage earners and the toilers of the country in the position of appearing to act as a lawless mob or in other ways as violators of the law." Local unionists and socialists supplemented national efforts by denouncing the "political censorship of moving pictures" and calling for the abolition of all city and state boards.[63]

These heated class battles over censorship testified to the mounting belief in the power of film. Movies were no longer simply "an instrumentality of recreation," AFL delegates declared in 1916, but had "a determining influence in directing and educating public thought and opinion." Enthusiastic responses to worker-made films and newsreels prompted cries from rank-and-file unionists and socialists for more films that would challenge conservative visions of working-class life. After months of delivering talks on the Socialist party's lecture circuit, road-weary E. W. Perrin concluded that his cause would be better served if he and his comrades made fewer speeches and more movies. "There is not a strike in America that could not be woven into a picture play," he argued in 1913, and told "with such a force as to carry conviction." Equally convinced that film could help sway public opinion, Little Rock trade unionist Andrew Hill implored his AFL brethren in 1916 to devise "some practical plan by which we can get labor's side of all questions before the general public through the motion pictures."[64]

Spurred on by these pleas, a small number of radicals and trade unionists set out to reach the screen on a more regular basis. The commercial success of *From Dusk to Dawn* inspired Frank E. Wolfe to promise his fans "to produce more Socialist pictures—twelve a year if necessary." In February 1915, he unveiled his plans to build a permanent movie studio at the socialist colony Llano del Rio. Upton Sinclair launched an equally pioneering campaign the following year. The aspiring filmmaker contacted socialist leaders throughout the nation in hopes of raising enough money to set up an independent production company that would turn his film scenarios, "which have been too radical for regular producers," into commercial features. The AFL also considered another foray into the movie world as Gompers discussed working with producer Thomas Ince on a picture "setting forth the advantages of organized labor."[65]

None of these actions was guided simply by blind idealism. Wolfe and Sinclair were convinced their movies would be commercially successful, as well as politically useful. Audience demand was there. "If I had ten different big features depicting the class struggle," Wolfe insisted in 1914, "I could keep them all working." An equally confident Sinclair told *Appeal to Reason* editor W. H. Wayland that there were "no end of fortunes being made in the moving-picture business," and if audiences were offered "real vital material and revolutionary ideas, they could be gradually taken away from the regular moving-picture theatres." Once local exhibitors discovered that "labor plays pay," predicted another market-conscious socialist, they would "pay as much for rent for our films as for any others."[66]

These varied attempts to push the political direction of American film further to the left came to an abrupt halt in April 1917, when President Woodrow Wilson announced American entry into World War I. Cinematic efforts at class struggle, like many other forms of labor and radical resistance, were temporarily suspended as the demands of war assumed the center stage of national life. Yet eighteen months later, the movie industry and the worker film movement would emerge from the war profoundly changed. The death of Progressivism, the eruption of labor militancy, and the rise of an oligarchic studio system popularly known as Hollywood signaled the beginning of a new era of conflict between an increasingly conservative movie industry and an equally determined array of labor unions and worker filmmakers. The war in Europe had ended, but the battle for control of Hollywood—which began in 1914—would last until the end of the 1920s.

Part II

THE RISE OF HOLLYWOOD:
FROM WORKING CLASS TO
MIDDLE CLASS

5

When Russia Invaded America: Hollywood, War, and the Movies

THEY COULD be seen on movie screens throughout the land: secret Bolshevik agents sent by their Red masters to destroy American industry and ease the way for a Russian takeover of the United States. No business, no employer, no man, woman, or child was safe from these duplicitous fiends. Audiences saw Herman Wolff, Comrade Petroski, and Boris Blotchi travel to the silk mills of Paterson, New Jersey, the steel mills of Crucible City, the docks of New York, the coal mines of Colorado, and the shipyards of Seattle in hopes of "planting the scarlet seed of Terrorism in American soil." Aided by corrupt union leaders and IWW faithful, "the Bolsheviki of America," they succeeded in inciting strikes and violence among thousands of unwitting workers. "Bolshevism has attacked America," warned one screen hero in 1919, "and we've got to fight that as hard as if it was Germany, and fight it to a finish—or else turn our country over to those filthy, longhaired degenerate murderers whose creed is to stab in the back, dynamite homes, parcel their women among them as if they were cattle and attack any institution, government or religion that stands for sanity, morality and civilization."[1]

Could these enemies of democracy be stopped? Was there no one who could prevent Russia from invading America? Like scores of other films made between 1917 and 1922, *Life's Greatest Problem* (Blackton 1918), *The Transgressor* (Catholic Art Association 1918), *Bolshevism on Trial* (Mayflower 1919), *Everybody's Business* (1919), and *Dangerous Hours* (Ince 1920) dramatized many of the fears that gripped the postwar nation. "The Bolsheviki distrust the United States," a secret Military Intelligence report warned in May 1918, and their "disciples plan to remodel our government immediately." The widespread outbreak of strikes and labor militancy in 1918 and 1919 and concurrent rise of two American-based Communist parties heightened popular anxieties that the proletarian revolution had indeed crossed the Atlantic Ocean.[2]

Politicians, government agencies, and business leaders all offered solutions to the problems of labor militancy and Bolshevism. And so too did the movies. Nowhere was this more evident than in the nearly two hundred labor-capital films that flooded the screen between April 1917, when America entered the war, and the end of 1922, when fears of radicalism and labor militancy finally died down. The prominence of these films challenges conventional wisdom concerning the relationship between cinema, politics, and class during these tumultuous years. Film scholars have argued that politically engaged social-problem films, like the Progressive movement that spawned them, rapidly declined in the postwar era. "The working man as a subject for films disappeared after the war," insists Lewis Jacobs, "reappearing only when the depression reawakened interest in his milieu." After several years of war and deprivation, Americans, or so scholars have claimed, wanted to forget their problems and lose themselves amid cinematic fantasies of sex, consumption, and the fast life.[3]

A close look at the films of the era reveals that class-conscious productions were far more prominent and complex than scholars have suggested. Although certain kinds of social-problem films faded away, features about class conflict grew even more popular. At least 171 labor-capital movies were released between April 1917 and December 1922—an average of 30 a year compared to 22 a year released between 1908 and March 1917. These figures are especially remarkable considering that the total number of annual productions declined as feature films grew longer. Wartime and postwar events also precipitated dramatic changes in the dominant ideology of these movies. Nearly half the labor-capital films produced before the war were liberal (46 percent) and only a third (34 percent) conservative. However, during the five and a half years following American entry into war, conservative films hostile to unions and radicals composed 64 percent of all labor-capital movies, and liberal films supportive of workers and their struggles only 24 percent. Moreover, not a single radical film was produced by industry regulars during these years.[4]

To understand this pronounced shift in the politics of labor-capital films, we need to look beyond the screen and examine how the changing circumstances under which movies were produced affected the images and ideologies that appeared on the screen. Between 1917 and 1922, four developments interacted to shift cinematic discourses about class conflict and class relations in increasingly conservative directions: major transformations in the structure of the film industry; mounting public hysteria over perceived Communist threats; political pressure on filmmakers by federal agencies and state censors; and heightened labor militancy inside and outside the movie industry.

World War I marked a turning point not only in domestic and world politics but also in the evolution of the movie industry and its relations with government, business, and labor. It was during the war years that the modern entity we call "Hollywood" took form. By 1918, European film production was devastated by war and the United States reigned as the movie capital of the world. But this was a movie industry dramatically different from its prewar predecessor. The wide array of producers and ideas that characterized the early industry was greatly curtailed by the skyrocketing costs of production and the emergence of a powerful studio system that moved to eliminate all competitors. The creation of Hollywood, however, was a slow and contentious process. In order to establish and maintain control over national and international markets, studio leaders had to deal with tough industry competitors, anxious government officials, and disgruntled industry employees.

The labor-capital films that came out of Hollywood during these years were shaped by the new corporate orientation of the movie industry and by the hopes and fears of government officials. Much has been written about government efforts to use the movie industry in its Cold War crusade against Communism during the late 1940s and 1950s. What is not generally known is that a similar crusade was launched thirty years earlier when, in the wake of war and the Russian Revolution, federal agencies battled with movie-industry leaders over the content and ideological direction of their films. Government leaders saw radical and even liberal labor-capital films as possible threats to national stability and sought to purge them from the screen.

The rise of Hollywood marked a turning point in the way Americans would look at, and perhaps think about, radicalism and working-class movements. Over the course of the decade, studios and government agencies attempted to marginalize all independent efforts to depict a progressive leftist vision of American life. With conservative features constituting nearly two-thirds of the labor-capital films released between April 1917 and 1929, when "talking" pictures displaced silent films, unionism and radical alternatives to capitalism were repeatedly depicted as unacceptable agents of change. And what millions of viewers found unacceptable on the screen might well become unacceptable off the screen—especially in workplaces and voting booths.[5]

Over the next four chapters we will examine, respectively, the emergence of Hollywood and its impact on the politics of labor-capital films; the ways in which labor and radical organizations responded to these changes; how industry leaders expanded the class composition of audiences and helped redefine ideas about class relations; and the final attempts by worker filmmakers to carve out a permanent niche for oppositional films in America. I begin this part of the book by examining how the movie industry changed during the war and postwar years, the efforts of government agencies to influence the ideological content of commercial films, the heated labor struggles that beset the industry, and how these forces intersected to shape the subject matter and ideologies that dominated the screen, and perhaps American consciousness, between 1917 and 1922.

The Rise of Hollywood

In June 1914, an angry Serb assassinated Archduke Franz Ferdinand and changed the world forever. Within a few weeks Europe was engulfed by what become known as the Great War. By the time an armistice was finally declared in November 1918, the war had claimed the lives of more than 8 million soldiers, and had altered the course of European history. World War I also reshaped the rapidly developing film industry. In 1914, the United States produced slightly more than half the world's movies; by 1919, 90 percent of the films exhibited in Europe and nearly all of those shown in South America were made in the United States. Although Europeans slowly resumed production after the war, the United States remained the center of world's film industry.[6]

The rapid growth of American movie production signaled the rise of a new type of film industry and the birth of "Hollywood" as a metaphor used to describe it. By 1920, Hollywood was no longer just a place but a way of doing business. The large number of modest-sized, geographically scattered producers, distributors, and exhibitors that dominated the prewar era were steadily supplanted by an increasingly oligarchic, vertically integrated studio system based in Los Angeles and New York and financed by some of the largest banks and corporations in the nation. When we talk about a "Hollywood" production, we usually mean a film that is made by a big studio, costs millions of dollars, features famous movie stars and expensive sets, and is distributed to theaters throughout the world. Where a film is made matters less than how it is made. A low-budget film, even if filmed in Hollywood proper, generally remains outside the metaphorical world of Hollywood. In short, Hollywood connotes big business—nearly $1 billion of business in 1921.[7]

These transformations did not happen all at once, nor was it inevitable that American filmmakers would continue to dominate the world market. Someone had to be clever enough to make this happen. The wartime expansion of the industry was led by the aggressive independent producers who had challenged the Movie Trust, pioneered feature-length films, and turned Europe's tragedy into their opportunity. Embracing strategies employed by other big businesses, these emerging moguls created a studio system that made mass entertainment a commodity subject to mass production.[8]

The dramatic transformation of the movie industry from a nickel-and-dime operation into a complex big business is illustrated by the career and maneuverings of Adolph Zukor. Admired by some and hated by many, Zukor was the quintessential movie mogul, and Paramount, his brainchild, the quintessential studio of the teens and twenties. Zukor was not the first to make feature films, utilize movie stars, or organize a studio. But, as film historian Douglas Gomery notes, "he exploited those concepts more fully than others."[9]

Born in Hungary in 1873 and orphaned at an early age, Zukor emigrated to the United States in 1889, where he earned a living as a furrier. Ten years later, Zukor and his partner Morris Kohn left Chicago to seek new opportunities in New York City. Like several other moguls-to-be, Zukor entered the movie world through the arena of exhibition. When friends opened a small penny arcade on 125th Street in 1902, Zukor, fascinated by its success, "stood about observing the interest of the customers. This was my first experience in studying audiences, and I have been doing it ever since." A year later, Zukor and Kohn opened a penny arcade on 14th Street near the bustling entertainment center surrounding Union Square. By 1904, the men had closed their fur business and, taking in former fur salesman Marcus Loew as their partner, opened arcades in Newark, Philadelphia, and Boston, and an elegant movie theater in Manhattan. Other theaters quickly followed, and in 1909 Zukor merged his holdings with Loew under the name of Loew Enterprises.[10]

Freed from the daily responsibilities of running his exhibition venues, Zukor turned his attention to making movies. In 1912, Zukor and Broadway producer Daniel Frohman organized the Famous Players Film Company and made a series of profitable films that featured Broadway stars James O'Neill, Lily Langtry, and Mary Pickford in cinematic versions of their recent stage triumphs. This policy of signing prominent stars, which Zukor continued throughout his career, soon became an industrywide practice.

Having ventured into the worlds of exhibition and production, Zukor set his sights on distribution. In 1914 he signed a lucrative contract with the recently organized Paramount Company, promising to supply a half of the one hundred films the company distributed each year. Zukor, however, was not content to be just another player in the movie business. Like empire builders in other industries, he wanted to secure greater control—and profits—over all ends of the business. This meant combining production, distribution, and exhibition into a single company. He accomplished the first two steps in 1916 by merging with Jesse Lasky, Paramount's second leading producer, and then, through a series of skillful maneuvers, taking control of Paramount itself. By December 1916, the poor Jewish orphan from Hungary was president of the world's largest producer-distributor operation.

But Zukor had greater ambitions. He moved to enhance his control over exhibition by demanding that first-run and luxury house owners buy an annual package of Paramount films on unfavorable terms and without previewing them—block booking, as the practice was known. Angered by this new policy, a number of theater owners fought back by financing and distributing their own films through the First National Exhibitors' Circuit.

Zukor responded by securing a $10 million line of credit from the Wall Street investment house of Kuhn, Loeb, and Company in 1919 and embarking on a relentless campaign of theater acquisition and construction. Within two years, Paramount had employed threats, violence, and lots of cash to acquire control of 303 theaters—many of them among the most prestigious in their area. "The methods they are using," complained the general manager of a Louisiana theater chain, "are as near Bolshevism as anything I know of. They hope to gain a hold for each tentacle of their octopus by threats and brute financial force."[11]

Zukor's strategy of integration set a pattern that was replicated by his rivals and that dominated the industry well into the 1940s. Under Zukor's leadership, observed the *Film Daily*, Paramount reigned as "the United States Steel Corporation of the motion picture industry." Indeed, at the time of his death in 1976, the 103-year-old Zukor still served as Paramount's chairman of the board emeritus. There is an irony to this story. Zukor began his career as one of the Davids who, along with Carl Laemmle, William Fox, and several other independent producers, slew the Goliath Movie Trust. But having slain the giant, Zukor and his studio brethren in turn became giants bigger and more hated than the monster they had destroyed.[12]

The creation of Hollywood and the studio system (that is, the integration of production, distribution, and exhibition into a single company), as Zukor's career reveals, was a gradual process, not a sudden event. The outbreak of war in Europe offered unprecedented opportunities for rising entrepreneurs like Zukor, Laemmle, Fox, Loew, and Lasky. Yet to turn foreign disaster into domestic profit, industry leaders had to abandon the haphazard methods of the past in favor of more efficient modern business practices.

The first priority was producing films more quickly and in greater quantity. This was no easy task, for the increased emphasis on turning out elaborate multireel features with movie stars made production more complex and expensive. Stars such as Mary Pickford, Douglas Fairbanks, and Charlie Chaplin attracted more customers, but producers had to pay dearly for their services. As Pickford's fame rose, so too did her earnings: from $175 a week in 1911 to $1,000 a week in 1914 to $10,000 a week—plus a percentage of the profits—in 1916. Spiraling star salaries, combined with longer and more lavish productions, quickly drove up the cost of first-run feature films. In 1909, before the star system took hold, a one-reeler could be made for $1,000. Ten years later, five-reel features cost $40,000 to $80,000 to produce, and more elaborate six- to nine-reel "special" productions ran $200,000 or more.[13]

Companies soon devised new methods for cutting costs and increasing productivity. Like other modern industrialists, studio executives began placing greater emphasis on the division of labor and rationalization of production. The early improvisational system in which the filmmaker was a jack-of-all trades who often wrote, produced, directed, edited, and cast his own film was slowly replaced by what film scholars refer to as the "director-unit system" and then by the "central producer system." Cost accounting, not artistic expression, became the new corporate bywords. No longer were directors allowed to begin shooting with just a bare outline of a story. By 1916, everything was carefully planned and budgeted before filming began. Directors who did not follow instructions, or who came in over budget, soon found themselves looking for another job.[14]

Not every film was produced under this regimented system, of course, nor was every director reduced to the role of a "glorified foreman." Powerful individuals such as D. W. Griffith, Cecil B. DeMille, and Erich von Stroheim resisted the dictates of central authority and continued making films their own way well into the 1920s. Sharp-tongued director King Vidor was especially critical of the bottom-line mentality that permeated the studios during the 1920s and mockingly referred to the central producer system as the "sausage-factory method of making films." Nevertheless, the new emphasis on following solid business practices set the trend for the future. "After 1917," observes film curator Jan-Christopher Horak, "the film industry as a whole . . . conformed to American industrial norms by practicing a division of labor, scientific management, and consumer advertising."[15]

Changes in production were accompanied by the rise of Hollywood and its environs as the industry's main production site. In 1906, when the New York-based Biograph company became the first filmmaker to shoot in the area, Los Angeles was only one of many production locales. The search for more efficient ways to make films on a year-around basis soon led many eastern and midwestern companies to restrict or shut down their operations and head west. New York City remained the financial center of the movie industry, but Los Angeles quickly emerged as its production capital. By 1915, Los Angeles studios employed over 15,000 people and made between 60 and 75 percent of all American films. Four years later, the region's seventy-plus production companies turned out over 80 percent of the world's movies.[16]

There is a great deal of scholarly debate over why the film industry moved to Los Angeles. Although precise interpretations vary, it is clear that filmmakers were drawn to the region by a combination of factors: good year-round sunlight and favorable weather conditions; a wide variety of natural scenery—ocean, beaches, desert, mountains; plentiful and inexpensive land to expand studio operations; lower taxes; abundant labor, low wages, and relatively weak unions; and, for early independents, distance from the Trust monopolists. Although some companies moved to the nearby cities of Santa Monica, Glendale, Culver City, and Long Beach, Hollywood was the favored spot of early producers. "Nestled at the foot of the Santa Monica Mountains," explains one historian, Hollywood "offered easy access to the downtown business district, available lots for studios, comfortable bungalow housing for employees, and good locations nearby for Western action."[17]

Moving to Los Angeles provided ambitious filmmakers with a rare opportunity to exchange the cramped spaces of their eastern operations for what one film scholar dubbed "new palaces of production."[18] In March 1915, Carl Laemmle transformed a 230-acre chicken ranch located just north of Hollywood into the largest and most modern studio in the world. Universal City, a film studio so immense that it was categorized as a third-class city, contained two massive shooting stages, street sets and back lots for location work, film processing labs, cutting rooms, costume shops, construction yards, and its own zoo. Universal was only one of many sprawling new studios to take root in sunny southern California. Triangle, Ince, Lasky, Vitagraph, Metro, Hodkinson, and Fox all erected imposing facilities that tourists could easily have mistaken for factories.

Not all companies built large studios or employed the latest and most efficient production techniques, however. Dozens of small and modest-sized firms were content to rent space on studio lots and turn out several low-cost films a year. Those with more ambition than cash took offices along the Hollywood boulevards collectively known as "Poverty Row."[19] Varied audience tastes meant that clever producers would always have a place in the industry. Nevertheless, the power of independents and small studios greatly waned in the wake of increased efforts at industrial consolidation by their larger brethren.

Movies were now big business and, as in other big businesses, those who were successful increased profits and secured greater control over the market by expanding into other areas of the industry. Distributors moved into production, producers into exhibition, and exhibitors into production and distribution. Powerful exhibitors such as Fox, Loew, and the twenty-seven firms that formed the First National Exhibitors' Circuit in 1917 ventured into production by building or buying their own studios, while prominent film companies such as Universal and Goldwyn formed modest theater chains in which to show their products. Industry giant Paramount responded to increased competition by creating its own chain of theaters.[20]

All this ambitious expansion required money, more money than any single individual or company could raise. Some studios tried to expand through a series of mergers, but the most venturesome firms turned to the nation's financial and industrial communities for capital. "Wall Street," reported the socialist *New York Call*, "is financing a scheme to lift the motion picture industry from its uncertain status to the dignity of big business." The powerful investment banking house of Kuhn, Loeb, and Company helped fuel Adolph Zukor's expansionist dream by underwriting a $10 million stock offering for Paramount. Loew's, Pathé, Fox, Metro-Goldwyn-Mayer, and Universal followed Paramount's lead and had their stock listed on the New York Stock Exchange. Studios also raised capital through bank loans or direct investments by financiers. Fox got money from Prudential Life Insurance and New Jersey bankers; the Goldwyn Company from the DuPonts, Chase Bank, and Central Union Trust; Triangle from the American Tobacco Company; and scores of companies found a welcome hand and ready cash at Amadeo Giannini's Bank of Italy (later to become the Bank of America).[21]

This financial largess did not come without strings. Major investors expected a seat on the studio's board of directors and a say in the way its business was run. Goldwyn's board, for example, included the presidents of DuPont, Chase National Bank, Central Union Trust, and United Cigar Stores, and Marcus Loew's directors included W. C. Durant, head of General Motors, and Harvey Gibson, president of Liberty National Bank. By the early 1920s, Wall Street firms and major industrial corporations were represented in the boardrooms of virtually every major film company—a development that did not sit well with many company employees. "When we operated on picture money there was a joy in the industry," recounted Cecil B. DeMille, "when we operated on Wall Street money, there was grief in the industry."[22]

The increasingly big-business character of Hollywood affected not only the composition of the industry's participants but the politics of its films. Ideological changes, however, were not solely the result of the industry's internal transformation. From April 1917 until the early 1920s, another powerful force attempted to influence the course of Hollywood's development and reshape how its films addressed questions of class and class conflict: the government of the United States of America.

Uncle Sam and the Movies

On April 14, 1917, just eight days after declaring war, President Wilson created the Committee on Public Information (CPI) and charged its chairman, former muckraking journalist George Creel, with using the mass media to "sell the war to the American public." No stranger to the movies, the forty-one-year-old Creel wrote the scenario for *Saved by the Juvenile Court* and a number of stories that Broncho Billy Anderson turned into films. Although the CPI relied on a variety of media, Creel favored using film to mold public opinion. To that end, he pursued three policies: persuading key movie industry personnel to assist government agencies in their war work; having the CPI make its own films; and influencing the subject matter and political content of movies made by commercial filmmakers.[23]

Creel wasted little time putting his plans into action. In June 1917, he called upon the National Association of the Motion Picture Industry

(NAMPI) "to bring the motion picture industry into the fullest and most effective contact with the nation's needs." One month later NAMPI leaders responded to Creel's plea by sending to Washington, D.C. a delegation that was headed by prominent producer William A. Brady and director D. W. Griffith. Within a few days, a special War Cooperation Board was formed and representatives from the NAMPI were assigned to virtually every government agency to help produce slides, shorts, and trailers that would publicize their war work.[24] The people and companies leading the economic transformation of Hollywood—Zukor, Lasky, Laemmle, Fox, Loew, and Lewis Selznick—were also the industry's most active participants in government war work.

No government agency was more powerful or aggressive in its dealings with movie industry personnel than the CPI. Not satisfied with simply allowing film companies to produce his war films, Creel created his own Division of Films in September 1917 and began cranking out newsreels, short subject films, and feature-length movies. Some films were intended to rouse the patriotism of the general population, such as *Pershing's Crusaders* (1918) and *America's Answer* (CPI 1918); others were aimed at particular groups, such as *Labor's Part in Democracy's War* (1917), *Women's Part in the War* (1917), and *Our Colored Fighters* (1918). Creel also cooperated with the Treasury Department in recruiting Charlie Chaplin, Mary Pickford, Douglas Fairbanks, and other movie stars to help sell Liberty Bonds in movie theaters throughout the country.[25]

Initial relations between the movie industry and federal agencies proved cordial as studios discovered that there was a great deal of money to be made in producing, distributing, and exhibiting government films. But industry magnates soon learned that the government expected a quid pro quo in return for its lucrative "favors." Tensions mounted as the CPI pressured studios to promote particular visions of class relations in American society. Determined to counter enemy propaganda that portrayed the United States "as a Nation of dollar-mad materialists" and that publicized "news of strikes and lynchings, riots, murder cases, graft prosecutions, and all the public washings of the Nation's dirty linen," Creel asked studios to produce cheerful films that "presented the wholesome life of America, giving fair ideas of our people and our institutions."[26]

Too savvy to use strong-arm tactics, Creel relied on economic incentives and subtle threats to force studios into compliance. With European film production interrupted by war and foreign theaters clamoring for movies, huge profits could be made by sending American films abroad—old ones as well as new. To reach these markets, however, companies had to secure an export license for every film shipped overseas. CPI censors, who had the sole authority to grant these lucrative licenses, exercised their power by withholding them from films they deemed "harmful" to the Allied cause.[27]

Creel's ideological agenda was less a reflection of his personal politics than his firm belief that films promoting class harmony would enhance the war effort. In fact, the CPI chief was a long-time progressive; he championed the AFL-dominated American Alliance for Labor and Democracy and even sent its publicist, socialist filmmaker Frank E. Wolfe on a number of special assignments for the CPI. Nevertheless, he considered the liberal and radical social-problem films of the prewar era inappropriate for wartime. CPI censors repeatedly denied export licenses to films dealing with class conflict, political corruption, and other negative aspects of American life. Movies showing strikes and labor riots, hunger and poverty, or ghetto slum conditions were rejected on the grounds that they were a "bad testimonial to the value of democracy." *The Eternal Grind* (1916) was rejected because "it deals with a phase of American industrial life which is a blot on American institutions." *Little Sister of Everybody* (1918) was rejected because it showed a radical "inciting foreign-born laborers to rise against the owner of the mill where they are employed." *Her Man* (aka *The Woman Eternal*) was rejected because it "shows feudal conditions in the United States."[28]

Industry leaders also discovered that government agencies could control their very ability to carry on business. Although movie personnel initially managed to escape the draft, coal shortages in the winter of 1918 and the need for more soldiers led outraged Americans to demand the closing of movie theaters and the drafting of all eligible industry workers. After months of frantic lobbying, studio bigwigs persuaded the War Industries Board (WIB) to declare the movies an "essential industry" and exempt its employees from the draft. But in return, the WIB imposed a number of conditions that greatly strengthened the CPI's power. The industry's continued "essential" status, the WIB declared, depended upon its willingness to produce "only wholesome films." Indeed, a month earlier, the NAMPI curried government favor by agreeing to follow CPI guidelines governing the kinds of ideological statements acceptable for export. Filmmakers were cautioned "against making pictures" that contained "mob scenes and riots which might be entirely innocent in themselves but [could be] distorted and used adversely to the interests of the United States."[29]

Producers, distributors, and exhibitors may have privately balked at these efforts to control the subject matter and ideology of their films, but publicly they acceded to government demands and complied with CPI guidelines. Whether motivated by fear or patriotism, industry executives could not risk having their employees drafted, their theaters closed, or their profitable export markets taken away. The growing consolidation of the film industry was another powerful force working on behalf of compliance. With studios now involved in all ends of the business, the ideology of films was less important than securing their widespread distribution. Creel's victory was clear when Adolph Zukor announced in July 1918 that henceforth his company would "produce only plays of a cheerful nature" and "select only such subjects for production as will dictate to the peoples of foreign nations the qualities and spiritual texture which have been developed in American manhood and womanhood by the institutions which we are now striving to preserve."[30]

Studio leaders also understood that although Creel may have been hesitant to dictate the political content of domestic films, local and state censors were not. Government efforts to regulate ideology extended well beyond the federal arena as censorship boards repeatedly banned films that were deemed unpatriotic. When Los Angeles exhibitor Robert Goldstein refused the Assistant District Attorney's order to cut scenes in *The Spirit of '76*, he was arrested for violating the Espionage Act and sentenced to ten years in jail. As in prewar years, local censors were especially disturbed by films that portrayed class conflict. Frank Wolfe's *From Dusk to Dawn* (1913) and episodes of the serial *Patria* (1917) that showed Japanese and Mexican agents inciting labor violence were banned in several cities.[31]

As the war drew to a close, Washington abounded with rumors that the CPI's Film Division would soon be placed in charge of reorganizing all private production and distribution operations. "If the war had not ended when it did," insists one historian of the CPI, "the movie industry would no doubt have found itself under the strictest control from Washington, and the demand for 'wholesome pictures' presented more strongly than ever before, but still on the reasonable and self-apparent grounds of economy and conservation."[32]

The end of the war in November 1918 did not signal the end of government efforts to shape the ideological focus of American cinema. The Joint Committee of Motion Picture Activities of the United States Government and Allied Organizations, created after the armistice to monitor federal film activity, saw movies as valuable vehicles for addressing the nation's postwar problems. And few issues evoked more concern than the dual threats of labor militancy and Bolshevism.[33]

As the flush of foreign victory began to fade, American workers found themselves fighting domestic battles to maintain a decent standard of living. By 1919, rampant wartime inflation and lagging wages had reduced the average annual income for manufacturing, transportation, and coal-mine workers to less than half the figure the U. S. Bureau of Labor Statistics claimed was necessary to maintain an adequate level of health for a family of five. With government agencies doing little to help them, workers pursued justice through strikes and labor organizations. By the end of 1919, over 4.1 million workers belonged to unions (a 49 percent increase since 1916) and more than 4 million men and women had participated in 3,500 workplace stoppages—including a general strike in Seattle and a police strike in Boston. Class conflict even made its way into the sports world as player discontent with low salaries led several members of the Chicago White Sox to throw the World Series in 1919.[34]

The spread of Bolshevism between 1917 and 1919 intensified the growing climate of fear. The "Red terror," as it was dubbed by the press, swept east across Asiatic Russia and west into Germany, Poland, Hungary, and Bavaria. In March 1919, the Third International, a worldwide body of Communists from forty-one nations, met in Moscow and boldly proclaimed worldwide proletarian revolution as its goal. That same year, the American-based Communist party and Communist Labor party, though totaling fewer than 160,000 members, heightened domestic hysteria by endorsing the call for revolution. The dynamiting of Attorney General A. Mitchell Palmer's house in Washington, D.C., and numerous reports of mail bombs being sent to government officials seemed to confirm popular fears that the Red revolution would be a violent one.[35]

Critics of labor and the left wasted little time in linking rising labor militancy with the spread of Bolshevism. The fact that Gompers and the AFL were outspoken opponents of Bolshevism mattered little to their enemies. Ignoring the economic reasons that prompted most strikes, anti-union voices attributed labor unrest to the work of secret Red agents. Unionism, charged the editors of the *Open Shop Review*, "ranked with Bolshevism" as the "greatest crime left in the world." The National Association of Manufacturers and other leading employer organizations denounced the closed (union only) shop as "sovietism in disguise" and hailed the open shop as "100 Americanism."[36]

The haunting specter of the Russian Revolution and the widespread outbreak of strikes and labor militancy led federal and state agencies to adopt policies aimed at suppressing radicalism. Constitutional rights were violated and personal liberties trampled as thousands of socialists, communists, and Industrial Workers of the World (IWW) were arrested, jailed, or deported because of their political beliefs. The Red scare, observed electrical worker Laurence Todd, "began with nationwide raids directed by Attorney General Palmer," and reached "the high tide of hysteria" in January 1920 when, on a single night, Palmer ordered the arrest of 4,000 alleged Communists in thirty-three cities. "Among those running the country," explained screenwriter-to-be Lester Cole, "a panic set in: if the workers in Russia could take control what was there to prevent radical workers like the IWW from trying it here?"[37]

The vicious campaign initiated against both native- and foreign-born radicals by the Department of Justice and local "Red squads" is well documented. Less well known, however, are the more subtle ways in which the state used movies to curb the spread of radical and union activities. Wartime coal shortages led the Fuel Administration to make a film in December 1918 that attributed American deaths in Europe to the selfishness of union miners. In one scene, a dying doughboy tells a nurse, "The Germans did not defeat us. We were defeated by the miners at home. They are our murderers. If they had produced enough coal the factories would have been working and the ships would have been able to come over with plenty of ammunition."[38]

Not all agencies displayed such a strident anti-labor bias. The government was no more monolithic in its politics or filmmaking activities than Hollywood or working-class filmmakers. David Niles, chairman of the government's Joint Committee and head of the Labor Department's Motion Picture Section, condemned the Fuel Administration film as "a slander on labor" and lobbied to halt its release. But he was overruled by Fuel Administration members who "approved of the picture heartily and commended the scenario writer."[39]

Thwarted in one endeavor, Niles used his power to pressure large studios and smaller production companies into portraying unionists, radicals, and labor unrest in very particular ways. Although the twenty-eight-year-old, Boston-born Niles delighted in shrouding his personal life in mystery, he was no stranger to show business. He had directed movies in Hollywood and at Paramount's Long Island studio before joining the Labor Department. Niles's experience with the medium left him with a strong sense of its power. Insisting that the "motion picture can do more to stabilize labor and help bring about normal conditions than any other agency," he dispatched a letter to producers after the armistice requesting that they confer with him "prior to starting productions based on Socialism, labor problems, etc." "Constructive education," he told them, was preferable to "destructive propaganda." Portraying a screen villain "as a member of the IWW or the Bolsheviki is positively harmful, whereas portraying the hero as a "strong, virile American, a believer of American institutions and ideals, will do much good." Niles's "request" was accompanied by a series of incentives and threats. Those who cooperated with the Labor Department might receive valuable government endorsements; those who did not might open themselves to federal censorship. A number of current productions, he warned, "are being noted by the Department, and there may be some sort of Government supervision exercised before they are marketed." Several companies responded to Niles "request" and sent copies of scenarios and unreleased features for his approval.[40]

The unprecedented explosion of strikes and labor militancy that followed the war's end gave new urgency to Niles's work. In addition to monitoring Hollywood productions, government agencies also monitored its personnel. In 1918, as in the late 1940s, rumors of Communist infiltration of the movie industry spread throughout the country. R. M. Whitney, director of the ultraconservative American Defense League, told how a plan was formulated in Moscow to enlist the "stage and screen as mediums through which

Communist propaganda could be fed to the public . . . and Moscow stood ready to spend whatever money was necessary to further such a movement." Government agents, Whitney reported, had gathered secret files on Charlie Chaplin, Norma Talmadge, Will Rogers, William de Mille, and other industry figures "known to be in hearty sympathy with Communism and to be close friends of Communists." William de Mille recounted how, after his name was found on a list of people invited to dine with Communist trade union organizer William Z. Foster, he was interrogated by two Justice Department agents. When he confessed that the dinner was arranged by Charlie Chaplin, "a look of satisfaction passed between the two men; they had probably known all the time; it would have gone ill with me had I lied."[41]

Although some federal agencies looked upon the movie industry with suspicion, others tried to recruit its key figures into the government's Americanization campaign. Begun well before the war, the campaign aimed at turning immigrants into fully assimilated "100 percent Americans." In December 1919, Secretary of the Interior Franklin K. Lane, acting with the approval of Congress, met with movie industry magnates in New York and secured their pledge to assist the government in using film "to carry on a nation-wide campaign to combat Bolshevism and radicalism" that would "crush the Red movement in America." Lane asked for films that would dissuade the immigrant laborer from listening to the voices of "violent discontent" and turn him into "a cheerful fellow-worker in the making of America."[42] Within several weeks, the newly constituted "Americanism Committee of the Motion Picture Industry of the United States," comprising the nation's leading production, distribution and exhibition firms, began circulating suggested scenarios to producers aimed at combating the "revolutionary sentiment so assiduously and insidiously being fomented in this country."[43]

The Americanism Committee ultimately fell short of its ambitious goal of releasing a film a week. Nevertheless, the few movies it did turn out received widespread attention and distribution. The committee's first and most prominent release, *The Land of Opportunity* (Selznick 1920), reveals its class biases by portraying industrialists as the true friends of workers. The villain, Merton Walpole, is a sleazy looking, idle "Bolshevik" millionaire who carries around a copy of *Classes versus Masses* by Yakem Zubko and spouts what fellow Civic Club members clearly regard as ridiculous radical cant. When he tells them, "The Courts—the government—faugh! You rich men buy them and then blind the eyes of the poor by your big gifts to flashy charities," they jump up and tell him he is "a Bolshevist." Walpole is eventually cured of his radicalism when the club's butler, a "real" worker, reveals how Abe Lincoln saved him from sure death. Moved by the story, Walpole tears up his radical tract, throws it in the fire, and decides to become a true American—one who accepts rather than tries to change the world.[44]

The political goal of its films, the committee declared, was to "educate immigrants in the ideals of America and promote obedience to law . . . [and] peaceful enjoyment of the fruits of labor." Yet in practice, observed the *American Economic League Bulletin*, their films advocated "an unquestioned docile acceptance of economic conditions as they are and an irresistible inclination to indulge in unrestrained violence toward all who would better them." Labor leaders and radicals agreed with the latter point of view. If only "poor Lenin" had seen these Americanization films, quipped one socialist daily, "he would doubtless never have 'believed that the existing state of things needed speedy alteration.'" The less sarcastic Samuel Gompers professed his belief in Americanism, but complained in October 1920 that "some of these films depreciate the value of labor in propagating Americanism."[45]

Gompers and his allies had reason to be concerned. At the same time that industry leaders were vying to capture a greater share of domestic and world markets, they found themselves pressured to join government campaigns to thwart Bolshevism and ease postwar labor tensions. Compliance was easy so long as it involved only sending in a few scenarios or producing a few financially insignificant Americanism films. The more important question was, how would studios deal with problems of unionism and Bolshevism in their own productions? Would they give in to government pressure? Would they resist? The answers were critical, for with Hollywood now dominating the world market, its visions of proper class relations reigned as the dominant cinematic visions of the postwar world. In a time of turmoil and confusion, labor-capital films could exert a powerful impact on the way in which millions of people looked at contemporary events. What people saw and thought became important concerns for industrialists, radicals, labor leaders, and government officials alike.

Red Studios

It would be a mistake to interpret cinematic ideology of this era simply as the product of an evil government twisting the arm of a reluctant, liberal film industry. Changing class relations within the studios also played a vital role in altering class relations on the screen. Industry leaders may have resented the pressures placed on them by federal officials, but when it came to dealing with labor issues, government fears of unbridled class conflict found a sympathetic response among many powerful studio executives. Strikes, militant unionism, and Bolshevism were not things that happened only "out there" in society. They also happened on the studio lots.

The anti-labor, anti-left films of the war and immediate postwar years were paralleled by the emergence of the movie industry as a major big business and by increased militancy among its workers. The largest Hollywood studios were now closer in their business practices to General Motors, Ford, and U.S. Steel than they were to the modest movie companies of a decade earlier. And so too were their labor problems. Hollywood's heightened emphasis on efficiency and cost-consciousness caused widespread discontent among its employees. The years between 1916 and 1922 saw the first sustained efforts at unionizing virtually all film industry jobs. The studio craft unions founded before the war—stage employees, carpenters, electricians, and building tradesmen—remained the dominant unions after the war. However, increased production and wartime labor shortages prompted new organizations among actors and actresses, movie extras, movie cowboys, scenic artists, cameramen, and film laboratory workers. The strategy of centralization adopted by emerging studios was also used by Hollywood workers, who established the Amusement Federation to represent all industry unions in May 1919. The Motion Picture Producers' Association (MPPA), which represented the industry's leading studios, responded to this upsurge by pledging to maintain the "principle of the open shop upon which the picture studios have hitherto been conducted" and by hiring spies to penetrate unions and report on their activities.[46]

Not all Hollywood producers were anti-union or anti-Red. Charlie Chaplin, a founding member of United Artists Corporation and well-known supporter of socialist causes, was repeatedly hailed by the labor press as one of the "biggest boosters of Organized Labor in Southern California." Many of the stars most popular with working-class audiences were also strong allies of organized labor. Studios run by William Hart, Mary Pickford, and Douglas Fairbanks gave preferential hiring to union members. Hart's foreman once fired a worker for not belonging to a union, while Pickford and Fairbanks were among the few who "signed up for the closed [all union] shop agreement." But these pro-union producer-stars were in the decided minority.[47]

With organizing activities on the rise and the MPPA determined to halt the spread of unionism, the relative labor harmony of the prewar years gave way to a series of bitter strikes, boycotts, and lockouts. A new era of contentious labor relations began in January 1918, when Roy Stephenson became business agent and de facto head of International Alliance of Theatrical and Stage Employees (IATSE) Local 33. Few union positions are as important as the business agent, for he or she is the one charged with building up membership and ensuring that employers honor all union agreements. And no business agent had a greater impact in Hollywood than Stephenson. Within days of his appointment, the portly labor leader was policing studio lots and demanding that foremen and producers raise wages, enforce union work rules, and hire more union members. Stephenson's highly combative style quickly made him the most hated unionist in Los Angeles. "Practically every

Studio said that they did not want to do business with me," he told his local that July. But the scrappy business agent forced them to do business. Under his tenacious stewardship, Local 33 became the most powerful union in Hollywood and its membership rose from 87 in January 1918 to 1,626 by the end of 1919.[48]

Stephenson's aggressive leadership also sparked Hollywood's first major strike. In August 1918, after executives at twenty-five studios refused IATSE's request for an "equitable" wage increase and began firing unionists "for nothing more than carrying our cards," 1,100 angry Local 33 members walked off their jobs. Although IATSE eventually won their demands, anti-union feelings in Hollywood ran so high that when stage employees went on strike again the following year negotiations had to be shifted to the studios' financial headquarters in New York City, where cooler heads prevailed. Hostilities between studios and their employees grew even more pronounced in 1919 and 1920 as Hollywood came under assault from building tradesmen, actors, film lab workers, and cameramen. Exhibitors also faced scores of strikes by projectionists, musicians, and attendants.[49]

Bitterness mounted on both sides of the labor-capital divide as workers fought to obtain a fair share of the industry's new wealth. Producers maintained a special dislike for IATSE because its members could cost them a small fortune by tying up so many different aspects of production. IATSE united motion picture machine operators, stage hands, carpenters, plasterers, electricians, painters, grips, and other studio workers in a single industrial organization—a move that frightened employers and infuriated rival craft unions. Although IATSE leaders disavowed any allegiance with radicals, the *Los Angeles Times* repeatedly referred to it as "one big union"—the slogan of the IWW. Ironically, a united front of studio unions could have turned Hollywood into a closed-shop industry, but persistent jurisdictional disputes among IATSE, building tradesmen, and electricians prevented it from happening. As electrical worker Shorty Wade complained: "We have as many varieties of unionism as Heinz, the pickle man."[50]

Tensions between employers and employees peaked in July 1921, when eleven major studios initiated a drastic set of wage cuts. Determined to face down pesky unions once and for all, studio heads locked out all disgruntled workers and refused to meet with federal mediators or negotiate with AFL national representatives. Years of competition for the screen were now replaced by cooperation off the screen as MPPA members united "to combat Labor Organizations." Hollywood moguls particularly despised union work rules that prevented studios from using employees in anything but specifically designated tasks. When Samuel Goldwyn's foreman fired several idle carpenters and ordered other workers to perform whatever simple tasks might arise, Roy Stephenson quickly forced him to rehire the carpenters "even if they were compelled to allow the men to sit around." Not surprisingly, the 1921 lockout was led by studio heads who had experienced similar difficulties with unions: William Brady, William Fox, Lewis Selznick, and Jesse Lasky. These were also the industry leaders in closest contact with government agencies during and immediately after the war.[51]

Previously divided studio unions responded to producer intransigence by organizing a Joint Studio Strike Committee and initiating the "most widespread and systematic boycott ever launched and carried on in the history of the labor movement of America." The committee sent out more than 15,000 letters and circulars to labor bodies in the United States, Canada, and throughout the world asking their members not to see any film or patronize any theater showing movies made by the "four firms [who] control the bulk of the industry": Famous Players-Lasky, Goldwyn, Fox, and Universal. An effective boycott would force producers to the bargaining table for, as the committee explained: "When the working people, who are the great majority of those who attend picture shows, refuse to view these scab-made pictures the natural result will be no sales of these unfair products."[52]

Despite letters from hundreds of cities reporting that the "boycott was becoming effective," the studio unions lost the strike. To make a complicated story short, local unity was shattered by the reemergence of jurisdictional disputes among the striking unions' national bodies and the subsequent return to work by local IATSE members. Although the strike and boycott remained in effect throughout 1922 and managed to hurt a number of smaller producers, it failed to bring the major studios to their knees. By the end of 1922, the new era of labor militancy had come to an end. In fact, the MPPA succeeded in reviving a civil war among studio unions that lasted until 1926 and steadily eroded their remaining power over the industry.[53]

The bitter class conflicts that beset the industry between 1917 and 1922 were accompanied by a pronounced shift in the political sympathies of labor-capital films. During the prewar era, when few strikes plagued producers, 46 percent of the 244 labor-capital productions were liberal, 34 percent conservative, 9 percent anti-authoritarian, 7 percent populist, and 4 percent radical. As industry labor policies grew more conservative, so did their films: 64 percent of the 154 labor-capital films released between April 1917 and the end of 1922 were conservative, 24 percent liberal, 6 percent populist, 5 percent anti-authoritarian, and 1 percent radical. Companies experiencing the most labor troubles—Fox, Vitagraph, Goldwyn, Universal, Famous Players-Lasky—were also the leading producers of anti-union, antiradical films.[54]

I do not wish to be so simplistic as to suggest that what happened on studio lots was directly translated to the screen. There were other reasons for the proliferation of anti-left imagery. Bolshevism may have been bad for democracy but it was good for business. Making anti-Bolshevik films, suggested one *Moving Picture World* reporter, offered opportunities for "reaping a cash reward while serving a further and equally vital purpose of patriotism." Indeed, some companies were organized especially to produce anti-Red films. The Macauley Master Photoplay Company promised a 15 percent return on capital to investors smart enough to "know how scared some rich men are of the specter of Bolshevism and who are determined to capitalize that fear for their own advantage." Director William deMille attributed the prominence of screen Reds to the industry's perpetual need for good villains—ones who could make audiences boo, hiss, and cover their eyes in fear: "We had to have villains, and there was that tremendous land, far too busy to protest and containing one hundred and sixty million potential menaces."[55]

The rising costs of filmmaking and heightened fears of box-office failure proved equally crucial in determining the kinds of ideological statements that reached the screen. As films grew longer and production costs higher, studio output dropped from several hundred one- and two-reelers to several dozen feature films a year. Consequently, the financial stakes involved in any one movie grew more significant. With major investors and Wall Street financiers now sitting on their boards and forcing even powerful companies like Paramount to hire cost-cutting efficiency experts, studio executives had to secure decent returns on their films or risk losing their jobs. Producers repeatedly expressed a desire to please audiences, but deciding what audiences wanted was often a matter of guesswork. Studios did know, however, that ignoring government "suggestions" regarding labor-capital themes meant risking domestic censorship and the loss of profitable foreign markets. Moreover, given the industry's negative experiences with unions, making films that reflected the anti-left views of state authorities and large capitalists seemed logical. "The producers are themselves employers," observed one radical critic in 1920. "They think as employers, and their product reflects the employers' position."[56]

The anti-union imagery coming out of Hollywood also reflected the growing anti-union attitudes that swept the nation. Led by a powerful coalition of 1,400 local Chambers of Commerce and the 6,000 corporate and individual members of the National Association of Manufacturers, employers responded to the labor upheavals of 1919 with a renewed open-shop drive aptly called the "American Plan." Presenting their movement as consistent with the government's Americanization campaign, open-shop advocates called for replacing allegedly corrupt labor unions with democratic company unions. Unable to resist these protracted attacks, unions saw their membership drop from 5 million in 1920 to 3.6 million in 1929.[57]

Red Films

Although many factors helped determine what viewers saw on the screen, one cannot help but notice that the rise and fall of labor militancy in studio films paralleled the rise and fall of labor militancy in studio lots and in workplaces across the nation. When union power declined after 1922, so too did the number of labor-capital productions.

Driven by a variety of motives and pressures, filmmakers were actively redefining images of class and class relations in postwar America. With movie industry ties to large-scale capital tightening and studio workers' demands intensifying, it seems little wonder that many studio executives delighted in offering hostile portraits of unionism and radicalism. Prewar conservative portrayals of unionists as simply lazy or corrupt were superseded by more dangerous postwar images of unions and their leaders as the dupes or willing agents of the Bolshevik plot to conquer America. The militant industrial unionism preached by the IWW (and favored, in a far milder form, by studio nemesis IATSE) was presented as the typical ideology of organized labor. "When radicals are pictured in the films," observed socialist film critic Louis Gardy, "they are not shown as champions of the people, but as traitors of the deepest dye."[58] The collective message of these now dominant conservative movies was that honest American workers did not need self-serving radical organizations but could bring their complaints to their employer, man to man. And the employer, of course, would respond favorably to the just grievances of individuals.

Nowhere was cooperation between producers and government agencies more evident than in movies depicting the dangers of the Red menace. Conservative and liberal filmmakers responded to the Americanism Committee's plea to publicize the "seriousness of the Bolshevistic threat" with dozens of films about Russia in the aftermath of revolution. These pictures rarely explained the causes of the revolution or the actual political agenda of the Bolsheviks. Rather, visual images of Reds and their revolution were designed to turn the stomach and strike fear into the hearts of all decent Americans. No longer did audiences see romanticized scenes of revolutionary peasants fighting an evil Czar. Revolution now meant Bolshevism, and Bolshevism meant death and destruction. When silver-tongued Boris Blotchi—"one of the bloodiest butchers of the Revolution"—speaks to his following of deceived workers and misguided liberals of the need to bring the glorious legacy of Bolshevism to America, *Dangerous Hours* (Ince 1920) director Fred Niblo quickly cuts away to scenes that expose audiences to the *real* Red legacy. We see firing squads shoot children; we see two soldiers tear the blouse off a woman and drag her away to be raped; we see a mother

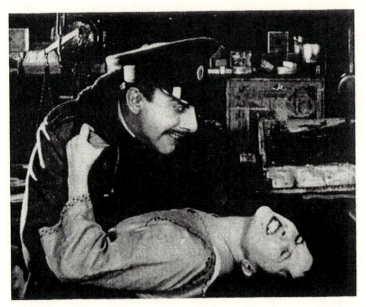

Conservative films such as *The New Moon* (1919) disparaged communists and communism with scenes of perfidious Bolshevik officers attacking vulnerable young women.

lying in the street dead, while Red armies callously march by her screaming baby. Visceral horror was also the strategy employed in films dramatizing the alleged Bolshevik decree nationalizing women—a supposed policy that made women the common sexual property of all party males and imposed the death penalty on any husband who resisted the edict. Indeed, who would not be repelled by repeated scenes of ugly Red officers pawing vulnerable young women? "The filthy and repulsive appearance of Russian alien characters" in these films, remarked one reviewer, "cause one to shrink and shudder."[59]

Filmmakers also played upon the popular fears of Russia's invading America. *Everybody's Business* (1919) typified Hollywood's zeal for portraying secret agents infiltrating "all our great cities . . . insidiously spreading the propaganda of terrorism and revolution." Lenin and Trotsky were repeatedly shown dispatching their Bolshevik lackeys to foment strikes and breed mass discontent among American workers. The Third International's call for world revolution was brought to life in *The Penalty* (1920), as audiences saw 10,000 disgruntled foreign workers, armed with rifles and pistols, await the signal to open fire on police and take over the city of San Francisco.[60]

The dominant cinematic discourse of the wartime and postwar eras de-picted strikes and labor militancy as the work of outside agitators, and wage earners as the dupes of a wide range of villains: German spies during the war, Bolsheviks after the war, and corrupt labor leaders at all times. Audi-ences grew to recognize secret agents by their foreign attire and IWW flun-kies by their scruffy appearance; workers on the screen, however, remained oblivious to the fiends in their midst. Though similar images of deceived workers could be seen in countless productions before the war, they as-sumed heightened importance after 1917, for worker foolishness now en-dangered the nation. Conservative feature films were especially scathing in their portrayals of union business agents, whom they stereotyped as men willing to take bribes from anyone. In *Dangerous Hours*, union leader Michael Reagan, an overweight, fiftyish Irishman who smokes fat cigars, is described as "a labor agitator and blackmailer who has profited repeatedly by selling out to the other side."[61] When a shipyard owner refuses to pay the double-crossing Reagan a bribe, he returns to helping his Bolshevik employ-ers incite strikes among the previously content shipyard workers. In some instances, hostile depictions of union officials were probably inspired by personal vendettas. The corrupt business agent in several films was played by portly men who looked remarkably like Roy Stephenson, the real busi-ness agent of IATSE Local 33.

Conservative films did not rule the screen unopposed. Liberal produc-tions continued to condemn exploitation, defend moderate trade unionism, and call for greater cooperation between labor and capital. But the lines between liberal and conservative, though fairly clear when focused on general depictions of workplace life, blurred in films portraying the rela-tionship between Reds and organized labor. Although *The Red Viper* (1919) *The Great Shadow* (1920) and *Dangerous Hours* (Ince 1920) all professed to be pro-worker, their directors used visual images that repeatedly placed anarchists, unionists, Bolsheviks, IWWs, and social reformers in the same contemptible category: men and women who seek to undermine—whether intentionally or unintentionally—the nation's well-being. Only unorga-nized workers are shown in a consistently positive light. Casting instruc-tions for a strike scene in *Dangerous Hours* call for the director to use "very good specimens of American workmen" to play unorganized workers, and actors who are "slightly foreign in appearance" as the "rag-tag army of the I.W.W." Progressive reformers, contemptuously referred to as Parlor Bolsheviks, are played by men and women who are "pale and anemic" and have "a general air of unhealthiness both mentally and physically about the majority of them."[62]

Filmmakers did not confine themselves to fantasies of revolution and invasion. Hollywood also offered viewers topical films that presented highly

Dangerous Hours (Ince 1920) showed Bolsheviks and misguided liberals conspiring against honest Americans.

Likewise, in *Bolshevism on Trial* (Mayflower 1919) foreign agents of Lenin and Trotsky dupe naive reformers, known as Parlor Bolsheviks, into helping the Bolshevik cause (note the Karl Marx-like character on the right).

embellished versions of recent labor conflicts. Bomb attacks against government officials, Red squad activities, vigilante assaults against IWW members, and major strikes in shipyards, western lumber regions, coal mines, copper mines, and steel mills moved from the nation's streets and workshops onto its movie screens. In this respect, postwar films played an especially powerful role in providing the general public with visual interpretations of contemporary turmoil. "The motion picture theaters and the newspapers," the *New York Call* insisted in 1920, "are the two most influential elements in educating the average man."[63] Yet cinematic versions of events often differed greatly from the events themselves as producers distorted actual occurrences to heighten dramatic tension or emphasize particular political perspectives.

The Seattle General Strike of 1919, which involved over 60,000 workers and featured the creation of a workers' council that strikers dubbed a "soviet," set off a wave of national paranoia that provided fertile ground for filmmakers. *The World Aflame* (1919) dramatized Mayor Ole Hanson's smashing of the Seattle strike, and *Virtuous Men* (1919), *Dangerous Hours* (Ince 1920), *The Great Shadow* (1920), and *Stranger's Banquet* (1922) explored shipyard strikes similar to the one that ignited the Seattle conflict.[64] Using the choreography of crowd scenes to deliver strong ideological messages, directors turned crowds of strikers into a dangerous mob by clustering large numbers of actors into a tightly bunched group and having them shake their fists or wooden bats at outsiders in a threatening manner. These films also echoed the claims of many employers by portraying strikes as the work of Bolshevik agents acting under orders from Moscow. The underlying causes of industrial unrest, such as postwar inflation and low wages, were simply ignored.

IWW organizing activities in western wheat fields suffered similar distortions in *Riders of the Dawn* (1920). Although the Great Plains was one of the few areas where Wobblies peacefully coexisted with employers, the film portrayed the IWW as murderous radicals bent on fomenting unrest. Transposing events that occurred during the Centralia, Washington, massacre of November 1919 onto the western wheat fields, the film ends with patriotic vigilantes defeating savage radicals in a violent gun battle. The organizing efforts that pitted the AFL against U.S. Steel, the nation's largest corporation, were also given an ahistorical twist in *The Undercurrent* (1919), a film that attributes the great steel strike of 1919 to the work of secret agents sent by Lenin and Trotsky. Events surrounding Bolshevik bomb plots against government authorities and subsequent Red squad raids were similarly distorted in *The Volcano* (1919). In one scene, New York Governor Al Smith is shown signing a bill prohibiting use of the red flag—a measure that he actually vetoed.[65]

Throughout the 1920s, directors of conservative labor-capital films such as *The Little Church around the Corner* (Warner Brothers 1923) choreographed crowd scenes with an eye toward emphasizing the frenzied, violent, and moblike character of working-class protests.

By constantly repeating images of Bolsheviks and radicals wreaking havoc on America, conservative and liberal labor-capital films helped legitimize the use of government force against its alleged enemies. The state-supported violence and domestic surveillance that were regular parts of the Red scare were presented on the screen as proper solutions to the machinations of leftist troublemakers. In *Dangerous Hours*, violence only occurs after radicals attack the police, while in *Bolshevism on Trial*, the day is saved by the arrival of the Coast Guard, which had kept the slimy Hermann Wolfe, "a professional agitator," under close surveillance during the previous year. If military force was needed "to knock the weak-kneed props from under red radicalism and IWWism in America," wrote one film reviewer, then force should be used.[66]

Despite their misrepresentations of actual events (or, perhaps, because of them), many of these films received enthusiastic endorsements from government officials throughout the country. *World Aflame* was shown at the Department of the Interior and endorsed by Governor Burnquist of Minnesota, and *Bolshevism on Trial*, *Dangerous Hours*, *The Red Viper*, and *The Volcano* were praised by a wide array of senators, governors, and state legislators. Only occasionally did a film go too far for government authorities. A publicity campaign by the producers of *Bolshevism on Trial* that asked theater managers to "stir up advance feelings against Bolshevism" by putting up red flags around their city and then hiring soldiers to tear them down prompted angry letters from Secretary of Labor Wilson to Postmaster General Burleson and Attorney General Palmer demanding they bring a halt such provocative activities. Pressure from the Yiddish press and Governor Al Smith forced the producers of *The Volcano* to alter its blatantly anti-Semitic plot. The hero's name was changed from Garland to Nathan Levison and the hook-nosed villain was now given the line: "I am not a Jew; I am a Bolshevik."[67]

The irony of these films is that they presented labor protests as the work of a powerful, well-organized left—whether Bolsheviks, communists, socialists, anarchists, or Wobblies. But in truth, postwar radical groups were devastated by years of government harassment and repression, and by bitter divisions within and between left organizations. In 1912, the Socialist party had 118,000 members and its presidential candidate Eugene V. Debs received nearly one million votes. In 1920, Debs was serving a ten-year sentence in an Atlanta jail for violating the Espionage Act, and party membership had fallen to 40,000. The dreaded Communist party had a total membership of 160,000—less than 1 percent of the nation's adult population. Similarly, the IWW, the screen's most vilified American organization, saw its ranks plunge from 100,000 in 1917 to 58,000 by the early 1920s. To put these figures in perspective, when the American Legion was founded in May 1919 it immediately enrolled 650,000 members.[68]

Leftists and trade unionists were infuriated as they watched their organizations being attacked on the screen. They knew they were not the dupes of outside agitators. Strikes and protests were rooted in workers' efforts to obtain a decent standard of living for themselves and their families. The quest for justice, not mass manipulation, was the driving force behind class conflict. But what could they do? Hollywood reached far more Americans with its interpretations of events than did labor periodicals. Whatever the truth might be, it was the scathing stereotypes of mobs and manipulators, not upright union men and women seeking justice, that dominated the screen.

By the early 1920s, Hollywood had turned against labor and the left—on screen and off—with unprecedented hostility. But repeated visual links between Bolshevism and unionism did not go uncontested by organized labor. "This kind of bunk," protested angry trade unionists in Bremerton, Washington, "is being used to discredit labor, which is declared to be too radical." AFL convention delegates denounced these films as instruments of "misrepresentation in the American-wide campaign against labor and labor organizations." Some did more than just complain. The aggressive campaign by government authorities and movie industry personnel to reshape the ideology of labor-capital films sparked the rise of a new series of labor struggles for the screen. Unionists and radicals across the nation rose up to challenge the ideological domination of Hollywood films by organizing production, distribution, and exhibition networks that would bring "the aims and hopes of the worker . . . before the masses in a most impressive and lasting manner." Men and women who had waged war to make the world safe for democracy now embarked on a crusade to make the screen safe for labor and the left.[69]

6

Struggles for the Screen: The Revival
of the Worker Film Movement

THEY COULD be seen on movie screens throughout the land: greedy capitalists and their ruthless hirelings bent on extorting profits and exploiting
employees. No wage earner, no man, woman, or child was safe from these
heartless fiends. Audiences watched obese textile boss Mr. Mulius work
poor Stefan Breznac to death and then seduce his daughter in the back seat
of a chauffeur-driven car; they watched the cruel forelady in a printing factory drive sweet Mary to exhaustion and then fire the caring Ann when she
came to her friend's aid; they watched absentee coal mine magnates and
factory owners use private armies, scab labor, and government Red squads
to break up unions, destroy workers' homes, and force employees to bow to
their autocratic will.

Could these enemies of democracy be stopped? Was there no one who
could halt these abuses of power and help honest working people make a
decent living? The answer to these questions could be found at the movies.
Like other worker-made films of the postwar era, *The Passaic Textile Strike*
(International Workers' Aid 1926), *Labor's Reward* (American Federation of
Labor 1925), *The Contrast* (1921), and *The New Disciple* (1921) contested
Hollywood representations of contemporary labor struggles and offered
audiences markedly different ways of understanding and resolving class
conflict. Beginning in July 1918, working-class organizations across the
country, from the teeming metropolis of New York to the quiet town of
Vallejo, California, created production companies and made films that
presented audiences with their political visions of a more democratic
postwar nation. "Tens of thousands of people," predicted one labor filmmaker, "will be reached and converted by these films who might otherwise
remain unaroused."[1]

At no time in the history of the movie industry were struggles for the
screen more intense than in the decade after World War I. Hundreds of
small producers, distributors, and exhibitors found themselves battling an
increasingly powerful studio system bent on absorbing or destroying all
competitors. As the range of producers decreased, so, too, did the choices
exhibitors—and audiences—could make. Exhibitors either accepted films
from large production-distribution companies like Paramount or suffered
the consequences. "You take that thing they shoved on us some time ago,

'Bolshevism on Trial,'" explained one irate New York theater owner. "Now,
I'm not a Bolshevik, but I hate to run a rotten series of pictured lies simply
because some big power has produced it and presents it so that I have to
take that picture or close my theater for the day."[2]

Declining control over the screen evoked similar concerns from other
industry figures. The bottom-line business mentality of big studios and their
Wall Street backers led a number of prominent stars to start their own companies. Mary Pickford, Douglas Fairbanks, Charlie Chaplin, and D. W.
Griffith denounced the growth of "certain combinations and groups of persons and corporations" that aimed to "dwarf the artistic growth of the motion picture." In January 1919, they formed United Artists, an organization
that would "protect the independent producer and the independent exhibitor against these commercial combinations."[3]

Disgust over the proliferation of anti-labor films also led radicals and
unionists in Hollywood, New York, Seattle, Chicago, and elsewhere to organize their own film companies. The leaders of this movement, like their
prewar predecessors, were not filmmakers per se, but labor and radical activists who used film to provide the public with positive portrayals of unionism, socialism, and the "true aspirations of labor." The dramatic changes
that gripped the postwar movie business made their undertaking considerably more complicated than it had been a decade before. Independent producers now had to clear three major hurdles in order to reach the screen.
First, they had to raise sufficient funds to finance a film, then they had to
make movies good enough that people would pay to see them, and finally
they had to persuade exhibitors to show their products. Class-conscious
labor companies faced the additional problem of overcoming the powerful
opposition of capitalists, censors, and government agencies. After being
warned that worker filmmakers were producing pictures for the "purpose of
inciting class feelings" and hatred against employers, J. Edgar Hoover dispatched federal agents in 1921 to monitor and undermine the efforts of
these fledgling companies.[4]

The quest to create a successful working-class film movement seemed
crazy to many observers. With large studios tightening their hold on the
industry, the chances of any new company getting its films into first-run
theaters seemed a long shot indeed. Not only did worker filmmakers challenge Hollywood's increasing control of the industry, but they also challenged its fundamental assumptions regarding the kinds of movies audiences wanted to see. Did audiences simply want to forget the hardships of
everyday life and lose themselves in fantasies, as industry leaders seemed to
believe? Or would audiences also turn out in large numbers to watch the
contemporary struggles of workers, as worker filmmakers predicted? Once
again, a new David rose up to challenge Goliath. And once again, Goliath
learned that a slingshot could be a powerful weapon.

Seeing Red

Anyone who believes that moviegoing during the silent era was a passive experience or that audiences meekly accepted what they saw on the screen would certainly have gotten a strong reaction from Emmanuel Lopez. Going to the movies, as the New York City laborer learned, could be a very dangerous ordeal. In September 1919, the forty-one-year-old Lopez went to the elegant Strand Theater on Broadway and 47th Street to see Samuel Goldwyn's latest anti-Bolshevik film, *The World and the Woman*. As the movie shifted from a Cinderella love story set in Czarist Russia to a reenactment of the Russian Revolution, Lopez attracted the attention of nearby patrons by cheering the Bolsheviks while everyone else "hissed them." His constant enthusiasm for the Reds soon proved too much to bear. When Lopez applauded an intertitle reading "Down with Religion, the Church, and Priests," he was attacked by the men sitting next to him. And when he defiantly yelled to his assailants that he was a Bolshevist and "proud of it," a riot broke out. "Several women fainted and others ran screaming toward the door." Lopez was quickly arrested and taken to the West 47th Street Police Station. When he appeared in court the next night, he was fined $10 for disorderly conduct and given a lecture by the local magistrate, who condemned Bolshevism and suggested that the Red-loving Lopez leave the country. Poor Emmanuel Lopez: he left his home to go to the movies and wound up getting arrested for being beaten up![5]

Movie audiences, as Lopez and his assailants would testify, took their films seriously. This held true for political activists as well as apolitical wage earners. Radicals and unionists did not spend all their free time reading Karl Marx or debating political issues. They also loved going to the movies and gossiping about movie stars. The same delegates who demanded American recognition of the Soviet Union at the Indiana Federation of Labor convention in 1924 also called for the reinstatement of scandal-plagued actor Fatty Arbuckle into the movies. Even that most die-hard of radical periodicals, the communist *Daily Worker*, placed its movie columns directly across from its editorials.[6]

Few films excited the passions of audiences as much as the anti-Red, anti-labor pictures of the era. Conservatives praised them, leftists condemned them, and general audiences booed, cheered, and, in some instances, "laughed at the . . . struggle" between unbelievably evil Bolsheviks and their equally unbelievably virtuous foes. Yet, when it came to assessing the impact of these films on public opinion, few labor and radical leaders were amused by what they saw. "The average picture of the struggles of workers—especially themes dealing with strikes," complained the editors of the *New York Call*, "is poisonous in its vicious distortion of these struggles. . . . They do harm, infinite harm, to the cause of labor." Robert Buck, editor of the *Chicago New Majority*, fumed that movies had been "captured and used by the enemies of the workers to lull the people to sleep and make them mutely and humbly accept their present unsatisfactory lot."[7]

Rank-and-file trade unionists were equally quick to condemn films that disparaged their cause. In Seattle, where workers discussed the latest movies while standing around the union hall, a labor spy overheard a heated conversation about *The New Moon* (1919) in which one worker complained: "They have now started a campaign of pictures trying to create a hatred between the Russians and the American working men, but I think we will be too wise for them this time . . . instead of the pictures making us hate the Russians we will like them the better." Unionists in Bremerton, Washington argued that anti-Red films were clearly intended to undermine labor's cause in the public eye by insinuating "that American labor will carry out the same program should they come into power."[8]

There was, however, no single "labor" view of Hollywood films. Political differences between moderate and militant trade unionists prompted bitter disagreements over movies. *The World Aflame* (1919), which depicted the Seattle General Strike as the work of Bolshevik agitators and ended with capitalists and loyal trade unionists uniting to defeat the vile Reds, received rousing endorsements from AFL leaders throughout California. On the other hand, the Seattle Labor Council, whose members participated in the strike, were outraged at the film's blatant distortion of events and condemned it as the worst kind of "anti-labor photoplay."[9]

Whatever their political disagreements, few unionists or radicals doubted the power of a medium that reached over 50 million Americans each week—nearly one-half the nation's population—by mid-1920s. It was not the reaction to any one film that most concerned the labor faithful, but the collective impact that scores of conservative labor-capital films would have on shaping public opinion about workers and their organizations. Those familiar with the workings of unions might reject reactionary cinematic diatribes. But, as one labor periodical pointed out, the vast majority of Americans still did not belong to unions and "few people even attempt to understand the labor movement." With 80 percent of all moviegoers in 1924 coming from "poor or only moderately well off" backgrounds, postwar audiences were dominated by unorganized blue and white-collar workers, many of whom had little first-hand knowledge of unions or radical organizations. "There are some who, every time they think of unionism, immediately think of anarchists and bolsheviki," observed the editors of the *United Mine Workers' Journal,* and "it is unfortunate also, that there are employers in this country who encourage just such a belief on the part of the public."[10]

The deleterious effects of features were compounded by weekly newsreels that presented audiences with biased depictions of ongoing strikes and labor troubles. Hugo Riesenfeld, manager of several Broadway movie palaces, explained how newsreels were especially important in molding public opinion, for they had the "ability to present a living image to the audiences, to recreate happenings that a newspaper, even with its illustrations, can only suggest." Despite their seemingly neutral, reality-based products, newsreel companies could manipulate public perceptions of events by choosing what footage they sent to exhibitors. Indeed, what was not seen on the screen could be as important as what was shown. Universal, Fox, Pathé, and other newsreel companies, explained one critic, edited their films to depict "the employers' side" of events and "do not present pictures of strikers being clubbed down. . . . In the [recent] rail strike, the scenes were of armed guards and college boy strikebreakers, but never of strike meetings or labor conditions."[11]

The same anger that prompted fist fights inside movie theaters also sparked widespread calls for union and radical families to demand that local theaters stop showing politically offensive films. "Hokum peddlers and anti-labor propagandists," suggested one Chicago daily, "should be soaked in the only place where they have any feelings, at the box office." Threats of boycotts and calls for establishing labor-owned movie theaters did have an effect on some smaller houses. Neighborhood theaters, suggested Riesenfeld, were more likely to bow to union pressure than movie palaces because the "threat of an out and out Labor Film theater in working-class sections does not look cheerful to smaller exhibitors." This proved true in Steubenville, Ohio, where union protests against "the distorted anti-labor propaganda" in the *Stranger's Banquet* resulted in the film's withdrawal from the Victoria Theater.[12]

Local efforts to pressure exhibitors were accompanied by national campaigns aimed at persuading producers to alter the ideological content of their films. Angered by films that repeatedly "ridiculed and falsified" their cause, delegates to the AFL convention in June 1920 instructed the Executive Council to file protests with the country's leading producers, distributors, and exhibitors. Universal, Fox, Pathé, and other companies responded to AFL protests by denying the delegates' charges. Universal, insisted vice president R. H. Cochrane, had never "permitted its pictures to be used as propaganda for or against organized labor or any other movement, excepting only . . . during the war." Concerned about a possible boycott by union families, National Association of the Motion Picture Industry members promised to work with AFL leaders on eliminating offensive films. Yet three years later, the AFL was still condemning Hollywood's "continued attempt to misrepresent labor."[13]

Whereas some unionists lobbied exhibitors or wrote letters to studios, others called on the nation's wage earners to move from movie patron to movie producer. If conservatives could make films that vilified labor and

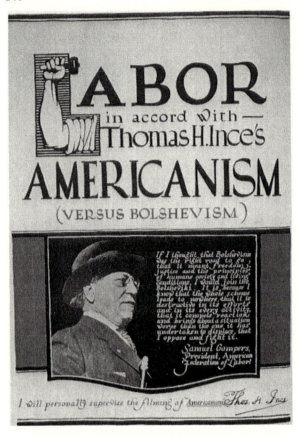

American Federation of Labor president Samuel Gompers hoped to counter attacks on organized labor by endorsing anti-Bolshevik, pro-union films such as *Americanism (versus Bolshevism)*, later renamed *Dangerous Hours* (Ince 1920).

radical organizations, then workers could make films that would "advance the true interests of every genuine reform movement" and "inspire men and women to want a less imperfect society." And so they did.[14]

Making Movies

Although the aims of the revived worker film movement were similar to those of its prewar predecessors, they faced more formidable logistical problems. Workers could no longer make commercially viable films for a few thousand dollars. Audiences were now accustomed to more elaborate

Hollywood films and expected good production values (good acting, costumes, sets, lighting). Good production values, however, required money. Large studios rarely put out features for less than $60,000 and even low-budget films of the early 1920s cost $25,000 to $35,000. Thus, making films that audiences would pay to see meant raising tens of thousands of dollars. Since banks and Wall Street financiers were unwilling to lend money or float stock offerings for labor film companies, aspiring producers had to solicit funds from politically sympathetic investors. Once they did that, worker filmmakers still faced the onerous task of finding distributors and exhibitors outside the increasingly monopolistic studio system to handle their features.[15]

As the movie industry grew more tightly organized, so too did the worker film movement. Labor's postwar struggles for the screen differed from earlier efforts in three key respects: sporadic films by individuals and small groups were superseded by movies and newsreels made on a more regular basis by incorporated production companies; the films were focused even more closely on current workplace and political battles; and the most successful companies adopted the business strategies of successful studios by creating new distribution and exhibition networks for their products.

Labor's foray into the world of studio production began in the summer of 1918 when members of the Brotherhood of Railway Trainmen entered into an unprecedented arrangement to buy their own Hollywood studio. Relying on the services of David Horsley, the studio's former owner, the Motive Motion Picture Company (MMPC) set out to produce movies and newsreels to "mould public opinion for the benefit of Organized Labor and to bring about reforms by the pressure of public opinion." Though nominally headed by former railroad workers George Williams (president) and Ben Lyon (secretary-treasurer), the driving force behind this remarkable venture was David Horsley, the company's director-general. Part hustler, part visionary, Horsley began making movies in 1907 at his New Jersey studio and ventured west in 1911 to open Hollywood's first studio, the Nestor Studio. A year later, he joined Carl Laemmle in creating Universal. Horsley, who grew up in a coal mine region near the Scottish border, considered himself a socialist—having been converted to the cause after reading Sinclair's *The Cry of Justice*. It was his avid concern with contemporary politics, as well as his sharp eye for a good business deal, that led Horsley to sell his five-acre studio on Main and Washington Streets to the railroad workers.[16]

The MMPC was founded in the midst of a heated national debate over the future of the country's railroad system, which had been placed under government control during the war. Intent on using the screen to promote the workers' cause, Horsely, Williams, and Lyon devised an ingenious plan to sell his studio to the "subordinate lodges of the Brotherhood." In September 1918, they sent circulars to railroad union locals throughout the country announcing the creation of a company "by former members of the Brother-hood of Railway Trainmen to produce a series of Motion Pictures" advocat-ing the nationalization of railroads and substantial raises for its workers. Company stock was sold at five dollars a share and investors were promised that the MMPC would "distribute large returns, not only in dividends but stabilize labor conditions and maintain, or raise the present standard of pay, which is none too large."[17]

The MMPC began its operations with a series of publicity releases worthy of any Hollywood studio. Horsley gained immediate national attention by signing Upton Sinclair to write a twenty-part serial dramatizing the "strug-gles of organized labor to obtain justice and a living wage." The company also garnered credibility with movie industry figures by hiring Francis Ford to produce its films. An experienced actor, director, and producer, Ford curried labor support by pledging he would not employ anyone "who does not carry a union card."[18]

Company officials moved to capitalize on their initial publicity by travel-ing around the country to meet with national labor leaders and sell stock to railroad lodges. By the end of 1918 they had sold several thousand dollars' worth of stock and secured promises of more money to come. In March 1919, the MMPC released its first production, a newsreel of the "Govern-ment Control" parade staged by Los Angeles railroad workers on Washing-ton's Birthday. The film premiered at the People's Theater, where it did "a rushing business." In June, the 187,000-member-strong Brotherhood of Railway Trainmen passed a resolution officially endorsing the company; delegates to the AFL Convention were also urged to "give their support and aid in every proper way" to the new venture.[19]

The MMPC seemed to have everything going for it: a studio in which to make its films, an experienced executive to run the studio, a well-known producer, and a famous writer. Yet despite its promising start, the company never made another newsreel, much less a feature-length film. Part of its decline was due to managerial incompetence and part to the difficulties of being an independent labor film company. With Horsley frequently diverted by his other business interests, the burden of running the studio's daily operations fell to Williams and Lyon—a task for which they were ill equipped. Williams, who was entrusted with the critical responsibility of selling stock, was more interested in fun raising than fundraising. While traveling in Philadelphia he boasted of sleeping with two women in ex-change for promises of acting jobs; after another trip to San Francisco, he brought three aspiring starlets back to the studio "and took naked pictures of them."[20]

Williams' sexual dalliances aside, the main problem the MMPC faced was the same one that confronted most small independent filmmakers: money. After the initial rush of orders, stock sales trickled to a few hundred dollars a month, barely enough to pay the studio's gas and electric bills. "I cannot understand why the train men are not coming through better," Horsley complained to Lyon. The answer was simple: railroad workers wanted to see the company's films before they would invest their limited funds, yet films could not be made without first obtaining sufficient investments. "As soon as the laboring men see our product on the screen," Lyon assured Horsley, "they will all want some of the stock." Assurances, however, did not pay the bills.[21]

Desperate for funds, Horsley spent most of the summer of 1919 in New York City, approaching friends at Universal and Pathé in hopes of lining up a distribution deal with a sizable advance. But distributors refused to buy the company's twenty-part serial "until they [had] seen some of them, at least three episodes." The MMPC also faced a barrier that other independents did not: it was a *labor* film company, and that made investors even more wary. "It is impossible to underwrite here," Horsley wrote that August, "as you have to look to people who would naturally be classed as 'Capital' and they can't see anything in helping people who haven't the spirit to help themselves. Capital naturally figures that if they [workers] will not take enough interest to buy a share of $5 stock, that they will not cooperate in demanding the pictures at the box offices."[22]

Unable to make a distribution deal, Horsley returned to his New Jersey studio in September and began producing comedies and tending to his other interests. In December, the MMPC's board of directors suspended Horsley, who was still drawing $200 a week in salary, for "his failure to devote his time and attention to the business." The board tried to revive company fortunes, but without a substantial influx of capital there was little they could do. By March 1920, the Motive Motion Picture Company was dead.[23]

The MMPC's failure did not discourage unionists and radicals from launching similar efforts. "Other groups have sprung up in past months in the Middle West," reported one labor periodical in May 1920, "and New York has three or four groups which propose to enter upon the competitive field to supply pictorial propaganda." The most successful were the Seattle-based Federation Film Corporation (FFC) and the New York-based Labor Film Services (LFS). In November 1919, nine months after the city's general strike, Seattle trade unionists initiated what they called a "twentieth century movement for the Emancipation of Labor" by founding the FFC. The company pledged to use film to "demonstrate the constructive aims of labor and combat the propaganda against the labor unions now being spread by employing interests and capitalists in an effort to reduce the workers to a state of wage-slavery again."[24]

Described by a local labor spy as "one of the most far-reaching moves ever started by organized labor," the FFC grew out of Seattle labor's commitment to worker cooperatives. The city was the leading cooperative center of the postwar era and by the end of 1919, its trade unionists owned a newspaper, savings and loan association, several union halls, a movie theater, and even a stock brokerage firm. Given these experiences running other enterprises, it is not surprising that the FFC was much better organized and managed than the MMPC. Like the MMPC, the FFC was a joint stock venture "owned and controlled by organized labor." Whereas Horsley had tried to raise funds among national unions who knew little about him or his organization, the FFC focused on raising money from city and state labor organizations. Company stock, which totaled $100,000 at par value, sold for $10 a share, and a minimum of 51 percent was reserved for union members.[25]

Although the FFC's worker-run executive board remained deeply involved in company financial operations, it hired a Hollywood professional, John Arthur Nelson, to plan and supervise productions. The choice of Nelson seemed sound, at least at first. Like Horsley, the forty-six-year-old Nelson was a dynamic figure with socialist leanings and an impressive Hollywood résumé that included writing, producing, and directing for Universal and Warner Features. He ran his own film company, and had published *The Photoplay: How to Write, How to Sell.* But Nelson also had a sleazy past that probably remained unknown to his Seattle employers. He was arrested for misappropriation of stockholders' funds while serving as vice-president of the U.S. Film Company in 1915, and again several years later for smuggling arms and horses across the Mexican border. In both cases, the charges against Nelson were eventually dropped.[26]

Whatever his past indiscretions, Nelson proved a shrewd businessman, something the company needed to succeed. During the winter of 1919–1920, Nelson spent much of his time attending local union meetings to publicize and sell stock in the FFC. "We have an opportunity," he told intrigued listeners, "of reaching and educating the non-union man of today who can be made the loyal union man of tomorrow." Well-made labor films, he insisted, could have reversed the outcome of the recent strike against U.S. Steel and "made victory possible by showing up the causes and abuses behind the strike, showing them up to Mr. General Public so that he would have added his great influence on their side." Nelson also spoke of the company's long-range plan to build a studio in Seattle that would serve as home to other film companies and help generate revenues needed to finance more FFC features.[27]

By the spring of 1920 the FFC's goal of putting "radical ideas across on the screen" was no longer just a dream. Repeated visits to union meetings brought in over $16,000 in stock sales, and when the company signed two exhibition deals for $18,000 in May, Nelson set off for Los Angeles, where he rented studio space and began shooting the FFC's first feature film, *The New Disciple.* In November 1920, one year after the company's formation,

Nelson screened a rough cut of his film to the board of directors. In May 1921, *The New Disciple* opened to rave reviews at Seattle's Class "A" Theater; six months later Nelson scored a major coup by arranging for a Broadway run at Shubert's Lyric Theater, just one-half block from Times Square. The FFC was clearly on the rise and its dream of challenging Hollywood suddenly seemed possible.[28]

At the same time that Nelson was beginning production in Los Angeles, radicals and militant trade unionists in New York were organizing the Labor Film Services. The most ambitious of all the postwar labor film companies, the LFS planned to produce and distribute an elaborate array of feature films, short subjects, and newsreels "portraying the worker's life in the mines, in the slums, on the farms, in the railroads, on the picket lines, etc." These projects would be funded through the sale of company stock, initially offered at $10 a share. To insure that the LFS remained in the hands of working people, company bylaws stipulated that members of labor and radical organizations would always control at least 51 percent of its stock and no individual would be allowed to own shares with a par value of more than $1,000.[29]

In June 1920, three months after its founding, the company's board of directors chose Joseph D. Cannon as their field director. Described by the *New York Call* as a "fine, white-haired, young-hearted, unquenchably enthusiastic miner" who "has won the hearts of all who have met him," Cannon was a longtime warrior on behalf of numerous radical causes. Born in 1871 to a coal mining family in Locust Gap, Pennsylvania, he began working in the local mines at the age of eight, and became a foreman by twelve. In 1898 he left Pennsylvania and became an organizer for the Western Federation of Miners (renamed the International Union of Mine, Mill, and Smelter Workers in 1916). Over the next two decades, Cannon played a key role in organizing copper, iron, and steel workers, directing the Cooperative League of the USA, and raising funds for striking steel workers and Irish nationalists. The mine workers' leader was also an important figure in the Socialist party. He ran for Congress in Arizona in 1906 and 1908, and for senator, congressman, and governor of New York in 1916, 1917, and 1920. Cannon could also be found at countless rallies speaking out on behalf of women's suffrage, Irish independence, and equality for black workers. The indefatigable Cannon served on the Executive Board of the AFL's mining department from 1914 to 1920, where he voiced his steadfast opposition to the conservative policies of Samuel Gompers.[30]

It is easy to see why the LFS wanted Cannon. But why did Cannon want to head a fledgling film company? The answer was simple. Having spent years on the Socialist party's lecture circuit, Cannon, like Frank Wolfe before him, found its traditional methods of propaganda unable to reach mass audiences. Film, however, offered a powerful new means for educating the unconverted. Laura Cannon, Joe's wife, acquainted him with the medium's potential when she delivered a rousing speech and visual presentation on behalf of the Wage Earners' Suffrage League at the Los Angeles Socialist Movie Theater in 1911. When the Western Federation of Miners produced films of the Calumet Copper Strike and Christmas tragedy in 1916, Joe followed his wife's lead and arranged screenings throughout New York. Four years later, when the LFS offered him an unprecedented opportunity for political education, he quickly accepted. As one company circular noted: "Fifty million Americans attend the movies every week. The LABOR FILM SERVICE will reach them in behalf of LABOR."[31]

Joe Cannon brought to the job an organizing skill and breadth of vision unequaled by any other labor film executive. He knew that if the LFS was to succeed as an agent of mass culture it needed to build a broad base of support among audiences and investors. To that end, the LFS leader quickly surmounted the long-standing ethnic and political divisions that plagued New York's unions, and obtained endorsements and stock subscriptions from the United Hebrew Trades, the Italian Chamber of Labor, and the Irish-dominated Central Federated Union. Cannon also received vocal and financial support from local liberals and a wide spectrum of leftists, including Norman Thomas, Scott Nearing, Morris Hillquit, and Sidney Hillman; the city's socialist actors; and his old IWW friends. "Dividends will be paid—good dividends," he assured potential investors. But he also promised that "we will not permit the desire for profit to become the main consideration in our work."[32]

Cannon believed that the fastest way to attract investors was to show them what a labor film looked like. Rather than waiting months or years to raise enough money to make a feature film, the LFS produced and released its first newsreel in July—just several weeks after Cannon's arrival. A month later it premiered the *Animated Labor Review*, a weekly newsreel covering "every phase of the workers' life in the shop, in the factory, in his union, during strikes, and on the picket line." Cannon's decision to make a quick public impact with newsreels resulted in brisk stock sales at screenings and the donation of a year's free film laboratory services by one mightily impressed patron. The *Animated Labor Review* was followed in October by a short film entitled *A Watcher at the Polls*. Appearing in the midst of Cannon's 1920 campaign for governor of New York, the movie showed foreign-born citizens how to vote and taught Socialist poll watchers how to detect the "election frauds and manipulations practiced by the old party politicians."[33]

However popular its newsreels and short film may have been, the LFS's success in challenging Hollywood and altering public opinion ultimately lay in its ability to produce first-run feature films. Cannon was blessed with a stroke of good fortune, for his longtime friend John W. Slayton brought him both the script and the money to fund such a project. A union carpenter and member of the Socialist party since 1898, Slayton labored for more than three decades as a speaker and writer in various party propaganda campaigns. Like Cannon, the Pittsburgh radical grew frustrated with soap-box polemics that failed to excite anyone but the party faithful. I want "to reach the non-unionist," he told a reporter in March 1918, "and we know the best place to do that is in the motion picture house." Slayton wrote a screenplay entitled *The Contrast* about the lives and struggles of coal miners, and spent the next three years traveling to union meetings in Pennsylvania, West Virginia, Ohio, and New York raising money to make his movie. By January 1919 he had sold $16,000 worth of stock in The Contrast Photoplay Company to nearly a hundred labor and radical organizations. He then convinced the LFS to contribute the rest of the financing and handle the film's distribution; Cannon agreed to serve as its producer. Working on a rapid schedule, the LFS began filming in January 1921. Three months later a special screening was held in Pittsburgh in Slayton's honor, and in May the film opened in New York and points west.[34]

The successful completion of *The Contrast* was quickly followed by the LFS' announcement that it had secured the rights to produce Upton Sinclair's *The Brotherhood of the Rails* (the scenario he wrote for the MMPC) and planned to release a new version of *The Jungle*. The LFS seemed poised to make its presence known to movie audiences throughout the nation.[35]

The FFC and LFS were soon joined in their efforts by several other organizations. The most active challenge to Hollywood's portrayals of Bolsheviks and Russian life was mounted by the International Workers' Aid (IWA). Originally known as the Friends of Soviet Russia, the organization was founded by radicals and left philanthropists in New York in August 1921 to collect money and clothing for famine victims in Russia. Several months later, the IWA set out to win greater public sympathy for their cause by hiring William F. Kruse to make films and newsreels depicting life in the Soviet Union. Born in Hoboken, New Jersey, in November 1894, the "Camera Man of the American Communists," as Kruse later became known, was the son of a grain elevator worker and grew up a "die-hard Republican" in Jersey City. Converted to socialism at the age of seventeen, the talented Kruse subsequently toiled as a playwright, sheet metal worker, Socialist lecturer, movie reviewer, director of the Young People's Socialist League, filmmaker, and student at a "thoroughly disrespectable, very effective night law school" in Chicago.[36]

Kruse's fascination with Hollywood films convinced him that popular culture could be used as a powerful tool for the left. The "tremendous propaganda power of the hundred thousand projectors," he wrote in 1924, "outshines all the newspapers, magazines, lecture platforms, and public libraries put together." Working with Soviet newsreels and footage that he and other American Communists shot during trips to Russia, Kruse produced a series of pioneering documentaries—*Russia through the Shadows* (1922), *The Fifth Year* (1923), *Russia in Overalls* (1923), *Russia and Germany: A Tale of Two Republics* (1924)—that exposed American viewers to scenes of "life in Russia that had never before been brought before the people." The loathsome Bolsheviks of Hollywood melodramas were shown here as ordinary people who worked hard and, like many Americans, enjoyed the simple pleasures of dancing, sailing, bicycling, and horseback riding. Kruse and the IWA also served as the American distributors of Russian feature films.[37]

While Kruse and the IWA hacked away at conservative stereotypes of Russians, delegates to the AFL convention in 1921 responded to repeated screen attacks against organized labor by ordering the Executive Council to investigate the viability of opening a movie studio and chain of theaters to make and show films portraying the "true principles, objects and activities of organized labor." Although the project was ultimately deemed too costly, the AFL made a five-reel feature film in 1925, *Labor's Reward*, which it used as the centerpiece of a national organizing campaign.[38]

Several other labor and radical organizations took a more modest cinematic path and, as we will see in subsequent chapters, produced nontheatrical films that were shown in union halls, schools, and small neighborhood theaters. But of the many fledgling labor companies that challenged Hollywood, only four—the FFC, LFS, IWA, and AFL—succeeded in producing newsreels and theatrical features during the early 1920s. Although each organization raised sufficient capital to make a film, there was no guarantee that anyone would go see it. To attract significant numbers of paying customers, labor film companies had to turn out entertaining features that nonunion people would enjoy watching; films that viewers would recommend to their friends and perhaps even see a second time. How, then, did these polemicists of the screen go about attracting mass audiences? What kinds of movies did they make and how did they manage to combine politics and entertainment?

Activist Entertainment

Entertainment in the pursuit of activism was the common goal of all worker film companies. The FFC, LFS, AFL, and IWA strove to create films that were as cinematically proficient as Hollywood productions, but whose visual politics differed from anything viewers were likely to see in conservative or liberal features. Whereas Hollywood concentrated on rewriting the history of the immediate past, labor films presented history in the making and did so from the workers' point of view. Cinematic depictions of miners' strikes, textile strikes, attempts to create worker cooperatives, and efforts to organize women wage earners all made it to the screen in the same period that these events were actually happening. In telling these stories, labor films offered viewers something that most postwar Hollywood films did not: a broad context for understanding the conflicts portrayed on the screen. Audiences saw how labor militancy was sparked by the unjust actions of employers and not by the secret machinations of Bolshevik agents or union agitators.

The four main labor features of the era—*The New Disciple* (1921), *The Contrast* (1921), *Labor's Reward* (AFL 1925), and *The Passaic Textile Strike* (IWA 1926)—gave voice to workers' desires, dreams, and discontents and did so, as John Nelson remarked, "in a manner which will not only amuse and entertain, but edify as well."[39] Filmmakers used melodrama, love stories, and documentary footage to parry conservative attacks that associated labor with the 3 R's—Reds, radicalism, and revolution. Taken collectively, these movies recast the dominant political vocabulary of the day and laid out new cinematic interpretations of contemporary class conflict. Yet, while challenging Hollywood's vision of the world, worker films differed from each other in form and ideology.

At first glance, these movies did not look very different from Hollywood films. All paid careful attention to lighting, acting, directing, and editing. Nelson and Cannon knew that unless their films were technically proficient they stood little chance of making it into first-run houses. Though he was operating on a relatively limited budget, Nelson used his industry contacts to assemble an impressive crew. He hired William Pigott, a longtime friend with 250 film credits, to write *The New Disciple's* scenario and Ollie Sellers, a former production manager at Triangle, to direct it. Starring roles went to upcoming actor Pell Trenton, who, ironically, had just starred in Metro's anti-Bolshevik comedy *The Uplifters*, and actress Norris Johnson, who had played lead roles in recent Ince and Goldwyn productions. The supporting cast featured veteran performers Alfred Allen, Margaret Mann, Walt Whitman, and even included a brief appearance by "Boris of Sezanoff," a Russian wolfhound reputedly owned by the former Czar. Equally intent on insuring visual professionalism, Cannon gathered a retinue of experienced but lesser known players—Dorothy Bernard, Tom Cameron, Dan Duffy, and Jerry Devine—to fill key roles. Guy Hedlund, one of D. W. Griffith's early ensemble actors, was hired to direct the film.[40]

While *The New Disciple* and *The Contrast* confronted the "present relentless open-shop drive against labor and labor organizations," they did so in a manner that reflected the differing aesthetic and political sensibilities of their producers. *The New Disciple* brought Seattle labor's faith in worker cooperatives before the moviegoing public in a form intended to appeal to the millions of non-unionists and middle-class viewers. The most experienced filmmaker in the worker movement, Nelson created a movie that was on the cutting edge of changing Hollywood styles. *The New Disciple* mixed aspects of labor-capital melodramas that emphasized class conflict with aspects of increasingly popular society films that focused on romance between the classes. But unlike these latter productions, the class struggles in Nelson's movie were never lost amid the joys and tears of cross-class romance.[41]

Presenting its message within the framework of a love story between John McPherson, a factory worker's son, and Mary Fanning, a factory owner's daughter, *The New Disciple* shows how worker cooperatives could restore the harmony between employer and employee that was shattered by wartime capitalist profiteering. During the course of the romance between its two class-crossed lovers, the six-reel film repeatedly challenges the anti-Bolshevik, anti-labor paranoia of Hollywood films by presenting radicals, closed shops, and worker cooperatives as agents of justice, and portraying open shops, Red squads, and the American Plan as loathsome efforts to undermine democratic values.

The movie opens in the small town of Harmony, where harmony indeed prevails between factory owner Peter Fanning and his employees, and where love blooms between Mary and John. Reversing the usual casting choices of anti-labor films, director Sellers cast the handsome Pell Trenton to play John, the beautiful Norris Johnson to play Mary, and Alfred Allen, an overweight, balding actor who looks like the sinister union business agent of anti-union features, to play Peter. Class harmony is shattered and love threatened as the outbreak of war turns Fanning into an avaricious war profiteer (one of the new disciples of misbegotten wealth), his wife Marion into an effete society leader, and John into a soldier who goes off to fight for peace and democracy.

When John returns from war, he finds his town and love threatened by growing class hostilities. Tensions on both sides are inflamed by the appearance of the familiar outside agitator. The agitator, however, is not a Bolshevik or union leader, but a spy from a competing Trust who poses as Peter's friend while secretly plotting to drive him out of business. Fanning is tricked by the spy into rejecting his employees' demand for a fair wage and responds to their ensuing strike by instituting a lockout. The film proceeds to show audiences what strikes and lockouts look like from the workers' point of view. Conservative depictions of strikers as violent mobs are countered by scenes of thoughtful men who calmly deliberate the likely consequences of their actions. Instead of an amoebalike mass of indistinguishable faces blindly following a single leader, we see employees seated in an auditorium, raising their hands and patiently waiting their turn to discuss their common course of action. During the meetings and subsequent strike not a single threatening gesture is ever made against their employer. But far from romanticizing the strike, the film shows the miseries workers are forced to endure. We see children suffer and go hungry as strike benefits run out and shopkeepers refuse to grant workers any more credit. We see Fanning try to break the strike by ejecting families from company housing and then using scabs, stool pigeons, Red squad raids, and company unions to force them into submission. But his employees refuse to bend. Despite their travails, women and children stand solidly behind the union.

The strike and lockout eventually drive Fanning into bankruptcy and the rival Trust is poised to buy and then dismantle his factory. But love and jobs are saved by John. Identified as a "radical" throughout the film, John explains to Mary—whose father has prohibited her from seeing her "Red" boyfriend—that radicalism is a relative concept: "Twenty years ago [Theodore] Roosevelt was called a radical." The "radical" idea he espouses is the same one that many FFC investors had used to win strikes and break lockouts: worker cooperatives. In Seattle, unionists and farmers lowered consumer costs and protected producer markets by organizing the Co-Operative Food Products Association. In Harmony, Peter persuades strikers and local farmers, who will lose their customers if the factory is shut down, to pool their capital and organize a cooperative. Happiness is restored as the cooperative succeeds in buying the factory and the repentant Fanning, realizing the foolishness of his ways, consents to the marriage of Mary and John. Romance aside, the final message is that collective struggle could restore justice.[42]

The Contrast presented viewers with a different cinematic form and political agenda. Set in the strife-torn coal regions of West Virginia, it favored social realism over romance, docudrama over melodrama, and advocated industrial unionism and militant workplace action as the best weapons against capitalist oppression. This preference for hard-hitting social realism was dictated by the extraordinary drama of ongoing events. Mingo County, West Virginia, the setting for this film, was engulfed in a virtual civil war as absentee coal mine owners and their hired gunmen ruled and murdered with relative impunity. Newspapers rarely reported atrocities committed against miners or offered any analysis of the causes of hostilities. "The great mass of news relating to West Virginia," complained AFL leader Samuel Gompers, "conveys the impression that lawless bands of miners roam the state without reason except unjustified bitterness against mine owners." The high drama of these struggles provided fertile material for dozens of Hollywood productions that usually presented distorted views of events.[43]

The Contrast corrects these distortions through a mixture of dramatic plotting and documentary scenes. Relying on techniques perfected by his mentor, D. W. Griffith, director Guy Hedlund uses juxtaposition to portray the causes of worker discontent, cutting back and forth between scenes of the lavish lives of mineowners and the poverty and dangers faced by their employees. *The Contrast* also adopts Griffith's raw emotionalism and builds audience empathy by evoking anger against employers. In one scene, the film cuts from a frightened young girl rummaging through a garbage can for something edible to the inside of a coal owner's mansion where we see a maid leading a pampered dog into an elegant dining room and offering him a hot chicken dinner. "To be seen in any great city," proclaims the ensuing intertitle, "it costs $10 a day to feed this dog." Depictions of the murder of union organizers by company guards and destruction of the miners' tent camps expose the lawless actions employed by coal barons. The film ends on a hopeful note, with newly unionized workers winning their strike through their own efforts, and not, as was the case in most movies, through the sudden benevolence of employers.[44]

The Contrast and The New Disciple did, however, have one thing in common with Hollywood productions: their world of unionists and radicals was inhabited largely by white males. Judging from these films, one would scarcely know that women and people of color also engaged in strikes and organizing efforts. Labor's Reward and The Passaic Textile Strike remedied that imbalance. Made in conjunction with the AFL's union-label campaign, Labor's Reward was less concerned with depicting militant labor struggles than with publicizing the benefits of unionization and organized consumption. Produced and written under the auspices of Union Label Trades Department head John J. Manning, the five-reel film was shot at the Rothacker Film studios in Chicago and featured professional actors "of national note." Potentially boring messages about production and consumption are delivered within the context of a highly entertaining, extremely well-made love story revolving around Tom, "a fine specimen of manhood," who works in a union shop, and Mary, "a beautiful girl," who toils in an oppressive non-union bookbindery. During the course of their romance, the movie repeatedly contrasts the working and living conditions of union and non-union men and women. Scenes of unorganized factories show laborers oppressed by heavy work loads and autocratic bosses, whereas shots of workers in union shops show happy employees whose representatives amicably resolve all grievances with employers.[45]

More conservative in its labor politics than The Contrast or The New Disciple, Labor's Reward is far more progressive in its sexual politics. Women are presented as powerful individuals who display remarkable solidarity and a fierce determination to obtain better working conditions. When overworked Mary faints from exhaustion and is sent home without pay, her friend Ann asks the abusive forelady to give Mary a lighter load—a request that leads to Ann's immediate dismissal. Ann's shopmates go out on strike in support of their fired comrade and vow they "will not return to work until conditions are improved." Though poorly paid themselves, they all chip in to aid Mary and her invalid father. Tom helps the women organize a union and win their strike, but they, in turn, teach him the importance of organized consumption. When Mary asks her beau if his new hat has a

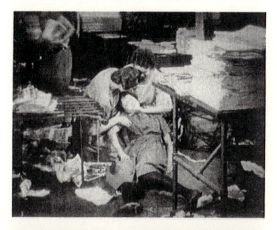

Unorganized workers in
Labor's Reward (AFL 1925)
are oppressed by unbearably
heavy work loads (top) and
autocratic bosses (middle),
while workers in union
shops resolve grievances
with employers in an amica-
ble manner (bottom).

union label, the suddenly sheepish Tom "realizes his mistake and demonstrates the courage of his conviction" by dashing out and exchanging it for a union-made product. Men in this film learn as much from women as women do from men.[46]

The Passaic Textile Strike (IWA 1926), the only labor movie that has survived virtually intact, was an important cinematic bridge between the melodramas of earlier worker-made films and the social realism that was to dominate radical films of the 1930s. Produced by Communist leader Alfred Wagenknecht, directed by professional still photographer Sam Russack, and distributed by the IWA, the seven-reel film chronicles the struggles of 16,000 striking New Jersey mill workers. A docudrama in the style of *From Dusk to Dawn* (1913) and *The Contrast*, the movie opens with studio-shot scenes that explain the causes leading to the strike. Stefan and Kata Breznac leave Poland and, as the intertitle tells us, come to the "Land of Opportunity only to find industrial oppression and bitter struggle." Subsequent scenes portray the hard-working Breznacs as people who want to be good Americans. Yet we see that their efforts to earn a living wage are futile in the face of repeated wage cuts at the textile mills. Family scenes shot inside actual Passaic tenements are a stark contrast to the sanitized screen images of D. W. Griffith's early films. Instead of Griffith's poor-but-clean apartment, we see a single room that crumbles before our very eyes; the paint is peeling and the walls are buckling. Poverty in Passaic was ugly, not neat.[47]

After playing out a melodrama in which Stefan dies of overwork, his daughter is raped by the callous mill manager, and his widow Kata is forced into the role of family breadwinner, the film switches to actual footage of the mill workers' quest for unionization and a decent standard of living. "We . . . got together a staff from the strikers and photographed the real happenings," explained producer Wagenknecht. "It was dangerous but it was genuine adventure, not the warmed-over thrills carefully dolled up by Hollywood methods." These documentary scenes offer powerful visual rebuttals to the anti-labor images of mainstream films. Caricatures of slovenly dressed men holding chaotic meetings are replaced by scenes of actual union gatherings that are peaceful, orderly affairs attended by men and women attired in suits and dresses. We never see one person leading all the rest. Leadership is shown as a collective experience, with women, blacks, Hispanics, and East and Central European workers addressing the crowds and marching in demonstrations. Forces of the state, not workers, appear as the instigators of violence and lawlessness. Remarkable documentary footage shot from rooftops shows police charging into lines of peaceful picketers and clubbing them until blood pours down their faces. The film ends in September 1926, as the strike leadership affiliates with the AFL's United Textile Workers' Union. The actual strike ended in November 1926, with the Botany mills agreeing to restore wage cuts and grant union recognition.[48]

The Passaic Textile Strike (International Workers Aid 1926) begins with a fictional recreation of events leading to the strike and stresses the care workers show for one another.

Newsreels were another powerful weapon in labor's cinematic arsenal. The LFS's *Animated Labor Review* and the FFC's *Labor News Weekly* and *Economic Digest* presented audiences with images of "workers and well-conducted labor enterprises" they were not likely to see elsewhere and coverage of events "left untouched by the capitalistic controlled news service." These newspapers of the screen featured stories about strikes, boycotts, Socialist party campaigns, and incidents of resistance by foreign workers. Working-class claims of government repression were authenticated in IWA films. Kruse's *Prisoners for Progress* (1925), a compilation of newsreels, featured scenes of "the police intimidating strike pickets in Paterson and Chicago, the militia in Herrin with machine guns covering the streets, the great prisons of Leavenworth and Sing Sing, inside and out, together with many of their political inmates, Haywood, Browder, Ruthenberg, Gitlow, and others." Taken collectively, these newsreels, insisted socialist movie critic Louis Gardy, presented the viewer with "a fuller knowledge of the day's events" and exerted "more influence than a shipload of features."[49]

Worker-made features and newsreels exposed viewers to ways of seeing contemporary class problems that challenged the dominant conservative discourse of postwar films and political life. Public opinion was not likely to be swayed by any one production. Rather, the possibilities for persuasion lay in the cumulative effects of labor films. These movies suggested that the

Documentary footage in *The Passaic Textile Strike* revealed the vital role women played in the strike.

The Passaic Textile Strike reversed dominant conservative labor-capital images by showing picketers holding peaceful protests even in the face of armed state authorities.

greatest threat to democracy came from state militias and employer-hired armies who invaded the nation's workshops and subjected wage earners to a tyranny more oppressive than any cinematically contrived Bolshevist regime. The instigators of violence were not secret agents sent by Lenin, but labor spies and provocateurs sent by employers to foment discontent and discredit peaceful efforts at change.

Strikes in these films are not caused by Reds, union organizers, or professional agitators. They are the result of ordinary people forced into action by unjust employers. Worker filmmakers, like their Hollywood counterparts, relied on costuming and careful choreography of crowd scenes to give visual authority to their messages. When the striking women in *Labor's Reward* decide to picket outside their factory, we see no tightly clustered masses wildly punching the air with their fists. Instead, the director spaces the women about twenty yards from each other and has them walk back and forth in an orderly fashion while the police look on.

Newsreels played an equally important role in humanizing the image of unionists and radicals. Non-union viewers used to seeing, and perhaps believing, Hollywood stereotypes could now gaze at the screen and see real men and women who looked like their neighbors, their fellow workers, and perhaps even themselves. Newsreels of union social activities revealed that the same class-conscious wage earners who attended speeches and went on strike were also mothers and fathers who enjoyed frolicking at picnics with their families. Even seemingly mundane footage of local buildings such as the New York Labor Temple and the Labor Film Services headquarters helped puncture longstanding caricatures of secretive radicals who only conducted their activities in dark basements.

By making movies and newsreels, worker filmmakers hoped to achieve what labor and radical organizations had not: to reach and sway a diverse, heterogeneous audience of working- and middle-class citizens, many of whom knew or cared little about unions, socialists, or communists. But to do so, producers had to secure widespread distribution and exhibition of their films. That, however, proved problematic and forced worker filmmakers into yet another series of struggles for the screen.

Showing Movies

Making movies, labor film companies soon discovered, was only half the battle. Finding theaters to exhibit them was equally difficult, for capitalist hegemony was established by controlling not just what was made but also what was shown. In order to reach a large national audience and secure a decent return on their investment, companies had to place their films in first-run houses. But access to these key theaters was increasingly restricted by the frenzied campaign of theater acquisition initiated by Paramount and its rivals after 1919, and by the frequent practice of booking only a particular studio's films into prestigious houses (block booking, as it was known). Of the 17,560 theaters devoted solely to showing movies in 1925, 12,700 were neighborhood houses, 3,140 downtown theaters, and 1,720 first-run theaters—and most of this last group was controlled by either studios or large theater chains.[50]

The reluctance of theaters "controlled by the movie trusts" to show films like *The New Disciple*, which they "declared to be 'too much Labor'," according to one union paper, forced worker film companies to develop new strategies for getting their movies to a mass audience. Unable to find national distributors, the LFS, FFC, and IWA marketed their own films, by either selling them to states rights distributors (who distributed films in specific geographic areas), striking deals with independent exhibitors, or arranging their own screenings. The FFC and LFS, for example, set up branch offices in several cities and hired agents to scour the countryside in search of sympathetic local exhibitors. The persevering Nelson succeeded in signing contracts with distributors in Washington, Canada, New York, Oklahoma, California, and Montana, and Cannon's innovative direct-mail campaign to 40,000 independent exhibitors, unions, and community organizations elicited positive responses "from Barbados to British Columbia and from the Cochrane to Mexico City."[51]

Worker film companies eventually succeeded in forging an alternative distribution system that relied on national networks of labor, radical, and ethnic organizations to market and arrange local exhibitions of their films. By the end of 1923, over 104 IWA branches and 200 labor bodies—including "Committees of Housewives Unions"—were serving as local distributors of worker films. The AFL went a step further and handled all arrangements for *Labor's Reward* on its own. It divided the country into five districts and assigned to each a four-man team composed of an advance agent who secured a local venue for showing the film, a machine operator, an entertainer, and a lecturer who followed each screening with a discussion of trade unionism.[52]

This unusual amalgam of independent distributors and local working-class organizations succeeded in placing labor films in neighborhood houses, large downtown theaters, and, on occasion, movie palaces. After *The New Disciple* had a successful two-week run at the Shubert's Lyric Theater on Broadway, Nelson and his agents booked the film into the St. Denis Theater in Montreal, Loew's Globe in Boston, the Liberty Theater in Detroit, the Aryan Grotto in Chicago, and dozens of other upscale theaters. *The Contrast*, *Labor's Reward*, and *The Passaic Textile Strike* secured few runs in first-class houses. They were shown mainly "in Union districts" and immigrant neighborhoods throughout the United States and Canada. The AFL offered free screenings in large cities and "little towns and villages" that it hoped to organize.[53]

When finding a sympathetic exhibitor proved impossible, worker film companies and their allies rented their own theaters or arranged for screenings in auditoriums, schools, or union halls. To attract large audiences, the LFS, FFC, and IWA created entertainment packages that included a worker-made feature, several comedies, labor newsreels, and a second-run Hollywood movie. "Three hours of education and entertainment," remarked one reporter, could be had for a mere twenty-five cents. Even free showings of *Labor's Reward* usually included live music and an array of local performers. Seattle viewers were treated to songs by John Moran, the "Irish blackbird," the nimble dancing of the Gartan sisters, and the "grimaces" of Hugh Glover. In Gebo, Wyoming, a "miner's son furnished the music, but being a delicate lad he had to pause quite often during the picture."[54]

Word-of-mouth information about these features quickly spread beyond cities and towns and into the nation's mining communities. "This is a Union Camp," a West Virginia theater owner wrote the National Board of Review of Motion Pictures in 1921, "and the miners want me to get The Contrast if I can and I promised I would if it was a good legitimate picture." Another mine district exhibitor urged Cannon to send *The Contrast* "at the earliest opportunity," for his patrons were "very anxious to have me run the film." When local exhibitors refused to show worker films, labor organizations in Pennsylvania, Illinois, Kansas, Kentucky, and Washington responded by opening their own movie houses.[55]

Labor companies had proven that they could make films and get them exhibited. But would anyone come to see them? To pose a serious challenge to Hollywood or alter popular understandings of contemporary labor struggles these films had to attract more than just thousands or even tens of thousands of viewers. Attendance figures are hard to obtain, for industry periodicals paid scant attention to worker-made films. The information we do have suggests that labor movies were patronized by mass audiences throughout the country. *The New Disciple*, the most widely distributed labor film, was seen by "at least 1 million" people within its first year. After playing "to crowded houses" during its two-week run on Broadway, the film broke attendance records in Montreal, Buffalo, and Detroit, and played to full houses in Boston, San Diego, Chicago, and other urban centers. The most accurate box-office records were kept by the AFL. During an initial forty-week run in 1925–1926, *Labor's Reward* was screened 591 times and seen by 479,500 people in thirty-six states and Canadian provinces. Demand for the film was so great that the AFL was forced to add two additional teams to tour the country and even then local arrangement committees continually complained of having "to turn away people in every town."[56]

Though modest in comparison to successful studio releases, these figures are remarkable when we consider the difficulties independent producers faced in exhibiting their movies. Only "5% of the pictures made in the United States are successes," the *World Almanac* reported in 1925, "50% failures, and 45% 'average.'" Despite industry opposition, worker films were shown in cities and small towns across the nation. Sometimes they played a few days, sometimes a few weeks, and sometimes they were brought back year after year. Daily audiences ranged from several hundred in small towns to several thousand in large cities. "In about 250 cities of all sizes and compositions," IWA leader William Kruse recounted in 1925, "we have shown anywhere from one to seven film programs, to an average [total] audience of 100,000 for each film."[57]

The modest success of these labor features revived interest in a number of older pro-labor films. In January 1922, the LFS released an updated version of *The Jungle* (1914) that contained several new scenes, all new titles, and editing changes supervised by Cannon and Sinclair. The film quickly sold over 5,000 advance tickets and drew "capacity audiences" during its opening run at New York's 5th Avenue Theater. In Los Angeles, audience demand for worker films led the owners of the Barn Theater to bring back Frank Wolfe's *From Dusk to Dawn* (1913) in September 1922.[58]

Reception and the Political Impact of Worker Films

However popular they may have been with some audiences, four labor features and a series of newsreels were not likely to alter the course of Hollywood production or American capitalism. They did, however, suggest what a fully developed worker-film movement might have achieved: production of scores of well-attended films that could challenge the dominant political discourse of American cinema and, by so doing, reorient the political consciousness of American citizens. The significance of the worker film movement is best measured not by attendance figures or the number of films it produced but by the powerful reactions it generated. In judging the political influence of movies, the intensity of audience reaction can be as significant as the quantity of product. One powerful movie, as D. W. Griffith's *Birth of a Nation* (1915) has shown, could have a far greater impact on society than dozens of minor films.

Assessing the reception and impact of any film or genre is a complex matter, for, as we saw in Chapter 4, there were different types of audiences and different arenas in which the impact of films were felt. Class, gender, racial, ethnic, and political loyalties all contributed to shaping how viewers judged a movie. Movie critics, movie audiences, and government authorities also responded to worker films in very different ways.

Predictably, worker productions were lavishly praised by labor and radi-cal periodicals. Movies such as *The New Disciple*, declared the *Chicago New Majority*, helped "counteract the vicious propaganda of the 'open shoppers' who have attempted to mold the minds of the public against organized labor." Working-class critics also praised labor features for their excellent direction, good acting, crisp editing, and high production standards. *The Contrast*, gushed one socialist reviewer, "had the sustained dramatic force and the complete pictorial beauty of Rembrandt." The only serious criticism of these films came from the Communist *Daily Worker*, which complained that *The New Disciple* "reeks with the 'social compact' reformist viewpoint."[59]

Though distasteful to communists, *The New Disciple* earned plaudits from the powerful New York daily press. "Surprisingly well done and is just what the producers promised it would be—something different," remarked the *Evening World*; "as interesting to the capitalist as to the labor man," added the *American*. Movie-industry periodicals, however, offered conflict-ing opinions, leading one to believe that aesthetic judgments were colored by a reviewer's political sympathies. *Photoplay* criticized *The New Disciple* for "mediocre direction and an indifferent cast," and the notably conserva-tive *Variety* blasted it as having "little entertainment value and even less value as propaganda." The *Moving Picture World*, however, stated that the FFC film was well directed, credibly acted, and possessed "a humanly inter-esting romance."[60]

Movie patrons had equally varied responses. Scenes of radicals, strikes, and union leaders in labor films and newsreels elicited clapping, shouting, whistling, and foot stomping from politically sympathetic patrons and boos and hisses from more conservative filmgoers. Reactions around the country were often so intense that they prompted fights between male viewers of different political persuasions. Women, though more restrained with their fists, were equally outspoken in their admiration for these films. Mrs. John Kennedy of Seattle's Farmer-Labor Women's Club suggested that for "those of the working class who find the average picture show weak and mawkish, *The New Disciple* will appeal as a plunge in the surf does after a swim in a warm pool, or as a taste of fine fresh fruit after molasses and mulch."[61]

The popularity of worker films proved that the dominant Hollywood belief that audiences only wanted to see classless escapist fantasies was wrong. Movie fans certainly enjoyed going to see films about flappers, swells, jazz clubs, and the fast life. Yet when given the chance, audiences also went to see films with serious political messages. Although worker-made films certainly contained strong doses of fantasy, the fantasies were those of the working class. Many people enjoyed seeing movies that showed men and women winning strikes, defeating employers, and taking control of industry and their own lives. Labor film companies, Cannon boasted, taught the "theatre world that there was a need for labor pictures and demand for labor pictures."[62]

Worker filmmakers wanted to change society, not just amuse it. In assessing the political significance of their films we must once again expand our concept of reception to include what happened outside the movie house. The impact of these productions was felt beyond the walls of the theater and involved far more people than just the immediate audience. Although worker-made films represented less than 1 percent of the six to seven hundred features produced annually during the 1920s, the fervid support and opposition they elicited testified that their impact far exceeded their modest number.

Union and radical leaders insisted that these films helped inspire and empower workers—especially those embroiled in bitter labor disputes. One Illinois labor leader explained that striking workers in his town who saw *The New Disciple* "found hope in the story of a like situation." In Seattle, the film aroused several unions "to combat local open shop campaigns." Repeated screenings of *Labor's Reward*, the AFL reported, attracted new union members and increased the "demand for union made goods." Labor organizer Ella Reeve "Mother" Bloor, who toured the country showing *The Passaic Textile Strike*, told how its stark images of police brutality against peaceful workers succeeded in "arousing a lot of public sympathy for the strike" and generating contributions that helped sustain the wage earners' struggle.[63]

These achievements stand in sharp contrast to the dire warnings issued by Frankfurt School critics of the 1930s and 1940s and subsequent generations of radical theorists. Film, they argued, was a conservative medium used by capitalists to homogenize class and ethnic differences and present bourgeois middle-class values as classless "American" values. Although films were eventually used in this way, worker filmmakers of the 1920s showed that this was not inevitable. Control of the medium, not the medium itself, is what determined its politics. Nelson, Cannon, and others used the homogenizing powers of film to broaden labor's appeal by presenting working-class values as "American" values. Their films told unorganized blue-collar wage earners and the rapidly expanding ranks of white-collar employees that their interests were closer to those of unions than they were to those of employers. After watching the LFS's recut version of Upton Sinclair's film, one mightily impressed viewer professed that if "some method could be devised whereby every unorganized worker in New York City could be prevailed upon to see *The Jungle*, if none other, great work could be done toward uniting labor into one unconquerable formation."[64]

Labor filmmakers also demonstrated that mass culture did not necessarily undermine autonomous class, ethnic, or gender identities. Workers and radicals used films to link and reinforce class, ethnicity, and gender. The

LFS and IWA organized special "Labor Film Festivals" in foreign-born working-class sections of New York, Detroit, and Chicago. Screenings were also sponsored by working-class ethnic associations—Ukrainians in New York; Finns in Minnesota, Michigan, and New York; Slovaks and Croats in Pennsylvania; Jews in Detroit and New York; and scattered groups of Hungarians, Russians, and Lithuanians—to raise money for strike funds or new buildings. Female trade unionists arranged showings of The Contrast, The New Disciple, Labor's Reward, and The Passaic Textile Strike to illustrate the close connections between women's and class interests.[65]

The worker film movement evoked aggressive responses from a wide range of government authorities. When The Contrast was shown in Pittsburgh in March 1921, slumped down in the back rows of the theater busily taking notes was one of J. Edgar Hoover's agents. The film, he warned his boss, was a "propaganda work" designed "to stir up antagonism and hatred between workmen and their employers." Hoover responded by assigning Bureau of Investigation agents (the predecessor of the FBI) to monitor the activities of key figures in the LFS, FFC, and IWA. Fear of labor films was so pronounced that Hoover and the U.S. Postmaster's Office conspired with the New York City police Red Squad in 1920 to deny the LFS a permit to publish their proposed Labor Film Magazine. Hoover also instructed his agents to gather copies—probably illegally—of all company correspondence. The most complete collection of LFS records can now be found in the Bureau's archives.[66]

The LFS also came under scrutiny from Department of Agriculture officials who pressured Cannon to delete from The Jungle several scenes that reflected poorly on the work of their agency—changes the filmmakers refused to make. Employers were equally concerned about the potential impact of this movement and feared, as New York Assemblyman Samuel Orr explained, that movies would "become too dangerous in the hands of workers." In Seattle, labor spies planted in local unions by employer associations kept their bosses apprised of the activities of the FFC and its leaders.[67]

The fierce determination of state and local censors to keep worker films off the screen further testified to official fears about the power of visual radicalism. Censorship was most severe in areas where class conflict was most pronounced. Ohio, Kansas, West Virginia, Pennsylvania, Maryland, New York, Washington, and South Carolina passed laws empowering local boards to ban or cut any films and intertitles "calculated to stir up . . . antagonistic relations between labor and capital" or "revolutionize our form of government through insidious propaganda." In Kansas, where coal miners' strikes raged, censors banned The Contrast, ruling that scenes "of a coal strike and an appeal of the strikers for railroad men to join in" incited class antagonisms by laying "too much stress upon the power of the strike and is chiefly labor union propaganda." In North Carolina, where textile troubles simmered, Durham officials refused to let *Labor's Reward* be shown in the municipal auditorium.[68] New York's Motion Picture Commission ordered the IWA to remove several provocative scenes and intertitles from *The Passaic Textile Strike*. Lines referring to a textile worker as "having been a good slave," "exploited by the mill owners," and suffering "from the mill owners' greed" were cut on the grounds "that they would 'tend to corrupt morals' and 'incite to crime.'" Commenting on the class bias of censors, William Kruse complained that regulations "never prevented hundreds of films from showing labor organizations as murderous, grafting brutes, while their capitalist opponents embodied all the virtues."[69]

It is said that a powerful movement makes powerful enemies. So it was with the worker film movement. Despite the opposition of movie industry figures, censors, and government agencies, it succeeded in making several movies and getting them shown in theaters throughout the country. By the mid-1920s, labor filmmakers seemed poised for greater success. Yet the euphoria surrounding their entry into the market proved short-lived. Just as labor films were reaching the screen, movies and moviegoing underwent a dramatic series of changes. Fantasy and politics were merging in ways that created yet another set of challenges that labor filmmakers had to confront.

7

Fantasy and Politics: Moviegoing and Movies in the 1920s

THE COLD March winds could not stop thousands of determined men and women from being part of movie history. They began gathering early in the day, and by 7 P.M. over 10,000 excited people stood at the corner of 7th Avenue and 50th Street. Housewives wrapped in their warmest winter coats, blue-collar workers in sturdy galoshes and long underwear, and young lovers cuddled in each other's arms all hoped to catch a glimpse of the rich and famous. It was March 11, 1927, opening night at the world's largest and most expensive movie palace, New York's $12 million Roxy Theater. Twenty years earlier, police were busily closing down seedy nickelodeons frequented by the city's immigrant and working-class population. But that night, 125 cops stood outside the theater to protect the arriving guests, including Mayor Jimmy Walker, movie stars Charlie Chaplin, Norma Talmadge, and Harold Lloyd, and "6,200 leaders in [the] city's commercial, professional, and artistic life." As they entered what the neon-emblazoned marquee announced to be "THE CATHEDRAL OF THE MOTION PICTURE," the most privileged guests flashed their engraved invitations to the ticket takers, while lesser luminaries clutched the special green tickets that cost $11 each (about $83 in 1990 dollars).[1]

Inside the theater was everything that manager and co-owner Samuel Lionel Rothapfel—Roxy to all who knew him—had promised. The massive Grand Foyer in the entrance hall was decorated with crystal chandeliers, five-story green marble columns, and the world's largest oval rug. At 8:30 P.M., the audience entered the cavernous auditorium and made their way to the 6,214 plush red seats, each with a monogrammed "R" on its back. At precisely 9 P.M. the lights dimmed, and from the mechanical pits rose three organ consoles attended by three organists who played several songs and then disappeared. Darkness fell over the theater and an ominous voice boomed forth:

> Ye portals bright, high and majestic, open to our gaze the path to Wonderland, and show us the realm where fantasy reigns, where romance, where adventure flourish. Let ev'ry day's toil be forgotten under thy sheltering roof—O glorious, mighty hall—thy magic and thy charm unite us all to worship at beauty's throne. . . . Let there be light.

Opening night at New York City's luxurious Roxy Theater (March 11, 1927) attracted an elite crowd of New Yorkers.

A sudden burst of light then revealed a 110-piece symphony orchestra. For the next hour and a half the audience was treated to a number of overtures, ballets, songs by the Roxy Chorus and Singing Ensemble, and a tune written by Irving Berlin especially for the Roxy opening. The cinematic portion of the evening began with greetings from President Calvin Coolidge, Vice President Charles Dawes, New York Governor Al Smith, and Mayor Jimmy Walker, and continued with the Roxy Pictorial Review, a compilation of the week's best newsreels. The feature film, *The Love of Sunya*, starring Gloria Swanson, seemed almost anticlimatic after such a dazzling array of live performances. When the evening ended shortly after midnight, a proud Roxy surveyed his palace and remarked: "Take a look at this stupendous theatre. It's the Roxy and I'm Roxy. I'd rather be Roxy than John D. Rockefeller or Henry Ford."[2]

Opening night at the Roxy, like opening nights at movie palaces around the country, was confined largely to the rich and famous. But the next morning, and for 365 mornings and evenings each year, the doors were thrown open to anyone willing to buy a ticket. Clerks, lawyers, waitresses, teachers, stenographers, plumbers, doctors, and factory workers enjoyed the same opulence and grand treatment accorded to movie stars, politicians, and aristocrats. Neighborhood theaters still continued to serve their largely working-class clientele. But the exhibitors who built luxury movie palaces during the 1920s expanded the class composition of the audience and ushered in what many heralded as a new age of democratic fantasy. "What greater democratic institution exists than the movie theater?" New York Socialist Assemblyman Samuel Orr asked in 1921. "It is there where rich and poor, young and old, men, women and children gather by the millions everyday throughout the land to laugh together and cry together."[3]

By the time the Roxy opened, movies and movie theaters were respected forms of mass culture that drew perhaps as many as 100 million people a week, a figure that nearly equaled the entire national population. Movies had long attracted the "masses," but in the 1920s they also attracted the "classes." Although some wealthy and middle-class folk frequented movies before the war, it was only in the postwar era that moviegoing became a *regular* part of their lives, especially for the latter. In the decade following the end of World War I, major studios and exhibitors set out to increase their profits and establish greater control over the industry by creating a cross-class entertainment experience designed to attract greater numbers of prosperous middle-class patrons, while retaining their steady working-class following. To that end, they erected exotic movie palaces and produced lavish films aimed at turning moviegoing into an experience that both transcended and reshaped traditional class boundaries.[4]

The creation of these seemingly democratic centers of entertainment, as the exuberant Samuel Orr failed to note, exacted political costs that went far beyond the price of a ticket. At the same time that worker filmmakers were trying to heighten class consciousness, movie industry leaders were merging fantasy and politics in a manner that eschewed class hostilities in favor of appealing to cross-class fantasies of luxury, comfort, and consumption. These fantasies took two distinct forms: movie palaces that brought different classes together to bask in the same opulent surroundings for several hours, and cross-class fantasy films that promoted glamorous but ultimately conservative visions of consumption and class interaction. The goal of these cross-class fantasies was not to integrate the classes in any lasting way, but to increase movie attendance and revenues by drawing them into the same theaters.

The 1920s marked a turning point in the history of the movie industry and in the formation of modern understandings of class and class relations. The proliferation of white-collar employees and the widespread participation of wage earners in a flourishing consumer economy created great confusion over modern class identities. Were white-collar employees middle class or working class? Should class status be based on one's work or one's ability to consume? Did class even matter anymore? Capitalists and socialists alike spoke about the blurred "lines of demarcation" between social classes and of the "powerful agencies that consciously and unconsciously aid in blurring the group lines of American society." Movies and movie theaters were among the most powerful of those agencies.[5]

Scholars such as Lary May see the 1920s and the rise of Hollywood as signaling the triumph of an emancipatory consumer culture over the highly restrictive Victorian culture that dominated American life at the turn of the century. Yet in emphasizing the "liberating" aspects of cultural change, scholars often overlook the more problematic political consequences of change. Although consumer goods certainly eased the lives of many citizens, Hollywood's emphasis on consumer fantasies marked a conservative retreat from the far more serious and ideologically diverse treatments of class conflict that characterized prewar filmmaking. As major studios shifted their attention toward building a broader audience, labor-capital films that highlighted struggles between the classes were supplanted by cross-class fantasy films that focused on harmony among the classes. I use the term "cross-class fantasy" to describe a broad category of films that stressed messages of class harmony and explored the interactions and romantic involvements between an upper-class and either working-class or middle-class protagonist. In emphasizing these themes, movie industry leaders reinforced a growing capitalist discourse that promoted a new perception of class identity—one rooted in the more alluring world of consumption than in the conflictual world of production. Taken collectively, cross-class fantasy films stressed individualism rather than collective action; acceptance rather than change; and contentment with one's class position rather than aspiring to something more.[6]

These dramatic changes in the content of movies and the nature of moviegoing presented worker filmmakers and class-conscious audiences with a new set of challenges. Could serious films about class struggle survive in such a climate of fantasy? Although many radicals and trade unionists expressed their contempt for the conservative politics of cross-class fantasy films, they enjoyed the luxurious amenities offered by the movie palaces that showed them. Would they indulge their yearnings for fantasy and go to movie palaces despite the politics of their films, or would they hold fast to their political beliefs and patronize neighborhood houses that, while far less fun, were more likely to show pro-labor films? The answer was critical, for if worker filmmakers and the theaters that screened their movies could not draw the already converted, they stood little chance of reaching the great mass of moviegoers.

Although movies had attracted great numbers of people since 1905, it was not until the 1920s that they became a genuine institution of mass culture—one that reached *all* Americans regardless of their class, race, gender, ethnicity, or geographical location. Consequently, movies grew even more important as vehicles of propaganda and political suasion. Never

before had so many people from so many different backgrounds seen the
same films at roughly the same time; and never before could so many people
be influenced by what they saw and experienced at the movies. Whether
Americans perceived class conflict as a continuing problem or as a past
concern that was now resolved might well depend upon the images that
dominated the screen.

It was during the 1920s that Hollywood and the studio system that
created it came to dominate the movie industry. For better or for worse,
corporate ownership of studios and movie theaters meant that leading
Hollywood studios exerted tremendous control over the fantasy lives and
political consciousness of millions of Americans. Understanding how this
came about requires us to look at the complex interaction of several interconnected forces: how changing attitudes toward work, leisure, and consumption affected people during the 1920s; how exhibitors capitalized on
these changes to expand their audience base; how studios orchestrated the
political messages viewers saw on the screen; and how these developments
effected the various groups struggling to challenge Hollywood's visions of
fantasy and politics.

Leisure, Consumption, and Class

In the nation's dominant political circles, the 1920s were known as the "Age
of Normalcy." The progressive spirit that marked the Wilson era waned in
the postwar decade as three successive Republican presidents—Warren
Harding, Calvin Coolidge, and Herbert Hoover—steered the nation on a
more conservative, business-oriented course. But life in the social arena was
anything but "normal" as new attitudes toward leisure and consumption
"revolutionized the habits of the people." A leisure revolution that began in
modest fashion at the turn of the century now swept the entire nation as
millions of men and women of all classes spent their time and money on a
wide array of goods and amusements. Commercial recreations achieved a
new patina of respectability in the 1920s as civic leaders in Cleveland,
Buffalo, Salt Lake City, Indianapolis, and elsewhere insisted that movies and
other previously suspect amusements for the masses now occupied "a large
and legitimate place" in the life of the nation's citizenry.[7]

Commercial recreation was not without its critics. Moralists throughout
the nation published books with such sobering titles as *The Threat of Leisure*
(1926) and continued to warn of the dangers of licentious entertainment.
"Some of them," explained one Indianapolis survey, "are idling, meander-
ing, gambling, trash-reading, razzy-jazzy-joy-riding, illicit sex practices,
marauding, bad gang activities, over-indulgence in mere amusements, recreation of the wrong kind, in the wrong places and at wrong times . . . [and]

that insidious disease known as 'sit-itis' alias 'spectatoritis.'"[8] Although they could not stop the spread of most commercial amusements, members of the ancien régime of culture did secure passage of the Eighteenth Amendment and Volstead Act which prohibited the manufacture, sale, or transportation of alcoholic beverages after January 1920. But Prohibition proved more an inconvenience than a barrier to the spread of night life and fun.

The leisure revolution that supporters hailed and critics condemned was part of a broader set of changes wrought by the rapid development of industrialization—changes that altered the nature of work, consumption, leisure, and class identity. The adoption of mass production techniques pioneered by Henry Ford and the heightened emphasis on division of labor proved successful beyond the average employer's wildest dreams. Dramatic increases in productivity led to lower prices and made consumer goods more affordable to tens of millions of grateful Americans. Between 1919 and 1929 workers turned out 20 million motor vehicles and 7 million radios, installed 6 million telephones, and electrified 9 million residences. During the course of the decade, the percentage of homes with radios rose from almost none to 40 percent, washing machines from 8 percent to 24 percent, vacuum cleaners from 9 percent to 30 percent, and refrigerators from 1 percent to 8 percent.[9]

The increasingly routinized and deadening qualities of the workplaces that created these goods also caused enormous discontent among wage earners. As work continued to lose its capacity to give a sense of inner satisfaction, people looked for self-fulfillment outside the workplace. And many found it in the worlds of goods and amusements. With the average work week shrinking (from 47.4 hours in 1920 to 42.1 hours in 1930) and the output of consumer products and inexpensive entertainments expanding, many Americans came to view work as a means to an end. This outlook was not confined to blue-collar workers but was equally pronounced among the white-collar minions of the "business class," who also experienced increasingly alienating workplaces. "For both working and business class," Robert and Helen Lynd noted in their 1929 study of "Middletown" (Muncie, Indiana), it "is more this future, instrumental aspect of work, rather than the intrinsic satisfactions involved, that keeps Middletown working so hard as more and more of the activities of living are coming to be strained through the bars of the dollar sign."[10]

That working class and middle class should express the same desires is not surprising. The blurring of class boundaries, already evident by 1900, as we saw in Chapter 1, grew far more pronounced in the 1920s as the maturing of industrial capitalism continued to alter the nation's occupational structure. The rapid expansion of corporations and service-sector businesses, and their attendant need for armies of managers, supervisors, accountants, clerks, sales people, and other kinds of "brain" workers generated an explosion of white-collar personnel. Between 1900 and 1930 no part of the nation's work force grew as quickly as its white-collar sector. While the total labor force expanded by 68 percent, the numbers of neatly attired white-collar men and women soared 225 percent. By 1930, white-collar personnel composed nearly one-quarter of the working population.[11] Workplaces also grew more highly feminized as the number of wage-earning women more than doubled between 1900 and 1930, from 5.3 million to 10.8 million. Many of these new jobs came in the clerical and service sectors, where employers lowered their costs by hiring women who, though often performing the same jobs as men, were paid less money.[12]

Changes in occupational structures and declining chances for self-employment transformed the way many white Americans talked about class. During the early part of the nineteenth century, when the vast majority of adult white males were self-employed farmers, artisans, or merchants (80 percent according to one estimate), "class" was discussed in terms of a large producing class that created wealth (this included working employers as well as employees) and a small nonproducing class that lived off the wealth of others (lawyers, bankers, and real-estate speculators). As the self-employed working population fell to about 33 percent in 1870, largely as a result of the rising number of massive corporations and declining number of independent farmers, many Americans began speaking about a modestly sized middle class comprised, as one labor daily explained, of "independent farmers, traders, professional men, and manufacturers," and an expansive working class that included virtually everyone else. The continued decline of self-employed Americans in the early twentieth century (to about 20 percent in 1940) and the rapid growth of white-collar personnel generated another change in the language of class. Newspaper editors, politicians, and businessmen began distinguishing between a blue-collar working class and a broadly conceived "new" middle class that, in addition to the "older" middle class, included "salaried professionals, managers, salespeople, and office workers employed in bureaucratic organizations." As wealthy Americans grew more visible, the term "upper class" was used to describe those who lived "on the interest of property already obtained, whether by work, inheritance or theft."[13]

In an age of diminishing prospects for self-employment—one of the two cornerstones of the long-standing American ideology of success (home ownership being the other)—moving from blue-collar to white-collar status, or from the working class to the middle class offered many people the appearance of upward mobility. Yet whatever people may have been called or called themselves, the lines between the collars and the classes was far less pronounced than public discourse of the era suggested. Business leaders (including movie personnel) often assumed white-collar "brain" workers were middle class, but this was not always clear to the white-collar workers themselves. In terms of status, numerous white-collar employees and low-level professionals such as teachers, nurses, and social workers believed they belonged to a higher class than blue-collar workers; yet in terms of income, they often earned less than skilled craftsmen. Family background was not always a good barometer of class identification, for, as noted in Chapter 1, many of the young men and women who entered the white-collar ranks came from working-class families and continued to live in working-class neighborhoods and marry blue-collar spouses.[14]

Whether the great mass of white-collar workers thought of themselves as working class or middle class was critical to the class struggles of the postwar era. The powerful anti-union American Plan campaign of the early 1920s succeeded in weakening the strength and size of organized labor. Labor leaders realized they might reverse this decline by convincing clerical and service-sector workers to join their largely blue-collar ranks. However, they were less likely to do so if these people thought of themselves as middle class and identified, as one radical daily explained, with "the charmed spheres of the ruling classes" rather than the world of the working classes.[15]

As the desire for goods and entertainment permeated all groups during the 1920s, consumption emerged as an important arena in which battles over competing visions of class identity were fought. Consumer goods certainly existed well before this decade and some historians trace the origins of the nation's consumer economy back to the eighteenth century. Yet it was not until the 1920s that the concept of a "consumer society" became part of the national lexicon. Although capitalists and labor leaders alike welcomed this development, they spoke about its significance in markedly different ways. Business leaders, advertisers, and politicians promoted a new discourse of class identity based on one's ability to consume rather than on one's occupation. Anyone who could afford a vaguely defined middle-class style of consumption was considered middle class—regardless of what collar they wore. Advertisers heralded the power of consumption to end class inequalities by creating a new cross-class democracy in which all Americans had equal access to goods. According to "Parable of the Democracy of Goods," as historian Roland Marchand calls it, the "humblest citizens, provided they chose their purchases wisely . . . could contemplate their essential equality, through possession of an identical product, with the nation's millionaires."[16]

Although capitalists used appeals to consumption to blur class divisions, labor leaders used them to reinforce the importance of united class actions. The steady decline in union membership and the wage earners' heightened cry for more goods and leisure time led American Federation of Labor stalwarts to place obtaining what was popularly known as the "American Standard of Living" at the forefront of union demands. This standard, explained Bureau of Labor Statistics head Royal Meeker, would provide workers "with all the necessaries, many of the comforts, and a goodly supply of the luxuries of life." Speakers at celebrations on Labor Day, the one day a year when unions commanded the attention of millions of Americans, repeatedly talked about labor's determination to secure what employers were unlikely to grant without a fight: higher wages and a five-day work week that would allow men and women more time to consume and relax. In his 1927 radio address, AFL president William Green called upon all working people, "whether professional, trained, skilled or unskilled," to join unions if they hoped to achieve a truly "American Standard of Living."[17]

Ideas about consumption, whether articulated by labor or capital, had great resonance in large part because many Americans *were* better off in the 1920s than in previous decades. Real wages and salaries for nonfarm employees rose more than 26 percent (depending on whose statistics one uses) between 1919 and 1929, and the Department of Commerce estimated that the average American family had a third more purchasing power in 1928 than before World War I. The greatest gains were made by professionals and white-collar workers who, after lagging behind skilled blue-collar workers in the prewar years, often outpaced them between 1920 and 1926. Prosperity and consumption, however, were never as widespread as employers suggested. While real earnings for skilled manufacturing workers rose a modest 12–15 percent, those of unskilled workers, who composed a third of the factory workforce, remained steady or declined over the course of the decade. African-Americans and other minority workers generally fared even worse than unskilled white workers. In many households the desire to consume outstripped the ability to do so. A Brookings Institute study of family earnings in 1929 found that only 29 percent of all families earned enough to achieve an "American Standard of Living"; 42 percent of all families earned less than $1,500—an amount barely enough to sustain a family of four.[18]

Lack of money, however, never stopped people from dreaming. It is "impossible to overestimate the role of motion pictures, advertising, and other forms of publicity," observed Robert and Helen Lynd, in raising people's desires for more goods and a continually better living standard. Yet even many professionals and white-collar workers found it difficult to fulfill those desires. Refrigerators, automobiles, and new furniture were all big-ticket items that required long-term savings or careful investigation of installment plan options. But there was one fantasy that could be fulfilled on a regular basis by all collars and classes: a night at the movies.[19]

Despite the ever-growing number of leisure possibilities in the 1920s, movies remained the nation's most frequented commercial entertainment. Movie box-office receipts soared from $301 million in 1921 to $720 million in 1929, a figure nearly four times greater than the combined receipts for all spectator sports and live theatrical entertainments. Movies remained so wildly popular because they remained so eminently affordable. With admission to most neighborhood theaters still a modest 10c to 50c, most Americans could afford to go to the movies. Movies were cheap enough that any working woman could take herself to a show without waiting for a man to ask. And women often did. Exhibitors and social surveyors frequently commented on the increased feminization of audiences in the 1920s—a fact they attributed to the rising number of female wage earners and the growing social freedom enjoyed by women.[20]

Selling entertainment was now very big business. But theater owners were no longer content with the nickels, dimes, and quarters of their long-time working-class patrons. Ambitious exhibitors wanted to devise a higher-priced entertainment experience so fantastic it would attract people from all classes. But how was this to be done? How could they lure people away from the neighborhood houses that so carefully catered to the class, ethnic, and gender needs of their patrons? Would people really pay $1 ($7.50 in 1990 dollars) to go to a *movie* theater? Although efforts to create a new movie experience were begun in the prewar years, it was not until the postwar era that exhibitors turned moviegoing into a genuinely cross-class entertainment. And few did so more creatively or successfully than two Jewish boys from Chicago.

Palaces for the People

For twenty years, Abraham Joseph Balaban and Sam Katz took the pulse of the people and made it beat faster. At a time when most theater owners were content to provide customers with a good movie, Balaban and Katz offered them an experience that indulged their fantasies and desires. No one, not even the celebrated Roxy, was more responsible for opening movies to a wider audience than these two sons of immigrants. In 1917 the partners owned only one theater. In 1925, when they sold their business to Paramount, they were making more money than any other chain and their methods were adopted by theaters across the nation. Their career reveals the rapid transformation of movie theaters from humble nickelodeons that served immigrant and working-class patrons to luxurious palaces that appealed to a broad array of Americans and in which movies were only a small part of an evening's entertainment.

Born in Chicago in 1889 to Russian Jews who ran a small grocery store, Abe Balaban entered the movie business in 1907 when he took a night job singing songs at the Kedzie, a 103-seat storefront theater in the city's westside Jewish ghetto. In January 1908 he used his family's savings of $178 to buy the Kedzie, and several months later, with more audacity than money, began building the 700-seat Circle Theater on Sawyer and 12th Street. Aided by his brother Barney, Abe attracted large crowds by supplementing his films with a four-piece orchestra and popular vaudeville acts such as Sophie Tucker and the Four Marx Brothers. This formula proved so successful that the brothers soon opened a film exchange and purchased an interest in three more theaters.[21]

Running the Circle taught the Balabans that to stay ahead of the competition they needed to offer audiences more show for the money and keep expanding into neighborhoods where people were hungry for entertainment and willing to pay for it. To carry this concept out on a grander scale, the financially strapped pair entered into partnership with Sam Katz in 1916. Also the son of Russian Jews, Katz grew up in a dreary west-side tenement and supported himself by, among other things, playing piano in a nickelodeon owned by Carl Laemmle. In 1912, he bought a small movie theater next to his dad's barber shop and by 1915 the twenty-one-year-old Katz owned three theaters. But Sam wanted to run a theatrical empire, not just several neighborhood houses. Together, the partners realized that dream by fashioning a theater chain built, as film scholar Douglas Gomery observes, on five key factors: "location, the theater building, service, stage shows, and air conditioning."[22]

Balaban and Katz developed an innovative strategy aimed at attracting a broad array of collars and classes. Instead of remaining in the crowded downtown entertainment district, they erected several luxury theaters in outlying areas that were being rapidly populated by middle-class and upwardly mobile working-class families. The Central Park, the partners' first theater, was built in suburban North Lawndale, "where immigrant Jewish families like the Balabans and Katzs moved in order to prove they had 'made it.'" A year later, on October 2, 1918, they opened the Riviera Theater on Chicago's fashionable North Side. That opening was followed in February 1921 by an even bigger luxury palace, the Tivoli, built on the South Side. The steady profits from these ventures soon allowed them to build several more suburban palaces and a massive theater in the downtown entertainment district. Not content with remaining a Chicago institution, B&K also acquired regional theater chains in the surrounding Midwestern states.[23]

Choosing the right location was critical to their success, but it was less important than the partners' ability to know what patrons wanted. Having seen the hardships endured by parents, relatives, and neighbors, Balaban and Katz understood that watching films was only a small part of the reason people went to the movies. People wanted fantasy, and the more fantastic the experience, the more willing they were to pay for it. The goal of B&K theaters, Abe explained, was to "make people live in a fairyland and to make them forget their troubles." Fantasy, as Balaban and Katz conceived it, was less an escape *from* something than an adventure *into* a wonderfully different world. Luxury, service, and entertainment at affordable prices became the dominant features of the B&K theater chain. They hired the best architects to design their theaters, the best musicians to play in them, the best art directors to create their stage shows, the most talented people to perform in them, the hottest jazz bands to set the place on fire, and the latest air-conditioning systems to cool it off.[24]

The key to their success, however, lay in persuading audiences to spend $1 to go to the Tivoli, Riviera, or Chicago rather than twenty-five cents to attend a more modest neighborhood theater. To that end, the partners tried to make their patrons feel that walking into a B&K theater was like entering another world—the world of the rich and pampered. Ornate outside façades dazzled people with exotic images and styles drawn from Spain, France, Italy, and the Orient, while inside, boasted Balaban, paintings, sculptures, "furnishings and fountains fit for museums and king's palaces were familiarly seen and used by our patrons." Customers were also offered a variety of comforts to make their visit more pleasant: spacious lounges near ladies and men's rooms; nurseries and playrooms where parents could leave their children; air-conditioning systems that provided welcome relief from hot, muggy summer nights; and a small army of uniformed ushers trained to attend to the moviegoers' every need and to treat even the rudest patron with a deferential "yes, sir" or "no, ma'am."[25]

Audiences enjoyed being surrounded by elegance and impeccable service, but it was the fabulous stage show that kept luring them back week after week. A typical show lasted two and a half hours and it hardly mattered that B&K (because they were not part of a studio) had "little access to Hollywood's top films." It was the stage show and not the film that drew the crowds. Weekly shows, the equal of many Broadway productions, cost $3,000 to $5,000 to mount; special holiday extravaganzas ran upward of $50,000. Whereas the former usually drew on local talent, holiday shows included the likes of Fannie Brice, Bill "Mr. Bojangles" Robinson, Sophie Tucker, John Philip Sousa, Paul Whiteman, Eddie Cantor, and the Marx Brothers.[26]

This mixture of elegance, style, and fun, observed the *Chicago Herald-Examiner*, turned the B&K theaters into the "meeting place of the aristocrat and humble worker." Yet although aristocratic pretensions graced the theaters' walls and interiors, democracy ruled the box office. Unlike legitimate theaters that charged a variety of prices depending on location, Balaban and Katz "established one price to make all men feel equal in the pocketbook." The partners refused "to establish financial class distinctions, or to divide our auditoriums by means of reserved sections which seem to be more desirable and exclusive [because] *the American people don't like this distinction.*"[27]

Success at the box office proved they were right. By 1925, B&K was the chain store of the movie business, dominating Chicago's luxury trade and controlling theaters throughout Illinois, Iowa, and Nebraska. The B&K "style," observed one-time associate Arthur Mayer, was "widely copied all over the country with even greater pomp, less taste—and similar profits." Adolph Zukor was so impressed by their operation that he merged Famous Players' Theaters with B&K in November 1925 and sent Sam Katz to New York to head up the new Publix Theater chain. By 1930–1931, Publix, using B&K methods, reigned as the largest exhibition circuit in the industry's history, drawing in 2 million people a day and grossing $113 million for the year.[28]

Balaban and Katz may have been the best at what they did, but they were certainly not unique. The age of the movie palace began in 1914 with the opening of the Strand Theater in New York. Yet it was not until the early 1920s that picture palaces, to quote the renowned king of malaprops Samuel Goldwyn, spread like "wildflowers." The battle for control of exhibition and its lucrative earnings began in earnest in 1919, when Adolph Zukor used the proceeds from Paramount's $10 million stock issue to fund his expansionist ambitions. It continued throughout the decade as First National, Fox, Loew's, Universal, Warner Brothers, and a number of smaller but powerful regional theater chains joined the fray. The number of movie theaters soon rose from about 15,000 in 1919 to 20,500 in 1928.[29]

The rise in the number of seats was much greater than these figures suggest, since the prime focus of this new wave of theater expansion was not the neighborhood movie houses but the larger, more profitable first-run theaters. Small and modest independent exhibitors of prewar years were soon pushed to the margins as wealthy studios and theater chains spent exorbitant sums constructing opulent cathedrals of entertainment that seated 5,000 to 6,000 people in the early 1920s. Loew's laid out more than $3 million ($22.3 million in 1990 dollars) for its Kansas City (Mo.) Midland Theatre, Paramount $3 million for its Times Square namesake, and the Stanley chain $2.5 million for the Baltimore Stanley. Deluxe houses were also built in smaller communities where companies like Universal faced "little competition from other producers who were building up . . . theaters in the metropolitan cities." By 1926, according to the editor of the *Motion Picture News*, "some 500 houses of the 'million dollar' type" were operating in 79 cities with populations over 100,000, and an equal number of a slightly "less expensive and luxurious grade . . . in the next group of cities, say down to 50,000."[30]

The rationale guiding this wave of palace construction was simple: a theater of 1,800 to 5,000 seats that charged $1, even if it had fewer shows per day, was likely to make significantly more money than a 300- to 500-seat neighborhood house that charged twenty-five or thirty cents. Studios had an additional financial incentive for expanding into exhibition: owning theaters provided them with an immediate market for their films. Even an occasional bad picture was likely to make a profit, noted one industry critic, for the "producer who also controls the theatres upon a substantial scale can exhibit to the public anything he wishes to exhibit."[31]

In retrospect it is clear that movie palaces proved extraordinarily success-ful. Yet it was not so clear during the late teens and early twenties. Exhib-itors knew what *they* wanted: a larger audience willing to pay higher ticket prices. But simply buying established theaters or building new ones was no guarantee of future success. Entrepreneurial ambitions, not democratic in-stincts, fueled the movement toward building a cross-class audience. Like Balaban and Katz, palace owners around the nation discovered they could do this by combining location, architecture, interior comfort, service, stage shows, and movies in a way that would satisfy their customers' taste for luxury and fantasy and make them come back for more. Silent movies may well have been a universal medium that required no English-language skills, but it was palace exhibitors who turned the movie theater into a universal gathering place where all classes could enjoy an evening together.

Not surprisingly, the key groups targeted by most exhibitors were pros-perous skilled workers (and their families) and the growing ranks of the amorphous middle class. Many of the "new" middle-class patrons that ex-hibitors courted were in fact the white-collar offspring of blue-collar fami-lies who had grown up watching movies in nickelodeons and neighborhood theaters. The exhibitors' task was less a matter of attracting new audiences unfamiliar with the medium than convincing adults to continue their child-hood leisure habits. They did that by building deluxe theaters in emerging suburban neighborhoods and in more traditional downtown entertainment districts. Expanding public transportation systems and growing ownership of automobiles in the 1920s made access to suburban theaters relatively easy and gave them "something of a city-wide attendance." Balaban and Katz advertisements boasted that no Chicagoan needed to travel more than half an hour to reach one of their wonder theaters. In Baltimore, Detroit, Mil-waukee, Seattle, Atlanta, and Pittsburgh new palaces also followed the pop-ulation movement into prosperous outlying areas.[32]

Exhibitors convinced people to spend the extra time and money required to travel downtown or into the suburbs by selling fantasy at an affordable price. Fantasy permeated every aspect of the moviegoing experience and was not, as in the past, confined largely to the screen. A new generation of theater architects, led by Thomas Lamb, John Eberson, and the Rapp broth-ers, designed palaces that boggled the imagination and transported patrons to the far corners of the world. Sparing no expense, they created reproduc-tions of famous buildings and styles that hitherto only very wealthy globe-trotters could afford to see. The exotic eventually grew so commonplace that one American tourist in India was heard to remark: "So this is the Taj

Mahal; pashaw . . . the Oriental Theatre at home is twice as big and has electric lights besides."[33]

From the moment customers entered the palace until the moment they left, exhibitors catered to their comfort by providing plush seats, courteous service, and clean surroundings. Footmen dressed in exotic costumes helped women out of cars and held an umbrella over them on rainy days. Once inside, a retinue of uniformed door men, elevator operators, page boys, nurses, and crisply attired ushers—or in the case of Grauman's theaters, trousered usherettes—made sure that customers received not the service they deserved, but the service they desired. The inside of the highly decorated auditorium was equally fascinating and offered a vast array of comforts. "No kings or emperors have wandered through more luxurious surroundings," remarked one contemporary writer. "In a sense, these theatres are social safety valves in that the public can partake of the same luxuries as the rich and use them to the same full extent."[34]

Exotic architecture, lavish furnishings, and ushers who catered to their every need satisfied all but the most finicky customers' craving for luxury and service. Yet for all this, the stage show reigned as the centerpoint of the movie palace experience. When asked what drew them to the movie theater, only 10 percent of the 1,600 Fresno residents surveyed by the Kinema Theatre in 1922 and 17 percent of the 600 students surveyed by Professor H. W. Hepner in 1928 responded "pictures." In both instances, and throughout the country, it was the musical stage show that won the hearts of patrons. Roxy Rothapfel's productions were so good, marveled one rival theater manager, that "the public will come whatever the weakness of his feature." Indeed, Roxy frequently slashed scenes from his feature presentation in order to leave more time for his stage shows—a practice followed by other palaces. At New York's magnificent Capitol Theater, noted one reporter, the "stage show lasted two hours while the movie rarely ran more than sixty minutes."[35]

At the best deluxe houses, there was no such thing as a "typical" stage show—especially in the mid-1920s, when a new wave of theater construction sparked competition for better and bigger shows. Audiences attending any of Sid Grauman's massive picture palaces were treated to an elaborate prologue (the name for his stage shows) specifically "devised to enhance the film that would follow." San Franciscans were entranced by Jack Partington's patented "Magic Flying Stages" that "lifted the grand symphony orchestra and gold-crusted organ consoles from the dark obscurity of the orchestra pit, and gave performers onstage a magic carpet to sing, dance, soar, sink, and vanish on." Deluxe houses also mounted productions designed to pique gender fantasies. Male patrons loved watching swim suit contests, beauty pageants, and chorus lines of long-legged dancers who radiated with "pep and personality." Female consumer dreams were fed by fashion shows

The exotic exterior of Grauman's Chinese Theater, Los Angeles (1929). This and the decor and amenities illustrated in the next three photographs helped attract a wide variety of classes to the lavish movie palaces of the 1920s.

Ornate interior of Brooklyn Paramount Theater.

Lounge area, Brooklyn Paramount Theater.

Polite ushers and doormen, Metropolitan Theater, Washington, D.C.

that featured millions of dollars in "luxuriant fur coats, cloaks and wraps, lavish displays of gowns, suits, hats and shoes—everything that Milady will own or covet next autumn."[36]

In no other arena of entertainment were high and low culture so closely intertwined as in the movie palace. Orchestras nearly the size and quality of city symphonies offered an eclectic mix of opera, classical music, ballet scores, popular show tunes, and jazz. Music was a critical part of the show, and during most of the 1920s movie theaters annually employed nearly 20,000 musicians—a third of the nation's musical work force. Popular orchestra leaders quickly developed their own loyal followings. Paul Ash, Chicago's "Rajah of Jazz," was so revered that he and "his merry-made musical gang," noted one labor newspaper, "are the prime attractions at McVickers, while the screen programs are rather secondary."[37]

Of course, movie palaces also offered patrons the latest Hollywood features. Since many urban palaces were owned by the studios that made these films, their new productions could only be seen in their theaters. By the end of the decade, Paramount owned or controlled 1,000 theaters, Fox 800, Warner Brothers 700, Universal 300, and Loew's nearly 200. Films usually premiered at a downtown palace, played a week, and then, after being held off the market for thirty to ninety days, moved to the first-run neighborhood palace. Those unwilling to wait several weeks or months to watch the most recent Douglas Fairbanks, Mary Pickford, Rudolph Valentino, or William S. Hart film *had* to visit a movie palace. The illusion of classlessness created in these theaters was often, as we shall soon see, reinforced by the films that played on their screens.[38]

To attract a cross-class audience exhibitors had to convince people that class did not matter, at least not in the movie theater. Though the ownership and control of palaces grew increasingly oligopolistic during the twenties, the theaters themselves maintained a steadfast atmosphere of democracy—at least for their white patrons. Unlike opera houses or symphonic halls, declared William Fox, in movie theaters "there are no separations of classes. Everyone enters the same way. There is no side door thrust upon those who sit in the less expensive seats. . . . In the movies the rich rub elbows with the poor and that's the way it should be." Though certainly self-serving, Fox was correct to a point. Any white man or woman who could afford the cost of admission was free to enjoy the same comforts, luxuries, and services as the palace's wealthiest patron. At New York's luxurious Rialto and Rivoli theaters, Roxy explained in 1918, "the man who comes to the theater on foot rubs elbows with the man who arrives in a limousine, and no favoritism is shown to either one or the other."[39]

Movie-theater democracy did have its limits. Like most arenas of American life, segregation was the rule and people of color were shunted off into distant balconies, inconspicuous orchestra seats, or excluded from the theater altogether. Those gaining admission were carefully watched by the armies of ushers who patrolled the aisles. Exhibitors considered such discrimination necessary in order to make middle-class customers, perhaps already nervous about potential lower-class seat mates, more comfortable. Racism also extended to theater employees. African-Americans and Mexican-Americans were rarely hired as uniformed ushers or ticket takers, but were relegated to less-visible and low-paying jobs such as messengers, maids, porters, or page boys.[40]

For audiences, however, the appeal of moviegoing transcended the prejudices of theater owners. Limited in their ability to join the festivities at white palaces, African-Americans, Asians, and Hispanics eagerly flocked to theaters that welcomed their trade. In Washington, D.C., African-Americans could choose from among fifteen movie houses (though only two were considered Class A theaters); in Chicago, the South State area between 26th and 39th Streets, popularly known as the "Stroll," served as the central entertainment district for black residents and featured a number of first-run houses. Movies remained equally popular among other people of color. The Japanese community of Los Angeles found a welcome respite at the Fuji-kan Theater on East First Street. The city's Hispanic residents congregated at downtown houses near the river, while Chicago's Mexican-American population patronized neighborhood theaters in the Back of the Yards area.[41]

Whatever the color of the audience, deluxe theaters provided men and women with a rare opportunity to forget their worries and indulge their fantasies. For a few hours, working-class and middle-class audiences could live like the rich and receive the respect and care they rarely saw at work or at home. Indeed, the very purpose of the palace was to allow fantasy and desire to run rampant; to create a magical place where, as one Balaban and Katz associate remarked, "men who worked hard all day in subordinate capacities and women escaping for a few hours from the bondage of stoves and diapers . . . might for a change be subordinated to." Lloyd Lewis captured the essence of the palace's class fantasies in a 1929 article for *The New Republic*. "When she goes home that evening, she will perhaps clean spinach and peel onions, but for a few hours, attendants bow to her, doormen tip their hats, and a maid curtsies to her in the ladies' washroom. She bathes in elegance and dignity; she satisfies her yearning for a 'cultured' atmosphere. . . . The royal favor of democracy it is: for in the 'de luxe' house every man is a king and every woman a queen."[42]

Neighborhood theaters remained an important part of community life, but they could not provide the kind of luxury, entertainment, and excitement that palaces did. Young working-class men viewed palaces as weekend treats for which they would dress up and to which they would take their dates. "Downtown [Los Angeles] had three big theaters until the mid-1930s," recounted former costume-union business agent Ted Ellsworth.

"Going to Grauman's Million Dollar Theater, the Metropolitan, or the Warner Brothers Theater on 7th and Hill was a special event" that he gladly traveled from distant Eagle Rock to attend. "We preferred this to the neighborhood theater for shows and entertainment." For young adults in Chicago, the downtown palace fulfilled a desire "to escape from the local community and to find adventure and romance in the larger outside world of the city."[43]

Working-class and ethnic patrons, as Liz Cohen and others have shown, exerted considerable control over the character of neighborhood theaters. Yet we should not romanticize the neighborhood theater. Contemporary patrons certainly did not. Audiences accustomed to the comforts of palaces grew increasingly disgusted by the run-down quality of many local houses. After attending a performance at a "much frequented" Manhattan neighborhood theater, socialist movie critic Louis Gardy complained that the "place was stuffy and the atmosphere was laden with uncongealed sweat. The seats were of the narrowest and were found only after the spectator had been standing about in the rear long enough to grow accustomed to the deafening noise and the darkness. There was no polite usher to point out a seat, no flashlight to show the way down the narrow aisle." Here, as in many other third- and fourth-run theaters, the pictures were old and the print condition so bad that patrons could see streaks across the screen. Residents in Seattle, Toledo, and Salt Lake City also complained that local houses were becoming hangouts for juvenile delinquents, loose women, and exceedingly loud children.[44]

Life inside the neighborhood theater was not always so bleak. Although poorly run theaters soon closed, other local houses kept a regular clientele by charging low prices—10, 20, or 30 cents as opposed to 50 cents for downtown theaters or $1 for palaces—and retaining, as Roy Rosenzweig notes, "much of the old informality and communality with their amateur nights and perennial giveaways of dishes, linens, and turkeys." Located within walking distance of most patrons' homes, neighborhood theaters were easier to get to than downtown houses and remained, even as late as 1938, "points at which intense social activity occurs." Movie fans who patronized palaces on weekends might still see a movie during midweek at a local theater.[45]

Astute palace managers understood the intimate appeal of the better neighborhood houses and tried to attract customers and build good will by accommodating a particular group's needs. Marcus Loew, for example, held Yom Kippur services at the Palace Theater in Brooklyn and the Avenue B Theater on the Lower East Side. Theater manager Hugo Riesenfeld provided free summertime entertainment for 400 Lower East Side children at the Rivoli and Rialto every Tuesday. In some instances, palaces became part of the political life of a city. In Pittsburgh, New York, Seattle, Detroit, and other urban centers exhibitors allowed socialists and unionists to hold fundraisers or meetings in their theaters.[46]

Through a combination of fantasy, luxury and comfort, movie palace owners built an audience that crossed political, class, ethnic, gender, and, in some cases, racial lines. By the middle of the decade, deluxe houses throughout the country were attracting a mix of what one DeQueen, Arkansas, theater manager called the "masses and classes." The investment bankers at Halsey, Stuart and Company, who preferred not to speak in class terms, observed that palaces were "drawing largely from new groups—the music lovers, the church people, 'society'—bringing new throngs to the theaters and creating an irresistible demand for more seating capacity." Recreational surveys of the era also described the emergence of a cross-class audience that attended movies on a regular basis. A 1929 Indianapolis survey revealed that weekly attendance was highest in neighborhoods dominated by "prosperous executives and owners of businesses" and only slightly lower in areas inhabited by "skilled labor, clerical and small business classes." Attendance rates were also high in neighborhoods "inhabited largely by colored people who were not very well off economically, the men of the families being of the unskilled and semi-skilled type of workers." A Salt Lake City survey taken the same year noted how young white-collar workers, especially women, spent a good part of their time and income on the movies. Offering more impressionistic evidence, documentary filmmaker Pare Lorentz insisted that the regulars he saw going to the movies in 1928 were the nation's "army of clerks."[47]

Exhibitors managed to build a middle-class audience while also preserving their traditional working-class clientele. Seattle's labor daily estimated that "working people" constituted 80 percent of the city's movie audiences in 1921 and that "most of the patrons" of its downtown theaters "belong to unions or are in sympathy with them." Movies were also among the most popular entertainments for working people in Los Angeles and nearby suburban areas like South Gate. In Worcester, Massachusetts, "working-class groups initially resistant to the lure of the nickelodeon," such as the city's Swedes and Irish Catholics, were drawn to the more respectable houses of the 1920s.[48]

Selling fantasy to the classes proved exceedingly profitable. The "Grauman Theatre of Los Angeles is now earning profits of 100 percent a year," financial analyst H. D. H. Connick told the Federal Trade Commission in 1923, "the Rialto in New York at the rate of about 80 percent a year; the Stillman in Cleveland at the rate of over 100 percent a year." By 1926 the nation's 2,000 first- and second-run houses accounted for half the country's weekly movie attendance—and palaces were most profitable of all theaters.

Sidney Kent, General Manager of Paramount, estimated that 75 percent of the company's exhibition revenues during the mid-1920s came from only 1,250 key deluxe houses.[49]

The success of new exhibition strategies presented studios and producers with a number of new questions: What kinds of films should they offer this new cross-class audience? Should they produce movies that catered to specific ethnic, political, class, and gender interests? Or should they make films less likely to offend the industry's increasingly heterogeneous clientele? In particular, how would filmmakers deal with the thorny issue of class conflict? Movies may not have been the most important reason people went to luxury palaces, but without movies the industry would surely collapse. Exhibitors could still earn profits if they showed several bad films; producers could not. Too many box-office disasters would lead to ruin for even the largest studio. Thus the decision of what to offer the public was not just a matter of catering to audience desires. It was a life-and-death proposition for the rapidly growing studio system and even more so for the independent production companies that hoped to survive long enough to challenge it.

Fantasy on the Screen

At the same time that luxury palaces were expanding the class composition of audiences, filmmakers were refashioning the ways Americans looked at class relations. In the 1920s, as in the 1910s, the industry's first priority was to make movies that would entertain audiences and earn money for their producers. Filmmakers turned out comedies, melodramas, mysteries, westerns, and adventure stories that played to the fantasies of the widest possible audience. Fantasy, of course, took many forms: the child who imagined himself or herself as a hero or heroine in the time of Robin Hood or Cleopatra; the young man who dreamed he was more sheikish than Rudolph Valentino; the young woman who saw herself dancing till dawn in Parisian night clubs. Yet when it came to the subject of class, the fantasies seen in 1920s films were markedly different from their predecessors. Labor-capital films that focused on conflict between the classes were superseded by cross-class fantasy films that emphasized love and harmony among the classes—a point of view seemingly more in tune with the mingling of classes that was occurring in the movie palaces themselves. Labor-capital films did not disappear from the screen, but by the mid-1920s they grew fewer in number and were rarely shown in the first-run theaters that gave films their greatest visibility and profits. Audiences may have still wanted to see these kinds of movies, but Hollywood producers were reluctant to make them.

In trying to reverse earlier depictions of audiences as passive receivers of mass culture, scholars have recently stressed the power movie patrons had in shaping the social environment of neighborhood theaters and interpret-ing the meaning of the films they saw. It is important, however, not to overemphasize the power of audiences; audiences were certainly free to ac-cept or reject the messages on film, but in the end their power was limited to choosing among the films that producers wanted to make.[50]

The question of whether audiences get the films they want is as old as the movie industry itself. Speaking before an International Sales Convention in May 1930, veteran movie mogul Carl Laemmle bluntly declared, "I don't care what you want or what I want, it is what the public wants that counts, because in the end they have to pay and they have the say." But unlike countless others who invoked similar platitudes, Laemmle quickly admitted that when it came to deciding *what* the public wants, "Nobody knows."[51]

Laemmle was right. There was no way of knowing what audiences really wanted because audiences may not have known themselves. Moviegoers wanted to be entertained, but entertainment could take many different forms. Producers tried shaping audience tastes by accustoming them to cer-tain kinds of films. Movie industry head Will Hays frequently spoke about the filmmakers' ability to shape popular fashions and consumer habits. "No longer does the girl in Sullivan, Indiana, guess what the styles are going to be in three months," he explained in 1927. "She knows, because she sees them on the screen." Likewise, the "head of the house sees a new kind of golf suit in the movies and he wants one. . . . Perhaps the whole family gets a new idea for redecorating and refurnishing the parlor—and down they go to the dealers to ask for the new goods."[52]

If audiences could get their ideas about fashion from the screen, why not their understanding of class relations? During the 1920s, producers both responded to and helped accelerate changes in the dominant class discourse by producing cross-class fantasy films that shifted attention away from the deadening world of production and toward the pleasures of consumption. Taken collectively, these films suggested that old ideas about class no longer mattered; that participation in a modern consumer society made class dif-ferences irrelevant. Filmmakers also shaped audience tastes and conscious-ness through the films they did not make. During the 1920s, they made fewer and fewer labor-capital films. Although many factors contributed to this shift in the class politics of American cinema, two were especially im-portant: first, industry leaders' belief that films stressing class harmony and consumer fantasies would help build a cross-class audience and increase attendance at the highly profitable movie palaces that showed them; and, second, their knowledge that opposition by censors made production of politically volatile labor-capital films a financially risky proposition. Film-makers, then, found themselves caught up in a complex effort to respond to audience tastes, while also accustoming them to new, less problematic, kinds of productions.

During the late teens and early 1920s, producers, like exhibitors, catered to the rapidly expanding, if somewhat amorphous, ranks of the middle class and assumed that working-class fans would continue going to movies regardless of what was shown. Postwar audiences, they insisted, wanted to forget about war and social problems and instead celebrate the flowering of peace and prosperity. Wartime service, industry leaders argued, acted as a temporary equalizer of classes and led many Americans to believe that they now deserved a taste of the good life. "Class distinctions had broken down," observed producer Benjamin Hampton. "The way of the rich was becoming the way of the land, and the people were suddenly interested in etiquette, in social forms, in behavior, in the standards and clothes and beauty lotions and habits that would help them to be like the people they admired." Although Hampton had an exaggerated sense of the breakdown of class distinctions, it was one shared by many of his peers.[53]

As postwar politicians, business leaders, studios, and voters succeeded in supplanting the idealism of prewar Progressivism with a new emphasis on materialism, producers and exhibitors shied away from making or showing hard-hitting social-problem films. "Picture palaces were designed to take people out of their mundane lives," observed silent-era scholar Kevin Brownlow, "not push them back in." It was the Cecil B. DeMilles and James Cruzes, not the Lois Webers or D. W. Griffiths, who best understood the changing needs of the industry. Money, sex, beauty, and luxury was the DeMille formula, and his films, in brother William's words, were "hailed with loud hosannas by the public of that day. . . . This was what the people as a whole wanted to see; a sumptuous and spectacular dramatization of the age of jazz, prohibition, and flaming youth." Studios quickly turned out features with such provocative titles as *Sex, Flapper Wives, Ladies of Ease, Gigolo, Reckless Youth, Jazzamania, Daughters of Pleasure, A Slave of Fashion, Extravagance, Success,* and *Money, Money, Money.*[54]

These flights of fantasy did not entirely monopolize the efforts of producers and studios. Postwar strikes and the fear of Red invaders kept class conflict fresh on the minds of Americans and kept labor-capital films on movie-theater screens. Yet as labor and radical activism declined after 1922, films about Reds, radicals, and unions no longer appeared quite as salient to Hollywood studios. Filmmakers also hesitated to make labor-capital films because censors threatened to ban them. By 1926, film censorship boards were operating in 100 cities and nearly a dozen states, each with different standards. Censors repeatedly acted against any producer—labor film company or Hollywood studio—who made features or newsreels that criticized capitalists or offered sympathetic depictions of working-class life and struggles. Pennsylvania censors demanded substantial changes in William S. Hart's *The Whistle* (Famous Players-Lasky 1921), a liberal film that exposed unsafe working conditions in textile mills. State censors also ordered Pathé,

Hearst, Gaumont, and Fox to cut scenes of newsreels showing ongoing strikes and labor agitation on the grounds that "they tend to incite riot and disorder." Sympathetic footage of coal miners' strikes in Ohio, Pennsylvania, Illinois, and West Virginia never reached the screen.[55]

Studios could, of course, refuse to comply with censors' demands. But doing so would mean delaying, perhaps even canceling, a film's release in any number of states. With the cost of an average feature film spiraling from $12–18,000 in 1918 to $40–80,000 in 1919, and to $300,000 in 1924 (plus tens of thousands more for advertising, publicity, and the like), producers took a much harder look at the kinds of politics they wanted to put on the screen. "The advance commitments of a company on its pictures are so heavy," Laemmle explained, "that one or two box-office failures may make serious inroads on the reserves built up during periods of success." This was especially true for struggling smaller companies to which, as Jack Warner emphasized, "every nickel counted." Potential losses were heightened for powerful moguls such as Zukor and Fox, for whom the delay of a film meant less product and less profit for their distribution and exhibition wings.[56]

The scandals that rocked the nation following the manslaughter trials of popular comedian Roscoe "Fatty" Arbuckle (who was accused of killing actress Virginia Rappe at an allegedly decadent party) and the suspicious murder of director William Desmond Taylor in 1921 drew closer attention to the values seen on the screen and prompted outraged cries for even greater censorship of motion pictures. Producers moved to avert more government censorship by organizing the Motion Picture Producers and Distributors Association (MPPDA) in 1922, hiring squeaky-clean Postmaster General Will Hays as its president, and agreeing to follow a voluntary censorship code in 1924 that Hays promised would maintain "the highest possible moral and artistic standards in motion picture production." With Hays's office rejecting scripts deemed "too provocative" and "anesthetizing anything political," and with "Wall Street watchdogs" (who handled shares for eleven movie corporations by 1925) constantly offering what Jesse Lasky and others felt was "much unappreciated advice," industry leaders grew even more conservative in their choice of productions.[57]

Given the enormous financial risks involved, producers decided to cut back on labor-capital productions. After all, studios were in the movie business and not, like worker film companies, in the consciousness-raising business. Between 1923 and 1929, when roughly 700 features were released each year, the movie industry (excluding labor film companies) produced only 48 labor-capital films, an average of seven films per year—a sharp drop-off from the 171 films released between April 1917 and December 1922 (an average of 30 films per year). When studio executives did approve a labor-capital film, they made sure it was one unlikely to earn the wrath of censors: 71 percent of the labor-capital films made between 1923 and 1929 (excluding worker-made films), and 79 percent of the 33 films made after the publication of the MPPDA code in 1924, took a decidedly conservative point of view.[58]

Hollywood continued to deal with class issues throughout the 1920s, but it presented its class visions in the form of cross-class fantasies rather than riskier labor-capital features. Like working-class films of the prewar era, cross-class fantasy films cut across established genres and included comedies, dramas, and melodramas. Yet unlike working-class films, they also included a group of movies that cinema scholars refer to as society films. These films, explained Richard Koszarski, "typically dealt with tribulations in the lives of the rich and famous and served as showcases for glamorous costumes and settings. Often a working-class character, usually female, would be introduced into upper-class society by some twist of fate. This allowed the filmmakers to demonstrate the moral superiority of the working class while lavishing attention on the glamorous life-styles of the wealthy."[59]

When it came to dealing with the "problems and possibilities of inter-class and intercultural relationships," the range of characters in cross-class fantasies was far greater than Koszarski's brief quotation suggests. Changes in the class composition of postwar audiences and the occupational structure of the workplace precipitated changes in the class composition and occupations of the protagonists seen on the screen. Whereas society films generally depicted upper-class and blue-collar interactions, and labor-capital films the conflicts between male factory workers and their employers, cross-class fantasy filmmakers expanded their scope to include the rapidly growing ranks of middle-class professionals, white-collar workers, and sales and service employees—people who were among the industry's most sought-after patrons.[60]

Filmmakers also recognized the growing presence of women in the work force and eagerly catered to their dreams and desires. Cross-class fantasies were generally less paternalistic than prewar working-class films, in which sweatshop and factory women were seen as helpless objects in need of protection. Instead, these films explored the experiences and fantasies of seemingly more independent women who worked as clerks, secretaries, stenographers, telephone operators, department store sales people, and owners of businesses who sometimes did better than the men they loved.[61]

When industry leaders said movies were looking up they were not just talking about profits. The blue-collar screen of the nickelodeon era grew increasingly white in the 1920s as "new" and "old" middle-class and upper-class protagonists came to dominate Hollywood films. Studio heads often assumed that white-collar workers wanted to see themselves living a middle-class life. A close examination of subject headings in one film catalog reveals that between 1921 and 1929 "society" films outnumbered labor-capital films 308 to 67. Fantasies about cross-class relations now proved more important and profitable than discourses about class conflict—at least in the minds of filmmakers.[62]

These films proved so popular because of the tremendous variety of fantasies they offered male and female audiences. Film critic Welford Beaton was struck by how many of these fantasies were geared to a new generation of white-collar workers: "the discouraged stenographer is inspired by the fact that the stenographer in the picture marries the boss, and the traveling salesman is given fresh hope when he sees Dick Dix or Bill Haines playing a salesman cop the millionaire's daughter in the final reel." Producers also offered fantasies for those who dreamed of getting lots of money without having to earn it. In *The Millionaire* (1921), Herbert Rawlinson plays a $25-a-week bookkeeper who suddenly inherits $80 million, and in *A Daughter of Luxury* (1922) Agnes Ayres is a homeless girl who discovers she is really a wealthy heiress.[63]

Dreams of wealth, mobility, respect, and luxury could all be found on the screen, but love between the classes remained the cornerstone of these films. All problems, both personal and societal, could be solved through love; and true love was strong enough to break down any class barriers. After all, class was an artificial construct, love was real. Cross-class fantasies offered viewers almost as many varieties of love as Heinz made condiments. Modern versions of Cinderella and Cinderfellar stories could be seen almost every week. But instead of love between a peasant and handsome prince or beautiful princess, love permutations in these films included mixes of urban-based blue collars, white collars, professionals, business owners, servants, the working wealthy, and the idle rich.

In the movies, if not in life, wealthy women showed a particular affinity for marrying white- or blue-collar men. In *Taking Chances* (1921) a wealthy capitalist's daughter spurns a rich financier in favor of her father's secretary, a former book salesman. More traditional Cinderella tales saw rich men marrying department-store clerks, chorus girls, and typists. Sometimes Prince Charming assumed the more modest guise of a successful professional (architect, doctor, lawyer) who weds a waitress or factory operative. Disguised identities often turned what appeared to be intraclass love into interclass love. In *Orchids and Ermine* (First National 1927) hotel telephone operator Colleen Moore, who dreams of "gold dust not cement dust," falls for Jack Mulhall, who is valet to a fabulously wealthy Tulsa millionaire. After initially resisting his advances, she consents to marry him only to discover that Jack is really the "Oil Baron"—he switched identities to avoid "all these money-mad women" and find someone who loved him for what he was.[64]

Whatever the combination, cross-class romances invariably offered audiences glimpses of the extravagant life styles and luxurious possessions of

In cross-class fantasies like *Orchids and Ermine* (First National 1927), a hotel operator (Colleen Moore) who dreams of "gold dust not cement dust" (top) eventually finds happiness with a millionaire oil man (Jack Mulhall, bottom).

the American aristocracy. DeMille and directors like him, argues Lewis Jacobs, thought "every shopgirl longed to be accepted as the heroine of the film, into the social circles of the rich, and sought a knowledge of table etiquette, how to dress, how to be introduced, how to order, and how to conduct oneself in general."[65] Most, if not all of these desires, could be satisfied in a good cross-class fantasy. Factory and tenement settings, so popular in earlier social-problem films, now gave way to films set in lavish hotels, magnificent mansions, fashionable clothing boutiques, and costly night spots where the rich liked to amuse themselves.

In telling their story of love between the classes, cross-class fantasies removed the overtly contentious political edge that accompanied most labor-capital films and offered a point of view that fit well into the conservative Republican politics of the decade. Individualism and personal fulfillment were the dominant ideological undercurrents of these films—a sharp contrast to the sense of collectivism and cooperation advocated by labor film-makers of the 1920s. Although acknowledging inequities of wealth and power in society, cross-class fantasies suggested that there was no need for unions or any kind of collective activity to achieve one's dreams. Love and moral superiority would lead the way to happiness.

These often subtle political themes were presented within seemingly liberal calls for cross-class tolerance and mutual respect: whatever the barriers and distance separating them, working class, middle class, and upper class could learn from one another. Yet in looking more closely at the values characters actually taught each other, these films reveal an extremely conservative and patronizing attitude toward class relations. Working people, whether blue collar or white, were inevitably portrayed as salt-of-the-earth types who taught the wealthy the value of hard work. The rich, in turn, instructed these good-hearted but socially inept folk in manners, grace, and the proper way to consume luxury. The most conservative films offered their working-class characters—and viewers—a taste of the good life, but in the end suggested they were ultimately happier loving and consuming within their own class. Thus, while movie palaces brought the classes together, cross-class fantasy films pulled them back apart.[66]

No one brought these conservative messages to the screen with greater success than Cecil B. DeMille. In his skillful hands, working hard, wanting a taste of luxury, and remaining content within one's class seemed the natural thing to do. His movies helped justify the dominant class system by suggesting that its openness lay in the realm of consumption rather than in movement across class boundaries. The son of a minister, DeMille was born in August 1881 to a prominent family in Ashfield, Massachusetts. DeMille entered the movie business in 1913 when he assumed the position of director-general of the Jesse L. Lasky Feature Play Company. A successful film-maker before the war, he grew even more prominent afterward. DeMille gained his postwar reputation as an innovative director of society comedies and dramas. One film critic praised him for opening up "a whole new world for the films, a world that middle-class audiences, newly won to the movies by the luxurious theaters then springing up, wanted to see."[67]

DeMille imbued his productions with a conservative political edge that reflected his personal politics. Dubbed by Kevin Brownlow as "perhaps the most conservative figure in Hollywood," DeMille (unlike his liberal brother William) remained a rabidly anti-union, anti-Communist Republican most of his life. He rejected films that focused on mass movements in favor of making movies that concentrated on individuals. "The audience is interested in people," he wrote in his autobiography, "not masses of anonymous people, but individuals whom they can love or hate, in whose fortunes they can feel personally involved." Working people craved entertainment, not political sermons. "Your poor person," he declared in 1925, "wants to see wealth, colorful, interesting, exotic." Yet whatever his professions, the poor people watching the minister son's films also had to sit through his sermons.[68]

Saturday Night (Famous Players-Lasky 1922) offers us a glimpse into the political mindset of DeMille and his many imitators. The movie opens by focusing on four discontented protagonists who fantasize about leading a better life. Pretty Irish laundress Shamrock O'Day (played by Edith Roberts) "is a modern Cinderella who is tied to Drudgery and Cotton Stockings and longs for French Perfume and a French Maid." Her handsome next-door neighbor Tom McGuire (Jack Mower) is "a Chauffeur, who is so fed up on the Corned Beef and Cabbage of Life, that he longs for a little of the Caviar." On the more upscale side of town live the equally discontented Iris Van Suydam (Leatrice Joy), "one of the Lilies in Life's Hot-House—who 'Toils Not, neither does she Spin,'" and her wealthy fiancé Richard Prentiss (Conrad Nagel), "who is just as tired of the Silken Women of her class, as she is bored with the Men of his." Cross-class love quickly blossoms when Shamrock delivers laundry to Richard's magnificent mansion and winds up clumsily falling down his staircase and sprawling clothing in every direction. Richard immediately falls in love and drives her home. When Iris sees the two leave, she flies into a jealous rage and decides that if Richard can drive a laundress, she can picnic with a chauffeur. Of course, she turns out to be a reckless driver and Tom winds up saving her life and falling in love. After passing out, Iris awakens in Tom's arms and declares: "Tom, I have just learned how much more important Red Blood is—than Blue!" Tom, swell guy that he is, responds: "I don't blame you, you poor kid! You just haven't been brought up right."[69]

Meanwhile, back at the mansion, a lavish ball is in progress and audiences could delight in watching tuxedoed men and expensively gowned, diamond-bedecked women gracefully dancing to the sounds of a large orchestra. Richard spots Shamrock, who has returned with his laundry, and leads her out to the dance floor. Mom is aghast, his sister ashamed, and the guests amused. But Richard does not care one fig. Likewise, the besmitten Iris asks Tom to take her away "where I can cook for you, and sew for you, and just be your Wife!" An intertitle quickly warns: "Romance laughs at the heavy Chains of Tradition. But Society metes out swift punishment to those who Break the Chains." Both couples defy the strictures of their class and get married. Shamrock moves into a luxurious bedroom in the mansion (which we see in great detail), while Iris gets to live in a small, noisy apartment next to the elevated line.

The rest of the film dwells on the seemingly humorous situations that arise from these class-crossed marriages. Each character continually lives up to the class stereotypes drawn by DeMille. When a maid prepares a midweek bath, the startled Shamrock tells her in ungrammatical English that "it ain't Saturday night." Lacking proper table manners, she embarrasses everyone at a fancy dinner party. Iris has an equally tough time being a working-class housewife. She is unable to cook or clean, and when she lights up a cigarette at a disastrous dinner party Tom angrily barks: "Cut the smokin'! Do you want my Friends to think you're fast?" Both husbands are constantly embarrassed by their wives' inability to adjust to their new situations. Whatever their class prior to marriage, women in this film are clearly expected to adopt the class characteristics of their husbands after marriage.

Through a combination of misadventures, Tom and Shamrock wind up spending a happy evening together stuck atop a Coney Island ferris wheel, where they manage to fall in love. Richard goes looking for her at Tom's apartment and when the errant couple finally arrive, Shamrock tells him of her new love. "Dick, dear, it ain't our fault! I like Tom because he likes Gum, and Hot-Dogs, and Jazz! Just as you, and Iris, like High-Brow Operas, and Olives—and such." All conversation is halted when a fire breaks out in the building. During the ensuing confusion, Tom rushes off with Shamrock and when Richard comes back to rescue Iris she confesses, "In the end, Dick—it's always—Kind to Kind." The film cuts to seven years later, and, in two consecutive scenes, we see Tom and Shamrock having fun with their three kids at Coney Island, while Iris is dressed in a gorgeous black gown, surrounded by wealth, servants, and an admiring Richard.

The conservative undertones of Saturday Night and its patronizing attitudes toward working-class life are apparent throughout the film. Wealth and luxury, DeMille argues, do not bring contentment; whatever people think they might want, they will be happier marrying and consuming within their own class. Different classes may come to love one another, but they cannot live together in an intimate setting. Such conservative messages

In Cecil B. DeMille's *Saturday Night* (Famous Players-Lasky 1922), Irish laundress Shamrock O'Day (Edith Roberts) gets to move into the mansion of her rich husband (top), while the wealthy but spoiled Iris Van Suydam (Leatrice Joy) marries a chauffeur and has to move into his modest one-room flat (bottom).

were not unique to *Saturday Night* and could be seen in other DeMille films such as *Male and Female* (1919) and *Manslaughter* (1922).

DeMille's brand of conservatism was only one of many varieties seen in cross-class fantasies. Be satisfied and content with your lives was the message that accompanied the frequent salt-of-the-earth portrayals of working-class protagonists. Many of these films advanced a nostalgic reverence for the dignity of work and the work ethic that workers either rejected or found hard to achieve off the screen. It was precisely because work had lost so much of its meaning that people wanted shorter work days and more leisure. Working-class men and women preferred the allures of the new consumer ethos to the old Protestant work ethic that stressed the importance of frugality, self-denial, and deferred gratification. Yet in Hollywood movies, work and the work ethic were portrayed as powerful forces that could redeem and transform the idle rich. In the course of promoting these twin values, producers conceded a sense of moral superiority to hard-working blue- and white-collar audiences, while also offering them a voyeuristic look at the decadent but fascinating lives of the filthy rich.[70]

Upward mobility was another area where film fantasies outpaced the realities of work life. Since the nation's beginnings, rising up to own a business served as a benchmark of independence and success. Yet as massive factories and highly capitalized corporations replaced artisan shops and small manufactories during the nineteenth and twentieth centuries, the percentage of self-employed Americans steadily declined. In the movies, however, success and independence were easily attained if one worked hard and persevered. *Sure Fire Flint* (1922) typified capitalist fantasies of upward mobility. A poor soldier who comes home and labors at a number of unskilled jobs gets a big break when he returns a coat filled with money to a steel mill owner. Flint's honesty earns him a job in the mills and "almost overnight," notes one reviewer, he rises to the position of manager, foils a robbery, and then marries the boss's daughter.[71] Plumbers, blacksmiths, factory workers, and superintendents were all featured in similar rags-to-riches films.

Women figured prominently in these films as passionate upholders of the work ethic. Gender stereotypes crossed class lines as wealthy and poor women alike insisted that their men work. An artist's model in *The Woman He Married* (1923) refuses to marry a young millionaire until he is able to do something other than spend money and smoke gold-tipped cigarettes. In *Wealth* (1921), a young illustrator marries an idle rich man and begs him to work and accomplish something with his life. When he ignores her, she leaves him; but he wins her back when he follows her advice. According to this film, remarked one labor reviewer, the "trouble with wealth is . . . it gives you no chance to develop character, it leaves you a spineless creature and worst of all, it does not allow you to perform what is known as 'a man's work.'" The daring reviewer quickly added that he "would risk the danger and accept any number of millions of dollars which might be willed to us by kind uncles."[72]

The work ethic was meant to apply to men of all classes, but not to all women. Poor women were expected to help support their families. This was made abundantly clear in films about ghetto life, like *Humoresque* (Cosmopolitan 1920) and *His People* (Universal 1925). But gender, class, and the work ethic created an uncomfortable mix when it came to looking at middle-class career women. Cross-class fantasies took a decidedly anti-careerist perspective and showed the misfortunes that befell women who preferred careers to raising families. They may have become successes in business, but they were failures as women. This was especially true for women who proved more driven than their husbands. As the advertisement for *This Freedom* (1924), a film about a successful female banker, warned: "The story of home or a career and the resulting chaos caused by a woman too ambitious for her own welfare."[73]

Not all cross-class fantasy filmmakers assumed such reactionary positions. Even by the late 1920s, Hollywood movies did not present a monolithic view of class relations. Like labor-capital films, a number of cross-class fantasies contained a biting anti-authoritarian edge that poked fun at the values and aspirations of various classes. Few actors were better at skewering the arrogant pretensions often found among the rising cadre of white-collar supervisory personnel than Harold Lloyd. The Charlie Chaplin of the middle class, Lloyd was especially popular with blue-collar and low-level white-collar audiences. Chicago trade unionists praised his films for offering "wholesome fun with a punch" and starting "the beholder thinking in the right instead of the wrong direction." In *Safety Last* (Roach 1925), the bespectacled Lloyd plays a bumbling sales clerk who always runs afoul of—but ultimately bests—the store's extraordinarily pompous head floorwalker, Mr. Stubbs, a man who has grown "Muscle-bound," as an intertitle tells us, "From patting himself on the back." The film not only mocks the autocratic floorwalker, but also the overbearingly ambitious young men who are confident they will rise quickly through the white-collar ranks to become great successes.[74]

Comedian Buster Keaton lampooned middle-class norms in a somewhat different fashion. "Where Lloyd accepted middle-class order and made comedy from the foolish antics of the man on the make," observes film historian Robert Sklar, "Keaton's existence within the same social setting was predicated on a recognition of not his but *its* absurdities." The ethos of upward mobility and limits of cross-class love are wonderfully parodied in *Cops* (1922), *The Navigator* (1924), *Sherlock Jr.* (Keaton 1924), and *The General* (Schenck 1927).[75]

Moviegoers who wanted to see hard-hitting portrayals of class relations were not likely to find them in the cross-class fantasies that played to the cross-class audiences who flocked to the nation's movie palaces each week. When it came to dealing with class tensions these films were notable for what audiences did not see: strikes, radicals, union organizing, and mass movements. Love and inner happiness, not conflict and class struggle, were the preferred themes of these films. Working-class and white-collar audiences were repeatedly told how superior they were to the upper classes; yet these movies also advised them to do nothing to remedy the situation in which the so-called superior class was being oppressed by the inferior class. Look and desire, but be satisfied with your lot was their collective message. Working-class viewers, remarked one labor weekly, were constantly being told "that you must be content to be poor and not kick about it."[76] By portraying class interactions in such a way, cross-class fantasies helped legitimize the class hierarchies and inequalities that dominated American society.

Watching films in the same environment did not mean that different classes accepted and assimilated the same ideas. Producers may have homogenized the politics of their movies, but not the political perspectives of all moviegoers. The nation's labor press blasted Cecil B. DeMille as a "subtle propagandist for the enemies of the workers." The *Chicago New Majority* bitterly complained how in *Saturday Night* "all working men and girls eat with knives and are brutish, selfish boors," while "all finer feelings are monopolized by those of gentle birth. . . . Workers stink and bathe only on Saturday night. Only the gentle-born are sweet and clean." The paper's editor conceded that DeMille's movies were technically beautiful, but he accused the director of being "one of the most dangerous propagandists against the public welfare, connected with any established publicity channel. He slides across continual arguments for things as they are, in his elaborately staged photoplays." Working-class movie critics were equally critical of the conservative view of gender roles that permeated many cross-class fantasy films. One labor reviewer denounced *The Famous Mrs. Fair* (1923) for preaching the "reactionary doctrine that a woman has no business trying to have a career, that her place is to slave in the home and take orders from her husband."[77]

Audiences enjoyed the fantasies of the movie palace but not necessarily those of the films that played there. Although producers insisted that people preferred escapist cross-class fantasies to more serious films, movie patrons often expressed a very different point of view. When audiences at New York's Rialto, Rivoli, and Criterion Theaters were asked in June 1923 what kinds of films they wanted to see, they responded in a four-to-one ratio that they preferred "simple true-to-life stories rather than spectacular and fantastic ones and pictures that instruct and provoke thought rather than pictures whose sole purpose is amusement." Specific comments included "More natural stories—less 'hokum,'" "Omit the false impressions of life," and "Less concentration on wealthy class and their aristocratically spectacular life, simple stories of actual people with intelligent direction." Likewise, when the *Saturday Evening Post* asked readers in 1928 whether they preferred "Pictures That Have Lavish Settings, Costumes, Fashions . . . [or] A Simple Story Well Told?" a majority of respondents favored the latter.[78]

These limited surveys suggest that producers did not always respond to audience demands. Many patrons still enjoyed seeing serious films about workplace life such as King Vidor's *The Crowd* (MGM 1928), which offered a bleak portrait of the faceless, routinized world of the white-collar worker. Yet although moviegoers may have wanted to see more labor-capital films, producers were hesitant to make them. The opposition of external censors, in-house censorship by studios and the Hays office, and the prospect of losing one's job if a producer failed to make money on a film, proved far more influential than audience surveys in deciding what films would be made. "Seventy-five percent of the motion pictures shown today are a brazen insult to human intelligence," actor Rudolph Valentino, the heartthrob of millions, complained in 1923. "This is because the trusts play the cash register, and that is all that they worry about."[79]

Patrons wanting to see more serious stories about class relations were most likely to fulfill their desires at neighborhood theaters that continued to screen old and new labor-capital films. Yet these theaters held less and less appeal for the millions of moviegoers who grew accustomed to watching films in an atmosphere of luxury, comfort, and fantasy. Although many people went to the movies simply to be entertained and cared little about the ideological content of films, class-conscious fans who read unfavorable reviews in the labor press found themselves having to decide what was more important, fantasy or politics? Although most moviegoers probably never thought about these issues, this dilemma was played out in what was undoubtedly the most class-conscious American city of the postwar era, Seattle, Washington.

Fantasy or Politics?

In August 1919, six months after a general strike that involved 60,000 people and three months before the formation of the Federation Film Corporation (producers of *The New Disciple*), Seattle workers entered the world of motion picture exhibition by founding the Seattle Union Theater Company (SUTC). One of the city's many experiments in labor capitalism, the company was organized by *Seattle Union Record* editor Harry Ault and local labor leader Frank Rust. Adopting the catchy slogan, "Make Your Fun Pay You a Profit," the SUTC was incorporated at $1.5 million and its 30,000 shares were offered to "bona fide members of trade unions." Like the FFC, the SUTC's goal was to counter anti-labor propaganda by offering movie-goers films "in which the labor side of the plot was presented in a true light." Recognizing that people wanted to be entertained, not just instructed, the company promised to build a palatial 3,000-seat theater that would screen only "such propaganda plays . . . that have power to grip the imagination and interest of the average man and woman." Area residents found the prospect of a luxurious class-conscious movie theater so appealing that they bought over $20,000 in stock within a week of its initial offering.[80]

Seattle's worker exhibitors envisioned merging fantasy and politics by opening a movie palace where audiences would enjoy "comfortable seats that really rested," see "pictures with a plot that appealed to the worker," and hear music that "sent them home humming the tunes." Creating such fantasies, however, proved more costly than the fledgling company could afford. Instead, it purchased a small downtown theater on 3rd Avenue near Pike and, on July 9, 1920, opened the Class A, the city's first worker-owned movie house. During its first several months, the theater screened a mix of recent pro-labor and liberal films, older labor-capital films, and a general array of first- and second-run films that featured the likes of Harold Lloyd, William S. Hart, and Mary Pickford—all for twenty-five cents, as compared to the fifty cents charged by luxury houses. Political activity on the screen was often accompanied by political activity inside the theater, as Farmer-Labor party candidates delivered speeches and held fundraisers prior to election day. Attracted by an advertising campaign that stressed the highly class-conscious character of its offerings, local residents flocked to the Class A in record numbers. Business was so good that six months after opening the theater, the company declared a 10 percent dividend on its capital stock.[81]

Convinced of its glowing future, the SUTC purchased four more small downtown theaters in November 1921. This decision to expand operations rather than upgrade the Class A proved disastrous. So long as the Class A showed good political films and a decent array of other first-run features, patrons were willing to put up with its less than luxurious and cramped environment. The politics of film, in this instance, was an equal, if not greater lure, than the fantasies of the palace. However, running four more theaters stretched the company's budget to such an extent that they abandoned expensive first-run features in favor of showing cheaper second- and third-run films. Worse yet, they stopped showing labor-capital films—even old ones. Seattle's class-conscious moviegoers soon stopped going to SUTC theaters. Although the exact financial details are unclear, the company defaulted on its mortgage payments and, sometime between January and July 1922 went out of business.[82]

Seattle's experience suggests that exhibitors who offered a mixture of political films and entertaining current productions could attract a steady clientele. Workers might well choose to go to the neighborhood theater for their politics and to the palace for their fantasy. This scenario, however, probably only held true for people who went to the movies several times a week and lived in heavily unionized areas. For men and women who saw moviegoing as a special weekend event, neighborhood theaters simply did not hold the same appeal as palaces. When forced to choose between politics or fantasy, most adults undoubtedly chose the latter—and that included committed trade unionists as well as the vast numbers of non-unionists. Despite their antipathy for DeMille and his ilk, unions and labor newspapers never called for boycotts of palaces showing conservative cross-class fantasy films. Indeed, labor and radical newspapers that were so critical of most aspects of capitalist development were enthusiastic supporters of movie palaces. The *Chicago Federation News, New York Call, Los Angeles Citizen, Seattle Union Record*, and *Milwaukee Leader* covered every local palace opening and offered rave reviews of palace stage shows. No neighborhood theater ever received this kind of attention. The Chicago paper was so enamored of Balaban and Katz's "wonder-theatres" that its coverage of B&K galas often appeared on the editorial page.[83]

Choosing fantasy over politics was not an indication of "false" or "misguided" consciousness. Rather, it reflected a preference for the direct pleasures of the palace over the vicarious thrills of watching films. Basking in the luxuries and comforts of the palace offered immediate physical delights that few movies could replicate. And savvy theater managers knew that. When evening programs threatened to run too long, successful exhibitors like Roxy Rothapfel cut the film rather than the stage show. Enjoying consumerist fantasies or movies about sex, jazz, and the fast life did not mean that audiences rejected labor-capital films. They rarely got a chance to see them.

This understandable desire for fantasy did, however, entail certain political costs. The massive patronage of palaces that showed cross-class fantasy films probably led producers to believe that audiences wanted more of these productions. Such patronage also meant fewer customers for neighborhood theaters, and fewer customers meant bankruptcy for many of the local houses that were most likely to run worker-made and pro-labor films. Most important, the prominence of cross-class fantasies and the declining number of liberal labor-capital films meant that the view of class relations seen by hundreds of millions of Americans took a decidedly conservative turn in the 1920s.[84]

The growing taste for fantasy posed another problem. In addition to fighting powerful studios and theater chains bent on monopolizing production and exhibition, labor film companies also had to respond to dramatic changes in audience expectations. The rise of movie palaces and wildly expensive, lavishly produced films had captured the imagination of moviegoers. Could labor filmmakers do the same? Could they rise up to the task of putting class conflict on the screen in a manner that would attract heterogeneous mass audiences and not just the already converted? Or, would Hollywood squash these pesky little competitors and, in so doing, establish itself as the sole guardian of the nation's political conscience?

8

Lights Out: The Decline of Labor Filmmaking and the Triumph of Hollywood

IN FEBRUARY 1928, a little-known movie studio electrician proposed a scheme that could have changed the political direction of American film and the course of the film industry. Labor-film companies, observed Patrick Murphy of Electrical Workers Union Local #40, were on the brink of extinction: they had plenty of ideas for movies but lacked the money to make them and access to theaters to exhibit them. Yet this problem could be solved with one simple act: turn the auditoriums in the nation's 1,500 labor temples (buildings that served as headquarters for several local unions) into movie theaters and offer customers a regular program of theatrical releases. By so doing, organized labor would suddenly possess the largest exhibition chain in North America. Control of so many screens would also give them a powerful role in deciding the kinds of films that would be produced. Studios would be far more inclined to make pro-labor films if labor temple managers promised to show them. The lucrative prospect of a guaranteed 1,500-theater run would also attract a bevy of investors eager to provide the temples and labor film companies with the capital to "write, produce and display its own film stories." With adequate financing, labor filmmakers could make star-studded features that would lure millions of people into temple auditoriums. By combining production, distribution, and exhibition, Murphy mused, the labor movement could eventually build "their own studios" and perhaps turn Hollywood into a different kind of dream factory, one that emphasized working-class fantasies.[1]

Producing multi-million dollar films or opening multi-million dollar movie palaces was beyond the financial reach of workers, but producing modestly budgeted films and opening modestly equipped movie theaters was not. Throughout the 1920s, radicals and unionists like Patrick Murphy fought to bring about significant changes in the kinds of movies people saw and where they saw them. As Hollywood producers began shying away from class-conscious films, cinematic battles between labor and capital were fought with renewed fervor in the nation's schools, churches, factories, and voluntary associations, where nontheatrical films made by workers and capitalists were seen by tens of millions of men, women, and children.

Changing the course of the movie industry, however, proved far more difficult than workers anticipated. As we have seen, the three most successful labor film companies of the era all turned out at least one feature-length production during the early 1920s. Duplicating those efforts in the face of a rapidly evolving movie industry proved infinitely more difficult. In order to survive, let alone prosper, movie producers—whether they were labor filmmakers, independents, or even once-prominent studios like Vitagraph—had to battle the growing power of the Hollywood studio system: a system so tightly controlled that the federal government under the conservative aegis of Presidents Calvin Coolidge and Herbert Hoover brought antitrust suits to dismantle it in 1927 and 1929. Labor filmmakers faced the additional burden of battling local and state movie censors who were determined to keep provocative pro-labor messages off the screen.

Despite momentary glimmerings of a promising future, only one of the three labor film companies survived until the end of the decade. By 1930, virtually no oppositional filmmaker had the resources to reach the screen on a regular basis. Examining the struggles of labor filmmakers, their successes and their failures, offers important insights into the many obstacles faced by any group wanting to produce movies for mass audiences. It also suggests how success might have been achieved even in the face of considerable opposition. Understanding how independent filmmakers especially highly politicized filmmakers, dealt with their problems, allows us to see what it would have taken to create a different kind of movie industry—for then and perhaps even for now.

Fighting for Survival

Guarded optimism was the outlook inside the headquarters of New York's Labor Film Service (LFS) and Seattle's Federation Film Corporation (FFC) in 1922. Company directors Joe Cannon and John Nelson were pleased with the initial success of *The Contrast* (1921) and *The New Disciple* (1921). Yet neither executive could afford to rest on his modest laurels. One feature film was simply not enough to sustain a labor film company, let alone a labor film movement that hoped to keep pace with the Hollywood establishment.

Despite the odds, the charismatic leaders remained confident of continued success. In addition to releasing a recut version of *The Jungle*, Cannon announced plans to produce Upton Sinclair's *The Brotherhood of the Rails*, an original screenplay "based on the life of the railroad worker." The LFS executive was also negotiating with German playwright Gerhart Hauptmann for the motion picture rights to his play, "The Weavers," and with the Interchurch World Movement for the rights to visualize their recent report on the United States Steel strike. Likewise, the Seattle-based Nelson spoke boldly of the imminent start of a *Labor News Weekly* that would place "two hundred cameramen . . . at strategic points throughout the United States and Canada to capture for the new film service the visual doings of labor." The former Warners director also remained hopeful of building a studio in Seattle to shoot future productions.[2]

Cannon and Nelson lacked neither vision nor ambition. What they did lack was money. American audiences had come to expect well-made films that featured elaborate costumes, interesting sets, and good production values. But well-made films cost money, and labor filmmakers had a hard time obtaining financing. It took the LFS and FFC approximately thirty-six months and eighteen months, respectively, to raise the $40,000 needed to finance their first films. Obtaining capital for a second production proved even more daunting. By 1925, a modest six-reel film cost at least $60,000 ($447,000 in 1990 dollars); first-run studio productions averaged around $200,000 and more elaborate films with established movie stars cost around $1 million.[3]

Cannon and Nelson soon found their fundraising efforts hampered by four key problems: the enormous time taken up dealing with distributors and exhibitors; persistent problems with censors; lack of returns to company stockholders; and the inability to attract new investors. Tight finances meant that Cannon and Nelson had to handle virtually every aspect of company operations unassisted. By contrast, Famous Players-Lasky employed six hundred people just to oversee sales and distribution. Without a staff to help them and unable to find a national distributor or theater chain willing to handle labor pictures, Cannon and Nelson spent months negotiating deals with states rights distributors (firms that handled exhibition rights on a state-by-state basis) and local labor bodies throughout the country. Many of the smaller companies he worked with, Cannon complained, seemed "unable to do anything" and were plagued by gross "mismanagement." Worse yet, instead of the usual fifty-fifty producer-distributor split, Cannon was occasionally forced to concede 60 percent of the gross to his distributors.[4]

A patchwork combination of states rights exhibitors, local unions, and radical organizations managed to get LFS and FFC films to the screen, but they did not generate large revenues for the production companies. "To make money," Cannon noted, "we must get into the bigger houses." Yet since many large theaters showed an exclusive run of studio films, the former mine workers' organizer found his greatest demand coming "mostly from smaller houses." Bad luck also plagued the LFS as the poor quality of its reissued print of *The Jungle* caused several exhibitors to cancel potentially lucrative runs at large urban theaters. By September 1922, five months after its release, the LFS had netted only $840 in exhibition fees.[5]

Cannon's logistical and financial problems were further complicated by frequent battles with censors. As censorship of labor-capital films grew more pronounced in the early 1920s, the fiery socialist found himself forced to spend considerable time getting his productions past local boards. When he previewed *The Contrast* and *The Jungle* before the National Board of Review of Motion Pictures, one member "became almost choleric" and "branded the JUNGLE as the most un-American picture that was shown." To placate the Board, whose approval was essential to reassuring politically leery exhibitors, Cannon was forced to change several intertitles on Sinclair's film, which entailed a further outlay of already scarce resources.[6]

Cannon's clash with censors in Kansas proved even more costly and time-consuming. *The Contrast*, which showed militant West Virginia coal miners winning a strike, appeared in the midst of a prolonged battle between Kansas miners and mine owners. The State Board of Censors banned the film in August 1921 because it laid "too much stress on the power of the strike and is chiefly labor union propaganda." The LFS fought back by hiring an attorney and suing the State Board on the grounds that it had "no right to reject a film dealing with a social question." Determined to stop a movie it feared would encourage further labor violence, the State Board took the unprecedented step of having Kansas Attorney General Richard Hopkins argue the case. "This is the first court hearing on a picture dealing with the industrial situation," *Variety* reported in February 1922, "and the fact that the state was represented by the attorney general shows that it is considered of great importance." The case dragged on for two years and was resolved in the LFS' favor only after the company agreed to eliminate "several scenes of violence during a strike, of a scene showing the funeral of a striking workman, and of a scene showing a minister denouncing labor at a meeting of capitalists."[7]

Instead of reaping profits from its first film and beginning production on another, the LFS found itself fighting for survival. "We have been pretty hard pressed," an unusually downcast Cannon confessed to Sinclair. "Money is awfully tight and this has retarded us at every stop, and now, more so than ever." The LFS field director had planned to finance *The Brotherhood of the Rails* with the revenues generated by *The Contrast* and *The Jungle*, but Cannon had underestimated the capital reserves a new company needed to stay afloat while it waited for profits to come in. Even under the best of circumstances, observed New York bank president and movie financier Dr. Attilio Giannini, it took the average "producer from a year to two years to get his full returns from any one picture." Exhibition delays caused by censors meant that returns would take even longer to accumulate.[8]

Once Cannon realized that he was unlikely to see any profits for quite a while, he began looking for other sources of funding. But where? Small companies turned to sympathetic bankers like Giannini for loans, while large studios such as Paramount, Fox, and Universal found Wall Street investment houses willing to raise millions of dollars on their behalf. Neither source, however, was inclined to invest in films explicitly dealing with class conflict at a time when censors moved to keep such films off the screen. Cannon approached a number of potential investors and European distributors, but without success. "There is an undercurrent in the moving picture world," he grumbled in August 1921, "that Labor pictures must be kept from the screen, and on several occasions the mere statement that a picture dealt with Labor conditions shut off further negotiations."[9]

With the usual sources of funding closed off to him, Cannon returned to the unionists and socialists who had originally invested in the company. But they proved no more willing than outsiders to give him money. When he began selling stock in July 1920, Cannon promised that "Dividends will be paid—good dividends." But two years later, not a single dividend had been paid. Problems with censors and distributors made prospects for future dividends equally unlikely. Labor investors were no more interested than capitalist investors in throwing good money after bad.[10]

The long-term success of the LFS required Cannon to focus all his considerable energies on fundraising activities. But by the beginning of 1923, the more immediate problem of feeding his family forced the white-haired labor activist "to take some outside work to keep things going." He spent the next several months dividing his time between the LFS and his new job working for the Box Makers' Union. Cannon managed to struggle on for another year, but it soon became evident that he could not keep the company alive. In September 1924, Sinclair, angry at the company's repeated defaults on his scheduled royalty payments, pulled *The Jungle* from the LFS and began distributing it on his own. A year later, in an article discussing the fate of labor films in America, International Workers' Aid film director William Kruse lamented the passing of the "bankrupt 'Labor Film Service'."[11]

In Seattle, the Federation Film Corporation's prospects for survival were complicated by similar difficulties in securing distributors and financing, exacerbated by the seemingly criminal activities of its director. Like Cannon, John Nelson pieced together a distribution network that relied heavily on the assistance of state and local labor councils. Sustaining this tenuous network, however, proved virtually impossible. Unionists around the nation were willing to arrange a single showing, and sometimes even a return engagement, of *The New Disciple*—the film about worker cooperatives. But their own pressing needs and the declining fortunes of organized labor in the 1920s made them unwilling to spend more time promoting labor film interests. To his credit, Nelson secured bookings throughout 1923, 1924, and 1925. Yet despite his supposedly extensive industry contacts, the silver-tongued screenwriter-director-producer was unable to forge a national distribution deal for *The New Disciple* or for his proposed newsreel series, the *Labor News Weekly*.[12]

Money proved even more problematic and soon emerged as a source of bitter contention between Nelson and company investors. The chances of generating capital for subsequent projects were complicated by the FFC's close financial ties with the labor-run Seattle Union Theater Company (SUTC). When the SUTC went belly-up in 1922, not only did the FFC lose a sizable source of capital but it incurred the wrath of small investors like A. W. Blumenthal of Chehalis, Washington, who lost what was to him the considerable sum of $105 (about $820 in 1990 dollars). Not surprisingly, Nelson's appeals for further funds fell on deaf ears. As SUTC board member E. B. Ault confessed to the livid Blumenthal, "[I'm] sorry that either you or I ever had anything to do with the SUTC, and trust that we will both have more sense in the future than to invest in any stock company."[13]

The mounting problems of running a labor film company and the lack of personal financial rewards ultimately proved too much for Nelson. The man was ambitious, but his ambitions were more for himself than for the FFC. By the beginning of 1925, the FFC had ceased its operations and Nelson was again living in Los Angeles, where, instead of making movies, he began publishing *The National Pictorial*, a new "monthly illustrated magazine designed to bring about a better understanding between capital, labor, and the public conscience." Chicago trade unionists were duly impressed with the first issue, which appeared in May, and expressed their confidence in "this pictorial magazine edited by this able writer and thorough student of human nature."[14]

Seattle unionists, however, were bitterly divided over whether Nelson was a true friend or a con artist. Residual anger over the failure of the FFC erupted at a Central Labor Council meeting in September 1925, when delegates from several unions denounced Nelson for failing "to make any accounting to their organizations for the thousands of dollars put into the venture by the unions here." Nelson's "loyal friends rushed to his defense, declaring that his sincerity is above reproach and that he lost heavily on 'TND.'" Given his prior arrest for misappropriating stockholders' funds while working as vice-president of U.S. Films in 1915 and his wartime arrest for smuggling guns and horses, it seems likely that accusations of malfeasance on Nelson's part were well grounded. Moreover, given the number of theaters in which it played and the many box office records it set, *The New Disciple* should have generated significant returns. Yet, as with the LFS, no dividends were ever paid to stockholders. Nelson, however, despite claiming to have lost money, did well enough to start up a new magazine. When the prince of chutzpah asked the city's Central Labor Council to endorse *The National Pictorial* that September, his former friends angrily refused.[15]

Not all was glum on the labor cinema scene. The financial constraints that hastened the demise of the LFS and FFC led communist activist and International Workers' Aid (IWA) movie head William Kruse to devise a strategy that kept radical films on the screen through the end of the decade. Like other labor film company leaders, the one-time playwright, lawyer, sheet metal worker was committed to helping workers "develop a motion picture field" that would combat the "pro-capitalist pictures" of Hollywood. Yet because most of the funds raised by the communist-dominated IWA were channeled into relief efforts, Kruse received far less money than either Cannon or Nelson.[16]

The New Jersey-born communist made up in ingenuity what he lacked in money. As the *Daily Workers'* movie industry analyst, Kruse was keenly aware of the difficulties independent producers faced in financing and distributing feature films. Instead of struggling to make one or two elaborate features, he focused on turning out a large number of relatively inexpensive documentaries and newsreels. As Hollywood features drifted toward fantasy, documentary filmmakers were garnering international acclaim. Robert Flaherty, generally considered the "father" of American documentaries, attracted widespread attention with the release of *Nanook of the North* (1922), a staged study of Eskimo life on Canada's Hudson Bay, and *Moana* (1926), which documented the lives of eastern Samoan islanders. In Russia, Dziga Vertov, Lev Kuleshov, Sergei Eisenstein, and Vsevolod Pudovkin rejected Flaherty's often staged sentimental lyricism in favor of a more class-conscious presentations of "life as it is lived." This politicized emphasis on social realism also permeated French, English, and German documentaries of the late 1920s.[17]

The IWA's turn to documentary was dictated more by pressing economic considerations than by a desire to imitate the political style of their communist brethren. When asked in a 1975 interview whether his reality-based films were influenced by other documentarians, Kruse replied: "I'd be kidding you if I intellectualize this. I had so much celluloid, so much audience, and my job was to bring the two together." So far as Kruse was concerned, "I was the first man to whom the term, the film as document was applied. It was before even Flaherty got his." Using raw footage provided by the Soviets and scenes he shot in the United States and abroad, the "Camera Man of the American Communists" managed to produce five feature-length "news films" by September 1925, including the well-received *Russia through the Shadows* (1922), *The Fifth Year* (1923), and *Prisoners for Progress* (1925). Kruse also turned out three one-reel documentaries and a number of newsreels released as special "Film Editions of the *Daily Worker*."[18]

Although eight films and several newsreels exceeded the combined output of the LFS and FFC, Kruse knew he needed more products to sustain a serious working-class film movement. Limited in his potential output as a producer, in 1922–1923 the Chicago-based radical set up a distribution company in New York, Intercontinental Films, and became the sole American distributor of Russian-made features. During the next several years, Kruse sponsored showings of films such as *Polikushka* and *Commander Ivanov*, which he cleverly renamed *The Beauty and the Bolshevik*, which attracted widespread attention. By October 1925, Kruse was distributing over twenty foreign films and newsreels that, according to the IWA's Berlin-based founder, Willi Münzenberg, were seen by "25 million people" throughout the world.[19]

Despite his modest success as a producer and distributor, Kruse, like Cannon and Nelson, wanted to go beyond the already converted and reach a heterogeneous mass audience. Yet he believed the best way to do that was by first building a loyal following among ethnic and working-class audiences. Instead of spending months trying to line up deals with large theater chains or national distributors, Kruse focused on placing his films in areas populated by his most likely constituency: mining camps, small industrial towns, and second- and third-run houses in blue-collar urban neighborhoods. Exhibitors in small towns who were "dependent upon labor support," he reported, "rented our pictures as part of their regular program." In large cities, declining revenues caused by the popularity of movie palaces drove many smaller houses out of business and made surviving financially pressed exhibitors receptive to IWA entertainment—which included a combination of Kruse's films, Russian-made features, and an assortment of newsreels. The manager of a Detroit theater that "has had poor business in his house for months, was breathless at the size of our crowd." Convinced he could "clean up big," he quickly asked Kruse for two more dates.[20]

Kruse understood that the IWA's long-term success depended on the continued willingness of ethnic and working-class organizations to arrange exhibitions in local theaters. Rather than expecting the working-class faithful to do this out of the kindness of their hearts, Kruse offered his local agents a share of the proceeds. "Labor! Make Money by Showing RUSSIAN MOVIES," declared one IWA advertisement. Being rewarded for doing good political work proved a great incentive. Finnish workers organized one-night bookings in small towns such as Rock, Michigan, and Sebeka, Minnesota, while Chicago communists arranged to show IWA programs at small theaters in the city's "Russian, Slavic, and Jewish sections."[21]

By the fall of 1925, Kruse's efforts at building a working-class film movement proved a mixed success. Spared the enervating rigors of raising capital to finance large-scale productions, the IWA leader forged a distribution network that brought his programs into 250 communities and attracted an average audience of 100,000 for each film. *The Fifth Year*, Kruse's most financially successful production, earned over $40,000 for the IWA. Local sponsors also raised tens of thousands of dollars that they used to support ongoing strikes or to finance the construction of labor temples and ethnic halls. When compared to the single-feature life of the LFS and FFC, these were notable achievements. Yet Kruse was under no illusions about the overall dimensions of his "success." The IWA, he confessed in September 1925, had made little headway in seriously challenging Hollywood films or studio control of exhibition. "Our enemy reaches fifty million people a week. . . . We reached ten thousand a week, once."[22]

Far from being discouraged, Kruse was determined to continue his cinematic struggles. Movies, he reminded his allies, offered "tremendous revolutionary possibilities" for attracting people who proved difficult to reach "by our ordinary propaganda weapons." But the IWA's optimistic film head never got a chance to finish what he started. Kruse traveled to the Soviet Union sometime in late 1925 or early 1926 and remained there until 1927, studying at the Lenin School and serving as an unofficial consultant to the Mezhrabpom-Rus motion picture works. Soon after his return to the United States he and several dozen comrades were expelled from the Communist party following an ideological clash with Joseph Stalin and his supporters.[23]

Kruse's departure, both to Russia and from the Communist party and IWA, was a serious blow to IWA fortunes, but it did not halt its filmmaking activities. When forty-five-year-old German émigré Alfred Wagenknecht took over as head of the American section of the Workers' International Relief (the IWA's new name), he also assumed oversight of the organization's cinematic endeavors. Although not a filmmaker, Wagenknecht had cofounded the Communist *Daily Worker* and understood the powerful role the mass media played in shaping the political consciousness of the nation's citizenry. Wagenknecht and the WIR aimed at the "50 per cent of the public" who did not go to the movies because, as Hollywood director King Vidor explained, they were "bored with the same old familiar formulas." The "only way to reach them," Vidor suggested, "is through a specialized type of film played in smaller theaters." And that is precisely what the WIR did.[24]

WIR filmmakers of the Wagenknecht era turned out documentaries that challenged the class biases of American newsreels. Tremendously popular during the mid-1920s, newsreels were regularly shown in 85 to 90 percent of the nation's nearly 20,000 theaters and probably reached a larger audience than any single feature. But newsreels were as heavily censored as feature films. Longtime labor activist Reverend Charles Stelze told how Pennsylvania authorities repeatedly forced news companies to cut "scenes showing the strikers in the coal regions of Pennsylvania struggling to secure their rights" or "depicting the terrible conditions under which they lived . . . the only picture scenes permitted being those showing the calling out of the militia to quell 'disorder.'" New York and Kansas censors ordered

Pathé and Selznick News to remove all scenes of strike activity at Herrin, Illinois, while another state board demanded that scenes of Communist leader William Foster be eliminated "because he had shown himself a bad actor in the steel strike."[25]

The Passaic Textile Strike (IWA 1926), *The Miners' Strike* (1928), and *The Gastonia Textile Strike* (1929), the three most important IWA/WIR films of the post-Kruse era, contested distorted newsreels by offering audiences feature-length documentary accounts of ongoing labor struggles. Taken collectively, the three productions were an important cinematic bridge between the melodramas of earlier worker-made films and the social realism that would dominate radical films of the 1930s. Instead of presenting political messages in the form of romantic melodramas, IWA/WIR documentaries offered straightforward depictions of class struggles as they were happening.[26]

Resembling newsreels in their content, *The Miners' Strike* and *The Gastonia Textile Strike* functioned more like entertainment films in their use of narrative and editing to build dramatic tension. Set in the strike-plagued bituminous coal fields of Ohio and Pennsylvania, *The Miners' Strike* chronicled sixteen months of bitter struggle by 150,000 miners and their families. Produced by Wagenknecht (who also produced *Passaic*) and shot by Sam Burke, the seven-reel film was made in cooperation with the communist-led National Miners' Relief Committee—the organization that helped the miners when the United Mine Workers' Union refused to fight against a devastating series of wage cuts. By showing scenes of men working deep inside mine shafts, of actual "catastrophes in non-union mines which swept away hundreds of lives," and of the destitution faced by impoverished families forced to live in tents, the film exposed viewers to a world as foreign to many as those inhabited by Flaherty's Eskimos or Samoans.[27] But this was not a foreign land, it was America, and that was precisely the point filmmakers wanted to make.

Working within a documentary format did not mean simply presenting events as they happened. Utilizing techniques similar to those employed by Russian filmmaker Sergei Eisenstein, Barbara Rand and Caroline Drew edited the movie in a manner aimed at encouraging viewers to identify with the strikers. By cutting back and forth between the hardships faced in workplace and home, *The Miners' Strike* showed in stark visual terms the adverse effects capitalist exploitation had upon the lives of working-class families. Audience sympathies were heightened by carefully chosen scenes of families being evicted from ramshackle company-owned homes "reminiscent of middle age serfdom," and "police clubbings and arrests" of peacefully picketing men, women, and children. Yet workers were not shown solely as victims. The film also included footage of their "parades and mass meetings," of cooperative efforts within tent colonies, of fights with mine guards, and of "miners' children waylaying a scab and beating him up with fists, sticks, and stones."[28]

A year after mine workers began their battle, 1,700 textile workers in Gastonia, North Carolina, went out on strike to protest increased work loads and wage cuts that reduced their pay to $10 to $12 a week. WIR organizers, accompanied by cameraman Sam Brody, traveled to Gastonia in July 1929 to aid in relief efforts and to document the strike. Like D. W. Griffith's early populist films, the one-reel *Gastonia Textile Strike* tried to raise viewers' ire with scenes of police and National Guardsmen terrorizing picket lines of women and children; of armed mobs demolishing union headquarters; and of families living "out on the streets after eviction from the company-owned homes." The film also contained graphic scenes of "wretched conditions in the workers' settlements and portray[ed] the emaciated appearance of the mill workers, many of whom are suffering from pellagra."[29]

Though successful as pioneering documentaries, these two productions marked the end of the IWA/WIR as an effective filmmaking body. It was Kruse who had built the production and distribution wings of the IWA and forged its modest but growing national exhibition network. Without his energy and contacts, the IWA's cinematic department, which was always secondary to the organization's relief efforts, was never the same again. When *The Passaic Textile Strike* was released in September 1926, Kruse's networks were still strong enough to place it in theaters, union halls, auditoriums, and schools across the country. But it was the last IWA/WIR production to enjoy such widespread distribution. Although *The Miners' Strike* and *The Gastonia Textile Strike* continued to be shown during the early 1930s, neither received the publicity nor generated as many donations as earlier films.[30]

The difficulties of sustaining an oppositional film movement were also complicated by repeated battles with local and state authorities. Virtually all of Kruse's productions and many of his imported Russian films provoked rabid reactions by censors who "so cut the films," gloated anti-communist activist R. M. Whitney, "that they were at last reduced to nothing but lantern slides." Pennsylvania officials ordered the IWA to make thirty-four cuts in *Russia through The Shadows*—twenty-two of which, reported one labor daily, "were found to be based entirely on anti-labor political prejudice." Chicago censors banned *Prisoners for Progress* (1925) because it might "incite riot and disorder," and *The Miners' Strike* because it was "prejudicial to a class of citizens, setting them open to scorn and ridicule; incites to riot, telling the audience to break the laws of our country." When the WIR district secretary complained to Windy City officials that coal and iron police really did beat up strikers, the censors confessed: "Yes, yes, it is awful, but you know we cannot afford to show the officers of the law in this light."[31]

It is difficult to know how many moviegoers might have gone to see IWA/ WIR films, because local authorities frequently pressured exhibitors not to run them. Charles Roberts, who owned a small theater in Monessen, Pennsylvania, described how police burst into a showing of *Russia and Germany* "with guns and ammunition displayed" and arrested him, his projectionist, and several customers and charged them all with "encouraging sedition." Captain William "Red" Hynes, head of Los Angeles' notorious Red Squad, boasted to a Congressional committee in 1930 about how he had "succeeded in stopping the showing" of WIR films by informing theater managers of the organization's communist leanings and suggesting they needed to "protect themselves against suit, or anything." When asked by the committee, "Under what law did you do that?" he smugly replied, "There is no particular law." Given the considerable opposition they faced from police and censors, and the limited financial returns they were likely to receive from arranging exhibition venues, WIR locals and sympathetic theater owners steadily reduced their participation in the organization's film ventures. By 1930, the WIR's ability to challenge Hollywood features or newsreels was marginal at best.[32]

Another Path, Another Battleground

The decline of the WIR and collapse of the LFS and FFC did not signal the end of labor filmmaking, however. Although no group was able to duplicate the ambitious feature films of the New York and Seattle companies, workers continued to make movies throughout the 1920s. But the same constraints that plagued Cannon, Nelson, and Kruse forced other labor organizations to alter the kinds of films they made and the venues in which they were exhibited. As Hollywood shied away from labor-capital productions after 1922, cinematic battles between labor and capital were carried on in the form of nontheatrical films (often thought of as "educational" films today) made by workers, capitalists, and government agencies. Exhibited in schools, churches, settlement houses, civic auditoriums, YMCAs, factories, union halls, mining camps and occasionally in movie theaters, these relatively inexpensive films were ideologically more dangerous than lavish studio features. Movies seen in schools or churches had an aura of truth and authority about them that films seen in fantasy-laden movie palaces did not.

Nontheatricals grew especially popular in the 1920s among organizations that wanted to reach large audiences for a modest amount of money. Lacking the stars or elaborate production values of Hollywood features, they cost only about $2,500 a reel to produce instead of tens of thousands of dollars. The declining costs of portable movie projectors and rapid growth of companies specializing in the distribution of nontheatricals made it easy to show these productions in a wide variety of settings. By 1923, 30,000 movie projectors were installed in churches, schools, labor temples, industrial plants, YMCAs, and the like. Six years later the estimated number of nontheatrical venues ranged from 65,000 to 100,000 (as compared to 21,000 commercial theaters), and the patrons for these films reached into the tens of millions. Unfortunately for unionists, noted one radical daily, many of the "so-called educational pictures" that played in these venues were "purely anti-labor propaganda."[33]

The companies most active in crushing unions and implementing the American Plan during the 1920s were also the most aggressive in producing nontheatricals aimed at teaching the worker, especially the immigrant, how "to conduct himself as a thinking individual" and not as part of a class. The Northern Pacific Railway Company responded to union militancy and calls for nationalizing railroads by setting up its own motion picture division to make films dealing with the "present phase of industrial unrest; the menace of what is popularly referred to as 'Bolshevism.'" The Ford Motor Company used the *Ford Educational Weekly* to discourage ethnic loyalties and promote the ideology of classless Americanism.[34] Prominent open-shop advocates such as U.S. Steel, General Motors, and Peabody Coal Company assisted federal agencies in turning out films, such as *The Story of Steel* (Bureau of Mines 1924) and *When a Man's a Miner* (BM 1924), that merged governmental messages of "safety first" with sympathetic portrayals of corporate concern for workers.[35]

Manufacturing companies drew on this vast array of industrial and government films to educate, entertain, and forestall unionization among their employees. Ford, Simonds Manufacturing, and scores of other firms built special screening rooms and ran a mix of nontheatricals, newsreels, and comedies as part of their lunchtime or evening industrial recreation program. Other companies arranged to have films shown at local YMCAs. Employee pacification was the implicit goal of these free programs. "In industrial plants where films were shown," observed one English visitor, "the men have remained more contented than they otherwise would be. Besides, the films took them away from Socialist and union meetings."[36]

As in the prewar era, the National Association of Manufacturers (NAM) took the lead in carrying big business's message to a diverse, movie-hungry public. In the fall of 1922, they opened a Motion Picture Bureau and launched a vigorous drive to provide, at no charge, carefully selected nontheatrical films to factories, schools, churches, and community groups. NAM's propaganda efforts were aided by the rapid growth of companies specializing in the distribution of nontheatrical films. The Instructive Film Service, formed for the sole purpose "of overcoming strife, strikes, and unrests of all sorts," reached millions of additional viewers by placing business-made films in regular movie theaters. Small neighborhood houses and luxurious palaces often supplemented their programs with films made by U.S. Steel, Westinghouse Electric, and the National Coal Operators Association. "If the regular theater program is loaded with anti-labor propaganda," William Kruse complained in 1924, "the non-theatrical program is saturated with it."[37]

Labor and radical organizations responded to these cinematic assaults by producing and distributing their own nontheatricals. Hoping "to acquaint the public with the less militant phases of trade union character," the International Typographical Workers' Union (ITU) produced a three-reel documentary in 1925, *His Brother's Keeper*, that contrasted the "lot of the down-and-out [nonunion] worker of a few decades ago" with the many social and economic benefits currently enjoyed by ITU members. The ITU film opened with scenes of the union's beautiful 300-acre, $3 million retirement home in Colorado Springs, Colorado. Viewers were given a quick tour of the home's comfortable quarters, dining facilities, library, croquet courts, and nearby mountain streams. Impressed by what he saw, one *Boston Globe* reviewer quipped that the film "should have as a subtitle 'The Realization of a Trade Union Vision.'"[38]

Adopting a far less idyllic style of filmmaking, Alfred Hoffman, southern organizer for the United Textile Workers of America, produced a hard-hitting nontheatrical in the summer of 1927 that documented the bitter textile strike in Henderson, North Carolina. Hoffman's highly polemical one-reel movie "caught all the atmosphere of the fight—the young cotton factory hand telling the crowd never to give up the fight for the 12 1/2 percent raise, the steel wire fence with its high volt charge . . . [and] machine gunners from the North Carolina National Guard." Claims of employer benevolence that dominated government and capitalist nontheatricals were countered here with scenes of the "cowpath street, oozing with mud; the [company-owned] frame shack houses, with a census showing one-third leaking. No plumbing; folks walk a block to a quarter of a mile to open wells."[39]

Nontheatricals did not have to be expensive or well made to be politically effective—especially when audiences could see them at no charge. "People like to go to free things," explained Boot and Shoe Workers' Union representative Collis Lovely, and once "they turn out . . . there will be an opportunity to reach them and tell them the truth, make them understand the present condition." Lovely told the AFL's Union Label Committee in May 1925 of the tremendous success his union experienced as a result of making and exhibiting its own film: "During the three years they had the picture they saw more people wake up about the union label than in the twenty-five years before." Adopting a slightly different and cheaper path, federal postal employees, Brooklyn laundry workers, and New England cigarmakers publicized wage demands, defended strikes, and resisted open-shop drives by producing elaborate slide shows and exhibiting them in local movie houses.

Though modest in comparison to feature films and nontheatricals, these presentations proved so effective that Brooklyn laundry owners threatened local exhibitors who refused to "discontinue showing the union's slides." Unionists and radicals in Los Angeles, Chicago, St. Louis, Philadelphia, Seattle, and other cities also capitalized on the widespread popularity of movies by screening films to attract people to meetings and fundraisers.[40]

Favorable audience responses to nontheatricals occasionally prompted unions to venture into the theatrical arena. One of the most ambitious cinematic efforts of the early 1920s was undertaken by the members of United Mine Workers' Union (UMW) Local 323, who were determined to depict the bloody Mingo County, West Virginia, coal strikes in the form of a big Hollywood-style production, complete with famous movie stars. For many years, Mingo County, the setting for *The Contrast* (1921), was plagued by bloody strikes and a state government that, as one newspaper observed, abdicated its authority "in favor of private armies of deputy sheriffs and outside detective agencies" employed by the coal owners. Only one lone sheriff, Sid Hatfield, dared oppose these armed thugs. In a dramatic gunfight on May 19, 1920, that left twelve dead, Hatfield helped stop company gunmen from taking over the town of Matewan.[41]

When West Virginia authorities decided to indict Hatfield for murder, the mine workers rushed out and hired a motion picture company to make a film heralding the sheriff's courage. The one-reel nontheatrical, *Smilin' Sid*, which starred Hatfield and featured a dramatic reenactment of his shoot-out with Baldwin-Felts agents, was shown at local mining camps and strikers' tent colonies around the state. When the UMW tried running it at a movie theater in the small town of Princeton, West Virginia, headquarters of the Baldwin-Felts agency, the local sheriff, according to county prosecutor Howard Lee, "feared that its showing might precipitate a riot between mine guards and union sympathizers and notified the theater owner . . . that the picture could not be shown in the county." The picture was so successful in boosting striker morale that a Baldwin-Felts detective stole the union's only copy. The detective agency struck a far more devastating blow in August 1921, when Baldwin-Felts assassins gunned down an unarmed Sid Hatfield outside the county courthouse.[42]

The theft of their film and subsequent acquittal of the gunmen drove the members of Matewan-based UMW Local 323, led by Sid's brother C. Willis Hatfield, to develop a script for a seven-reel feature "woven around the assassination of Sid Hatfield." Their plan was to bring the "struggle between West Virginia miners and the operators with their gunmen" to the attention of a national audience. Willis traveled to Seattle in April 1923 hoping to persuade the FFC to produce his movie. When the almost defunct company proved unable to accommodate him, the tenacious unionist went directly to Hollywood and managed to interest western movie star William S. Hart in the project. "Bill Hart," the *Chicago New Majority* told its readers that June, "is reported to have declared the scenario, as sketched by Sid's brother Willis, is the best he ever heard of. An English film concern is after the movie rights."[43]

Neither Hart nor the English company followed through on their initial interest. Although there are no documents explaining the project's ultimate demise, it is likely that Hart, whose relatively mild factory melodrama *The Whistle* (1921) came under the censor's knife, and the English producers considered this highly political venture too risky—especially since they were being asked to finance it. Willis continued traveling around the country trying to raise funds from unions, but with little success. It was not until 1987, when screenwriter-director John Sayles made *Matewan*, that Willis' dramatic story of class struggle finally appeared as a first-run feature film.[44]

The problems encountered by Hatfield and UMW were by no means unique. By the late 1920s, the enormous difficulties of financing, distributing, and exhibiting theatrical films forced all independents either into the shadows of Hollywood studios or into nontheatrical production. Even well-financed organizations like NAM could not break into the theatrical world. Although unions and radical organizations occasionally produced newsreels that were shown in local theaters, the larger struggle to establish an important niche in the theatrical world appeared doomed.

Last Chances

For more than two decades, workers, radicals, and trade unionists struggled to make films that would entertain, educate, and politicize millions of Americans. The demise of their quest to create a permanent oppositional cinema can be attributed to four key factors: the high cost of making feature films and the reluctance of relatively wealthy organizations to help finance or endorse them; the combined opposition of industry leaders who refused to distribute or exhibit labor films, and state officials who censored them; the reluctance of union audiences and officials to engage in "cultural" struggles over movies; and the coming of "talkies" and the emergence of the radio.

But it is important not to shrug off the collapse of labor filmmaking as the inevitable consequence of changing market conditions and the increased power of the studio oligarchy. There were three critical moments when far-sighted unionists and aspiring labor filmmakers proposed measures that would have changed the fortunes of the worker film movement: in the immediate postwar era, when several fledgling labor companies approached the AFL for help; in 1921, when rank-and-file convention delegates called on the AFL to open its own film studio; and in 1927, when the electricians' union advocated creating a national chain of labor-owned movie theaters. We need to examine these and understand not only why things turned out the way they did, but the possibilities for what could have been.

The first critical moment for labor filmmakers occurred between September 1918 and February 1921, when labor militancy was high and half a dozen worker-owned or supported film companies were struggling to establish themselves. At this time, it was still possible to make very low-budget films for $10,000 (about $75,000 in 1990 dollars) and more modest features (without movie stars) for $40,000 to $60,000 (about $300,000 to $450,000 in 1990 dollars). Yet with banks and capitalist investors unwilling to help them, most fledgling labor companies found such a sum beyond their reach.[45]

Desperate for help, four companies approached the one source that could have provided the financing and endorsements they needed: the American Federation of Labor. In September 1918, railroad worker-turned-studio president George Williams met with Samuel Gompers and asked for help on behalf of the newly launched Motive Motion Picture Company (MMPC). "Gompers assured us the support of his organization . . . both morally and financially," a company officer wrote MMPC screenwriter Upton Sinclair. The support never came. The following June, the MMPC appealed directly to AFL convention delegates. Seymour Hasting, delegate for the Motion Picture Players' Union and a close friend of MMPC Director-General David Horsley, asked the AFL simply to "endorse the plans of this company to produce motion pictures in the interest of labor."[46]

Gompers and the AFL were also approached that summer by Carl Clancy, a Los Angeles-based filmmaker and member of the actors' union. Clancy reported that his film, *The Smouldering Volcano*, "produced by the members of the Motion Picture Players' Union . . . under the direction of the Clancy-Super-Play Corporation," was a "big, thrilling, dramatic entertainment" that would be the nation's "first all union-made motion picture." Clancy had already raised $33,000 and asked the AFL to loan him the $32,000 needed to complete the project. Explaining how the movie featured "a union-man for its hero" and made "union-men the country over the savior of the nation's industries preventing their destruction by anarchists," Clancy promised to return the money and "a big interest in the profits" within a few months of its release. Avis Harriman, a former Hotel and Restaurant union organizer who went on to write and produce comedies for Universal, presented the labor body with an even more modest request. After moving to Vallejo, California, and setting up a labor film company that would bring "the aims and hopes of the worker . . . before the masses in a most impressive and lasting manner," Harriman asked the AFL for an official endorsement—something the city's central labor council had already granted. In return, he promised to set aside ten percent of the company's net profits "to build and maintain a home for disabled and destitute workers." AFL leaders received another request for help in February 1921, when after screening *The New Disciple* for Gompers and the Executive Council, John Nelson asked the labor body to endorse the film.[47]

Given the AFL's long-standing concern with the proliferation of anti-union films, labor producers fully expected the organization to assist them. From 1910 onward, AFL convention delegates had repeatedly denounced movies that presented "untruthful representations of labor's cause" and demanded that the Executive Council formulate "some practical plan by which we can get labor's side of . . . all questions before the general public through the motion pictures." Labor filmmakers presented the organization with a splendid opportunity to do just that. But Gompers and the Executive Council proved unwilling to associate the AFL with "radical" elements at a time the labor body was struggling to portray itself as a legitimate "American" organization. Because he was unable to control the content of the films, Gompers refused to provide any of these neophyte companies—many of whom maintained close ties with socialists—with money or endorsements. Labor filmmakers were simply told: "We appreciate the efforts being made to produce pictures showing labor's side in industrial disputes upon the screen, but so far as endorsement, this is a matter we can not do."[48]

The enthusiastic support of the AFL at this critical juncture would have given these companies a chance to test their films in the marketplace and, if they proved successful, to make several more. Aside from their enormous propaganda value, well-marketed labor films had the potential to earn a good deal of money. The "12 1/2 million members of labor unions in English speaking countries," Clancy explained to AFL Vice President Frank Morrison, formed "a tremendous guaranteed-in-advance audience for just such a union-labeled picture." If every AFL member took just one friend and they each paid ten cents to see a labor film, the movie would gross $600,000. To persuade distributors and exhibitors that unionists would patronize these films, production companies needed an official endorsement from the AFL and its 3 million potential customers—over 10 million if their families are included. "Without this endorsement," Vallejo labor leader P. H. Peterson warned Gompers in November 1920, "the big producers would kill this picture and it would be an impossibility, almost, to get a showing." Worker film companies could hardly expect to get the support of wary industry personnel if they could not even get the support of their own kind. Peterson's dire predictions of industry opposition in the face of AFL apathy proved correct. Lacking an AFL endorsement, labor filmmakers did indeed have great difficulty lining up financiers, distributors, and exhibitors. Consequently, instead of being part of a postwar cinema that featured a wide array of working-class producers, most of these aspiring labor companies went out of business.[49]

The worker film movement was also undermined by Gompers' personal vendetta against Joe Cannon and James Duncan, leader of Seattle's Central Labor Council and a supporter of the FFC. The two radicals led a movement to unseat Gompers as AFL president at the 1919 convention and, a year later, when Gompers denounced Bolshevism, they led a convention floor fight calling for recognition of the Soviet Union. Gompers' desire for revenge proved greater than his desire to challenge Hollywood. Cumberland, Maryland, coal miners were apparently dissuaded from investing in the LFS after receiving a frosty letter from Gompers. Likewise, when a Bureau of Investigation agent interviewed Gompers' ally Peter Brady about Cannon in January 1921, the New York City labor leader happily turned over a scathing AFL report that blasted the socialist for advocating "syndicalism and . . . sovietism" and opposing "legitimate trade union organization." Perhaps it was merely coincidence, but that same week Cannon was denied a permit to publish *The Labor Film Magazine*. The FFC's close association with the Duncan-led Seattle Central Labor Council (whose charter Gompers threatened to revoke) proved equally damaging to its chances of obtaining an AFL endorsement.[50]

Rampant hostility against communism and left-wing unionism further weakened the possibilities of enticing powerful AFL affiliates to finance or endorse labor movies. The United Mine Workers' Union, which in 1919 denounced Hollywood's continual efforts to associate unionism with "anarchism and bolshevism," seemed a natural champion for a staunchly pro-miner film such as *The Contrast*. But the UMW, like numerous other unions of the 1920s, was even more vociferous in its attacks against the kind of unsanctioned wildcat strikes and radical industrial unionism portrayed in the LFS film. UMW president John L. Lewis and his allies were equally hostile toward William Kruse, whom they disparaged as a member of the "Communist 'inner circle' in the United States," and the communist IWA/WIR, which they vilified for "distributing disloyal and revolutionary doctrines and propaganda . . . [and] promoting labor unrest and discord." In all fairness to Lewis and Gompers, their decision to purge communists from their ranks was partially a defensive response to the radicals' efforts to replace conservative union leaders with their own elected officials—"boring from within" as the strategy was known. "The most dangerous foe of our unions is not the champion of the open-shop," AFL stalwart Paul Scharrenberg insisted in 1921. "It is the small group that disrupts from within." For many trade union leaders, internal battles against "Reds" seemed far more important than common class struggles against anti-labor films.[51]

Although the radical leanings of most labor film hopefuls doomed them in the eyes of AFL leaders, it did not necessitate the death of labor filmmaking. A second opportunity to save the worker film movement came at the 1921 AFL convention, when rank-and-file unionists, led by Sacramento laundry worker Roy Burt, passed a resolution calling on the Executive Council to investigate the possibility of opening a studio that would make films depicting "the true principles, objects, and activities of organized labor." The studio "would pay for itself and its maintenance," Burt argued, "through the rental of its films to the exhibitors as well as the returns from the box office receipts of a chain of moving picture houses owned or leased by the Local and International unions throughout the country." Only by producing and exhibiting their own films, he concluded, could labor hope to combat the "hundreds of pictures that have portrayed in a derogatory way the labor leaders and those who were advocating organization of the laboring people to better their own conditions."[52]

Burt's vision of a studio devoted to producing labor films proved too expensive for the AFL leadership. After a year of investigating the matter, the Executive Council reported in June 1922 that the cost of building and equipping a studio would run at least $225,000, plus an additional $27,000 per year to pay for its maintenance. Leasing a studio proved equally exorbitant: at least $160,000 a year. None of these figures included the "salaries of actors and other expenses in the taking of a picture," expenses which they estimated could run from $10,000 to $1 million depending on the nature of the film and its stars. "We venture to suggest," the council concluded, "that this is not a field of activity into which the A.F. of L. can enter profitably either from a financial or practical viewpoint and, therefore, report adversely to the proposal of having the A.F. of L. enter into the field of producing motion picture films." The Executive Council also vetoed the possibility of launching a chain of labor movie theaters and spoke of the "almost insurmountable difficulties that present themselves in such a large business enterprise."[53]

The Executive Council succeeded in stifling further cries for labor-owned studios or theaters until November 1927, when members of the Hollywood electricians' union called on organized labor to "produce and display its own film stories." Writing in the columns of the *Journal of Electrical Workers*, Patrick Murphy, secretary of International Brotherhood of Electricians' (IBEW) Local #40, argued that the labor film movement could be revitalized by turning the nation's labor temples into movie theaters. Of the 6,500 labor temples and meeting halls in the United States and Canada, 1,500 contained large auditoriums that required little expense to prepare them for exhibition—just a movie projector and screen. Since few exhibitors controlled more than several hundred theaters, this would make the labor temples the largest movie chain in the country. "It can easily be seen that our proposition is a paying one, right off the jump," Murphy explained, "because we would have more releases than any other company in the world."[54]

By handling distribution as well as exhibition, the labor chain could eventually generate sufficient profits to "support and maintain its own moving picture producing" companies. The prospect of screening movies to a guaranteed market of 1,500 theaters would undoubtedly attract a swarm of eager investors. "When you show capital that you have the means to dispose your pictures," insisted one Local #40 member, "you can get all the financial backing you want."[55] With adequate funding, advocates claimed, labor filmmakers could lure mass audiences into their temples by hiring a Douglas Fairbanks, Mary Pickford, or Clara Bow to star in their productions. Big stars would make their movies more appealing, and more appealing labor movies might also make labor unions more appealing. By exerting control over all three areas of the movie business, organized labor could play an important role in determining the kinds of films that would be made. Hollywood studios and independent filmmakers would be far more inclined to produce pro-labor pictures if they could strike a deal with the union theater chain.

Would the IBEW plan have made labor producers as powerful as big Hollywood studios? Not likely, but it could have paved the way for a profitable company that, like Columbia, Fox, or Universal, specialized in producing B-movies for a niche market. William Fox, for example, built his fortune by making inexpensive melodramas and action pictures "to please the patrons of his unpretentious houses." The electricians envisioned pursuing a similar strategy. They would begin with six or seven films a year specifically tailored for working-class audiences. Only later would they branch out and try to reach "every class." All productions would emphasize entertainment rather than crude propaganda "because labor union people don't enjoy propaganda pictures any more than does the general public."[56]

Initial response to the IBEW proposal was quite enthusiastic. The idea was endorsed by a number of labor newspapers and, coming in the midst of a looming actors strike and Federal Trade Commission action against Paramount, "by some of the biggest independent producers in Hollywood, along with well known directors, stars and writers." *Film Spectator* editor Welford Beaton trumpeted the plan and predicted that its success would see the same producers who presently denounced the viability of labor films "crawling on their bellies to those whom they now spurn." Yet supporters also agreed with the editors of the *Chicago Federation News* that success was predicated on the "financial support" and steadfast commitment of local and national union leaders. "Labor allowed the first genuine labor movie, 'The New Disciple,' to perish for want of support." It could not afford to do so again.[57]

Unfortunately, Gompers' successor William Green and other leading union officials did not consider cultural struggles over movies a very important issue. Given the limited money they had to spend on organizing activities, especially during the 1920s, when membership was dwindling and unions were under constant attack from open-shop forces, AFL bigwigs were unwilling to support an activity they deemed peripheral to "real" labor struggles. Take the case of Dave Beck. The one-time Seattle labor leader began his career organizing the city's laundry drivers, was elected president of the city's Joint Council of teamsters in 1923, and eventually rose to become president of the International Teamsters Union in 1952. When I interviewed Beck in hopes of obtaining a first-hand account of Seattle labor film activities, he was able to recount his organizing campaigns but could not remember a single thing about the Federation Film Corporation, John Nelson, or *The New Disciple*. When I continued asking him about movies of the period and whether he remembered the ways in which unionists were portrayed, he brusquely snapped "Movies? Who gives a fuck about movies! . . . Why waste your time on something that don't affect your organization? You're a damn site better spending that money on organizing."[58]

Beck's response is quite significant. Here was a man as serious about organizing the unorganized as any labor leader in the country. Yet movies meant little to him. This attitude was undoubtedly shared by many other AFL leaders. Though they might grow momentarily angry about anti-union films, doing something about them occupied a low priority. Clashes between rank-and-file members who called for greater labor participation in film and officers who resisted it can be explained in part by generational differences. Born in the middle or end of the nineteenth century, men like Samuel Gompers (born 1850), William Green (1870), or John L. Lewis (1880) did not grow up watching movies as children and consequently did not fully appreciate their powerful hold on the imagination. Like Beck, they never quite understood that what mattered most was not film's effectiveness as an organizing tool, but its effectiveness in shaping the way millions of Americans thought about labor unions and their struggles. In all fairness to the AFL, many older radicals were equally dismissive of film's political effectiveness. "The road to revolution," declared the IWW's *Industrial Worker*, "is not made easier by the movies. It is still primarily a question of organization."[59]

Union audiences also share responsibility for the decline of the labor film movement. Despite its reluctance to engage in producing or exhibiting films, the AFL repeatedly asked its members not to patronize movies that were "prejudicial and unfair to Labor." Had the millions of men, women, and children with ties to radical or labor organizations exercised their considerable consumer power by demanding pro-labor films and boycotting theaters that ran anti-labor features, things might have been different. But the fantasy elements of entertainment ultimately proved more important to their daily lives than its political content or consequences. West Virginia electrician Bob Keck told how one fellow unionist chided his brethren in 1928 for "coming under the spell of the luxuries of life; the movies, the automobile, and the radio, and reminded us that after becoming an addict to these luxuries, we become oblivious to the source from whence they came—organized and collective bargaining." Indeed, trade unionists who were militant in their workplace activities proved unwilling to carry class struggles into movie theaters. Movie operators' locals around the country frequently complained about union families who, despite pleas and fines from local labor councils, continually patronized anti-union movie houses.[60]

With local and national union leaders unwilling to spend the money needed to convert labor temples into movies theaters, and rank-and-file unionists unwilling or unable to force them into doing so, the electricians' proposal was left to die, and with it died the last hopes for forging a powerful worker film movement.

Hollywood Triumphant

In reviewing the fate of the worker film movement, it would be a mistake to blame its decline solely on the internal failings of organized labor. As we have seen in earlier chapters, factors outside the labor movement were also crucial in thwarting worker filmmakers. The rise of the studio system and national theater chains in the postwar era shifted control of production, distribution, and exhibition operations into the hands of a few vertically integrated companies. "Unless an independent producer sells his product to one of the Big Three [Famous Players-Lasky, Associated First National, and Metro-Goldwyn-Mayer]," filmmaker Murray Garsson explained in 1925, "he is shut out of the opportunity of having his picture gross a revenue sufficient to cover the cost of production." Although reporters still spoke of the "inherently democratic" character of the movie industry, the Federal Trade Commission (FTC) thought otherwise. In 1928, it charged the ten distributors who handled 98 percent of all films shown in the United States with violating antitrust laws; a year later it charged Paramount, Metro-Goldwyn-Mayer, Fox, and Warner Brothers with the same offense for producing 90 percent of the feature films made in the United States.[61]

Survival in the new Hollywood was predicated on two key factors: the quality of a company's films and its ability to finance them. Though their scenarios may well have interested audiences, the politics of labor-company films made it virtually impossible for them to obtain financing. And by 1927, exhibition was virtually monopolized by large chains or studios with little interest in screening films that expressed "the labor point of view." Politically sympathetic local theater managers outside the chains found it impossible to show independent films, labor or otherwise, for "block booking" practices required them to fill their entire annual program with a particular studio's releases or receive no films at all. Even such a powerful star as Mary Pickford complained that block booking forced United Artists to take her pictures to the "cheap houses on side streets instead of picture theaters, thereby losing money."[62]

Many readers may be tempted to dismiss these economic arguments and simply attribute the demise of the labor film movement to its inability to satisfy changing audience tastes. This would be a mistake. The old cliché that successful filmmakers succeed by giving the public what they want needs to be tempered by the realization that many producers never got a chance to test their products in movie theaters.

Government opposition posed yet another problem for working-class filmmakers. Censors were unlikely to accept *any* class-conscious film no matter how popular it may have appeared. New York, Maryland, Kansas, Ohio, and Kansas censors aimed their most severe diatribes not at wanton displays of cinematic sexuality, but at movies—such as *The Contrast, The Passaic Textile Strike, Breaking Chains* (1927) and *The Miners' Strike*—which they accused of stirring up "antagonistic relations between capital and labor" and seeking to "undermine and revolutionize our form of government through insidious propaganda." Censors' fears of class conflict even extended to films that were several years old. When the IWA tried to re-release *The Jungle* (1914) in 1927, New York censors ruled it "immoral" and demanded three pages of detailed cuts before they would approve it. The IWA was forced to eliminate intertitles such as "They grind up the workers as well as the animals in their great machines. . . . The workers are the slaves of greed," and "Jurgis, lacking in class consciousness, attempts to go to work. His fellow workers prevent him and he is taught his first lesson about the great class struggle." Likewise, when the WIR attempted to release a recut version of *The Gastonia Textile Strike* (1929) in 1932, censors ordered them to eliminate intertitles such as "The Southern workers rise" and "Down with oppression," and cut scenes of "strikes, strikers and riots in United States—this includes all views of strikers and sympathizers picketing, marching, all demonstrations of marchers with banners."[63]

Given such intense opposition, it is hardly surprising that few labor filmmakers managed to produce a first, let alone a second, film. Two developments encouraged workers to embrace other media to spread their message: the arrival of "talkies" and the radio. With the success and rapid spread of sound in the late 1920s and early 1930s, it became too expensive for labor and radical organizations to make movies that would attract mass audiences. *The Jazz Singer* (1927), for example, cost $500,000 and subsequent productions ran considerably higher. The popularity of these talkies was so great that silent films, as one Chicagoan explained in 1931, quickly became an anachronism to be found only in small towns and rural areas. Even if they could raise the money to make a "talkie," there was still the problem of where to show it. Neighborhood theaters were the most likely venue for labor films. Yet the high costs of wiring theaters for sound—$10,000 to $30,000 depending on its size—and the onset of the Great Depression in 1929 forced many local houses to close down or sell out to chains like Publix or Balaban and Katz. Unions that had been reluctant to equip labor temples for silent films were even more unlikely to wire their auditoriums for sound.[64]

But worker struggles to produce mass culture went on. The same impulse that led unionists and radicals into film led others to embrace a new medium—radio—that was cheaper, more accessible, and reached a vast audience with less fuss and bother. Instead of spending several years raising funds and securing distributors and exhibitors, workers could simply write a script, go on the air, and enter the homes of millions of potential listeners. A new age of cultural politics was inaugurated in the mid-1920s as unions, central labor councils, and socialists across the nation began broadcasting regular programs over local stations that regaled listeners with songs, ethnic music, variety acts, and news of strikes, demonstrations, and important political events. The perceived power of the new medium was so great that the Chicago Federation of Labor opened its own radio station, WCFL, in July 1926. A year later, socialists in New York City launched WEVD (named after Eugene V. Debs). Yet the conflicts with industry and government agencies that characterized worker struggles over film were replicated in their struggles over the airwaves. Oligarchic national networks like NBC and CBS gradually absorbed community stations and forced workers off the air, while capitalists and their allies pressured federal officials to revoke the licenses of WCFL and WEVD.[65]

What Ever Happened to . . . ?

For a few brief years, a diverse group of worker filmmakers pursued a common dream of bringing labor's struggles for justice to the screen. With the demise of that dream, they scattered in a variety of directions. After the collapse of the Labor Film Service, Joe Cannon spent the next thirty years working on behalf of labor and the left. During the 1920s he served as Executive Secretary of the New York Socialist party and as an organizer and business representative for unions in the cleaning and dyeing, paper box, and doll industries. The 1930s saw the fiery radical joining with the newly created Congress of Industrial Organizations (CIO) in its efforts to organize the unorganized. From 1937 until his retirement in 1946, he served as a CIO field representative, chairman of its Distillery Workers Organizing Committee, and Kentucky regional CIO director. Cannon also continued his political work by testifying before various legislative bodies on behalf of labor bills and helping to launch the New York branch of the American

Labor party in 1936. The seventy-one year old activist died at his home in Flushing, New York, in January 1952.[66]

John Nelson's life took a decidedly downward turn following his departure from Seattle's Federation Film Corporation. His efforts to launch a national labor pictorial magazine in 1925 quickly petered out, and the one-time director was forced to take a job training Great Danes for the movies. In May 1928, Nelson returned to the public limelight when he was charged with kidnapping his former girlfriend, Jean Weston, an artist's model and movie extra, strapping her to a bed in his North Hollywood home, and branding "an obscene word on her stomach." After a steamy trial worthy of the *National Enquirer*, Nelson was acquitted of kidnapping charges. But the publicity apparently brought an end to his career and nothing further is known about his life.[67]

Unlike Cannon or Nelson, IWA film head William Kruse continued his career in the movie business, though in a very different role. After his expulsion from the Communist party, Kruse went to work making educational films for the Bell and Howell Company and remained there the next seventeen years, heading up a number of departments. When the company's film library was sold to Universal in 1946, Kruse went along with it and worked as a vice president in the studio's nontheatrical division. Abandoning the Communist party but not his commitment to political activism, the pioneering filmmaker pressured Bell and Howell to negotiate with unions and liberalize its hiring practices. In 1936, after Upton Sinclair and Sergei Eisenstein's efforts to make *Que Viva Mexico!* fell apart, Kruse, who was friends with both men, took the raw footage and cut it into a one-reel film, *Mexican Symphony* (1936), which was shown in a number of venues and included in the Bell and Howell catalog. In 1971, the National Audio-Visual Association awarded the former "Red" a special commendation honoring his fifty years of activity in the field.[68]

Upton Sinclair's filmmaking partnership with Soviet director Eisenstein was only one of the many interesting ventures that marked the subsequent career of this extraordinary radical. Although he failed to finish *Que Viva Mexico!*, Sinclair's ambitions to reach the screen again were fulfilled. His tragic story about alcoholism, *The Wet Parade*, was produced by MGM in 1932, and an earlier novel, *Damaged Goods* (1913), was made into *Marriage Forbidden* (1937) by the Criterion Pictures Corporation. No socialist characters appeared in either film. In between his cinematic activities, the protean novelist-journalist-filmmaker-politician-orator ran for governor of California on the Socialist ticket in 1926 and 1930, and again in 1934 as the Democratic candidate. In one of life's great ironies, Sinclair's close defeat in the 1934 election was caused in large part by a series of phony newsreels produced by MGM under the direction of Irving Thalberg. The pictures succeeded in scaring voters with staged scenes of thousands of tramps being lured to California by the supposedly easy life they would have under Sinclair's End Poverty in California plan. Disappointed but undaunted, Sinclair spent the remaining thirty-four years of his life writing and speaking out on behalf of a wide variety of radical causes. The ninety-year-old socialist died in Bound Brook, New Jersey, in November 1968.[69]

Self-proclaimed socialist David Horsley, cofounder of Hollywood's first studio and the leading force behind the Motive Motion Picture Company, went into semi-retirement after the collapse of the labor film venture, apparently living off earnings from the family's film laboratory in Bayonne, New Jersey. He did, however, pursue his political ambitions in Los Angeles by mounting unsuccessful campaigns for mayor in May 1929 and for Congress (as a Republican) in July 1932. Horsley died at his home near Hollywood in February 1933 following a lingering illness. He was sixty at the time.[70]

After the AFL refused to help fund his all-union film company, Carl Stearns Clancy abandoned his efforts at labor filmmaking and went to work writing titles for Robert Flaherty's enormously successful documentary *Nanook of the North* (1922). Instead of spending his career making movies about working people, as he had hoped to do, Clancy wrote scenarios for such films as *The Headless Horseman* (1922), *Six Cylinder Love* (1923), and *The Adventurous Sex* (1925). In 1928, Clancy produced *The Viking Ship, A Saga of Surging Seas*, a documentary account of the voyages of Leif Erickson.[71]

These men, and the many anonymous individuals who supported them, fought to challenge Hollywood representations of class conflict and offer viewers alternative ways of understanding the reasons for strikes and unions. Like committed activists of past and present, Cannon, Nelson, Kruse, and earlier labor filmmakers understood that nothing in history is inevitable. Certainly there was nothing inevitable about the ideological direction of American film. During the first two decades of the twentieth century, movies were as much a potential weapon of working-class resistance as a form of capitalist propaganda. The low costs of production and relatively easy access to the screen allowed a wide variety of groups and classes outside the industry to make movies that visualized their politics. Consequently, early audiences were exposed to a wide array of ideological visions that expressed the radical, liberal, conservative, populist, or anti-authoritarian perspectives of their producers. Yet as the nature of the industry changed, so, too, did the kinds of political subjects and ideological statements audiences were likely to see. The rise of "Hollywood" brought an end to an unprecedented era of political diversity. Suffragists, child labor reformers, birth control advocates, religious groups, corporations, and worker filmmakers were forced off theatrical screens as it became increasingly difficult to produce and exhibit their films.

The story of the rise and fall of the first generation of labor filmmakers ends in 1930; struggles for the screen did not. Ideological hegemony and economic control of the entertainment industry are never total, but are constantly shifting depending on technological change and who is challenging whom. Industry leaders continued to face challenges from a wide range of competing groups: employees who waged bitter battles over unionization and workplace control; independent exhibitors who called for antitrust legislation to end studio control over production and distribution; religious and reform groups that pressed for greater film censorship; and ethnic, racial, labor, and women's media-monitoring groups that sought to alter their depiction on the screen. Although early labor film companies were beaten back, subsequent generations of politically engaged filmmakers rose up once again to challenge the kinds of cinematic politics available to millions of viewers. In so doing, they, like their predecessors, provided audiences with something more than just entertainment. They offered people a vision of how the world could be—something certainly worth the price of admission.

The Movies Talk But
What Do They Say?

As the evening grew darker, hundreds of men, carrying union placards and torches, waited restlessly for their absent union leader to tell them what to do: should they continue their strike or go back to work? When he finally arrived, the Svengali of Labor worked his way through the crowd, shaking hands with the faithful, and then stepped up onto a platform to give a rabble-rousing speech. Gathered around him were a sea of men all dressed in dark clothing and closely bunched together. As the union leader got angrier and more animated, the men began punching the air with their fists. Within minutes, the tough-talking orator turned the peaceful crowd into a frenzied mob. His speech concluded, the union leader stepped off the platform and started marching toward company headquarters, followed closely by his loyal troops. As they advanced, the menacing mob was met by an army of company goons carrying wooden bats and ready for battle. Blood soon streamed across the ground as men on both sides of the labor-capital divide beat each other to a pulp; the less fortunate were set on fire with torches or smashed in the face with broken bottles. Massive explosions rang out as unionists overturned and then torched company trucks. Chaos, anarchy, and death were the legacies of this strike. At least eight unionists died that night. But for what?

Like countless films before, this labor-capital movie provided little information about why the men were striking. Instead, it focused on the drama and violence of the strike. Audiences saw unionists who proved incapable of measured response. Whatever the justice of their cause, once these men decided to go on strike they turned into a mob and their actions quickly devolved into mass violence. Although the film also showed episodes of management-induced violence, viewers were nevertheless left with a familiar conservative vision of unions as violent, lawless bodies, and union leaders as men unable to control themselves or their members. This is not, however, just another scene from another 1920s silent film featuring some long-forgotten minor actor. It is a scene from the 1992 film *Hoffa* (20th Century Fox) featuring megastar Jack Nicholson in the title role.[1]

Movies have "talked" since 1927, but when it comes to dealing with class conflict they have not said much that differs from their silent predecessors.

The conservative images and political discourse that characterized films of the late teens and twenties—images of corrupt union leaders and outside agitators stirring up previously contented workers, of frenzied labor mobs out of control, of radicals advocating violence and foreign "isms"—continued to dominate labor-capital films for the next seventy years. The triumph of the Hollywood studio system in the late 1920s and its ability to dominate the industry for decades meant that audiences would rarely be exposed to the wide range of ideological perspectives on class conflict that characterized the prestudio era.

Studio power was never absolute, of course. Independent producers and studio mavericks continued to challenge conservative visions of proper class relations, but their films generally occupied the periphery and not the center stage of the movie industry. And although leading studios of subsequent decades produced movies that critiqued the evils of monopoly capital and offered sympathetic portrayals of working people, few of their productions contained the radical politics or unabashedly pro-union messages that were common in early silent films. Populist films that condemn the miseries caused by individual capitalists have remained a popular legacy of the silent era, but films that challenge capitalism have virtually disappeared from the screen.

After devoting several hundred pages to thirty years of film history, I will not presume to analyze seventy years of sound films in a single chapter. Rather, I wish to revisit some of the themes raised in the Preface and examine how movies have continued to shape, not merely reflect, our visual understanding of workers, their organizations, and what it means to be working class. I want to ask why the conservative visions of class relations created in the silent era continued to dominate films of the sound era. At the same time, I also want to explore the possibilities for a revived worker-film movement in our own times. Would audiences today turn out to see radical or militantly liberal films about class and class conflict in America? What would filmmakers have to do to make this happen?

Although the conservative portrayals of the silent era dominated the sound era, dominance should not be equated with permanence. By disentangling some of the material factors that shaped cinematic ideology and looking at some of the problems class-conscious filmmakers encountered between the 1930s and 1990s, we can see how things could be different in the future. Labor-capital films may have declined in number, but they continue to intrigue producers and audiences. *Hoffa*, after all, was a major motion picture about a *labor* leader. It is possible, as we shall see, that audiences could once again be exposed to a wide spectrum of political ideologies that examine and offer solutions to the class problems that plague American life.

Continuing Visions of Class

In the seventy years since movies began to talk, Americans have remained confused and uncertain about the meaning of class. When *Fortune* magazine asked its readers in 1940 "What word would you use to name the class in America you belong to?" 27.5 percent said they did not know, while the remaining 72.5 percent offered over a dozen different class categories to describe themselves, the most frequent being middle class. Similar surveys taken in the 1950s and 1960s reveal "that most Americans think that classes exist, but there is little agreement about their nature and number, and there is great variation on how people of the same income and occupational level identify themselves." The same holds true today. America remains a nation with no meaningful language of class. As Linda Dittmar observes: "It is easier for us to talk about 'poverty' than about exploited classes, about 'termination' and 'downsizing' than about firings, about 'the economy' but not about class conflict." When Americans think about class, Barbara Ehrenreich recently explained, they "see the middle class as a universal class, a class which is everywhere represented as representing everyone."[2]

Certainly movies are not solely responsible for this situation. But seventy years of bombardment by negative images in sound pictures and television have contributed to shaping the modern paradox of class: we continually praise the sanctity of the work ethic but hold working-class people and their organizations in contempt. The dominant message of American film, black-listed writer John Howard Lawson observed in 1953, is "that working class life is to be despised and that workers who seek to protect their class interests are stupid, malicious, or even treasonable." Twenty-eight years later, Ken Margolies, writing in *Screen Actor*, observed how "organized labor's image on film ranges from inaccurate to sordid. Union leaders are depicted as outside agitators, inept nice guys, or 'big cigar' corrupt bosses. They provoke violent strikes, misuse union funds and dictate to the members." Likewise, Ford Foundation executive Robert Schrank concluded: "Blue-collar workers generally come across on television as sappy, dopey or foolish, and the labor movement is often portrayed as primarily involved with gangsters, cut-throats, thieves and bomb throwers."[3]

With such negative images of working-class life, is it any wonder that so many Americans cling to the image of themselves as middle class? And who in their right mind would want to join a union when their leaders are repeatedly depicted as corrupt and their rank-and-file members as blue-collar dolts? Why, then, would anyone want to think in class terms, at least in terms of being part of the working class?[4]

Labor-capital filmmakers of the silent era created many of the images of class that inform, or confuse, us today. But the range of these early ideological visions, like that of American politics, contracted over the years. Conservatism has dominated the sound era, with liberalism a distant second, and populist and anti-authoritarian films making only occasional appearances; radical films are hardly seen at all. In looking at labor-capital films from the 1930s to the present, one can identify four enduring themes: the indeterminate causes of class conflict; the working class as good-natured but easily manipulated dupes; union leaders or radicals as the ones who dupe them; and the need for outside intervention to solve contentious labor-capital problems. Taken collectively, these images have provided Americans with decades of condescending portrayals of what it means to be working class and have made being middle class a far preferable alternative.[5]

Conservative labor-capital films from *Black Fury* (Warners 1935) to *Reaching for the Sun* (1941) to *Slaughter on Tenth Avenue* (1957) to *Hoffa* (Fox 1992) rarely offered viewers insights into the underlying causes of class conflicts. Audiences saw lots of angry workers, but very little of the daily frustrations, injustices, or dangers of workplace life that led people to risk losing their jobs, their savings, and their lives in protest. Filmmakers preferred instead to concentrate on the more dramatic story of violence and confrontation; to present texts without contexts. By not exploring the roots of class conflict or union efforts to reach peaceful compromises, filmmakers turned their blue-collar protagonists into greedy, ungrateful, and violent people. "The view of the worker in the mass media," a 1973 government commission reported, "is that he is the problem, not that he *has* problems."[6]

The most long-standing conservative image of the silent era is undoubtedly the depiction of working people as easily manipulated by union leaders, outside agitators, or Reds. Adopting the basic plot line of countless silent films, producers, directors, and writers of the sound era repeatedly showed how wage earners were stirred into frenzied action by a corrupt union leader or some vile agitator—either a Red agent or malcontent employee. Implicit in this conservative scenario is the idea that American workers were quite happy with their good fortune. Consequently, there is no reason for strikes other than to line the pockets of venal working-class leaders (often seen driving Cadillacs, as in *On the Waterfront* and *Hoffa*) or to further the interests of Communists seeking to destroy America. In either case, the men and women who follow these people are made to seem very foolish if not down right stupid.[7]

During the 1930s, Hollywood studios gave the corrupt labor leader of the silent era a new partner in crime: the mobster. Union leaders, Mafioso, and other gangsters were repeatedly shown feasting off union funds and using threats of strikes to extort money from honest employers. This cinematic partnership between organized crime and organized labor lasted for decades. *Never Steal Anything Small* (1959), starring James Cagney, the criminal supreme of 1930s gangster films, opens with a prologue that informs viewers: "This picture is sympathetically dedicated to labor and its problems in coping with a new and merry type of public enemy, the charming, well-dressed gentleman who cons his way to a union throne, and never needs to blow a safe again."[8]

As agitation came from the outside, so too did salvation. Conservative (and even many liberal) films repeatedly presented blue-collar workers as incapable of calm deliberation. Even when workers have just grievances, as in *The Molly Maguires* (Paramount 1970) or *F.I.S.T.* (United Artists 1978), they do not know how to handle their passions and therefore their protests inevitably turn violent. Working people are rarely given the ability to articulate or resolve their problems; blue-collar reason rarely triumphs over blue-collar violence. Instead, filmmakers trotted out the old staple solutions of the silent era: labor problems could best be solved by clergy (*On the Waterfront* (1954)), government agencies (*Black Fury* (1935)), suddenly enlightened bosses (*The Devil and Miss Jones* (1941)), lawyers (*Our Leading Citizen* (1939)), or the clear-headed girlfriends of confused strike leaders (*I Believed in You* (1934)). The implicit message of these films was that while honest workers deserved rights and protection, they were not likely to find them in working-class organizations.

Not all "talkies" were hostile to workers or unions. Studios also turned out a small number of labor-capital productions that offered sympathetic depictions of the injustices working people suffered at the hands of errant employers, police, and politicians. Liberal, populist, and anti-authoritarian perspectives on class conflict appeared in *Our Daily Bread* (1934), *Modern Times* (Chaplin/United Artists 1936), *Dead End* (1937), *Grapes of Wrath* (Fox 1940), *How Green Was My Valley* (Fox 1941), *The Devil and Miss Jones* (RKO 1941), *The Whistle at Eaton Falls* (1951), *The Garment Jungle* (1957), *Bound For Glory* (United Artists 1976), and *Norma Rae* (Fox 1979). Yet, like liberal films of the silent era, many of these productions empathized with the plight of individuals but not with their efforts at collective action (*Norma Rae* being an exception). Nor did they attempt to explain the larger forces responsible for the hardships endured by millions of wage earners. Class problems were still portrayed in terms of corrupt individuals rather than a corrupt system. Consequently, all difficulties could be resolved either by the intervention of outsiders who called for harmony between labor and capital or by a remarkable individual whose sheer force of will could save the day. Frank Capra's populist fantasies, for example, may have made viewers feel good, but they proposed solutions that had little chance of succeeding off the screen. Capra's "belief in the small proprietor and nostalgia for a less complicated past," argues historian Frank Stricker, "excluded a faith in working-class movements" and "ultimately could not stand up to the task of defeating big capitalists and modern technology."[9]

To understand how movies shape popular consciousness, it is important to know what viewers did not see, as well as what they did see. Every year in hundreds of union halls, rank-and-file unionists carefully discuss whether they should strike for a better contract. Yet few modern labor-capital films show workers engaged in such calm deliberations; few show unions negotiating better living standards for their members; and fewer still show men and women who clearly understand the economic and emotional hardships that strikes entail. Did filmmakers discard such common scenes of daily life because they felt audiences did not want to see them, or were class-conscious images kept off the screen by people who considered them too dangerous for Americans to see?

The Shaping of Cinematic Ideology

The vision of class relations that dominated American cinema from the 1930s to the present was not necessarily the "best" or most progressive vision, but the one put forth by those able to exercise the most power. By 1930, eight studios—Paramount, Fox, MGM, RKO, Columbia, Universal, Warner Brothers, and United Artists—succeeded in beating back their opponents and seizing control of most ends of the business. "The Big Eight," note historians Clayton Koppes and Gregory Black, "reaped 95 percent of all motion picture rentals in the United States in the late 1930s" and controlled "80 percent of the metropolitan first-run houses, and all exhibition in cities of more than 1,000,000 population." The triumph of the studio system, however, made filmmakers even more susceptible to pressures that could cost them money.[10]

What was seen on the screen was never entirely divorced from what was happening in the world at large or on the studio lots. Pressure from external and internal censors, labor troubles within the studios, the return of yet another Red scare, and the studios' determination to avoid losing money all affected the kinds of politically charged class images that appeared or failed to appear on the screen. Film scholars have shown how several powerful conservative organizations, incensed by what they judged to be the excessively liberal moral and political tone of Hollywood films, pressured studios into creating the Production Code Administration (PCA) in 1934 and appointing conservative Catholic journalist Joseph Breen as its head. Thereafter, all scripts had to be submitted to the PCA and no studio was likely to handle a film without its approval. Despite the public furor over sex and violence, Breen and local censorship boards were even more troubled by graphic displays of class conflicts. "Time and time again," writes film scholar Peter Stead, "the left-wing journals showed how a blind eye had been turned to the gangsterism and sexuality which the Code was meant to outlaw whilst all suggestions of political radicalism were banned."[11]

The massive upsurge of strikes and union organizing that swept the Depression-ridden nation during the 1930s and early 1940s heightened censors' fears of class conflict and prompted greater self-censorship within the studios. The evolution of *Black Fury* (Warners 1935) offers a wonderful example of how outside pressure transformed a pro-union screenplay that was highly critical of coal mine owners into a politically conservative film. The original script, based on Judge Michael Musmanno's true story, opens with a scathing attack on the coal owners. After exposing viewers to the poverty and unsafe working conditions endured by miners, the script cuts to a scene of mine owners ordering an undercover agent to infiltrate the union and stir up a strike. When the company agitator succeeds, the owners bring in scabs (who are paid less than union laborers) and an army of coal and iron police. The latter's cruelty leads to a violent confrontation with strikers in which thirty-five people are killed.

The lawless activities of the mine company are eventually defeated through the efforts of the film's hero, union leader Jan Volkanik. When President Franklin Roosevelt learns of the bloody battle between miners and police, he asks Volkanik to come to Washington and explain the situation to Labor Department officials. After describing the events that led to the strike, the shrewd unionist tells the government how to solve this and similar conflicts: make the owners agree to a shorter work week, a minimum wage, and honest dealings with unions. Jan's testimony is quickly followed by a cut to a newspaper headline that reads: "NRA drafts code to settle troubles in the coal field." The film's message is clear: when given a chance, workers and their leaders can solve labor-capital problems in a fair and honest way.[12]

But that chance never came—at least not on the screen. After reading the script, written in the midst of militant organizing efforts by the United Mine Workers' Union, Warner Brothers' executive Robert Lord was certain it would encounter problems with censors. "You know, the capital-labor subject is an extremely touchy one with them," he told the studio's head of production. The members of the National Coal Association were equally touchy about the subject. Their executive secretary wrote PCA head Breen and movie industry leader Will Hays demanding changes in the screenplay. Breen forwarded the complaint to Jack Warner, along with the recommendation that he alter the film "to establish the fact that the miners have little to complain about" and to show that "working conditions while not ideal . . . are getting better all the time." Local censors, he reminded Warner, had repeatedly banned strike footage from newsreels. Bowing to pressure, the studio ordered a rewrite and instructed its writer to "bend over backwards to eliminate anything unfavorable to the coal mining industry."[13]

The released version of *Black Fury* bore little resemblance to the original screenplay. Jan Volkanik, renamed Joe Radik (and played by Paul Muni) was transformed from a savvy union leader who commands the respect of miners and Washington politicians into a vengeful drunk who persuades the men to strike only after his girlfriend runs off with a company police-man. The film never mentions any of the employer-created problems that led miners to organize and strike. Instead, the company is shown providing men with decent wages and working conditions. The strike, now portrayed as the work of a corrupt industrial detective agency, is finally settled by the benevolent intervention of the government and not by the union's leader.

Despite the marked dilution of its class politics, *Black Fury* proved too radical for many censors. It was banned in Maryland and Chicago for being "inflammatory and conducive to social unrest," and encountered problems with censors in New York and Pennsylvania. Warner Brothers responded to repeated run-ins with censors by dropping its publicity cam-paign and, in the words of Muni's biographer, sweeping the film "under the carpet. . . . It was as if Hollywood were saying, 'Fine! Be socially con-scious—but not that much!'"[14]

With pressure groups, state censors, and industry watchdogs like the PCA opposed to mildly controversial labor-capital films, let alone militant ones, many studios decided either to give their films more conservative messages or not make them at all. With exhibition generating two-thirds of the industry's income, studios that owned theaters could not risk having censors keep their products from reaching the screen. Although studios continued to make films about working-class life, they kept provocative themes about class conflict to a minimum. Even the "best of Hollywood films about the working class—Warner's 'social conscience' epics," observe Al Auster and Leonard Quart, "never went beyond depicting workers as a mixture of urban ethnics, taxi-drivers, bellhops, and chorus girls all looking for the main chance—a world of elegance that was epitomized by a snap brim hat, a doublebreasted suit, and a diamond pinky ring."[15]

Studio labor problems of the 1930s and 1940s also affected the industry's view of radicals and unions. When screenwriters and actors tried to orga-nize in the mid-1930s, producers charged that their efforts were "led by Communist" and "Eastern Reds." Studio heads refused to believe that writ-ers and actors needed the kind of protection and benefits that unions ob-tained for their members. "Plumbers may need unions," quipped MGM's Irving Thalberg, "but not artists."[16] Chicago mobsters were far more suc-cessful than "Reds" in penetrating Hollywood, and they did so with the cooperation of the industry's most important studios. Long before *The God-father's* Don Corleone uttered his now famous words, mafia thugs were making exhibitors and studio heads offers they could not refuse. The mob-industry connection began in Chicago in 1932 when theater-chain magnate

Barney Balaban agreed to pay International Alliance of Theatrical and Stage Employees Union (IATSE) Business Agent George Browne and his partner, racketeer William Bioff, a lump sum of $20,000 plus $150 a week for cutting union wages by 25 percent. When Frank "Nitti" Nitto, Al Capone's main man in Chicago, got wind of the deal, he demanded half the take and then arranged to have Browne elected president of IATSE at its 1934 national convention.[17]

The mob extended its tentacles into Hollywood in January 1936, when industry leaders granted IATSE control over all studio jobs except for sound technicians. The union's national officers agreed to hold down labor costs by accepting low wage increases for studio workers and suppressing potential strikes. In return, Bioff received $50,000 from each of the major studios and $25,000 from the minor studios. "Anyone who resigns from this operation," Bioff warned his new studio partners, "goes out feet first." The IATSE-mobsters kept their end of the bargain until 1941, when Bioff and Browne were convicted of extortion and sentenced, respectively, to ten and eight-year terms in federal prison. Joseph Schenck, head of 20th Century-Fox and the producers' liaison with Browne and Bioff, was also sentenced to a year and a day in prison. Although the studios tried to distance themselves from the scandal, a federal judge castigated them for participating "with full knowledge of the facts in the activities of Browne and the Nitti group."[18]

Finally freed from mob intimidation, members of the Conference of Studio Unions (CSU), IATSE's rival, moved to restore democratic unionism and reverse years of low pay by launching a series of militant strikes between 1945 and 1947. Studio heads responded by once again casting the dissidents as "Red" agitators and Communist dupes. In a scene that could have come right out of the original script of Black Fury, Warner Brothers hired private police in October 1945 and issued them guns, hoses, steel bolts, and tire chains to help local police beat back striking workers. The violence of the strike and the studio's eventual capitulation to union demands for a 25 percent wage hike, explained Jack Warner's biographer, ended his interest in making films in praise of the "little man." Warners lost the strike, but it won the proverbial war. By 1947, the studios, aided by Screen Actors' Guild president Ronald Reagan, had effectively destroyed the CSU and restored IATSE to unrivaled prominence.[19]

Throughout the 1930s and 1940s, studio leaders repeatedly defeated democratic unionism both off and on the screen. They did so by aiding the growth of the mob-IATSE connection and opposing unionists who tried to rid the labor movement of corruption and mob influence. Of course, the industry's complicity in this story was never alluded to on the screen. Instead, Hollywood spent the next several decades turning out films—from Racket Busters (1938) to On the Waterfront (Columbia 1954) to F.I.S.T. (United Artists 1978) to Hoffa (Fox 1992)—that depicted all unions as mob-infested organizations that did little good for the average worker. "Certainly, there is nothing wrong with portraying union corruption," remark two cinema scholars, "as indeed some unions have been and are corrupt." However, Hollywood, perhaps smarting from its own unsavory past, has presented mob control of labor as the norm and made unions the scapegoat for what has gone wrong with "the American Dream." Yet according to a 1982 presidential commission on organized crime, "fewer than four hundred of the country's seventy thousand locals, less than 1 percent, had been suspected of such [mob] influence."[20]

The government's postwar anti-Communist crusade proved equally important in shaping depictions of unions, radicals, and working-class militancy. In his opening remarks at the 1947 House of Un-American Activities Committee (HUAC) hearings, Chairman J. Parnell Thomas spoke of "the tremendous effect which moving pictures have on their mass audiences" and argued that "what the citizen sees and hears in his neighborhood movie house carries a powerful impact on his thoughts and behavior." Thomas was determined to make sure that Americans would not leave their neighborhood theaters talking about "isms" or "class conflict." He and his committee set out to rid the screen of all taints of radicalism and the film industry of all suspected radicals.[21]

The story of HUAC, of the Red Scare of the late 1940s and early 1950s, and of the blacklisting by studio leaders of all employees suspected of being Communists has been told by dozens of writers. I would simply add that the intense pressures placed on Hollywood by government bodies strengthened the industry's proclivity to link unionism with radicalism and corruption, and to denigrate the individuals and organizations that spoke sympathetically about class and class conflict. The two hundred anti-communist films made between 1948 and 1953 included productions such as *I Married a Communist* (1950), which showed Communists instigating labor strife among San Francisco longshoremen, and *I Was a Communist for the FBI* (1951) which portrayed school teachers, blacks, and laborers as easy targets for communist agitators. The intersection of Communist hysteria, consensus ideology, and postwar affluence, argues film scholar Peter Biskind, led filmmakers to depict working-class discontent as "a psychological, individual issue, not a social or class issue . . . prosperity, along with the witch-hunt, had made class struggle obsolete."[22]

After a brief resurgence following Senator Joe McCarthy's downfall in the mid-1950s, labor-capital productions virtually disappeared from first-run theaters until the 1970s. The social and political activism of the 1970s inspired producers to turn out a small number of films, such as *The Front* (Columbia 1976), *Bound for Glory* (United Artists 1976), *Norma Rae* (Fox 1979), *Reds* (Paramount 1981), and *Silkwood* (Fox 1983) that, taken collectively, attacked Red-baiters and offered unabashedly positive portrayals of unions, labor organizers, and radicals. At the same time, however, an even greater number of films presented millions of Americans with disparaging visions of working-class organizations, their leaders, and their goals. *F.I.S.T* (United Artists 1978), *Blue Collar* (Universal 1978), and *Hoffa* (Fox 1992) perpetuated images of the union-mob connection, and other films took equally hostile swipes at unions, strikes, and organizing efforts. Even the King, Elvis Presley, ridiculed union leaders several years earlier in *The Trouble with Girls* (1969). After being accused by a moronic union steward of having to drink "to forget the corrupt acts you daily perpetuate on the working class," the bemused plant manager (Elvis) tells her, "I think I should have you put in a home for the silly."[23]

In addition to preserving old stereotypes, films like *Blue Collar* and *F.I.S.T.* also promoted new ones such as "Big Business, Big Unions, they're all the same!" As *Blue Collar* writer-director Paul Schrader told one reporter: "In my mind, the government, the company, and the unions are all the same. They are the Captains of Industry, who rule the world." Schrader and others who express similar sentiments forget one key fact: business can fire workers, workers cannot fire business. Schrader's cinematic images of the comparable greediness of union leaders and corporate heads grossly distorts differences in their power and wealth. The average salary of the chief executive officer at 424 of the nation's largest corporations in 1994 was $4.3 million. The average salary of the sixty highest paid union leaders was about $160,000. Given such disparities, writes *Los Angeles Times* reporter Harry Bernstein, "it might seem both embarrassing and ineffective for companies to urge their workers to reject unions because of greedy union leaders." The same could be said of many filmmakers.[24]

Oppositional Filmmaking Revisited

Hollywood's domination of American cinema during the sound era did not spell the end of radical or oppositional filmmaking. Unions, radicals, and independent filmmakers continued to make movies, but they usually did so on the margins rather than at the center of mass culture. During the 1930s and 1940s, leftist film organizations such as the Workers' Films and Photo League, Nykino and Frontier Films produced newsreels that exposed American audiences to scenes of strikes and demonstrations they were unlikely to see in commercial newsreels. Likewise, worker-made documentaries and docudramas such as *Millions of Us* (American Labor Productions 1936), *The Wave* (1937), *People of the Cumberlands* (Frontier Films 1937) and *Native Land* (Frontier Films 1942) showed "unemployed man's awakening to the reasons for organized action in strikes and to the meaning of 'scabbing.'" These films, as one of their producers explained, "aimed to educate workers in the benefits of a union, the harm of strikebreaking, the power of united action." This new generation of radical filmmakers differed from their silent predecessors in two key respects that ultimately limited their effectiveness: they were filmmakers who happened to be radicals rather than people based in the labor or other mass movements who used film to mobilize members and potential members; and, they generally produced documentaries that reached relatively small audiences rather than more costly fiction films aimed at a broad public.[25]

After years of reaching audiences through radio, labor unions resumed their filmmaking endeavors in the late 1940s, but they produced nontheatricals that circulated largely among the already converted. Union-made films such as *Union At Work* (Textile Workers' Union of America 1949), *With These Hands* (International Ladies Garment Workers' Union 1950), *Twenty-Five Hours* (Amalgamated Meat Cutters and Butcher Workmen of North America 1954), *We the People* (AFL-CIO 1959), and scores like them, although popular with unionists, never achieved the broad-based commercial exhibition of worker films of the 1920s such as *The New Disciple* (1921) and *The Contrast* (1921). Consequently, their messages were scarcely heard by the millions of Americans who poured into the nation's movie theaters. From the 1970s onward, the AFL-CIO and a number of national unions abandoned the big screen in favor of producing television shows for local stations and lobbying network and studio executives to provide more progressive depictions of workers, their lives, and their struggles.[26]

It would be a mistake to attribute the decline of radical and labor filmmaking solely to misguided production strategies (i.e. making nontheatricals instead of theatricals) or to a lack of audience interest. Filmgoers, as I have argued throughout the book, rarely got a chance to see, let alone to express their desire for more radical films. In the sound era, as in the silent era, leftist filmmakers repeatedly clashed with a wide array of government and industry officials who were determined to keep class-conscious films off the screen. The difficulties encountered by the producers of *Salt of the Earth* (Independent Productions Corporation and International Union of Mine, Mill, and Smelter Workers 1954) and *Matewan* (Cinecom International/Red Dog Films 1987) provide two examples.[27]

In 1951, after serving a jail term for refusing to answer HUAC questions about his political loyalties, blacklisted screenwriter Herbert Biberman founded his own company and secured financing from the International Union of Mine, Mill, and Smelter Workers to make a movie about a recent zinc mine strike led by Mexican-American unionists in Silver City, New Mexico. Written by blacklisted and former Academy Award winner Michael Wilson, directed by Biberman, coproduced by fellow blacklist member Paul Jarrico, starring Mexican actress Rosaura Revueltas, and featuring many local union members, *Salt of the Earth* is one of the most progressive Amer-

ican films ever made about the ways in which a strike transforms the strikers, their families, and their community. Indeed, in no other American film
are the interconnections of class, race, and gender so powerfully drawn.[28]

Far more than just another movie about just another strike, *Salt of the
Earth* builds its dramatic tension by interweaving three simultaneous stories: the class conflicts between miners and mineowners, the racial conflicts
between Mexican-Americans and Anglos, and the gender conflicts between
the male miners and their wives. Like worker films of the silent era, these
highly political themes are presented in the form of a drama that focuses on
Ramon Quintero (Juan Chacon) and his wife Esperanza (Revueltas). The
movie opens with compelling scenes of the hardships endured by miners
and their wives at work and at home. When Ramon tells his wife of the
union's plan to demand safer working conditions, Esperanza replies: "If
you're asking for better conditions why can't you ask for decent plumbing
too?" But Juan, who patronizes his wife just as the Anglo mine owners patronize their Mexican employees, brusquely responds that the union has
"more important demands." For Juan and his union brethren, demands for
class justice are clearly separate from and far more important than what they
see as women's demands.[29]

When the Anglo boss orders the men to return to work after an explosion, the miners go out on strike. Company claims that the strike was
caused by "Reds" are countered by scenes of union meetings where men
calmly deliberate before voting on any action. Depictions of union picketing
contain none of the violence or loss of control seen in studio productions,
but show workers who are determined to achieve justice without the use of
fists or guns. When the company proves unable to incite the men to violence, they obtain a court injunction that orders the union to stop its picketing campaign.

The strike appears lost until the miners' wives and daughters, despite
opposition from many union men, vote to take their place on the picket
lines. Forced to assume the daily tasks of cleaning, cooking, and child care,
the men soon come to see housework not as "women's" work, but as work.
Class solidarity becomes strongest at the moment that men realize that they
have treated their wives as poorly as the company has treated them. "There
are two kinds of slavery," one recently enlightened house husband tells
Juan, "wage slavery and domestic slavery." Finally joined together as equals,
the men and women go on to defeat the company and achieve new respect
and love for one another.

Salt of the Earth's call for class, gender, and racial equality generated rabid
reactions among many powerful figures. During the course of filming, the
movie company was harassed by local vigilantes who shot at them, by U.S.
immigration authorities who arrested and deported actress Revueltas—even
though she had a passport and work permit, by IATSE's West Coast head,
Roy Brewer, who tried to prevent union crews from working on what he

claimed was a Communist film, and by Congressman Donald Jackson who, though he had neither seen the film nor read the script, spent twenty minutes denouncing it on the House floor and warned that if "shown in Latin America, Asia, and India it will do incalculable harm not only to the United States but to the cause of free people everywhere." And this was only the beginning of Biberman's problems. After completing shooting, he had great difficulty finding a lab willing to process the film. Once he overcame that problem, Biberman encountered stiff opposition from distributors who refused to handle it, from IATSE projectionists who refused to screen it, and from first-run exhibitors who refused to exhibit it. Although the film opened to favorable reviews and large crowds at New York's Grande Theater in March 1954, the concerted opposition of so many forces proved too great and the movie quickly disappeared from mainstream theaters.[30]

Like worker filmmakers of the 1920s, Biberman discovered that one simply could not earn a living producing leftist films about class conflict in America. Despite frequent public protests about excessive cinematic displays of sex, violence, and crime—whether in the 1920s, 1930s, or 1990s—such films rarely encountered the kind of fanatical opposition that accompanied *Salt of the Earth*. Little wonder, then, that few studios or independent filmmakers were willing to make such films when the chances of getting them shown and earning back their investment, let alone making a profit, seemed so slight.

One filmmaker who dared to offer audiences an entertaining radical production about class violence in America was writer-director John Sayles. *Matewan* (Cinecom International/Red Dog Productions 1987), based on the true story recounted in Chapter 8, portrays the efforts of striking West Virginia coal miners to defeat a powerful, anti-union coal company in 1920. What makes *Matewan* a radical film rather than a liberal one is its unambiguous sympathies for socialists and unionists, its clear depiction of capitalists and state authorities conspiring against organized labor, and its message that individual needs can best be fulfilled through collective class action. Yet Sayles understood that most filmgoers would not pay to see a movie unless it was entertaining. Consequently, like worker filmmakers of the 1920s, he presents his political messages in the form of an action-packed movie that builds to a dramatic climax right out of *High Noon* (1952) in which the sheriff and his union allies walk to the center of town and shoot it out with coal company gunmen.

Bringing this picture to the screen, however, proved to be a difficult and time-consuming task. Unable to find a studio willing to finance a leftist film whose hero was a socialist, Sayles and coproducers Peggy Rajski and Maggie Renzi spent three years raising the money needed to make the movie. As Sayles recounts, they finally pieced together the nearly $4 million needed for this "low-budget" film "from a combination of my money, distributor's money, outside investors' money, and home-video presale money."[31]

Unfortunately for Sayles and aspiring political filmmakers, low box office returns helped perpetuate the long-standing industry belief that audiences do not want to see class-conscious stories. The film's limited financial success, however, might be attributed less to public disfavor than to poor distribution and publicity. Audiences never got a fair chance to see the film. "In Hawaii," recounts William Puette, "the film was shown for [only] one week at the theater next to the state university, even though it showed to overflow crowds on the same premises as part of the famed East-West Center Film Festival."[32] My own experience is also telling. Unable to attend a performance during its initial run in Los Angeles, I tried to see *Matewan* several months later when it returned to one theater for a brief time. Unfortunately, the movie was only playing at 2:00 pm, the middle of the work day. So, I left work early on a Monday and showed up at the theater only to be told that it played just on Tuesdays and Thursdays. Consider how well *any* major studio production would do if it was shown on such a limited basis.

Despite the many problems faced in marketing radical films such as *Salt of the Earth* and *Matewan*, American filmmakers did not stop producing movies about class conflict. During the 1970s and 1980s, the bulk of these productions were made by documentary filmmakers rather than more mass-market oriented fiction film companies. *Union Maids* (New Day Films 1976), *Harlan County, U.S.A.* (Cabin Creek Films 1977), *With Babies and Banners* (New Day Films 1978), *The Wobblies* (First Run Features 1979), *The Life and Times of Rosie the Riveter* (Clarity Educational Productions 1980), *American Dream* (Cabin Creek Films 1989), and *Roger and Me* (Dog Eat Dog Film Production 1989) present moving accounts of strikes, organizing efforts, and corporate greed from the 1930s to the 1980s. Shying away from simplistic populist visions of one man rising up to defeat the larger forces of corruption, these films reveal the hardships entailed by working-class resistance and stress the need for entire communities to act in concert. Movies like *Union Maids* and Academy Award winner *Harlan County*, write Al Auster and Leonard Quart, "show men and women whose idealism and commitment remain strong after years of struggle and defeat. . . . These workers still believe in a dream, one that stresses collective decency, democracy and egalitarianism."[33]

Fast Forward: Thinking about the Future

Given the many obstacles faced by class-conscious filmmakers of the past, is it reasonable to expect a more optimistic future? Is a revived worker film movement still possible? Would Americans pay to see radical or even strongly liberal films about class and class conflict? Indeed, why should anyone care about the future of labor-capital films or about movies that challenge the dominant vision of America as a classless society?

American filmmakers have helped create a culture whose citizens either no longer view class as an important part of their lives or define the middle class so broadly that class no longer seems to matter. Whether rightly or wrongly, Americans see their ability to consume as a vital, if not dominant factor, in determining their class identity. Many perceive work simply as a means of achieving more goods, and unions as a relic of the distant past, something once necessary but now either an anachronism or a barrier to progress. Likewise, class conflict is a concept professionals and white-collar workers associate with blue-collar wage earners. Yet most citizens fail to realize that the high levels of consumption that have helped define modern notions of being middle class have come from embracing rather than fleeing from working-class organizations. The high wages, pension plans, paid vacations, and health care benefits enjoyed by so many Americans today were not *given* to employees by benevolent employers, as conservative labor-capital films continually suggested. They were *won* by workers and their unions either through collective bargaining or workplace militancy. Consumerism and unionism are not antithetical. Despite the deprecating messages of conservative films, unions have struggled to have their members share the wealth, not the poverty, of the modern world.

As we get ready to enter a new century, many "middle-class" Americans find themselves in a precarious position. The age of economic abundance and unbridled optimism that characterized much of national life in the 1950s and 1960s has given way to a new age of scarcity and pessimism. With poverty rising, high-wage jobs disappearing, and companies downsizing, millions of citizens find themselves in jeopardy of falling out of the "middle class." In a special March 1981 article entitled "America's Middle Class: Angry, Frustrated and Losing Ground," *U.S. News and World Report* noted that with "the exception of those in strong unions, most workers have made little or no progress over the last decade"—and that included numerous professionals as well as the vast army of white-collar and sales personnel, who all claim the identity of middle class. Fifteen years later, an article in *Newsweek*, "It's Hip to Be Union," suggested that economic troubles were prompting a wide spectrum of Americans to realize that unions were "needed more than ever."[34]

Labor-capital films will continue to matter so long as people continue to seek a better life. The worker film movement of the silent era grew out of a commitment to address and offer solutions to the complex problems facing working Americans. Frank Wolfe and Joseph Weiss did not make *From Dusk to Dawn* (1913) and *What Is To Be Done* (1914) in order to convert Americans into zombielike followers of foreign "isms" or to present unions and socialism as good things in and of themselves. Nor did they and other worker filmmakers wish to disparage the importance of individualism. Rather, their goal was to show how individual fulfillment could best be realized through collective action. We need to remember what they tried to tell us: that a people who are determined to change the world, a people who see the need to start with *me* but progress to *us* can accomplish momentous things.

Worker filmmakers and labor-capital films could once again play an important role in contemporary political life and attract large audiences. But to succeed, filmmakers would have to follow the advice offered by electrical worker Patrick Murphy nearly seventy years ago: audiences will only turn out to see leftist movies about class conflict if they are fun to watch. Unionists, he observed, "don't enjoy propaganda pictures any more than does the general public."[35] Audiences today would go to see labor-capital films if they were as entertaining as other features playing at the time—especially if their cast were headed by a popular movie star. Studios undoubtedly agreed to make films like *F.I.S.T.*, *Norma Rae*, *Reds*, and *Hoffa* because Sylvester Stallone, Sally Field, Warren Beatty, and Jack Nicholson agreed to star in them.

If Hollywood is afraid of going "working class," then the working class could go Hollywood. The best chance for a revived worker film movement is likely to come from well-financed mass organizations like the AFL-CIO rather than from poorly funded independent producers. Although union membership has fallen to less than 16 percent of the work force, its lowest level since the 1920s, the nearly 14 million members of the AFL-CIO still constitute a sizable body. The recently revitalized labor body could take a lesson from its silent-era predecessors and produce movies that would bring labor's message to the general public and to the people they are now trying to organize. Indeed, many of those targeted by today's unions are similar to the groups who once flocked to the nickelodeons: immigrants, women, blue-collar workers, service workers, and wage earners in search of a better life. By placing a special $10 assessment on its members, the AFL-CIO could immediately raise nearly $140 million, enough to make several big-budget films with big stars. Money and movie stars will not guarantee a film's success. But they would offer the AFL-CIO a chance to reach millions of Americans who might not otherwise listen to their message.[36]

Film is as important today as it was in 1910. Movies can help us imagine a different world, perhaps even a better world and a better life. Yet too many filmmakers use their remarkable powers in trivial ways. They can transport us to distant galaxies but they rarely send our imagination to areas that could alter our lives. We live in age where the adage "You can't fight City Hall" seems to dominate political life; an age in which voter turnout is abysmally low and shrinking; an age in which Americans feel powerless to change forces they often cannot see or understand. They feel powerless because there *are* powerful forces aligned against them, and because they have no *vision* of how things could be different. Imagine a cinema which, in addition to entertaining people, offered them a blueprint for change; a cinema that offered people—whether they call themselves working class or middle class—some idea of what to do and how to fight back in a work world that is constantly "downsizing" and making it harder to achieve the last remaining pillar of the American dream, home ownership. Like Frank Wolfe's long forgotten silent drama, *From Dusk to Dawn* (1913), movies could once again inspire people to change the world and *show* them how to do it.

Vision is a gift, a gift held by the best writers, the best orators, and the best filmmakers. Committed filmmakers could help replace the current politics of despair with the politics of hope, and replace the politics of pessimism with the politics of possibilities. That is the ultimate genius of cinema: it can take a politically blind population and offer them the gift of sight.

Appendix I

Select Filmography

THE FOLLOWING is a select list of surviving theatrical and nontheatrical silent films that I found especially useful in describing various aspects of class relations, class conflict, and working-class life in America. Some of these films can be found in several archives, but I list only the place where I viewed them. An increasing number of silent films are now available on video or can be seen on cable television stations such as Turner Classic Movies. The year cited is generally the film's release date. The following are abbreviations for film repositories and production companies:

AM & B   American Mutuoscope and Biograph
BM   Bureau of Mines, U.S. Department of the Interior, Washington, D.C.
EH   The George Eastman House, Rochester, New York
LC   Library of Congress, Washington, D.C.
MOMA   Film Studies Center, Museum of Modern Art, New York
NA   National Archives, Washington, D.C.
UCLA   Film and Television Archive, University of California, Los Angeles
USC   Cinema/Television Library, University of Southern California,
            Los Angeles
video   films available on video or seen on cable television

The Adventurer (Mutual 1917) video

Amarilly of Clothes Line Alley (Pickford 1918) LC

An American in the Making (BM 1913) NA

America's Answer (Committee on Public Information 1918) NA

Beggar on Horseback (Famous Players-Lasky 1925) LC

Behind the Scenes in the Machine Age (Women's Bureau 1931) NA

Behind the Screen (Mutual 1916) video

Bell Boy 13 (Ince 1923) UCLA

The Big Idea (Pathé 1924) UCLA

Bill Joins the WWWs (Komic 1915) LC

Bolshevism on Trial (Mayflower 1919) LC

The Bomb (Gaumont 1907) LC

Boomerang (National Film Corp. 1919) EH

The Burning Question (Catholic Art Association 1919) USC

By Man's Law (Biograph 1913) USC

Censorship and Its Absurdities (Edison 1915) LC

A Child of the Ghetto (Biograph 1910) LC

Children of Eve (Edison 1915) LC

Children Who Labor (Edison 1912) MOMA

Coal Heavers (Hepworth 1904) LC

The Coal Strike (AM & B 1905) LC

The Coal Trust and the Winter Sun (Inkwell c. 1910–1919) LC

A Corner in Wheat (Biograph 1909) LC
The Cossack Whip (Edison 1916) EH
The Count (Mutual 1916) video
Courage of the Commonplace (Edison 1917) LC
The Crime of Carelessness (Edison 1912) MOMA
The Crowd (MGM 1928) video
The Cry of the Children (Thanhouser 1912) EH
The Cure (Mutual 1917) video
The Customary Two Weeks (Edison 1917) LC

Dangerous Hours (Ince 1920) LC
Dough and Dynamite (Keystone 1914) LC
The Dressmakers Accident (AM & B 1903) LC
The Dynamiters (IMP 1911) LC

Easy Street (Mutual 1917) video
The End of the Road (American Social Hygiene Association 1919) NA
The Eternal Mother (Biograph 1912) USC
The Eviction (Gaumont 1904) LC

False Gods (Rothapfel 1919) LC
Fighting Odds (Goldwyn 1917) MOMA
The Fireman (Mutual 1916) video
First Love (Realart 1921) LC
The Floorwalker (Mutual 1916) video
Ford Weeklies (Ford Motor Company 1918–1924) NA
From the Submerged (Essanay 1912) LC

The General (Schenck 1927) video
Girl Shy (Lloyd 1924) video
The Girl at the Cupola (Selig 1912) LC
The Gold Rush (Chaplin 1925) video
The Good Boss (Pathé Frères 1910) LC
The Great Mine Disaster (Éclair 1911) LC
Greed (MGM 1925) video

His Mother's Boy (Ince 1917) UCLA
His People (Universal-Jewel 1925) LC
The Hoodlum (Pickford 1919) Silent Movie Theater, Los Angeles
Hot Water (Lloyd 1924) video
How Hubby Got a Raise (Biograph 1910) LC
Humoresque (Cosmopolitan 1920) UCLA
The Hypocrites (Bosworth 1914) LC

The Iconoclast (Biograph 1910) LC
The Idle Class (Chaplin 1921) video
The Idler (Pathé Frères 1908) EH
The Immigrant (Mutual 1917) video
In the Watches of the Night (Biograph 1909) LC
The Incendiary Foreman (Pathé Frères 1908) LC
The Incorrigible Dukane (Famous Players 1915) EH
Intolerance (Wark 1916) USC
The Italian (N.Y. Motion Pictures 1915) LC

Johanna Enlists (Pickford 1918) EH

The Kid (Chaplin 1921) video
The Kleptomaniac (Edison 1905) LC

Labor's Reward (American Federation of Labor 1925) UCLA
Land of Opportunity (Selznick 1920) LC
Lawrence Mills, Lawrence Mass (Edison c. 1904–5) LC
Life's Greatest Problem (Blackton 1918) LC (re-released as *Safe for Democracy*)
The Lily of the Tenements (Biograph 1911) LC
The Little Church around the Corner (Warner 1923) LC
Live and Let Live (BM 1924) NA

A Man's a Man (Solax 1912) EH
The Mark of Zorro (Fairbanks 1920) LC
Martin Eden (Bosworth 1914) LC

The Mill Girl (Vitagraph 1907) MOMA

The Miller's Daughter (Edison 1905)
MOMA

The Miner's Lesson (BM 1914) NA

The Miser's Heart (Biograph 1911) LC

More Pay—Less Work (Fox 1926) UCLA

Morganson's Finish (Tiffany 1926) LC

The Mother and the Law (Griffith 1919)
UCLA

The Musketeers of Pig Alley (Biograph
1912) USC

Never Weaken (Pathé 1923) video

The Nihilists (AM & B 1905) LC

The Non-Union Bill Poster (Paley &
Steiner 1905) LC

The Non-Union Paper Hanger (AM & B
1902) LC

Nurse Marjorie (Realart 1920) LC

Old Isaacs the Pawnbroker (AM & B
1908) MOMA

One A.M. (Mutual 1916) video

One Is Business, the Other Crime (Biograph 1912) LC

One Kind of Wireless (Edison 1917) LC

One Night and Then (Biograph 1910) LC

Orchids and Ermine (First National
1927) LC

Orphans of the Storm (Griffith 1921) EH

Our Children (Children's Bureau 1919)
NA

Passaic Textile Strike (International
Workers Aid 1926) MOMA

Patria (Wharton 1917) MOMA

The Pawnshop (Mutual 1916) video

Pay Day (Chaplin 1922) MOMA

The Paymaster (AM & B 1906) LC

Physical Culture Lesson (AM & B 1906)
LC

The Pillars of Society (Thanhouser 1911)
EH

A Plain Song (Biograph 1910) LC

Playing Dead (Vitagraph 1915) LC

A Poor Relation (Klaw & Erlanger 1914)
LC

The Ragamuffin (Lasky 1916) EH

The Reckoning (AM & B 1908) LC

Revolution In Odessa (Pathé Frères 1906)
MOMA

The Rink (Mutual 1916) video

Robin Hood (Fairbanks 1922) UCLA

Rose O'Salem Town (Biograph 1910)
MOMA

The Royal Pauper (Edison 1917) LC

Safety Last (Roach 1923) MOMA

Safety Lessons in Metal Mining (BM
1914) NA

Sanitation in Mining Villages (BM c.
1915) NA

Saturday Night (Famous Players-Lasky
1922) EH

The Sausage Machine (AM & B 1902)
LC

Sherlock Jr. (Keaton 1924) video/cable

Shoes (Bluebird 1916) LC

Simple Charity (Biograph 1910) LC

The Skyscrapers (AM & B 1906) LC

Smouldering Fires (Universal 1925) LC

Song of the Shirt (AM & B 1908) LC

Speedy (Lloyd 1928) video

Spirit Awakened (Biograph 1912)
MOMA

The Steel King (World Film Corp. 1919)
LC

The Story of Asbestos (BM 1921) NA

The Story of Lead Smelting (BM 1925)
NA

The Story of Steel (BM 1924) NA

Straight from Paris (Equity 1921) LC

Suffragette in Spite of Himself (Edison
1912) LC

The Tempest (Schenck 1928) EH

The Test of Friendship (AM & B 1908)
LC

Tol'able David (Inspiration 1921) UCLA

Tour of the Thomas Ince Studios (Ince
1922) MOMA

Traffic in Souls (IMP 1913) LC

The Transgressor (Catholic Art Association 1918) UCLA

The Triumph (Famous Players-Lasky 1924) EH

The Tunnel Workers (AM & B 1906) LC

Two Cents Worth of Happiness (U.S. Post Office 1921) NA

The Two Paths (Biograph 1911) LC

Twelve Points of Safety (BM 1926) NA

The Unbeliever (Edison 1918) LC

Union Iron Works (Edison 1898) LC

The Unwritten Law (Lubin 1907) EH

The Usurer (Biograph 1910) LC

The Vagabond (Mutual 1916) video

The Voice of the Violin (AM & B 1909) MOMA

The Volga Boatman (DeMille 1926) EH

The Wages of Sin (Klaw & Erlanger 1914) LC

What Demoralized the Barber (Edison 1901) LC

What Shall We Do with Our Old? (Biograph 1911) UCLA

When a Man's a Miner (BM 1924) NA

When Wages Stop (BM c.1923) NA

The Whistle (Hart 1921) LC

Who Pays? (Balboa Amusement Co. 1915) Episodes #9, 12, UCLA

Why Worry? (Roach 1923) cable

Within the Gates (Women's Bureau 1930) NA

Witness Mockefeller (Inkwell c. 1910–1919) LC

Won through Merit (Edison 1915) NA

Work (Essanay 1915) MOMA

The Workman's Lesson (Edison 1912) LC

Appendix II

Sources and Methods for
Writing Film History

To UNDERSTAND the forces that shaped the subject matter, ideology, and politics of American film, scholars need to continue reconceptualizing their approach to writing film history and expand their vision of what constitutes a useful source. The histories of the worker film movement and of the protracted class battles surrounding early American cinema have remained underexplored for so many years largely because cinema scholars tended to ignore nonfilm sources such as labor newspapers, union records, and government documents, while working-class and political historians slighted the important role that movies played in shaping attitudes toward class and class conflict. With the recent publication of several volumes in Scribner's History of American Cinema and historically grounded works by Miriam Hansen, Charles Musser, Douglas Gomery, and others (see Preface note 9), the long-standing chasm between history and cinema studies is slowly being bridged. But more needs to be done. Writing good film history demands that greater numbers of scholars adopt an interdisciplinary approach that integrates text and context, theory and empiricism, and visual and written sources. But where does one start their research and what kinds of sources should one look at?

Although specific approaches and sources for writing film history will vary depending upon the questions one asks, this bibliographical essay offers one possible research model for unraveling and analyzing the complex forces that shaped the dominant ideology and political direction of American film. Why, for example, did silent films about class conflict take the ideological forms they did? Who is responsible for shaping the politics of American films? How did clashes among worker filmmakers, movie industry leaders, studio workers, government agencies, censors, audiences, and employers' associations affect the kinds of political messages people were likely to see on the screen? How and why did cinematic depictions of class relations change over time? What does a close examination of the movie industry tell us about the ways in which a broadly conceived "ruling class" establishes and maintains hegemonic control over mass culture?

To answer these questions we need to venture beyond the screen and examine the circumstances under which real men and women shaped the course of the film industry. The ideological content of silent film cannot be understood apart from the economic, political, and class struggles that gripped the movie industry and American society at various points in time. In researching and writing this book, I employed an interactive, materialist model of historical analysis that envisioned movies and their ideologies as the products of the *simultaneous development and intersection* of several closely related forces. My readings in cultural theory and research in the history of the movie industry helped me identify five factors that were especially vital in shaping the class character of American cinema: the evolving structures and needs of the movie industry; the changing composition of its audience; the general political climate in which the movie industry operated; the specific pressures government officials placed on filmmakers to alter their ideological messages; and the changing nature of labor relations within the studios. I began my research in linear fashion by trying to understand the history of each of these factors. Yet I also knew that while each factor evolved in its own distinct way, like the circles in a Venn diagram they also overlapped at certain points to create a common field of intersection. My research goal was to identify those points of intersection and see how they interacted to shape the images and ideologies audiences saw on the screen.

Writing good film history requires moving back and forth between empirical research and reading theory, for "facts" rarely speak on their own. Recent works in cultural studies can help scholars understand what to look for and how to interpret their findings. Indeed, these lively debates sharpened my understanding of the political significance of mass culture and helped me clarify the interplay of culture, politics, power, and class. Reading through the often complex, jargon-laden theoretical literature on film and mass culture can be a daunting task. Yet understanding these debates is important, for they show how movies can be used to support or challenge the dominant political ideas of a society. To help readers unfamiliar with this literature, I offer a brief synopsis of some of these debates.

Since the late 1920s, American scholars of mass culture, and of movies in particular, have generally focused on one of five themes: mass culture as a form of social control or escapism; how movies shape or reflect society; the presentation of "images" on the screen of women, blacks, immigrants, or ethnic groups; how the so-called masses reinterpret and use mass culture to serve their own needs; the material circumstances involved in producing mass culture. Until the past few decades, theorists and historians neglected the last two themes and emphasized what they viewed as the "manipulative" powers of mass culture. Movies, radio, and television were seen as activities imposed on audiences. There was little sense of how ordinary men and women responded to these new cultural endeavors; workers were simply seen as easily duped, passive consumers of culture.

These early views of mass culture and their implicit contempt for the intelligence of audiences are partly attributable to the long-standing influence of Frankfurt School theorists and uncritical applications of Antonio Gramsci's concept of hegemony. Writing in the 1930s and 1940s, when European fascism and American mass culture appeared to pose major threats to democracy, German theorists like Max Horkheimer, Theodor Adorno, Leo Lowenthal, and Herbert Marcuse (collectively known as the Frankfurt School) portrayed mass culture as a degraded entity used by ruling groups to manipulate, pacify, and control populations. Having fled from Nazi Germany to America, they saw parallels between European totalitarian regimes and the hidden manipulations of Hollywood; they saw how Adolph Hitler and Joseph Stalin had used film to glamorize their systems and how Hollywood studios used film to glamorize capitalism. Even in America, they argued, ruling elites and powerful capitalists employed mass culture to set the dominant values of society and deflect major political challenges to the status quo. These elites also used mass culture to homogenize ethnic and working-class values, and to portray bourgeois values—that is, values set by the dominant capitalist elite—as classless "American" values. Among the Frankfurt School, only Walter Benjamin stressed the liberating possibilities of mass culture and its potential uses by workers to promote greater class consciousness. But until recently, his theories and influence were overshadowed by those of his colleagues.

Those interested in learning more about the Frankfurt School might begin with the following works: Tom Bottomore, *The Frankfurt School* (London 1984); Martin Jay, *The Dialectical Imagination: A History of the Frankfurt School and the Institute of Social Research, 1923–1950* (Boston, 1973); David Held, *Introduction to Critical Theory: Horkheimer to Habermas* (Berkeley, 1980); Susan Buck-Morss, *The Origin of Negative Dialectics: Theodor W. Adorno, Walter Benjamin and the Frankfurt School* (Sussex, England, 1977). For key works by Frankfurt School members, see Herbert Marcuse, *One Dimensional Man* (London, 1968); Theodor Adorno, *The Culture Industry* (London, 1991); and the sources cited in Preface note 7.

These dark views of mass culture were kept alive by New York intellectuals of the 1940s, 1950s, and 1960s, many of whom were affected by the anti-communist Cold War mentality of the times, and by radical scholars of the 1970s and 1980s. Expressing the fears of the former group, sociologist Bernard Rosenberg speculated in 1957 that "mass culture threatens not merely to cretinize our taste, but to brutalize our sense while paving the way to totalitarianism" (see Rosenberg, "Mass Culture in America," in Bernard Rosenberg and David Manning White, eds., *Mass Culture: The Popular Arts in America* [Glencoe, Ill., 1957], 9). During the 1970s and 1980s, radicals like Stanley Aronowitz and Stuart and Elizabeth Ewen drew on social control and *embourgeoisment* critiques to produce works echoing Marcuse's early view that mass culture was a dangerous entity capable of the "systematic moronization of children and adults alike" (Marcuse quoted in Donald Lazere, "Introduction: Entertainment as Social Control," in Lazere, ed., *American Media and Mass Culture: Left Perspectives* [Berkeley, 1987], 7). Cinema scholars influenced by the work of French Marxist Louis Althusser also portrayed film as a bourgeois medium that served as a powerful tool of what Althusser called the "ideological state apparatuses" (Louis Althusser, "Ideology and Ideological State Apparatuses [Notes toward an Investigation]," in Althusser, *Lenin and Philosophy and Other Essays* [New York, 1971], 127–86).

The problem with these analyses has less to do with the theories than with the ways in which many scholars have applied them. The fascination with Antonio Gramsci's concept of hegemony offers one important example. This Italian Marxist saw hegemony as a dynamic process by which a ruling class maintains power through its skillful use of social and cultural institutions—rather than military force—to gain the willing consent of the ruled. A successful hegemonic culture remains successful by incorporating all challenges to its authority and by making the ideology of ruling elites appear as the natural way of life. In the case of the movies, this was done by controlling what was seen on the screen as well as what was not to be seen (films and newsreels that challenged the authority of capitalists and capitalism fell into the latter category).

Historians have found the concept of cultural hegemony an especially useful theoretical approach to understanding the links between politics, culture, ideology, and power. Those unfamiliar with Gramsci's work should start with T. J. Jackson Lear's excellent piece, "The Concept of Cultural Hegemony: Problems and Possibilities," *American Historical Review*, 90 (June 1985), 567–93; also see Richard Butsch, "Introduction: Leisure and Hegemony in America," in Butsch, ed., *For Fun and Profit: The Transformation of Leisure into Consumption* (Philadelphia, 1990), 3–27. Gramsci's writing on hegemony can be found in *Selections from the Prison Notebooks of Antonio Gramsci*, edited and translated by Quintin Hoare and Geoffrey Nowell Smith (New York, 1971). Useful secondary works on Gramsci and hegemony include Carl Boggs, *Gramsci's Marxism* (London 1976); Roger Simon, *Gramsci's Political Thought: An Introduction* (London 1982); Anne Showstack Sassoon, ed., *Approaches to Gramsci* (London, 1982); Perry Anderson, "The Antinomies of Antonio Gramsci," *New Left Review*, 100 (November 1976–January 1977), 5–78.

Unfortunately, hegemony has become the buzzword of modern cultural analysis, a concept that many know but whose actual operation few can describe. A teleological determinism has penetrated numerous analyses of mass culture. That is, knowing how things turned out, scholars assume the triumph of bourgeois hegemony over emerging forms of mass culture and simply chart its subsequent development. In so doing, they ignore the historical process by which a particular group of capitalists defeated rival capitalists to establish their control over the movie industry; they also ignore how workers and radicals fought with industry personnel and government officials to secure greater power and influence over motion pictures.

Over the past few decades, a new generation of scholars has challenged monochromatic portrayals of workers as the dupes of mass culture. They have looked closely at the actual historical workings of hegemony and the clashes between rulers and the ruled. European and American writers, as I state in the Preface (see sources cited in note 8), demonstrate the variety of ways in which the "masses" received and transformed cultural forms to serve their own interests. Gramsci, observes Suzanne Desan, "overestimated the capacity of the elites to impose 'cultural hegemony' on the masses and underestimated the resilient ability of the lower classes to limit and reformulate these cultural impositions" (Desan, "Crowds, Community, and Ritual in the Work of E. P. Thompson and Natalie Davis," in Lynn Hunt, ed., *The New Cultural History* [Berkeley, 1989], 60). Although these writers have taken our understanding of the class battles surrounding mass culture to a new level, they still tend to portray mass culture as something produced from above. Consequently, they overlook important moments when audiences grew so angry over the political content of movies that they went out and produced their own films.

To understand the changing ideology and political focus of American cinema, and to answer the questions I laid out at the beginning of this essay, we must first understand the changing historical circumstances under which filmmakers and the film industry operated. The problem with the Frankfurt School is that its participants looked at the movie industry of the 1930s and 1940s, when a powerful Hollywood studio system was in place, and *assumed* it had always been that way. But film is not an inherently conservative or bourgeois medium. Although movies ultimately came under the control of big business, it was not foreordained that they should do so. Someone or some group had to make it happen. The researcher's task, then, is to integrate theoretical insights with empirical research in order to show how real-life struggles among workers, radicals, movie industry personnel, federal agencies, local authorities, and others shaped the development of the film industry and the ideological content and direction of American film.

The sources mentioned in the following discussion are not an exhaustive listing of all works in the field. Rather, I offer a few key secondary works to help researchers get started, and a more thorough discussion of useful and often underutilized primary sources. Those wanting more extensive citations will find them in my notes. Readers interested in seeing a more detailed application of my interactive model of historical analysis can consult my article, "Beyond the Screen: History, Class, and the Movies," in David James and Rick Berg, eds., *The Hidden Foundation: Cinema and the Question of Class* (Minneapolis, 1996), 26–55.

Anyone beginning research in the silent era would do well to get a strong grounding in the basic social and economic history of the movie industry. The best one-volume introduction to film history is still Robert Sklar's *Movie-Made America: A Cultural History of American Film* (New York, 1975, revised 1994). Sklar does a superb job linking analyses of class, ethnicity, and gender to his study of the economic evolution of the movie industry and the changing content of its films. Lary May's *Screening out the Past: The Birth of Mass Culture and the Motion Picture Industry* (New York, 1980), provides an excellent analysis of the changing cultural content of silent films and the constant battles between movie industry leaders and their critics. Garth Jowett's *Film the Democratic Art: A Social History of American Film* (Boston, 1976) offers another fine overview of the silent and sound eras. For useful histories of the silent era written by early industry participants, see Terry Ramsaye, *A Million and One Nights: A History of the Motion Picture Through 1925* (New York, 1926); Benjamin Hampton, *A History of the Movies* (New York, 1931); and Fred J. Balshofer and Arthur C. Miller, *One Reel a Week* (Berkeley, 1967).

Readers wanting a more comprehensive examination of the industry, its films, audiences, and problems should consult Scribner's three-volume history of the silent era: Charles Musser, *The Emergence of Cinema: The American Screen to 1907* (New York, 1990); Eileen Bowser, *The Transformation of Cinema 1907–1915* (New York, 1990); and Richard Koszarski, *An Evening's Entertainment: The Age of the Silent Feature Picture 1915–1928* (New York, 1990). For works that explore connections among changing film styles, changing technologies, and the changing material demands of the movie business, see David Bordwell, Janet Staiger and Kristin Thompson, *The Classical Hollywood Cinema: Film Style and Mode of Production to 1960* (New York, 1985); Barry Salt, *Film Style and Technology: History and Analysis* (London, 1992); and Thomas Elsaesser, ed., *Early Cinema: Space, Frame, Narrative* (London, 1990).

Those interested in learning more about the business side of the industry should start with the following secondary sources: Howard T. Lewis, *The Motion Picture Industry* (New York, 1933); Mae D. Huettig, *Economic Control of the Motion Picture Industry: A Study in Industrial Organization* (Philadelphia, 1944); Tino Balio, ed., *The American Film Industry* (Madison, 1976); Suzanne Mary Donahue, *American Film Distribution: The Changing Marketplace* (Ann Arbor, 1987); and Janet Wasko, *Movies and Money: Financing the American Film Industry* (Norwood, N.J., 1982). Two extremely useful first-hand looks at the changing business demands of the film industry are Joseph P. Kennedy, ed., *The Story of the Films* (Chicago, 1927), and

Howard Thompson Lewis, *Cases on the Motion Picture Industry. Harvard Business Reports, Vol. 8* (New York, 1930). For surveys that trace the rise of the studio system, see Douglas Gomery, *The Hollywood Studio System* (New York, 1986); Thomas Schatz, *The Genius of the System: Hollywood Filmmaking in the Studio Era* (New York, 1988); and Neal Gabler, *An Empire of Their Own: How the Jews Invented Hollywood* (New York, 1988).

Biographies and autobiographies, though often self-serving, offer an excellent entry point into the world and the motivations of the people who built the film industry. Works I found most useful include William C. de Mille, *Hollywood Saga* (New York, 1939); Cecil B. DeMille, edited by Donald Hayne, *The Autobiography of Cecil B. DeMille* (Englewood Cliffs, N.J., 1959); Upton Sinclair, *Upton Sinclair Presents William Fox* (Los Angeles, 1933); Samuel Goldwyn, *Behind the Screen* (New York, 1923); John Drinkwater, *The Life and Adventures of Carl Laemmle* (New York, 1931); Jesse L. Lasky with Don Weldon, *I Blow My Own Horn* (London, 1957); King Vidor, *A Tree Is A Tree: An Autobiography* (Hollywood, 1981); Joseph P. Eckhardt and Linda Kowall, *Peddler of Dreams: Siegmund Lubin and the Creation of the Motion Picture Industry 1896–1916* (Philadelphia, 1984); and Jack L. Warner with Dean Jennings, *My First Hundred Years in Hollywood* (New York, 1965).

Movies, of course, could not survive without movie theaters. The history of theaters and changing exhibition practices are most thoroughly explored in Douglas Gomery, *Shared Pleasures: A History of Movie Presentation in the United States* (Madison, 1992), and Ben Hall, *The Best Remaining Seats: The Golden Age of the Movie Palace* (New York, 1988). Carrie Balaban's *Continuous Performance: The Story of A. J. Balaban* (New York, 1942) is a wonderful account of how Abe Balaban went about fulfilling the fantasies of movie audiences.

The lack of audience surveys for the silent era makes it is difficult to offer definitive statements about the composition of early film audiences, their desires, and their reactions to particular movies. This is one area of film history where much work remains to be done. Recreation surveys commissioned by local governments during the early decades of twentieth century discuss the kinds of people civic leaders believed were going to the movies and the impact film had on their lives (see my citations in Chapters 1 and 7). Those interested in more detailed studies of the changing class composition of audiences should begin with the recent debate sparked by the publication of Ben Singer's "Manhattan Nickelodeons: New Data on Audiences and Exhibitors," *Cinema Journal*, 34 (Spring 1995), 5–35, and responses ibid., 35 (Spring 1996), 72–128 (also see the sources I cite in Chapter 1 note 23).

Audiences, as recent scholarship has shown, did not passively accept everything that was shown on the screen. People's responses to films were shaped by their class, race, gender, ethnicity, religion, and political beliefs. The most interesting accounts of working-class reception of silent films can be found in Roy Rosenzweig, *Eight Hours for What We Will* (Cambridge and New York, 1984); Kathy Peiss, *Cheap Amusements* (Philadelphia, 1985); Lizabeth Cohen, *Making a New Deal* (New York, 1990); Miriam Hansen, *Babel & Babylon* (Cambridge, Mass., 1991). For a provocative debate over the power of audiences, see Lawrence Levine, "The Folklore of Industrial Society: Popular Culture and Its Audiences," and subsequent responses in *American Historical Review*, 97 (December 1992), 1,369–1,430. William Marston Seabury's *The Public and the Motion Picture Industry* (New York, 1926) shows how the rise of the studio system greatly limited the audience's power to influence the kinds of films that producers would make. William Uricchio and Roberta E. Pearson, *Reframing Culture: The Case of Vitagraph Quality Films* (Princeton, 1993) and Sumiko Higashi, *Cecil B. DeMille and American Culture: The Silent Era* (Berkeley, 1994) reveal how certain studios and filmmakers set out to shape the composition of audiences by producing movies designed to attract middle-class customers.

As researchers shift their focus from audiences to films, they will find themselves overwhelmed by thousands of books and articles covering a wide range of topics. Movies dealing with class relations are usually discussed under the broad heading of "social-problem" films. Those interested in a work that combines a good economic history of the industry with a highly readable survey of silent-era social-problem films should read Lewis Jacobs, *The Rise of the American Film: A Critical History* (New York, 1968). The key text for anyone interested in a more thorough exploration of social-problem films is Kevin Brownlow, *Behind the Mask of Innocence* (New York, 1990). I recommend following that with Kay Sloan, *The Loud Silents: Origins of the Social Problem Film* (Urbana, 1988). For a more focused analysis of the class content of American cinema, see the essays in the previously cited collection edited by James and Berg, *The Hidden Foundation*.

The role of working people as the subjects and, to a lesser extent, producers of silent films is most fully discussed in Peter Stead, *Film and the Working Class: The Feature Film in British and American Society* (London, 1989), and in the aforementioned works by Brownlow and Sloan. For brief but useful overviews of cinematic depictions of workers, see William J. Puette, *Through Jaundiced Eyes: How the Media View Organized Labor* (Ithaca, 1992), and Sara U. Douglas, *Labor's New Voice: Unions and the Mass Media* (Norwood, N.J., 1986). The activities of radical filmmakers during the late 1920s are examined in U. S. Congress, *Investigation of Communist Propaganda. Hearings before a Special Committee to Investigate Communist Activities in the United States of the House of Representatives. 71st Cong., 2nd sess.* (Washington, D.C., 1930–1931). For an excellent critique of American cinema by one of the most perceptive radical critics of the time, see Harry Alan Potamkin, *The Compound Cinema* (New York, 1977).

Working people were a dominant part of the moviegoing public throughout the silent era. Their history as audiences and as producers of films deserves far more scholarly attention. Anyone interested in doing primary research in this area should start by consulting the Thomas Brandon Collection at the Film Studies Center, Museum of Modern Art. Brandon's unpublished manuscript, "Populist Films," is by far the most detailed survey of silent films by and about workers and radicals. In the course of his research, Brandon collected primary and secondary materials on all aspects of the film industry. Among other things, the collection contains Upton Sinclair's correspondence with movie industry personnel and labor film companies (photocopied from the Upton Sinclair Collection, Lilly Library, Indiana University); detailed reports from state and local censorship boards; interviews with radical filmmakers of the 1920s, 1930s, and 1940s; articles from labor and radical periodicals; and extensive lists and synopses of films by and about workers. This is a gold mine of information. MOMA has compiled an excellent guide to the collection.

Labor and radical periodicals are an invaluable source of information about working-class responses to films and workers' efforts to produce their own movies. Indeed, the bulk of my information about the worker film movement was drawn from these periodicals. I found the *New York Call* the most informative of all periodicals. The *Los Angeles Citizen* is especially valuable for tracing the history of studio labor relations and for describing worker films. The *Seattle Union Record* and the *Chicago New Majority* (later renamed the *Chicago Federation News*) were the most useful sources for the wartime and postwar eras. The Chicago *Daily Worker* and New York *Daily Worker* paid close attention to radical filmmaking in the 1920s. Numerous articles written by William Kruse were very helpful in drawing links between economic and political change within the movie industry. Other periodicals worth consulting are the *Cleveland Citizen, Milwaukee Social Democratic Herald, Milwaukee Daily Leader,* Girard, Ka. *The Appeal to Reason,* Los Angeles *Western Comrade, California Social Democrat, Los Angeles Labor Press,* Chicago *The Party Builder, Chicago Daily Socialist,* New York *The Socialist Review, The AFL Weekly News Letter, The American Federationist,* and *Journal of the Electrical Workers and Operators* (which assumed different names at different times).

The David Horsley Papers at the Margaret Herrick Library, Academy of Motion Picture Arts and Sciences, Beverly Hills, are the key source for those interested in charting the rise and fall of the Motive Motion Picture Corporation. The collection also contains valuable correspondence concerning the government's postwar Americanization campaign. Likewise, those interested in learning more about the Federation Film Corporation and the Seattle Union Theater Company should consult the union records and company spy reports housed in the Special Collections Department of the University of Washington Library.

Union records provide a wealth of information about organized labor's responses to mainstream and worker-made films, and their relations with a wide variety of movie industry personnel, censors, and government officials. The most accessible records are the published *Report of the Proceedings of the Annual Convention of the American Federation of Labor*. More detailed accounts of the issues raised at these meetings can be found in the American Federation of Labor Records: The Samuel Gompers Era, 1877–1937 (available on microfilm). Researchers will find the various Convention Reports (which contain follow-up correspondence for issues raised at the conventions) and the minutes of the AFL's Executive Council especially useful.

My understanding of changing labor relations within the studios was greatly enhanced by two manuscript collections: the Minute Books of the International Alliance of Theatrical and Stage Employees Union, Local #33, kept at the union's current headquarters in Burbank, California; and, the records of the Motion Picture Producers Association that can be found in the Hal Roach Collection, Special Collections, USC Library. The American Museum of the Moving Image in New York City also houses a considerable array of primary materials about movie-industry unions and their relations with employers. The *Combined Convention Proceedings National Alliance of Theatrical Stage Employees and Moving Picture Machine Operators of the United States and Canada: A Record of All Conventions Held Since the Inception of the Organization, July 1893* (New York, 1926) provides a detailed account of IATSE's battles with studio leaders and with other studio unions. For general histories of studio unions and changing relations between the industry and its unions, see the sources cited in Chapter 3 note 12, and Chapter 5 note 46.

The ideology of American films, as I noted earlier in this essay, was affected by the general political climate of the times and by the specific pressures brought to bear on industry personnel by federal, state, and local bodies. My notes contain numerous references to secondary sources dealing with the former theme. As for the latter, government records are a remarkably valuable and underutilized source of information about its role both in making films and in shaping the ideological content of Hollywood movies. The National Archives in Washington, D.C., houses an enormous array of materials that document relations between federal agencies, individual film companies, and movie-industry leaders. The Records of the Department of the Interior (Record Group 48) are one of the richest collections of documents detailing the filmmaking activities of the government. In addition to describing the vast collection of films made by the Bureau of Mines, often in cooperation with the nation's most anti-union corporations, these records also recount the wartime activities and pressures placed on studios by the Joint Committee on Motion Picture Activities of the United States Government and Allied Organizations and its postwar successor, the Joint Conference for Government and Allied Departments Engaged in Motion Picture Activities. The Records of the Department of Labor (RG 174) contain equally valuable data about government efforts to use film in its Americanization campaigns, pressures placed on studios making films dealing with labor-capital conflict, and the filmmaking activities of the department's Women's Bureau and Children's Bureau. The Records of the Committee on Public Information (RG 63) cover the government's wartime involvement with the movie industry and its efforts to shape the ideological content of American film. The remarks contained in the "Films Rejected for Export" file offer superb insights into the CPI's attitudes toward class conflict in the United States (see RG 63, file 30–B3).

The Investigative Case Files of the Bureau of Investigation (RG 65) are a key source for anyone interested in studying the activities of radical filmmakers. Some of my best materials about worker film companies came from the weekly reports of J. Edgar Hoover's agents. In addition to providing a great deal of information about the early history of the movie industry, the George Kleine Collection (Library of Congress) has a rich array of documents describing Americanization efforts by government filmmakers, studios, and nontheatrical producers (many of whom made decidedly anti-union films). More general discussions of the filmmaking activities of federal agencies can be found in Richard Dyer MacCann, *The People's Films: A Political History of United State Government Motion Pictures* (New York, 1973); U. S. Department of Labor, Women's Bureau, *Annual Report of the Director of the Women's Bureau* (Washington, D.C.).

Censors, police, clergy, reformers, and various lobbying groups also played important roles in shaping the political content of film. The activities of local and state censors were especially critical in this regard, for they helped define what was considered an acceptable or unacceptable subject for filmmakers. The growing secondary literature on censorship provides valuable insights into how a wide array of Americans responded to cinematic displays of class conflict, sexuality, crime, and other controversial issues. Useful earlier works on this topic include Ellis Paxson Oberholtzer, *The Morals of the Movie* (Philadelphia, 1922); Morris L. Ernst and Pare Lorentz, *Censored: The Private Life of the Movie* (New York, 1930); Lemar T. Beman, ed., *Censorship of the Theater and Moving Pictures* (New York, 1931); Edward de Grazia and Roger K. Newman, *Banned Films: Movies, Censors, and the First Amendment* (New York and London, 1982). For a more recent work, see Francis G. Couvares, ed., *Movie Censorship and American Culture* (Washington, D.C., 1996).

The best single source of archival material on censorship is undoubtedly the Papers of the National Board of Review of Motion Pictures, Special Collections, New York Public Library. This collection contains detailed discussions of individual films as well as correspondence with a wide array of concerned groups and individuals. There is a forty-four page guide to the collection that researchers can consult. A number of states appointed censorship boards that issued annual reports detailing what they considered appropriate or inappropriate cinematic themes. Many of these reports, as well as materials in the NBRMP papers, describe specific scenes or intertitles that censors ordered cut or altered. Among the most useful state reports are Commonwealth of Pennsylvania, *Report of the Pennsylvania State Board of Censors*; *Report of the Virginia State Board of Censors*; *Annual Report, Maryland State Board of Motion Picture Censors*; *Annual Report, Kansas State Board of Review*; Kansas State Moving Picture Censorship Commission, *Complete List of Motion Pictures Presented to the Kansas State Board of Review for Action*; and State of New York, *Annual Report of the Motion Picture Commission*. The exact titles of state reports often change over time.

Those working in film history also need to view the films they are writing about. It is difficult to understand the visceral power of movies or to interpret their ideological messages without seeing them. But what films should researchers see and where can they go to see them? Once a researcher determines the specific themes he or she wants to study, I suggest using secondary works and film catalogs to compile a list of appropriate films. The most comprehensive description of silent films is the six-volume guide compiled by the American Film Institute: Kenneth W. Munden, ed., *The American Film Institute Catalog of Motion Pictures Produced in the United States. Feature Films 1921–1930*, 2 vols. (New York, 1971); Patricia King Hanson, ed., *The American Film Institute Catalog . . . 1911–1920*, 2 vols. (Berkeley, 1988); Elias Savada, comp., *The American Film Institute Catalog . . . 1893–1910*, 2 vols. (Metuchen, N.J., 1995). Writers' Program of the Work Projects Administration, *The Film Index: A Bibliography*, 3 vols. (New York, 1941, 1985) offers excellent synopses of theatrical and nontheatrical films, as well as citations of movie reviews. Other works that contain useful information about silent films include Frank N. Magill, *Magill's Survey of Cinema: Silent Films*, 3 vols. (Englewood Cliffs, N.J., 1982); Richard Fauss, *A Bibliography of Labor History in Newsfilm*, 4 vols. (Morgantown, W. Va., 1980); Einar Lauritzen and Gunnar Lundquist, *American Film-Index, 1908–1915* (Stockholm, 1974); Craig Campbell, *Reel America and World War I: A Comprehensive Filmography and History of Motion Pictures in the United States, 1914–1920* (Jefferson, N.C., 1985).

Movie-industry periodicals are superb sources of information about specific films, audiences, and the film industry in general. I found *Moving Picture World* the most valuable of the silent-era periodicals; it is more balanced in its politics than the useful but far more conservative *Variety*. Researchers should also consult *Views and Film Index*, *Motography*, *New York Dramatic Mirror*, *Motion Picture News*, *Wid's*, and *Wid's Annual Year Book*. For published collections of reviews, see *New York Times Film Reviews, 1913–1968*, 6 vols. (New York, 1970); *Variety Film Reviews, 1907–1984*, 18 vols. (New York, 1986); also see Annette M. D'Agostino, comp., *An Index to Short and Feature Film Reviews in the "Moving Picture World"*: The Early Years, 1907–1915 (Westport, Conn., 1995). The Copyright Records Collection, housed in the Motion Pictures, Broadcasting and Recorded Sound Division of the Library of Congress, are yet another underutilized and incredibly rich source of information about silent films. This microfilm collection contains a wide assortment of materials sent by producers to the government's copyright offices: scenarios, press books, and reviews of tens of thousands of motion pictures.

There are a number valuable guides to help researchers locate repositories for surviving silent films. The most wide ranging of these is Ronald S. Magliozzi, *Treasures from the Film Archives* (Metuchen, N.J., 1988). For descriptions of films at the Library of Congress, see Kemp Niver, *Early Motion Pictures: The Paper Print Collection in the Library of Congress* (Washington, D.C., 1985); Kemp Niver, *Motion Pictures from the Library of Congress Paper Print Collection, 1894–1912* (Berkeley, 1967); *The George Kleine Collection*, prepared by Rita Horowitz and Harriet Harrison, with Wendy White (Washington, D.C., 1980); Howard Lamarr Wall, *Motion Pictures 1894–1912 Identified from the Records of the Copyright Office* (Washington D.C., 1953) and *Motion Pictures 1912–1939* (Washington D.C., 1951); *Catalog of Holdings of the American Film Institute Collection and the United Artists Collection at the Library of Congress* (Washington, D.C., 1978). The holdings of Film Studies Center, Museum of Modern Art are surveyed in Jon Gartenberg, *The Film Catalog: A List of Holdings in the Museum of Modern Art* (Boston and New York, 1985). The Library of Congress has compiled an Internet Guide to Research Centers and Film Archives around the world: http://lcweb.loc.gov/film/arch.html. Those unable to travel to distant archives should consult Robert Klepper, *Silent Films on Video: A Filmography of Over 700 Silent Features Available on Videocassette* (Jefferson, N.C., 1996).

Unfortunately, there is only a handful of archives that contain significant numbers of silent films. The largest of these is the Motion Picture, Broadcasting, and Recorded Sound Division of the Library of Congress. Although there is no single published guide to this collection, the Division's card catalog contains a complete list of its holdings. The other two major film repositories are the Department of Film, Museum of Modern Art, New York, and the George Eastman House, Rochester, New York. The UCLA Film and Television Archives has an excellent collection of early films; a list of their inventory has been put online and can be accessed at UCLA. USC has no published guide to its film collection, but there are photocopied lists of their holdings. The Motion Picture, Sound, and Video Branch, Special Archives Division of the National Archives, Washington, D.C., contains the nation's most underutilized collection of silent films. Researchers will find among its massive collection of mainly nontheatrical films a vast quantity of movies made by government agencies and industrial corporations, and an extensive collection of sound-era films produced by the AFL-CIO and its member unions. There is a massive card catalog describing individual films as well as a forty-five page typewritten finding aid, "Motion Pictures in the National Archives (1900–1930)."

Movies continue to play an important role in shaping the way Americans look at and think about their world. But how films do so and why they advance the political images they do remain mysteries to most moviegoers. The challenge of film history is to reach beyond the academic community and demystify the workings of the cinematic world. Film historians can provide citizens with the critical skills they need to contextualize, analyze, and criticize the images and ideologies they see on the screen. By so doing, scholars can help Americans understand how these images affect our views of the past and the possibilities for the future. This is an intellectual goal and civic duty worth pursuing.

Abbreviations

AFI	American Film Institute
AFL Convention	Records of the American Federation of Labor Convention, American Federation of Labor Records: The Samuel Gompers Era (microfilm edition, 1979), Microfilming Corporation of America
AFL Proceedings	*Report of the Proceedings of the Annual Convention of the American Federation of Labor*
AFL Records	American Federation of Labor Records: The Samuel Gompers Era (microfilm edition, 1979), Microfilming Corporation of America
AMPAS	Academy of Motion Picture Arts and Sciences, Beverly Hills, Ca.
Beck Papers	Broussais C. Beck Papers, Special Collections, University of Washington, Seattle, Wa.
Brandon Coll.	Thomas Brandon Collection, Films Studies Center, Museum of Modern Art, New York City
CLC	Central Labor Council, Seattle, Wa.
Copyright Records, LC	Copyright Records, Motion Pictures, Broadcasting and Recorded Sound Division, Library of Congress, Washington, D.C.
CPI	Committee on Public Information
FFC	Federation (or Federated) Film Corporation
Historical Statistics	U.S. Department of Commerce, *Historical Statistics of the United States: Colonial Times to 1970*, 2 vols. (Washington, D.C., 1975)
Horsley Papers	David Horsley Papers, Academy of Motion Picture Arts and Sciences, Beverly Hills, Ca.
IATSE	International Alliance of Theatrical and Stage Employees
IBEW	International Brotherhood of Electrical Workers
ICF, NA	Investigative Case Files, Records of the Bureau of Investigation, National Archives, Washington, D.C.
IWA	International Workers' Aid
IWW	Industrial Workers of the World
LA Citizen	*Los Angeles Citizen*
LFS	Labor Film Service
MMPC	Motive Motion Picture Company
MOMA	Film Studies Center, Museum of Modern Art, New York
MPPA	Motion Picture Producers' Association
MPW	*Moving Picture World*
NA	National Archives, Washington, D.C.
NAM	National Association of Manufacturers
NAMPI	National Association of the Motion Picture Industry

NBRMP	Papers of the National Board of Review of Motion Pictures, Special Collections, New York Public Library
NY Call	*New York Call*
Records of the CPI	Records of the Committee on Public Information, National Archives, Washington, D.C.
Roach Papers	Motion Picture Producers' Association, Hal Roach Collection, Special Collections, University of Southern California, Los Angeles
SUTC	Seattle Union Theater Company
UCLA	Speical Collections, University of California, Los Angeles
UMW	United Mine Workers' Union
USC	Special Collections. University of Southern California, Los Angeles
UW	Special Collections, University of Washington, Seattle, Wa.
WIR	Workers' International Relief

Notes

Preface

1. Birmingham quoted in Arthur Marwick, *Class: Image and Reality in Britain, France and the USA since 1930* (New York, 1980), 311.

2. Steven J. Ross, *Workers on the Edge: Work, Leisure, and Politics in Industrializing Cincinnati, 1788–1890* (New York, 1985).

3. Sklar and May remain the starting points for anyone interested in the social history of early American film. Robert Sklar, *Movie-Made America: A Cultural History of American Movies* (New York, 1975, rev. ed. 1994); Lary May, *Screening out the Past: The Birth of Mass Culture and the Motion Picture Industry* (New York, 1980). The filmmaking efforts of American workers and radicals during the late 1920s, 1930s, and 1940s are described in William Alexander, *Film on the Left: American Documentary Film from 1931 to 1942* (Princeton, 1981); Russell Campbell, *The Cinema Strikes Back: Radical Filmmaking in the United States 1930–1942* (Ann Arbor, 1982); Charles Wolfe, "The Poetics and Politics of Nonfiction: Documentary Film," in Tino Balio, ed., *Grand Design: Hollywood as a Modern Business Enterprise, 1930–1939* (New York, 1993), 351–86; Bert Hogenkamp, "Worker's Newsreels in the 1920s and 1930s," *Our History*, pamphlet 68 (London, 1977); and special issue on "American Labor Films," *Film Library Quarterly*, 12 (1979). For the history of Labor Day, see Michael Kazin and Steven J. Ross, "America's Labor Day: The Dilemma of a Workers' Celebration," *Journal of American History*, 78 (March 1992), 1,294–1,323.

4. For works that examine radical and working-class filmmaking in Europe during the silent era, see Stephen G. Jones, *The British Labour Movement and Film* (London, 1987); Bert Hogenkamp, *Deadly Parallels: Film and the Left in Britain, 1929–1939* (London, 1986); Vance Kepley, "The Workers' International Relief and the Cinema of the Left 1921–1931," *Cinema Journal*, 23 (Fall 1983), 7–23; Richard Taylor, *The Politics of Soviet Cinema, 1917–1929* (Cambridge, Mass., 1979); Peter Kenez, "The Cultural Revolutions in Cinema," *Slavic Review*, 47 (Fall 1988), 414–33; Jay Leyda, *Kino: A History of the Russian and Soviet Film* (Princeton, 1983); Denise J. Youngbloood, *Soviet Cinema in the Silent Era, 1918–1935* (Ann Arbor, 1991); Denise J. Youngblood, *Movies for the Masses: Popular Cinema and Soviet Society in the 1920s* (New York, 1992); Bruce Murray, *Film and the German Left in the Weimar Republic: From Caligari to Kuhle Wampe* (Austin, 1990); Jonathan Buchsbaum, *Cinema Engagé: Film in the Popular Front* (Urbana and Chicago, 1988); Vance Kepley, Jr., "Cinema and Everyday Life: Soviet Workers Clubs of the 1920s," and Jonathan Buchsbaum, "Left Filmmaking in the West: The Interwar Years," in Robert Sklar and Charles Musser, eds., *Resisting Images: Essays on Cinema and History* (Philadelphia, 1990), 108–25, 126–48; also see sources in note 3.

5. Unfortunately, most silent films no longer exist. The compilers of one film catalog estimate the number of extant films at "between 10 and 20 percent." Patricia King Hanson, ed., *The American Film Institute Catalog of Motion Pictures Produced in*

the United States. Feature Films 1911–1920, 2 vols. (Berkeley, 1988), I: xv. Only two worker-made films have survived: *Labor's Reward*, made by the American Federation of Labor in 1925, and *The Passaic Textile Strike*, made by the International Workers' Aid in 1926. Overall, I was able to view 185 silent films. See Appendix I for a list of surviving films and their repositories. For recent histories of silent films by workers and radicals, see Kay Sloan, *The Loud Silents: Origins of the Social Problem Film* (Urbana, 1988); Peter Stead, *Film and the Working Class: The Feature Film in British and American Society* (London and New York, 1989); Kevin Brownlow, *Behind the Mask of Innocence: Sex, Violence, Prejudice, Crime: Films of Social Conscience in the Silent Era* (New York, 1990); Steven J. Ross, "Cinema and Class Conflict: Labor, Capital, the State, and American Silent Film," in Sklar and Musser, *Resisting Images*, 68–107; Steven J. Ross, "The Unknown Hollywood," *History Today*, 40 (April 1990), 40–46; Steven J. Ross, "Struggles for the Screen: Workers, Radicals, and the Political Uses of Silent Film," *American Historical Review*, 96 (April 1991), 333–67.

6. E. P. Thompson, *The Making of the English Working Class* (New York, 1963), 13; Philip J. Ethington, *The Public City: The Political Construction of Urban Life in San Francisco, 1850–1900* (Cambridge and New York, 1994), 55.

7. Readers interested in a more extensive discussion of scholarly debates over mass culture should consult Appendix II. For key works by Frankfurt School theorists, see Max Horkheimer and Theodor Adorno, "The Culture Industry: Enlightenment as Mass Deception," in *Dialectic of Enlightenment*, translated by John Cumming (New York, 1972); Herbert Marcuse, *Negations: Essays in Critical Theory*, translated by Jeremy Shapiro (Boston, 1968); Leo Lowenthal, *Literature, Popular Culture, and Society* (Palo Alto, Ca., 1961); for a dissenting view within the Frankfurt School, see Walter Benjamin, "The Work of Art in the Age of Mechanical Reproduction," in *Illuminations*, translated by Harry Zohn (New York, 1969). For conservative views on the dangers of mass culture, see the collection of essays in Bernard Rosenberg and David Manning White, eds., *Mass Culture: The Popular Arts in America* (Glencoe, Ill., 1957); Daniel Boorstin, *The Image; or, What Happened to the American Dream* (New York, 1962); also see Neil Jumonville, "The New York Intellectuals and Mass Culture Criticism," *Journal of American Culture*, 12 (Spring 1989), 87–95. For a survey of debates over the role of popular culture from Matthew Arnold to the present, see John Storey, *An Introductory Guide to Cultural Theory and Popular Culture* (Athens, Ga., 1993).

8. Stuart Hall, "Notes on Deconstructing 'the Popular'," in Raphael Samuel, ed., *People's History and Socialist Theory* (London, 1981), 232. For key examples, see Richard Hoggart, *The Uses of Literacy* (London, 1958); Thompson, *The Making of the English Working Class*; Raymond Williams, *Culture and Society 1780–1950* (New York, 1958); Raymond Williams, *Problems in Materialism and Culture* (London, 1980); Stuart Hall and Paddy Whamel, *The Popular Arts* (New York, 1964); Stuart Hall, Dorothy Hobson, Andrew Lowe, and Paul Willis, eds., *Culture, Media, Language: Working Papers in Cultural Studies, 1972–79* (London, 1980); Michael Green, "The Centre for Contemporary Cultural Studies," in Peter Widdowson, ed., *Re-Reading English* (London, 1982), 77–90; Tony Bennett, Colin Mercer, and Janet Woollacott, eds., *Popular Culture and Social Relations* (Milton Keynes, England, 1986). For writings on American culture, see Roy Rosenzweig, *Eight Hours for What We Will: Workers and Leisure in an Industrial City, 1870–1920* (Cambridge and New

York, 1983); Francis G. Couvares, *The Remaking of Pittsburgh: Class and Culture in an Industrializing City, 1877–1919* (Albany, 1984); Kathy Peiss, *Cheap Amusements: Working Women and Leisure in Turn-of-the-Century New York* (Philadelphia, 1986); Lizabeth Cohen, *Making a New Deal: Industrial Workers in Chicago, 1919–1939* (Cambridge and New York, 1990). For recent essay collections that demonstrate the myriad ways people from different fields approach the intersection of history, culture, theory, politics, and mass media, see Donald Lazere, ed., *American Media and Mass Culture: Left Perspectives* (Berkeley, 1987); Lawrence Grossberg, Cary Nelson, and Paula A. Treichler, eds., *Cultural Studies* (New York and London, 1992).

9. Charles Musser, *Before the Nickelodeon: Edward S. Porter and the Edison Manufacturing Company* (Berkeley, 1991); Charles Musser, *The Emergence of Cinema: The American Screen to 1907* (New York, 1990); Eileen Bowser, *The Transformation of Cinema 1907–1915* (New York, 1990); Richard Koszarski, *An Evening's Entertainment: The Age of the Silent Feature Picture, 1915–1928* (New York, 1990); Tom Gunning, *D. W. Griffith and the Origins of American Narrative Film: The Early Year at Biograph* (Urbana and Chicago, 1991); Thomas Elsaesser, ed., with Adam Barker, *Early Cinema: Space, Frame, Narrative* (London, 1990); William Uricchio and Roberta Pearson, *Reframing Culture: The Case of the Vitagraph Quality Films* (Princeton, 1993); Miriam Hansen, *Babel & Babylon: Spectatorship in American Silent Film* (Cambridge, Mass., 1991); David Bordwell, Janet Staiger, and Kristin Thompson, *The Classical Hollywood Cinema: Film Style and Mode of Production to 1960* (New York, 1985). For historians who analyze the forces shaping the politics of film, see Clayton R. Koppes and Gregory D. Black, *Hollywood Goes to War: How Politics, Profits, and Propaganda Shaped World War II Movies* (New York, 1987); Stephen Vaughn, *Ronald Reagan in Hollywood: Movies and Politics* (New York, 1994); Sumiko Higashi, *Cecil B. DeMille and American Culture: The Silent Era* (Berkeley, 1994).

Introduction

1. Matthew Josephson, *The Robber Barons: The Great American Capitalists 1861–1901* (New York, 1962), 338.

2. For overviews of American life during the late nineteenth century, see Robert Wiebe, *The Search for Order 1877–1920* (New York, 1967); Herbert Gutman, *Work, Culture, and Society in Industrializing America* (New York, 1977); Alan Trachtenberg, *The Incorporation of America: Culture and Society in the Gilded Age* (New York, 1982); Frederic Cople Jaher, *The Urban Establishment: Upper Strata in Boston, New York, Charleston, Chicago, and Los Angeles* (Urbana, 1982); Alice Kessler-Harris, *Out to Work: A History of Wage Earning Women in the United States* (New York, 1982); Leon Fink, *Workingmen's Democracy: The Knights of Labor and American Politics* (Urbana, 1983); John Bodnar, *The Transplanted: A History of Immigrants in Urban America* (Bloomington, 1985); Robert C. McMath, Jr., *American Populism: A Social History 1877–1898* (New York, 1993); Nell Painter, *Standing at Armageddon* (New York, 1987); Richard Slotkin, *Fatal Environment: The Myth of the Frontier in the Age of Industrialization 1800–1890* (New York, 1985).

3. MPW, October 30, 1908.

4. This incident is reported by Ellis Paxson Oberholtzer, *The Morals of the Movie* (Philadelphia, 1922), 71.

5. William de Mille, *Hollywood Saga* (New York, 1939), 82.

6. "The Ubiquitous Moving Picture," *American Magazine*, July 1913, quoted in Garth Jowett, *Film the Democratic Art* (Boston, 1976), 42.

7. *MPW*, October 30, 1908; New York *Daily Worker*, April 14, 1920. The class composition of early movie audiences, a subject of great debate among film scholars, is discussed in Chapters 1 and 7.

8. De Mille, *Hollywood Saga*, 21, 13; *Kinematograph and Lantern Weekly*, November 26, 1914.

9. The movies are, respectively, *What Is to Be Done?* (1914), *From Dusk to Dawn* (1913), and *The Passaic Textile Strike* (1926).

10. The cast of characters, in order, are Frank E. Wolfe, David Horsley, John Arthur Nelson, Upton Sinclair, Joseph D. Cannon, and William F. Kruse.

11. Maryland censors' report quoted in Morris L. Ernst and Pare Lorentz, *Censored: The Private Life of the Movie* (New York, 1930), 42. The mill workers' response to *The Blacklist* is reported in R. J. Caldwell to National Board of Censorship, December 7, 1916, Box 105 (Supreme Test), NBRMP. Caldwell mistakenly identified the film as *The Supreme Test*. For conversions to socialism, see Walter Millsap, "Llano Cooperative Colony," 20–21, transcript, U.C.L.A. Oral History Project, 1969, UCLA; P. H. Reesburg to Upton Sinclair, January 18, 1915, quoted in Thomas Brandon, "Populist Film," chapter 1, 30, file C34, unpublished manuscript, Brandon Coll.; for Seattle workers, see *NY Call*, June 29, 1922.

Chapter 1
Going to the Movies

1. For attendance figures see Russell Merritt, "Nickelodeon Theaters 1905–1914: Building an Audience," in Tino Balio, ed., *The American Film Industry* (Madison, 1976), 63; New York *Daily Worker*, April 14, 1924.

2. Frederic C. Howe, "What to Do with the Motion Picture Show: Shall It Be Censored?" *The Outlook*, 107 (June 20, 1914), 412–16, quoted in Kay Sloan, *The Loud Silents: Origins of the Social Problem Film* (Urbana, 1988), 6.

3. Film scholars have devised many innovative approaches to analyzing the ideology and structure of movies, but they have been less attentive to examining how audience reception was affected by the varied settings in which films were viewed. For collections and review essays that offer a spectrum of approaches to film analysis and audience reception, see Bill Nichols, ed., *Movies and Methods: An Anthology*, 2 vols. (Berkeley, 1976, 1985); Gerald Mast, Marshall Cohen, and Leo Braudy, eds., *Film Theory and Criticism: Introductory Readings* (New York, 1991); Thomas Elsaesser, ed., *Early Cinema: Space, Frame, Narrative* (London, 1990); Ron Burnett, ed., *Explorations in Film Theory: Selected Essays from "Cine-Tracts"* (Bloomington, 1991); David Bordwell, *Making Meaning: Inference and Rhetoric in the Interpretation of Cinema* (Cambridge, Mass., 1989); David James and Rick Berg, eds., *The Hidden Foundation: Cinema and the Question of Class* (Minneapolis, 1996); E. Ann Kaplan, ed., *Psychoanalysis and Cinema* (New York, 1990); E. Deidre Pribram, ed., *Female Spectators: Looking at Film and Television* (London, 1988); Patrice Petro, "Reception Theories and the Avant-Garde," *Wide Angle*, 8:1 (1986), 11–17; Janet Staiger, *Interpreting Films: Studies in the Historical Reception of*

American Cinema (Princeton, 1992); Robert Arnold, "Film Space/Audience Space: Notes toward a Theory of Spectatorship," *The Velvet Light Trap*, 25 (Spring 1990), 44–52. For a study that looks at films and the spaces in which they were shown, see Miriam Hansen, *Babel & Babylon: Spectatorship in American Silent Film* (Cambridge, Mass., 1991).

4. For an overview of leisure activities in nineteenth-century America, see Rhea Foster Dulles, *A History of Recreation: Americans Learn to Play* (New York, 1965); Eric Lott, *Love and Theft: Blackface Minstrelsy and the American Working Class* (New York, 1993); Lawrence W. Levine, *Highbrow/Lowbrow: The Emergence of Cultural Hierarchy in America* (Cambridge, Mass., 1988); Steven A. Riess, *City Games: The Evolution of American Urban Society and the Rise of Sports* (Urbana, 1989); John Higham, "The Reorientation of American Culture in the 1890s," in John Higham, *Writings in American History* (Bloomington, 1970), 73–102. For life in Winona, see David O. Thomas, "From Page to Screen in Smalltown America: Early Motion Picture Exhibition in Winona, Minnesota," *Journal of the University Film Association*, 33 (Summer 1981), 3–13.

5. Wyckoff quoted in Daniel T. Rodgers, *The Work Ethic in Industrial America, 1850–1920* (Chicago, 1978), 75. The changing nature of work and the work ethic are also discussed in James B. Gilbert, *Work without Salvation: America's Intellectuals and Industrial Alienation, 1880–1910* (Baltimore, 1977).

6. *Historical Statistics*, 1: 164–73. Worker struggles for a shorter work day are described in Marion Cotter Cahill, *Shorter Hours: A Study of the Movement since the Civil War* (New York, 1932); David R. Roediger and Philip Foner, *Our Own Time: A History of American Labor and the Working Day* (London and New York, 1989); Roy Rosenzweig, *Eight Hours for What We Will: Workers and Leisure in an Industrial City, 1870–1920* (Cambridge and New York, 1983).

7. Statistics are taken from *Historical Statistics*, 1: 11–12, 14, 19. The Bureau of the Census defined "urban" as any community with a population greater than 2,500 people. The rise of commercial recreations in the late nineteenth and early twentieth centuries is described in David Nasaw, *Going Out: The Rise and Fall of Public Amusements* (New York, 1993); Kathy Peiss, *Cheap Amusements: Working Women and Leisure in Turn-of-the-Century New York* (Philadelphia, 1986); Gregory A. Waller, *Main Street Amusements: Movies and Commercial Entertainment in a Southern City, 1896–1930* (Washington, D.C., 1995); Richard Butsch, ed., *For Fun and Profit: The Transformation of Leisure into Consumption* (Philadelphia, 1990); Alan Havig, "The Commercial Amusement Audience in Early 20th-Century American Cities," *Journal of American Culture*, 5 (Spring 1982), 1–19; Rosenzweig, *Eight Hours*.

8. Alexis de Tocqueville, *Journey to America*, translated by George Lawrence (New Haven, 1960), 217. For the development of an American elite and its impact on cultural life, see Frederic Cople Jaher, *The Urban Establishment: Upper Strata in Boston, New York, Charleston, Chicago, and Los Angeles* (Urbana, 1982); Peter Dobkin Hall, *The Organization of American Culture, 1700–1900: Private Institutions, Elites, and the Origins of American Nationality* (New York, 1984); Paul DiMaggio, "Cultural Entrepreneurship in Nineteenth-Century Boston: The Creation of an Organizational Base for High Culture in America," *Media, Culture, and Society*, 4 (January 1982), 33–50; Lary May, *Screening out the Past: The Birth of Mass Culture and the Motion Picture Industry* (New York, 1980), 31–34; Levine, *Highbrow/Lowbrow*.

9. Daniel Horowitz, *The Morality of Spending: Attitudes toward the Consumer Society in America, 1875–1940* (Baltimore, 1985), 68–69.

10. The ranks of white-collar workers, according to one scholar, swelled from 3.4 million in 1900 to 7.9 million in 1920. Jurgen Kocka, *White Collar Workers in America 1890–1940: An Historical Perspective*, translated by Maura Kealey (London and Beverly Hills, 1980), 19, 291 note 45. I offer a more detailed analysis of the relationship between leisure and middle-class formation in Chapter 7. The question of class development and the rise of an American middle class has been discussed in hundreds, if not thousands, of scholarly works. For overviews of the changing language of class in nineteenth- and early twentieth-century America, see Martin J. Burke, *The Conundrum of Class: Public Discourse on the Social Order in America* (Chicago, 1995); Mary Ryan, *Cradle of the Middle Class: The Family in Oneida County, New York, 1790–1865* (Cambridge and New York, 1981); Sean Wilentz, *Chants Democratic: New York City and the Rise of the American Working Class, 1788–1850* (New York, 1984); Steven J. Ross, *Workers on the Edge: Work, Leisure, and Politics in Industrializing Cincinnati, 1788–1890* (New York, 1985); Ileen De Vault, *Sons and Daughters of Labor: Class and Clerical Work in Turn-of-the-Century Pittsburgh* (Ithaca, 1991); John S. Gilkeson, Jr., *Middle-Class Providence, 1820–1940* (Princeton, 1986); Stuart M. Blumin, *The Emergence of the Middle Class: Social Experience in the American City, 1760–1900* (Cambridge and New York, 1989); Philip J. Ethington, *The Public City: The Political Construction of Urban Life in San Francisco, 1850–1900* (Cambridge and New York, 1994); C. Wright Mills, *White Collar: The American Middle Classes* (New York, 1951); Robert Wiebe, *The Search for Order, 1877–1920* (New York, 1967); Burton J. Bledstein, *The Culture of Professionalism: The Middle Class and the Development of Higher Education in America* (New York, 1978); Pat Walker, ed., *Between Labor and Capital: The Professional Managerial Class* (Boston, 1979); Horowitz, *Morality of Spending*.

11. Levine, *Highbrow/Lowbrow*, 101; James Payton Sizer, *The Commercialization of Leisure* (Boston, 1917), 63–64. Class, ethnic, and racial patterns of opera and theater going are discussed in *NY Call*, March 16 and December 4, 1909, and February 22, 1910; the Drama Committee of the Twentieth Century Club, *The Amusement Situation in the City of Boston* (Boston, 1910); Michael M. Davis, *The Exploitation of Pleasure: A Study of Commercial Recreations in New York City* (New York, 1911); *Public Recreation; Transactions of the Commonwealth Club of California*, 8 (June 1913), 181–309; Eugene LeMoyne Connelly, "The First Motion Picture Theater," *Western Pennsylvania Historical Magazine*, 23 (March 1940), 4–5; Irving Howe, *The World of Our Fathers* (New York, 1976); Robert A. Slayton, *Back of the Yards: The Making of a Local Democracy* (Chicago, 1986); Francis G. Couvares, *The Remaking of Pittsburgh: Class and Culture in an Industrializing City, 1877–1919* (Albany, 1984); Nasaw, *Going Out*, 11, 49–51; Waller, *Main Street Amusements*, 40–46. For an excellent analysis of changing ethnic patterns of leisure during this era, see Rosenzweig, *Eight Hours*.

12. Statistics are taken from Havig, "Commercial Amusement Audience," 5. For contemporary accounts and attitudes toward these varied commercial amusements, see Annie Marion MacLean, *Wage-Earning Women* (New York, 1910); Frank Hatch Streightoff, *The Standard of Living among Industrial People of America* (Boston and New York, 1911); Louise de Koven Bowen, *Our Most Popular Recreation Controlled*

by the Liquor Interests: A Study of Public Dance Halls (Chicago, 1911); Juvenile Protective Association, *Recreation Survey of Cincinnati* (Cincinnati, 1913); Robert O. Bartholomew, *Report of Censorship of Motion Pictures and of Investigation of Motion Picture Theatres of Cleveland* (Cleveland, 1913); Francis North, *Indianapolis Recreation Survey* (Indianapolis, 1914); Mary Kingsbury Simkhovitch, *The City Worker's World in America* (New York, 1917); Cleveland Recreation Survey, *Commercial Recreation* (Cleveland, 1920). For histories of commercial recreation, see Robert W. Snyder, *The Voice of the City: Vaudeville and Popular Culture in New York* (New York, 1989); Robert C. Allen, *Horrible Prettiness: Burlesque and American Culture* (Chapel Hill, 1991); Elisabeth Perry, "Cleaning up the Dance Halls," *History Today*, 40 (October 1989), 22–26; John F. Kasson, *Amusing the Million: Coney Island at the Turn of the Century* (New York, 1978); Judith A. Adams, *The Amusement Park Industry* (Boston, 1991); and sources in note 7 above.

13. Davis, *Exploitation of Pleasure*, 34.

14. The Lumière brothers showed the first movies in Paris in December 1895. The evolution of early motion pictures is described in Charles Musser, *The Emergence of Cinema: The American Screen to 1907* (New York, 1990); Charles Musser, *Before the Nickelodeon: Edwin S. Porter and the Edison Manufacturing Company* (Berkeley, 1991); Gordon Hendricks, *The Kinetoscope: America's First Commercially Successful Motion Picture Exhibitor* (New York, 1966); Terry Ramsaye, *A Million and One Nights: A History of the Motion Picture through 1925* (New York, 1926); Robert Sklar, *Movie-Made America: A Cultural History of American Movies* (New York, 1994); Nasaw, *Going Out*, 120–53. The relationship between movies and vaudeville is discussed in Snyder, *Voice of the City*; Musser, *Emergence of Cinema*, 263–336. For the best overview of traveling road shows, see Charles Musser with Carol Nelson, *High-Class Moving Pictures: Lyman H. Howe and the Forgotten Era of Traveling Exhibition* (Princeton, 1990).

15. Connelly, "First Moving Picture Theater," 3. Thomas L. Tally's Electric Theater, which opened in Los Angeles on April 16, 1902, is often credited with being the first movie theater. However, Tally converted his theater into a vaudeville house six months later.

16. *Greater Pittsburgh*, June 1955, 19. Theater statistic for 1913 is taken from *Variety*, August 29, 1913. The evolution of nickelodeons is described in Eileen Bowser, *The Transformation of Cinema 1907–1915* (New York, 1990), 1–20; Garth Jowett, *Film the Democratic Art* (Boston, 1976), 30–33, 38–42; Charles H. Tarbox, *Lost Films 1895–1917* (Los Angeles, 1983); Q. David Bowers, *Nickelodeon Theatres and Their Music* (New York, 1986); Robert Kirk Headley, Jr., *Exit: A History of Movies in Baltimore* (Baltimore, 1974); Douglas Gomery, *Shared Pleasures: A History of Movie Presentation in the United States* (Madison, 1992), 18–33; Musser, *Emergence of Cinema*, 96, 125–28, 299–303; Sklar, *Movie-Made America*, 18–32; Nasaw, *Going Out*, 154–73; Waller, *Main Street Amusements*, 65–95. For exhibition in small towns, see Kathryn Helgesen Fuller, "'You Can Have the Strand in Your Own Town': The Marginalization of Small Town Film Exhibition in the Silent Era," *Film History*, 6 (Summer 1994), 166–77. The entry of Jews and women into the movie business is discussed in Neal Gabler, *An Empire of Their Own: How the Jews Invented Hollywood* (New York, 1988); Anthony Slide, *Early American Cinema* (Metuchen, N.J., 1994), 152–53; Karen Ward Mahar, "Women, Filmmaking, and the Gendering of

the American Film Industry, 1896–1928," Ph.D. dissertation, University of Southern California, 1995.

17. Quoted in Charlotte Herzog, "The Movie Palace and the Theatrical Sources of Its Architectural Style," *Cinema Journal*, 20 (Spring 1981), 30.

18. *Variety*, October 24, 1913. For Chicago and Arkansas theaters, see Slayton, *Back of the Yards*, 59; *NY Call*, December 24, 1913. The "democratic" quality of nickelodeons is discussed in Walter Prichard Eaton, "Class Consciousness and the 'Movies,'" *Atlantic Monthly*, 115 (January 1915), 51; May, *Screening out the Past*, 38.

19. *Variety*, November 28, 1913.

20. Author interview with Bill Edwards, May 31, 1989, Los Angeles; Jeff Kisseloff, *You Must Remember This: An Oral History of Manhattan from the 1890s to World War II* (New York, 1989), 508. For examples of municipally sponsored outdoor screenings, see *NY Call*, August 17, 1913, July 26, 1914; *LA Citizen*, January 13, 1911.

21. Lucy France Pierce, "The Nickelodeon," *World Today*, October 1908, quoted in Gerald Mast, ed., *Movies in Our Midst: Documents in the Cultural History of Film in America* (Chicago, 1982), 51; *MPW*, October 30, 1908; *Chicago Daily Socialist*, December 17, 1909; *California Social Democrat*, September 19, 1911.

22. Terry Ramsaye, "The Motion Picture," *Annals of the American Academy of Political and Social Science*, 127 (November 1926), 15; Thomas, "From Page to Screen," 9–10; Manhattan statistics in Davis, *Exploitation of Pleasure*, 21–31. A survey of movie audiences taken in Waltham, Massachusetts, in 1914 revealed that 63 percent were factory and mill workers, 18 percent belonged to the business community, 10 percent were clerks, and 8 percent were of the leisured class. Havig, "Commercial Amusement Audience," 8.

23. I date the emergence of movies as a regular part of middle-class life later than most film scholars. My reading of working-class periodicals of the time suggests that the class identity of white-collar workers was hotly contested before the war. For debates over the changing class composition of movie audiences, see Judith Mayne, "Immigrants and Spectators," *Wide Angle*, 5:2 (1982), 32–41; Garth S. Jowett, "The First Motion Picture Audiences," in Michael T. Marsden et al., eds., *Movies as Artifacts: Cultural Criticisms of Popular Film* (Chicago, 1982), 14–25; Ben Singer, "Manhattan Nickelodeons: New Data on Audiences and Exhibitors," *Cinema Journal*, 34 (Spring 1995), 5–35; and responses ibid., 35 (Spring 1996), 72–128; Musser, *Emergence of Cinema*, 415–47; Bowser, *Transformation of Cinema*, 1–20, 121–36; Sklar, *Movie-Made America*, 18–32; Jowett, *Film*, 30–50; Rosenzweig, *Eight Hours*, 191–220; May, *Screening out the Past*. For views that accord greater prominence to middle-class audiences during the prewar era, see Robert C. Allen, "Motion Picture Exhibition in Manhattan 1906–1912: Beyond the Nickelodeon," *Cinema Journal*, 18 (Spring 1979), 2–15; Merritt, "Nickelodeon Theaters," 59–82; for a critique of these works, see Robert Sklar, "Oh! Althusser! Historiography and the Rise of Cinema Studies," *Radical History Review*, 41 (Spring 1988), 11–35. My own findings come closest to those of Ben Singer's.

24. Barton W. Currie, "The Nickel Madness," *Harper's Weekly*, August 24, 1907, quoted in Mast, *Movies in Our Midst*, 49.

25. King Vidor, *A Tree is a Tree: An Autobiography* (Hollywood, 1981), 65; *NY Call*, February 7, 1914.

26. MacLean, *Wage-Earning Women*, 44–45. The practice of "nooning" is described in Juvenile Protective Association, *Recreation Survey of Cincinnati*, 26–27; Nasaw, *Going Out*, 163–64.

27. *NY Call*, October 15, 1913; *MPW*, February 22, 1908; George F. Kenngott, *The Record of a City: A Social Survey of Lowell, Massachusetts* (New York, 1912), 218.

28. For discussions of immigrant reception during this period, see Stuart and Elizabeth Ewen, *Channels of Desire: Mass Images and the Shaping of American Consciousness* (New York, 1982), 81–105; Hansen, *Babel & Babylon*; Mayne, "Immigrants and Spectators," 32–41.

29. Author interview with Rose Hobart, March 14, 1990, Motion Picture County House, Woodland Hills, Ca. Attendance figures for Chicago and Connecticut are taken from *Chicago Daily Socialist*, January 10, 1912, and Bowser, *Transformation of Cinema*, 2. Class patterns of moviegoing among children are discussed in Sizer, *Commercialization of Leisure*, 58.

30. The gendered uses of public space are described in Elizabeth Ewen, *Immigrant Women in the Land of Dollars: Life and Culture on the Lower East Side, 1890–1925* (New York, 1985), 208–16; Peiss, *Cheap Amusements*. For discussions of women who did not follow these roles, see Christine Stansell, *City of Women: Sex and Class in New York, 1789–1860* (New York, 1986); Carroll Smith Rosenberg, *Disorderly Conduct: Visions of Gender in Victorian America* (New York, 1985), 245–96.

31. Simkhovitch, *City Worker's World*, 128; *Jewish Daily Forward*, quoted in Howe, *World of Our Fathers*, 213. The gendered patterns of moviegoing are described ibid.; Ewen, *Immigrant Women*, 207–24; Hansen, *Babel & Babylon*.

32. Ralph Fletcher Carr, "Resources for Leisure Time: Motion Picture Theaters in Pittsburgh," *The Federator*, 10 (December 1935), 3; *Film Index*, February 29, 1908; *LA Citizen*, September 1, 1911. A New York survey estimated that 40,000 unescorted children went to the movies each day. Peiss, *Cheap Amusements*, 150.

33. MacLean, *Wage-Earning Women*, 45; Ognibene quoted in Elizabeth Ewen, "City Lights: Immigrant Women and the Rise of the Movies," *Signs*, 5 (Spring 1980), 58; Bartholomew, *Censorship of Motion Pictures*, 12; *NY Call*, January 1, 1916.

34. *Saturday Evening Post* quoted in Cleveland, *Commercial Recreation*, 22–23; Charles Stelze, "Movies instead of Saloons," *The Independent*, 85 (February 28, 1916), 311; Howe, *World of Our Fathers*, 214.

35. *Chicago Defender*, April 9, 1910, quoted in Mary Carbine, "'The Finest outside the Loop': Motion Picture Exhibition in Chicago's Black Metropolis, 1905–1928," *Camera Obscura*, 23 (May 1990), 16; Thomas quoted in Kisseloff, *You Must Remember This*, 276; *NY Call*, November 20, 1915.

36. Gregory A. Waller, "Another Audience: Black Moviegoing, 1907–16," *Cinema Journal*, 31 (Winter 1992), 10; statistics for black movie theaters are taken from *MPW*, October 4, 1913. The segregation of movie houses and evolution of black movie theaters are discussed in Carbine, "Finest outside the Loop," 8–41; Waller, *Main Street Amusements*, 161–79; Bowser, *Transformation of Cinema*, 9–10; Henry T. Sampson, *Blacks in Black and White: A Source Book on Black Films* (Metuchen, N.J., 1977); Dan Leab, "'All Colored'—But Not Much Different: Films Made for Negro Ghetto Audiences 1913–1928," *Phylon*, 36 (September 1975), 321–39; Richard Alan Nelson, *Florida and the American Motion Picture Industry 1898–1980*, 2 vols. (New York, 1983), 2: 390, 430, 459; Gomery, *Shared Pleasures*, 155–59.

37. Shimizu quoted in Junko Ogihara, "The Exhibition of Films for Japanese Americans in Los Angeles during the Silent Film Era," *Film History*, 4:2 (1990), 83. For Chicago theaters, see Lizabeth Cohen, *Making a New Deal: Industrial Workers in Chicago, 1919–1939* (Cambridge and New York, 1990), 124.

38. Simkhovitch, *City Workers' World*, 124; Marx quoted in Kisseloff, *You Must Remember This*, 171.

39. Rosenzweig, *Eight Hours*, 199. For recent discussions of how audiences shaped their moviegoing experiences to fit their needs, see ibid., 191–221; Peiss, *Cheap Amusements*, 139–62; Cohen, *Making a New Deal*, 120–31; Hansen, *Babel & Babylon*, 90–125.

40. Edward Wagenknecht, *The Movies in the Age of Innocence* (New York, 1971), 11; Francis R. North, *A Recreation Survey of the City of Providence, Rhode Island* (Providence, 1912), 29. The changing nature of early films and theater programs are described in Musser, *Emergence of Cinema*; Bowser, *Transformation of Cinema*; Tarbox, *Lost Films*.

41. Twentieth Century Club, *Amusement Situation in Boston*, 16. The sounds of the theater are also described in Bartholomew, *Censorship of Motion Pictures*, 17; Bowser, *Transformation of Cinema*, 124; Tarbox, *Lost Films*, 64; Bowers, *Nickelodeon Theatres*.

42. Jane Addams, *The Spirit of Youth and the City Streets* (New York, 1909), 87. For singing in theaters, see Davis, *Exploitation of Pleasure*, 24.

43. *Variety*, November 14, 1913; *LA Citizen*, February 25, 1916.

44. Lewis Palmer, "The World in Motion," *Survey*, 22 (June 5, 1909), 355.

45. Carbine, "Finest outside the Loop," 21–22; Waller, *Main Street Amusements*, 161–79; Sampson, *Blacks in Black and White*; Thomas Cripps, *Black Film as Genre* (Bloomington, 1978), 15–33; Thomas Cripps, "The Movie Jew as an Image of Assimilation, 1903–1927," *Journal of Popular Film*, 4:3 (1975), 194; Eric Goldman, *Visions, Images, and Dreams: Yiddish Film Past and Present* (Ann Arbor, 1983); J. Hoberman, *Bridge of Light: Yiddish Films between Two Worlds* (New York, 1991), 4–5, 26–37; Kevin Brownlow, *Behind the Mask of Innocence* (New York, 1990), 343–53, 384; Anthony Slide, *The American Film Industry: A Historical Dictionary* (New York, 1986), 46, 138, 140, 177; Ogihara, "Exhibition of Films," 81–87; Peiss, *Cheap Amusements*, 149–50; Hansen, *Babel & Babylon*, 100; *MPW*, January 4, 1908.

46. *NY Call*, November 6, 1908. Suffragist films are discussed in Shelly Stamp Lindsey, "*Eighty Million Women Want—?*: Women's Suffrage, Female Viewers and the Body Politic," *Quarterly Review of Film and Video*, 16:1 (1995), 1–22; Brownlow, *Behind the Mask*, 226–37; Sloan, *Loud Silents*, 99–123; *MPW*, March 14, 1916. Information regarding the exhibition of radical films can be found in Chicago *The Party Builder*, March 21, 1914; Walter Millsap, "Llano Cooperative Colony," 20–21, transcript, U.C.L.A. Oral History Project, 1969, UCLA; Steven J. Ross, "Struggles for the Screen: Workers, Radicals, and the Political Uses of Silent Film," *American Historical Review*, 96 (April 1991), 344–46.

47. *LA Citizen*, April 13, 1917; *Cleveland Citizen*, February 23, 1907; for Brooklyn socialists, see *NY Call*, November 6, 1908. For other examples of the use of theaters by unionists, socialists, and suffragists, see *LA Citizen*, March 11, 1910, September 15, 22, 1911; *Chicago Daily Socialist*, December 17, 1909, January 22 and June 8, 1912; *NY Call*, June 11, 1912, February 22, 1915. For a pioneering

analysis of the transformation and politicization of public space in modern western societies, see Jürgen Habermas, "The Public Sphere," *New German Critique*, 1 (Fall 1974), 49–55; Habermas, *The Structural Transformation of the Public Sphere: An Inquiry into a Category of Bourgeois Society*, translated by Thomas Berger (Cambridge, Mass., 1989).

48. Currie, "Nickel Madness," in Mast, *Movies in Our Midst*, 45; New York Society for the Prevention of Cruelty to Children, 1909, quoted in Nasaw, *Going Out*, 174, 288 note 1. For an overview of moral reform and its various approaches, see Paul Boyer, *Urban Masses and Moral Order in America, 1820–1920* (Cambridge, Mass., 1978); for moral reform in the movie industry, see William Uricchio and Roberta Pearson, *Reframing Culture: The Case of the Vitagraph Quality Films* (Princeton, 1993); Sumiko Higashi, *Cecil B. DeMille and American Culture: The Silent Era* (Berkeley, 1994); May, *Screening out the Past*.

49. Addams, *Spirit of Youth*, 82–83; *NY Call*, November 16, 1911. For a contemporaneous psychological analysis of the effects of film, see Hugo Münsterberg, *The Photoplay: A Psychological Study* (New York, 1916).

50. Kenngott, *Record of a City*, 218; David Nasaw, *Children of the City: At Work and at Play* (New York, 1985), 140; Bartholomew, *Censorship of Motion Pictures*, 12; *NY Call*, February 7, 1911.

51. Eaton, "Class Consciousness and the 'Movies,' " 52, 53, 50.

52. Henry James, *The American Scene* (New York, 1907), quoted in Levine, *Highbrow/Lowbrow*, 172; population statistics are taken from Raymond Mohl, *The New City: Urban America in the Industrial Age, 1860–1920* (Arlington Heights, Ill., 1985), 25. For nativism and Americanization campaigns, see John Higham, *Strangers in the Land: Patterns of American Nativism 1860–1925* (New York, 1970). The role that Jews and immigrants played in the movies is discussed in Gabler, *Empire of Their Own*.

53. Sklar, *Movie-Made America*, 18; Garth Jowett, "From Entertainment to Social Force: The Discovery of the Motion Picture 1918–1950," in Bruce A. Austin, ed., *Current Research in Film: Audiences, Economics, and Law*, 2 (1986), 10; Jack London, "The Message of Motion Pictures," *Paramount Magazine*, 1 (February 1915), reprinted in *Authors on Film*, edited by Harry M. Geduld (Bloomington, 1972), 105–6; *Chicago Daily Socialist*, December 13, 1909. The activities of socialist movie theaters are discussed in Chapter 4.

54. Juvenile Protective Association, *Recreation Survey of Cincinnati*, 25. The social control thesis and campaigns against allegedly immoral films are most fully explored in May, *Screening out the Past*; Musser, *Before the Nickelodeon*, 427–32; Higashi, *DeMille and American Culture*; Uricchio and Pearson, *Reframing Culture*; Sklar, *Movie-Made America*; Jowett, *Film*; Bowser, *Transformation of Cinema*, 37–52; special issue on "Hollywood, Censorship, and American Culture," *American Quarterly*, 44 (December 1992). The class dimensions of social control arguments are analyzed in Gareth Stedman Jones, *Languages of Class: Studies in English Working Class History 1832–1982* (Cambridge, England, 1983), 76–89.

55. Dollar equivalences are taken from figures in John J. McCusker, *How Much Is That in Real Money? A Historical Price Index for Use as a Deflator of Money Values in the Economy of the United States* (Worcester, Mass., 1992), 329–32. The rise of the feature film and the process of making movies respectable are described in Uricchio and Pearson, *Reframing Culture*; Higashi, *DeMille and American Culture*, 7–141;

Bowser, *Transformation of Cinema*, 191–233; Richard Koszarski, *An Evening's Entertainment: The Age of the Silent Feature Picture, 1915–1918* (New York, 1990), 63–190; Benjamin Hampton, *A History of the Movies* (New York, 1931), 101–45; Lewis Jacobs, *The Rise of the American Film: A Critical History* (New York, 1968), 81–201. For Kleine's view of his contributions, see George Kleine to Benjamin Hampton, September 12, 1927, Box 25, George Kleine Collection, Manuscripts Division, Library of Congress, Washington, D.C.

56. Will Irwin, *The House That Shadows Built* (New York, 1928), 151; *NY Call*, April 29, 1909. Emil Seidel, Milwaukee's Socialist mayor, was an advocate of films but expressed grave concerns about the safety of many nickel theaters; *MPW*, June 4, 1910. The dangers of movie theaters are described in Musser, *Emergence of Cinema*, 443–44; Koszarski, *Evening's Entertainment*, 12, 17; Robert A. Armour, "Effects of Censorship Pressure on the New York Nickelodeon Market, 1907–1909," *Film History*, 4:2 (1990), 115–17.

57. Roxy's early career is described in Gabler, *Empire of Their Own*, 95–100. For the rise of luxurious theaters and motion picture palaces, see Bowser, *Transformation of Cinema*, 121–36; May, *Screening out the Past*, 147–66; Hall, *Best Remaining Seats*, 26–68; Koszarski, *Evening's Entertainment*, 9–25; Douglas Gomery, "The Movie Palace Comes to America's Cities," in Butsch, *For Fun and Profit*, 136–51.

58. *NY Call*, April 5, 1914; Roxy quoted in Hall, *Best Remaining Seats*, 40.

59. *NY Call*, April 19, 1914. For descriptions of the amenities offered in these palaces, see *LA Citizen*, May 17, 1918, and sources in note 57.

60. Eaton, "Class-Consciousness and the Movies," 50; Watson quoted in Hall, *Best Remaining Seats*, 39–40.

61. Chicago *Daily Worker*, January 28, 1924. In 1922, only 9 percent of the nation's theaters contained more than 1,000 seats. Theater statistics are taken from May, *Screening out the Past*, 150; Hansen, *Babel & Babylon*, 100; Koszarski, *Evening's Entertainment*, 10–13.

Chapter 2
Visualizing the Working Class

1. Shepherd quoted in James Green, *The World of the Worker: Labor in Twentieth-Century America* (New York, 1980), 74–75. The Triangle fire and its aftermath are discussed in Leon Stein, *The Triangle Fire* (Philadelphia, 1962).

2. Ludlow quote in Louis Adamic, *Dynamite: The Story of Class Violence in America* (New York, 1935), 259. Death figures for the Ludlow massacre, which vary in different texts, are taken from H. M. Gitelman, *Legacy of the Ludlow Massacre: A Chapter in Industrial Relations* (Philadelphia, 1988), 18.

3. *The Crime of Carelessness* and *The Miner's Lesson* can be found, respectively, at MOMA and the Motion Picture Room, NA. For reviews of *The High Road* see *New York Dramatic Mirror*, May 5, 1915, *Motography*, May 8, 1915. A shooting script of *What Is to Be Done?* can be found in the Copyright Records, LC.

4. "Definition of Censorship Prepared by the National Board of Review of Motion Pictures. 1913," 2, Box 166, NBRMP. For a brief overview of the diversity of early producers and production sites, see Anthony Slide, *Early American Cinema* (Metuchen, N.J., 1994), 7–68.

5. For works that see radical filmmaking emerging in the late 1920s and 1930s, see Russell Campbell, *The Cinema Strikes Back: Radical Filmmaking in the United States 1930–1942* (Ann Arbor, 1982); William Alexander, *Film on the Left: American Documentary Film from 1931 to 1942* (Princeton, 1981); Bert Hogenkamp, "Worker's Newsreels in the 1920's and 1930's," *Our History* (pamphlet), 68 (London, 1977); and the special issue devoted to "American Labor Films" in *Film Library Quarterly*, 12:2/3 (1979).

6. I employ this citation system throughout the book. All years cited represent a film's release date rather than its production date. My analysis of early cinematic depictions of working-class life is based heavily on my viewing 100 films released between 1898 and April 1917 (when the United States entered World War I), and reading reviews for 605 working-class films released between 1905 (when the first nickelodeon opened) and April 1917. For a list of surviving films and their repositories, see Appendix I: Select Filmography.

7. In focusing on *The Birth of a Nation* and later works, scholars have tended to ignore the significance of Griffith's early Biograph years. My purpose here is not to be an apologist for Griffith's racism or Victorian romanticism, but to stress his often overlooked early contributions as a political filmmaker and staunch defender of the working class. My portrait of Griffith is drawn both from seeing many of his films and from the following sources: Iris Barry, *D. W. Griffith: American Film Master* (New York, 1940); Lewis Jacobs, *The Rise of the American Film* (New York, 1968), 95–119; Linda Arvidson, *When the Movies Were Young* (New York, 1969); Lillian Gish with Ann Pinchot, *The Movies, Mr. Griffith, and Me* (Englewood Cliffs, N.J., 1969); Harry M. Geduld, ed., *Focus on D. W. Griffith* (Englewood Cliffs, N.J., 1971); D. W. Griffith, *The Man Who Invented Hollywood: The Autobiography of D. W. Griffith*, edited and annotated by James Hart (Louisville, 1972); Lary May, *Screening out the Past: The Birth of Mass Culture and the Motion Picture Industry* (New York, 1980), 60–95; Richard Schickel, *D. W. Griffith: An American Life* (New York, 1983); Joyce E. Jesionowski, *Thinking in Pictures: Dramatic Structure in D. W. Griffith's Biograph Films* (Berkeley, 1987); Michael Paul Rogin, "'The Sword Became a Flashing Vision': D.W. Griffith's *The Birth of a Nation*," in Michael Paul Rogin, *Ronald Reagan, the Movie and Other Episodes in Political Demonology* (Berkeley, 1987), 190–235; Robert Lang, *American Film Melodrama: Griffith, Vidor, Minnelli* (Princeton, 1989); Russell Merritt, "Rescued from a Perilous Nest: D. W. Griffith's Escape from Theatre into Film," *Cinema Journal*, 21 (Fall 1981), 2–30; and, especially, Tom Gunning, *D. W. Griffith and the Origins of American Narrative Film: The Early Years at Biograph* (Urbana and Chicago, 1991).

8. Griffith quoted in Henry Stephen Gordon, "The Story of David Wark Griffith," *Photoplay*, 10 (June 1916), cited in Geduld, *Focus on Griffith*, 20.

9. Gish, *Movies, Mr. Griffith, and Me*, 62; *New York American*, February 28, 1915, in Geduld, *Focus on Griffith*, 29. Since directors were not credited at the time, it is difficult to determine the exact number of Griffith's Biograph films. Iris Barry and Tom Gunning estimate the number to range between 450 and 496.

10. *The Musketeers of Pig Alley* (Biograph 1912) is regarded as Griffith's most famous depiction of crime in the ghettos.

11. *MPW*, December 30, 1911. For Griffith and Los Angeles labor, see D. W. Griffith, "Motion Pictures Can Be Made to Help and Hearten Labor," *LA Citizen*,

February 25, 1916; "Minutes of the Meetings of Local 33, International Alliance of Theatrical and Stage Employees," September 8, 1922, Local 33 Headquarters, Burbank, Ca. For films promoting a vision of an independent proletariat, see *Simple Charity* (Biograph 1910) and *The Miser's Heart* (Biograph 1911).

12. Russell Merritt, "Nickelodeon Theaters 1905–1914: Building an Audience for the Movies," in Tino Balio, ed., *The American Film Industry* (Madison, 1976), 72.

13. For a brief overview of the complexities and contradications of the Progressive era, see Daniel T. Rodgers, "In Search of Progressivism," *Reviews in American History*, 10 (December 1982), 112–32.

14. McCormick quoted in Leon Fink, ed., *Major Problems in the Gilded Age and the Progressive Era* (Lexington, Mass., 1993), 319. For works that explore a variety of Progressive-era themes, see Alan Dawley, *Struggles for Justice: Social Responsibility and the Liberal State* (Cambridge, Mass., 1991); John Milton Cooper, Jr., *Pivotal Decades: The United States, 1900–1920* (New York, 1990); James Weinstein, *The Corporate Ideal in the Liberal State 1900–1918* (Boston, 1968); John D. Buenker, *Urban Liberalism and Progressive Reform* (New York, 1978); Martin Sklar, *The Corporate Reconstruction of American Capitalism, 1890–1916* (Cambridge, Mass., 1988); William Forbath, *Law and the Shaping of the American Labor Movement* (Cambridge, Mass., 1991); Robyn Muncy, *Creating a Female Dominion in American Reform 1890–1935* (New York, 1991); Nell Painter, *Standing at Armageddon* (New York, 1987); Robert Crunden, *Ministers of Reform: The Progressives' Achievement in American Civilization 1889–1920* (New York, 1982).

15. *NY Call*, May 25, 1913. For overviews of cultural change during this era, see Alfred Kazin, *On Native Ground* (New York, 1942); Henry May, *The End of American Innocence: A Study of the First Years of Our Time, 1912–1917* (Chicago, 1964); Douglas Tallack, *Twentieth-Century America: The Intellectual and Cultural Context* (New York, 1991); Edward Abrahams, *The Lyrical Left: Randolph Bourne, Alfred Stieglitz, and the Origins of Cultural Radicalism* (Charlottesville, Va., 1986); T. J. Jackson Lears, *No Place of Grace* (New York, 1981).

16. Weber quoted in Kevin Brownlow, *Behind the Mask of Innocence* (New York 1990), xxi–xxii; Vidor quoted in Raymond Durgnant and Scott Simmon, *King Vidor, American* (Berkeley, 1988), 27. For biographical sketches of Weber, see Ally Acker, *Reel Women: Pioneers of the Cinema 1896 to the Present* (New York, 1991), 12–16; Anthony Slide, *Early Women Directors* (South Brunswick and New York, 1977), 34–51. Social-problem films are discussed in Kay Sloan, *Loud Silents: Origins of the Social Problem Film* (Urbana, 1988); Peter Roffman and Jim Purdy, *The Hollywood Social Problem Film* (Bloomington, 1981); Charles J. Maland, "The Social Problem Film," in Wes D. Gehring, ed., *Handbook of American Film Genres* (New York and Westport, Conn., 1988), 305–29; Steven J. Ross, "The Unknown Hollywood," *History Today* 40 (April 1990), 40–46; Brownlow, *Behind the Mask*; Jacobs, *Rise of American Film*.

17. *Nickelodeon*, quoted in Tom Gunning, "Weaving a Narrative Style and Economic Background in Griffith's Biograph Films," in Thomas Elsaesser, ed., *Early Cinema: Space, Frame, Narrative* (London, 1990), 339; Goldwyn quoted in Brownlow, *Behind the Mask*, xviii.

18. Thomas Brandon, "Populist Film," chapter 1, 17, file C34, unpublished manuscript, Brandon Coll.; Brownlow, *Behind the Mask*, 433; Peter Stead, *Film and the*

Working Class: The Feature Film in British and American Society (London and New York, 1989), 23; Brandon figures quoted in Brownlow, *Behind the Mask*, 433.

19. Jacobs, *Rise of American Film*, 156; Eileen Bowser, *The Transformation of Cinema 1907–1915* (New York, 1990), 188. For other works that emphasize similar points of view, see James Combs, *American Political Movies: An Annotated Filmography of Feature Films* (New York and London, 1990), viii; Garth Jowett, *Film: The Democratic Art* (Boston, 1976); Sloan, *Loud Silents*; Gunning, *D. W. Griffith*. Miriam Hansen straddles the two sides, arguing on behalf of the political nature of early film but minimizing the number of movies expressly dealing with working-class life. Miriam Hansen, *Babel & Babylon: Spectatorship in American Silent Film* (Cambridge, Mass., 1991), 68–70.

20. Eugene Genovese and Elizabeth Fox-Genovese, "The Political Crisis of Social History: A Marxian Perspective," *Journal of Social History*, 10 (Winter 1976), 219. My analysis in this chapter and throughout the book is concerned mainly with exploring power in the public sphere, and especially the politics of class struggle. The number of political films would grow even greater if we included power in the private sphere—struggles between husbands and wives, parents and children, boyfriends and girlfriends. For an even more expansive vision of power, see Michel Foucault, edited by Colin Gordon, *Power/Knowledge: Selected Interviews and Other Writings 1972–1977* (New York, 1980).

21. There are no figures for the number of workers participating in strikes in 1910. Union statistics are taken from *Historical Statistics*, 1: 131, 138–39, 178–79. The evolution of labor and working-class history are explored in David Brody, "The Old Labor History and the New: In Search of the American Working Class," *Labor History*, 20 (Winter 1979), 111–26; David Montgomery, "To Study the People: The American Working Class," *Labor History*, 21 (Fall 1980), 485–512; Ava Baron, "Gender and Labor History: Learning from the Past, Looking to the Future," in Ava Baron, ed., *Work Engendered: Toward a New History of American Labor* (Ithaca, 1991), 1–46.

22. The 605 films I found represent only a small percentage of all working-class films. It was never my intention to create an exhaustive list of *all* films about working-class life (this is a project that deserves further attention by scholars). Rather, I began my research by reading through a variety of primary and secondary sources and compiling a list of only those films that seemed to deal explicitly with some aspect of class conflict. Thus, most working-class films never made it on to my list. The 605 films cited here (91 of which I have seen) were movies that initially appeared to explore class struggles. However, subsequent research revealed that many were about working-class life but not explicitly about class conflict. Anyone who doubts that that working-class films ran into the thousands should consult the subject indexes in American Film Institute Catalogs. These catalogs (which themselves include only a small percentage of all silent films) list a vast number of movies about work, working people, and working-class life. Indeed, my own computations suggest that working-class films probably accounted for at least 2,130 of the approximately 22,900 films released between 1911 and 1915. For a discussion of the methodology used to compute these figures, see Chapter 3 note 3.

In addition to the films themselves, the most useful sources of information in compiling this list were reviews in movie and labor periodicals, movie stills, film catalogs, and the tens of thousands of reviews, film scripts, and plot synopses that producers submitted to the federal copyright office in Washington, and which can be found on microfilm in Copyright Records, LC. The most helpful secondary sources included Philip Sterling, "A Channel for Democratic Thought," *Films,* 1 (Spring 1940), 8–14; Ken Margolies, "Silver Screen Tarnishes Unions," *Screen Actor* 23 (Summer 1981), 43–52; Roberta Pearson, "Cultivated Folks and the Better Classes: Class Conflict and Representation in Early American Film," *Journal of Popular Film and Television,* 15 (Fall 1987), 120–28; William J. Puette, *Through Jaundiced Eyes: How the Media View Organized Labor* (Ithaca, 1992); Craig Campbell, *Reel America and World War I: A Comprehensive Filmography and History of Motion Pictures in the United States, 1914–1920* (Jefferson, N.C., 1985); Brownlow, *Behind the Mask;* Stead, *Film and the Working Class;* Sloan, *Loud Silents;* Jacobs, *Rise of American Film;* Musser, *Emergence of Cinema;* Sklar, *Movie-Made America;* and especially Brandon, "Populist Film," MOMA. For a more thorough discussion of useful sources and film catalogs, see Appendix II.

23. Foreign films, which constituted 60 percent of the American market before the Trust, dropped to 10 percent by 1914. Gunning, *D. W. Griffith,* 146. For Solax production figures, see Anthony Slide, ed., *The Memoirs of Alice Guy Blaché,* translated by Roberta and Simone Blaché (Metuchen, N.J., 1986), 157–62. The Trust is discussed in greater detail in Chapter 3. The changing nature of production, distribution, and exhibition during the industry's early years are explored in Adolph Zukor, "Origin and Growth of the Industry," in Joseph P. Kennedy, ed., *The Story of the Films* (Chicago and New York, 1927, reprinted 1971), 55–76; David Bordwell, Janet Staiger, Kristin Thompson, *The Classical Hollywood Cinema: Film Style and Mode of Production to 1960* (New York, 1985); Charles Musser, *The Emergence of Cinema: The American Screen to 1907* (New York, 1990); Richard Koszarski, *An Evening's Entertainment: The Age of the Silent Feature Picture, 1915–1928* (New York, 1990); Charles Musser, *Before the Nickelodeon: Edwin S. Porter and the Edison Manufacturing Company* (Berkeley, 1991); John L. Fell, ed., *Film before Griffith* (Berkeley, 1983); Suzanne Mary Donahue, *American Film Distribution: The Changing Marketplace* (Ann Arbor, 1987); Benjamin Hampton, *A History of the Movies* (New York, 1931); Mae Huttig, *Economic Control of the Motion Picture Industry* (Philadelphia, 1944); Elsaesser, *Early Cinema;* Bowser, *Transformation of Cinema;* Balio, *American Film Industry.*

24. The number of new releases each year is discussed in Charles H. Tarbox, *Lost Films 1895–1917* (Los Angeles, 1983). For a first-hand account of the frenzied pace of early production, see Fred Balshofer and Fred C. Miller, *One Reel a Week* (Berkeley, 1967). For an account of early actualities, see Tom Gunning, "The Cinema of Attractions: Early Cinema, Its Spectators, and the Avant-Garde," *Wide Angle,* 8 (Fall 1986), 63–70.

25. *MPW,* July 9, 1910; "O'Kalem" quote is from Edward Wagenknecht, *The Movies in the Age of Innocence* (New York, 1971), 46–47. For the backgrounds and films of Lubin and Laemmle, see Joseph P. Eckhardt and Linda Kowall, *Peddler of Dreams: Siegmund Lubin and the Creation of the Motion Picture Industry 1896–1916* (Philadelphia, 1984); Linda Woal, "When a Dime Could Buy a Dream: Siegmund Lubin and the Birth of Motion Picture Exhibition," *Film History,* 6 (Summer 1994), 152–65; John Drinkwater, *The Life and Adventures of Carl Laemmle* (New York, 1931). Lubin

and Universal released movies such as *The Yiddisher Boy* (1908) and *The Heart of a Jewess* (1913), while Kalem shot a series of films in Ireland titled *The Colleen Bawn, Arrah-na-Pogue,* and *The Lad from Old Ireland.* Kalem also produced ethnic features for German audiences (*The Little Spreewald Maiden*) and Jewish ones (*A Passover Miracle,* 1914, which contained titles in English and Yiddish). For Kalem, see Anthony Slide, *Aspects of American Film History Prior to 1920* (Metuchen, N.J., 1978), 87–97. For the best overview of films for and about immigrants, see Brownlow, *Behind the Mask,* 301–423. The working-class focus of film companies and the class backgrounds of many early stars are discussed in Emanuel Julius, "Mary Pickford, Queen of the Movies," *NY Call,* June 7, 1914; Al Auster, "Mary Pickford (1893–1979), the Star the Working Class Found," *Cineaste,* 9 (Fall 1979), 42–43; Stead, *Film and the Working Class,* 31–36; Charles Musser, "Work, Ideology, and Chaplin's Tramp," in Robert Sklar and Charles Musser, eds., *Resisting Images: Essays on Cinema and History* (Philadelphia, 1990), 36–67; Robert Sklar, *Movie-Made America: A Cultural History of American Movies* (New York, 1994); Musser, *Emergence of Cinema,* 396, 479; Hansen, *Babel & Babylon,* 70.

26. The transition from nonfiction actualities to narrative films is discussed in Musser, *Before the Nickelodeon;* Gunning, *D. W. Griffith;* Bowser, *Transformation of Cinema,* 53–54.

27. Jacobs, *Rise of American Film,* 67.

28. *The Baltimore Sun,* quoted in Pearson, "Cultivated Folks," 122. The nature and sources of early comedies are described ibid., 179–84; Kalton C. Lahue, *World of Laughter: The Motion Picture Comedy Short, 1910–1930* (Norman, Okla., 1966); Kalton C. Lahue and Terry Brewer, *Kops and Custard: The Legend of the Keystone Films* (Norman, Okla., 1967); Eileen Bowser, ed., *The Slapstick Symposium* (Brussels, 1987); Henry Jenkins, *What Made Pistachio Nuts? Early Sound Comedy and the Vaudeville Aesthetic* (New York, 1992).

29. Films by Chaplin and John Bunny were especially popular with New York socialists, who showed them at various gatherings and fund-raisers; see, for example, *NY Call,* July 19, 1914.

30. *MPW,* December 21, 1907, quoted in Musser, *Before the Nickelodeon,* 429. The *Mirror* also distinguished between drama and melodrama: 34 percent of the films belonged to the former category, and 19 percent to the latter. *New York Dramatic Mirror,* August 13, 1910. The transition from comedy to melodrama is discussed in Musser, *Emergence of Cinema;* Bowser, *Transformation of Cinema;* Gunning, *D. W. Griffith;* for the dominance of melodrama during the teens and twenties, see Koszarski, *Evening's Entertainment,* 182.

31. *MPW,* August 22, 1908; *Report of the Pennsylvania State Board of Censors, June 1st, 1915 to December 1st, 1915* (Harrisburg, Pa., 1916), 7. The theatrical and literary roots of melodrama are explored in Peter Brooks, *The Melodramatic Imagination: Balzac, Henry James, Melodrama, and the Mode of Excess* (New Haven, 1976); David Grimsted, *Melodrama Unveiled: American Theater and Culture 1800–1850* (Chicago, 1968); Bruce A. McConachie, *Melodramatic Formations: American Theatre and Society, 1820–1870* (Iowa City, 1992); Lawrence Levine, *Highbrow/Lowbrow: The Emergence of Cultural Hierarchy in America* (Cambridge, Mass., 1988); Jacky Bratton, Jim Cook, Christine Gledhill, eds., *Melodrama: Stage Picture Screen* (London, 1994). For dime novels and working-class melodramas, see Michael Denning, *Mechanic*

Accents: Dime Novels and Working-Class Culture in America (London and New York, 1987). For filmmakers' efforts to develop more coherent cinematic styles, see Musser, *Before the Nickelodeon*, 359–97. The rise of the "classical" Hollywood style is described in Bordwell et al., *Classical Hollywood Cinema*.

32. Pearson, "Cultivated Folks," 125; Lang, *American Film Melodrama*, 18; Bowser, *Transformation of Cinema*, 45.

33. For a sampling of works on gender, ethnicity, and race in silent film, see Marjorie Rosen, *Popcorn Venus: Women, Movies, and the American Dream* (New York, 1973); Lester D. Friedman, ed., *Unspeakable Images: Ethnicity and the American Cinema* (Urbana, 1991); Randall Miller, ed., *Ethnic Images in American Film and Television* (Philadelphia, 1978); Lester D. Friedman, "Celluloid Assimilation: Jews in American Silent Movies," *Journal of Popular Film and Television*, 15 (Fall 1987), 129–36; Patricia Erens, *The Jew in American Cinema* (Bloomington, 1984); James M. Curran, *Hibernian Green on the Silver Screen: The Irish and American Movies* (Westport, Conn., 1989); Thomas Cripps, *Slow Fade to Black: The Negro in American Film, 1900–1942* (New York, 1977); Gary D. Keller, ed., *Chicano Cinema: Research, Reviews, and Resources* (Binghamton, N.Y., 1985); Daniel Bernardi, ed., *The Birth of Whiteness: Race and the Emergence of U.S. Cinema* (New Brunswick, N.J., 1996); and sources cited in Chapter 1 note 45.

34. Musser, *Before the Nickelodeon*, 11. For more extended discussions of cinematic treatments of poverty, see Brownlow, *Behind the Mask*, 264–99; Sloan, *Loud Silents*, 36–52.

35. Crosscutting refers to cutting back and forth between scenes that are happening simultaneously, whereas parallel editing refers to cutting between scenes that are separated by time. For discussions of these editing techniques, see Barry Salt, *Film Style and Technology: History and Analysis* (London, 1992); Richard Koszarski, ed., *The Rivals of D. W. Griffith* (Minneapolis, 1976); Bowser, *Transformation of Cinema*, 53–72; Bordwell et al., *Classical Hollywood*, 48–49, 210–12; Elsaesser, *Early Cinema*; Fell, *Film before Griffith*.

36. Quoted in Sklar, *Movie-Made America*, 57. For an extended analysis of *Song*, see Gunning, *D. W. Griffith*, 134–37.

37. For examples of Griffith's sanitized tenement flats, see *The Song of the Shirt* (Biograph 1908), *In the Watches of the Night* (Biograph 1909), and *A Child of the Ghetto* (Biograph 1910).

38. *MPW*, July 9, 1910.

39. The number of working women rose from 3.7 million in 1890 to 7.6 million in 1910. The number of married working women during this period more than tripled, from 515,000 to 1,891,000. *Historical Statistics*, 1: 133.

40. For a close reading of the cinematic techniques employed in *The Mill Girl*, see Eileen Bowser, "Toward Narrative, 1907: *The Mill Girl*," in Fell, *Film before Griffith*, 330–38. For a sampling of films about sweatshops, see *Song of the Shirt* (Biograph 1908), *A Child of the Ghetto* (Biograph 1910), *The Heart of a Jewess* (1913), *For His Father's Sins* (1914), *The Locked Door* (1914), *A Breath of Summer* (1915); for canneries, see *Children of Eve* (Edison 1915), *Out of Darkness* (1915); for cotton mills, see *The Cry of the Children* (Thanhouser 1912), *The Blood of the Children* (1914), *Eyes that See Not* (1915); for laundries, see *The Deception* (1910), and *The Invisible Enemy* (1916).

41. Drinkwater, *Laemmle*, 167–68. Laemmle was exposed to the horrors of child labor while visiting exhibitors in the Mississippi Valley. His company, Universal, produced *The Blood of the Children* (1914) and *The White Terror* (1915).

42. On Victorian attitudes and filmmakers, see May, *Screening out the Past*; the links between reformers, reformer films, and class fears are also discussed in Sklar, *Movie-Made America*; Jowett, *Film*; Brownlow, *Behind the Mask*; Sloan, *Loud Silents*.

43. *MPW*, March 9, 1912; Kay Sloan, "A Cinema in Search of Itself: Ideology of the Social Problem Film during the Silent Era," *Cineaste*, 14:2 (1985), 35. Other assessments of the film can be found in Brownlow, *Behind the Mask*, 428–29; Sloan, *Loud Silents*, 70–72. For further analyses of the limitations of these reform films, see ibid.; Ross, "Unknown Hollywood."

Chapter 3
The Good, the Bad, and the Violent

1. Between 1886 and 1895, state governors called out their national guard units 328 times, and at least one-third of these mobilizations were in response to "labor troubles." David Montgomery, *Citizen Worker: The Experience of Workers in the United States with Democracy and the Free Market during the Nineteenth Century* (Cambridge and New York, 1993) 95–96. Clashes among workers, employers, and government troops are described in Louis Adamic, *Dynamite: The Story of Class Violence in America* (New York, 1934); Richard O. Boyer and Herbert M. Morais, *Labor's Untold Story* (New York, 1955); Jeremy Brecher, *Strike* (San Francisco, 1972); James Green, *The World of the Worker: Labor in Twentieth-Century America* (New York, 1980); and Melvyn Dubofsky, *We Shall Be All: A History of the IWW* (New York, 1969). Statistics regarding strikes and work stoppages during this era can be found in *Historical Statistics*, 1: 179, and P. K. Edwards, *Strikes in the United States 1881–1974* (New York, 1981).

2. Thomas Schatz, *Hollywood Genres* (New York, 1981), 6; Eileen Bowser, *The Transformation of Cinema 1907–1915* (New York, 1990), 167. For early references to what were alternately called "labor," "labor-capital," or "labor movement stories," see advertisements in *Motography*, July 12, 1913, and advertisement for *The Power of Labor* in *Film Index*, September 12, 1908. Radical newspapers referred to the labor-capital film as a "proletarian playlet." *NY Call*, January 14, 1912. More elaborate discussions of genres can be found in Bowser, *Transformation of Cinema*, 167–89; William K. Everson, *American Silent Film* (New York, 1978), 205–37; Wed D. Gehring, ed., *Handbook of American Film Genres* (New York and Westport, Conn., 1988); and Schatz, *Hollywood Genres*.

3. My figure of 274 labor-capital films is a very conservative one. The movies I found are not the only ones that existed. Although I looked at more than 15,000 movie reviews and film catalog entries, I did not conduct an exhaustive search of every review listed in every trade periodical published between 1905 and 1930 (a project well worth pursuing by other scholars). Rather, as I read through film catalogs, labor newspapers, movie industry periodicals, film scenarios, and a variety of other primary and secondary sources, I wrote down the name of any film that seemed to deal with some aspect of labor-capital conflict. I then tried to locate and view as many surviving films as possible. I also went back to trade periodicals and

read reviews for every movie on my list. A movie did not have to be devoted entirely to the subject of class conflict in order to make my final labor-capital film list. I included any film that contained scenes of strikes, lockouts, union organizing, radical activism or political movements, clashes between workers and government troops or employer-hired armies, employer-employee negotiating sessions, and similar representations of overt class encounters or challenges to government authority. I placed movies that did not contain such scenes on my more general list of working-class films (see Chapter 2 note 22).

To offer readers an estimate of the number of working-class and labor-capital films, I did the following computations: Tom Brandon reports finding 4,249 film reviews in trade periodicals for 1914. The AFI catalog for 1911–1920, which includes only feature films of at least four reels or 4,000 feet, lists 452 movies for 1914. According to my research, at least 42 (9.3 percent) of the movies in the AFI catalog were working-class and 21 (4.6 percent) labor-capital films. If we assume that these percentages were the same for the remaining 3,797 shorter films not listed in the catalog, that would yield a total of 395 working-class and 195 labor-capital films released just in 1914 (that is, 9.3 percent and 4.6 percent, respectively, of 4,249 films). Using other sources, I found 41 labor-capital films made in 1914, 20 more than were listed in the AFI catalog. Although there are no exact figures for annual productions for the prewar era, Charles Tarbox estimates that there were at least 22,900 films released between 1911 and 1915 (this includes one-reelers as well as longer feature films). If we use the same ratios I found in the AFI catalog, that would mean there were about 2,130 working-class and 1,053 labor-capital films released during that five-year period. The ratio of working-class and labor-capital films to the total number of films listed in the AFI catalog remained fairly constant between 1914 and 1920: of the 5,189 releases included in the catalog, 371 (7.1 percent) were working-class and 218 (4.2 percent) labor-capital films. Brandon, "Populist Film," chapter 1, 17, file C34, Brandon Coll.; Charles Tarbox, *Lost Films 1895–1917* (Los Angeles, 1983), 47, 77, 111, 155, 211.

The sources most useful in creating this list included surviving movies, movie stills, press books, scenarios, manuscripts, and assorted archival materials housed at MOMA; Billy Rose Theater Collection, New York Public Library at Lincoln Center; the George Eastman House, Rochester; the Academy of Motion Picture Arts and Sciences, Beverly Hills; USC; UCLA; Motion Pictures, Broadcasting, and Recorded Sound Division, Library of Congress, Washington D.C.; records of federal agencies kept at NA; censorship reports contained in NBRMP; and the sources cited in Chapter 2 note 22. For a more comprehensive discussion of sources, see Appendix II.

4. A few caveats are in order. My ability to categorize films or offer precise numbers of films in each category was complicated by the disappearance of most of these early nitrate films. Without seeing a film, one is dependent on the widely varied political perspectives of movie reviewers. Films that certain critics dubbed liberal, others labeled conservative. Similarly, radical films praised by some for offering peaceful solutions were blasted by others for espousing violent socialism. Film catalogs, such as those produced by the American Film Institute, are helpful but problematic, for they depend on movie reviews and studio synopses widely considered unreliable. In order to circumvent these difficulties, my analyses of labor-capi-

tal films are based, whenever possible, on films I have actually seen. When movies were unavailable, I tried to reconstruct a film's visual politics by using the sources mentioned in the previous note. In cases where there were conflicting views of a film's politics, I relied on the perceptions of labor periodical reviewers. I assumed that they were closer to a working-class point of view than reviewers in *MPW* or *Variety*. For the problems of film catalogs, see Robert Sklar, *Movie-Made America: A Cultural History of American Movies* (New York, 1994), 88–89.

5. Thomas H. Dickinson, "Movies Changing the Face of the Nation," *New York Times*, July 1, 1923.

6. *MPW*, April 21, 1910; Frederic C. "Howe, "What to Do with the Motion Picture Show: Shall It Be Censored?" *The Outlook*, 107 (June 20, 1914), 412–16, quoted in Kay Sloan, *The Loud Silents: Origins of the Social Problem Film* (Urbana, 1988), 6.

7. For an overview of these theoretical debates, see Appendix II.

8. John Drinkwater, *The Life and Adventures of Carl Laemmle* (New York, 1931), 73. The original members of the Trust included Edison, Biograph, Vitagraph, Selig, Essanay, Lubin, George Kleine, Kalem, Pathé Frères, and Méliès. For histories of the Trust, its competitors, and its decline see Tino Balio, ed., *The American Film Industry* (Madison, 1976); Terry Ramsaye, *A Million and One Nights: A History of the Motion Picture through 1925* (New York, 1926, reprinted 1986); Benjamin B. Hampton, *A History of the Movies* (New York, 1931); Lewis Jacobs, *The Rise of American Film: A Critical History* (New York, 1968); Ralph Cassady, Jr., "Monopoly in Motion Picture Production and Distribution: 1908–1915," *Southern California Law Review*, 32 (Summer 1959), 325–90.

9. *Film Index*, January 30, 1909; Upton Sinclair, *Upton Sinclair Presents William Fox* (Los Angeles, 1933; reprinted New York, 1970), 24, 23. Nine of the eleven radical movies that I counted were made by independents. For Powers' early career, see I. G. Edmonds, *Big U: Universal in the Silent Days* (South Brunswick, N.J., and New York, 1977), 15. For a brief portrait of key Trust figures, see Lary May, *Screening out the Past: The Birth of Mass Culture and the Motion Picture Industry* (New York, 1980), 250–51. The lives and influence of Jewish movie industry personnel are discussed in Neal Gabler, *An Empire of Their Own: How the Jews Invented Hollywood* (New York, 1988).

10. Women involved with labor-capital movies included Hettie Gray (Baker), Ouida Bergere, Margueritte Bertsch, Alice Guy Blaché, Catherine Carr, Mrs. Sidney Drew, Bessie Eyton, Marion Fairfax, Julia Crawford Ivers, Agnes Johnson, Louise Keller, Anita Loos, Cleo Madison, Edythe Totten, and Lois Weber. The role of women in the silent film industry is discussed in Martin F. Norden, "Women in the Early Film Industry," *Wide Angle*, 6:3 (1984), 58–67; Ally Acker, *Reel Women: Pioneers of the Cinema 1896 to the Present* (New York, 1991); Anthony Slide, *Early Women Directors* (New York, 1977); Sharon Smith, *Women Who Make Movies* (New York, 1975); Richard Koszarski, *Hollywood Directors 1914–1940* (New York, 1976); Marjorie Rosen, *Popcorn Venus: Women, Movies, and the American Dream* (New York, 1973); Molly Haskell, *From Reverence to Rape: The Treatment of Women in the Movies* (New York, 1974); Karen Ward Mahar, "Women, Filmmaking, and the Gendering of the American Film Industry, 1896–1928," Ph.D. dissertation, University of Southern California, 1995.

11. Sloan, *Loud Silents*, 5.

12. The best histories of organizing efforts within the industry are *Combined Convention Proceedings National Alliance of Theatrical Stage Employees and Moving Picture Operators of the United States and Canada: A Record of All Conventions Held since the Inception of the Organization, July 1893* (New York, 1926); Robert Osborne Baker, *The International Alliance of Stage Employees and Moving Picture Machine Operators of the United States and Canada* (Lawrence, Kan., 1933); Alfred Harding, *Revolt of the Actors* (New York, 1929); Murray Ross, *Stars and Strikes: Unionization of Hollywood* (New York, 1941); Louis B. Perry and Richard Perry, *A History of the Los Angeles Labor Movement* (Berkeley, 1963); Michael Charles Nielsen, "Motion Picture Craft Workers and Craft Unions in Hollywood: The Studio Era, 1912–1948," Ph.D. dissertation, University of Illinois, 1985; Michael C. Nielsen, "Labor Power and Organization in the Early Motion Picture Industry," *Film History*, 2 (June-July 1988), 121–31. The organizational campaigns of actors are also described in *Chicago Daily Socialist*, August 25, 1910; *Variety*, July 25, 1913; *AFL Newsletter*, March 18, 1916; *LA Citizen*, March 24, 1916; *Los Angeles Labor Press*, April 21, 1916; *NY Call*, April 9 and August 25, 1916.

13. *Los Angeles Times*, *The Forty Year War for a Free City: A History of the Open Shop Movement in Los Angeles* (Los Angeles, 1929), 25. The *Times* incorrectly reported only seventeen companies as joining the MPPA; see *LA Citizen*, February 4, 1916; Perry and Perry, *Los Angeles Labor Movement*, 321–22. The early activities of the MPPA are described in the Hal Roach Collection, file 1 (1916–1918), USC.

14. *Variety*, June 26, 1914. Reports of IWW activities can be found in *MPW*, March 18, 1911; *NY Call*, April 21, 1913; Hyman Weintraub, "The IWW in California: 1905–1931," M.A. thesis, University of California, Los Angeles, 1947, 118, 308–9. The IWW also lent support to striking movie extras in 1916. It should also be noted that although Edison produced anti-labor films (such as *The Crime of Carelessness* [1912], *The Workman's Lesson* [1912], *The Courage of the Commonplace* [1917], and *One Kind of Wireless* [1917]), it also made a number of reformist films. It was unions rather than reform that Edison did not like.

15. Raymond Williams, *Keywords: A Vocabulary of Culture and Society* (New York, 1976), 128; Michel Foucault, *Power/Knowledge: Selected Interviews and Other Writings 1972–1979* (New York, 1980), 38. Foucault explains that whereas discourse presents itself as truth, ideology "always stands in virtual opposition to something else which is supposed to count as truth"; ibid., 118. For an excellent discussion of the multiple ways in which cultural scholars use terms like ideology and discourse, see Terry Eagleton, *Ideology: An Introduction* (London and New York, 1991); John Storey, *An Introductory Guide to Cultural Theory and Popular Culture* (Athens, Ga., 1993).

16. Preamble to IWW constitution, quoted in Mary Jo Buhle, Paul Buhle, Dan Georgakas, eds., *Encyclopedia of the American Left* (New York, 1990), 355. Haywood and Moyer were acquitted in 1907.

17. *NY Call*, October 19, 1913.

18. Quote from review of *The Molly Maguires, or, Labor Wars in the Coal Mines*, in *MPW*, December 3, 1908. For representative examples of conservative films, see *The Blacksmith's Strike* (1907), *The Ringleader* (1908), *Awakened Memories* (1909),

The Hero Engineer (1910), *The Strike at the Mines* (1911), *The Strike* (1912), *The Strike Breaker* (1913), *The Strike* (1914), *The Spender* (1915), *The Manager of the B and A* (1916), *The Girl and the Crisis* (1917).

19. *Moving Picture Stories*, January 24, 1913; *The Strike* quoted in Jacobs, *Rise of American Film*, 151.

20. The long-standing association of workers and mobs is discussed in Eugene E. Leach, "Chaining the Tiger: The Mob Stigma and the Working Class, 1863–1894," *Labor History*, 35 (Spring 1994), 187–215; Paul A. Gilje, *The Road to Mobocracy: Popular Disorder in New York City, 1763–1834* (Chapel Hill, 1987). For sources showing violent and peaceful images of labor, see William Cahn, *A Pictorial History of American Labor* (New York, 1972); Joseph L. Gardner, *Labor on the March: The Story of America's Unions* (New York, 1969); Judith O'Sullivan and Rosemary Gallick, *Workers and Allies: Female Participation in the American Trade Union Movement, 1824–1976* (Washington, D.C., 1975); District 1,199, National Union of Hospital and Health Care Employees and the Smithsonian Institution Traveling Exhibition Service, *The Working American* (Washington, D.C, 1979); Jonathan L. Doherty, ed., *Women at Work: 153 Photographs by Lewis W. Hine* (New York, 1981); Lewis W. Hine, *Men at Work: Photographic Studies of Modern Men and Machines* (New York, 1977); Rebecca Zurier, *Art for "The Masses": A Radical Magazine and Its Graphics, 1911–1917* (Philadelphia, 1988); Harry R. Rubenstein, "Symbols and Images of American Labor: Dinner Pails and Hard Hats," *Labor's Heritage*, 1 (July 1989), 34–49; Judith Ayre Schomer, "New Workers in a New World: Painting American Labor, 1830–1913," ibid., 3 (January 1991), 34–47.

21. For examples of lazy socialists, see *A Million Dollars* (1912), *Greater Wealth* (1913), and *A Daughter of the Poor* (1917). Reviews of *A Million Dollars* and *Greater Wealth* can be found in *Moving Picture Stories*, January 24, 1913; Sloan, *Loud Silents*, 50–51; *A Daughter of the Poor* in *Variety*, March 23, 1917, and *Wid's*, March 15, 1917.

22. An excellent analysis of these films can be found in Russell Campbell, "Nihilists and Bolsheviks: Revolutionary Russia in American Silent Film," *The Silent Picture*, 19 (1974), 4–36. For negative images of American anarchists, see *Gus and the Anarchists* (1915), *The Clarion* (1916), and *Fanatics* (1917).

23. *LA Citizen*, September 2, 1910. For movie industry reactions to labor complaints see *Moving Picture News*, October 8, 1910.

24. *Film Index*, May 20, 1911. Government figures only reported the causes of strikes for 1890–1905 and 1914–1916. *Historical Statistics*, 1: 179. *Awakened Memories* (1909) also shows the wife saving the family when her union-leader husband refuses to work; *MPW*, October 3, 1909. Comedies such as *Mr. Faddleaway Goes On Strike* (1911), *The Home Strike Breakers* (1912), and *Lazy Bill and the Strikers* (1912) deliver similar messages of savvy wives teaching their foolish husbands about the futility of strikes and importance of hard work.

25. *MPW*, April 13, 1912; for descriptions of Anderson's film, see ibid., September 23, 1911.

26. *NY Call*, January 9, 1913. Despite his radical politics, Miller directed for Edison, Vitagraph, Paramount, Jesse Lasky, and Famous Players-Lasky. For Miller's refusal to direct *The Fall of the Nation* and his socialist background, see ibid., August 22, 1915, and May 26, 1916; *New York Herald-Tribune*, November 11, 1949. Viola

Barry was the daughter of socialist politician J. Stitt Wilson and a member of the Los Angeles Socialist Theatre Company. *LA Citizen*, November 18, 1910.

27. *Appeal to Reason*, June 12, 1914. Two of the eleven radical films mentioned earlier were produced by worker filmmakers and will be discussed in the next chapter.

28. *Appeal to Reason*, June 12, 1914. Thomas joined the Knights of Labor around 1876–1877 and was an officer during the railroad strikes of 1877. During first decade of new century, he wrote plays that were praised by the socialist press in New York and Milwaukee. After the war, he changed his political loyalties and became head of the Producing Managers' Association (the theater owners' organization). *NY Call*, January 6, 1909, August 15, 1922; *Milwaukee Social Democratic Herald*, June 19, 1909; *New York Times*, August 13, 1934; Augustus Thomas, *The Print of My Remembrance* (New York, 1922); Brownlow, *Behind the Mask*, 473.

29. *Motography*, July 4, 1914. A copy of the press book, *All Star Features Corporation Presents Upton Sinclair's Powerful Story and Play "The Jungle"*, can be found in file J210, Brandon Coll.; it contains pictures from the film.

30. *Appeal to Reason*, June 12, 1914; *MPW*, June 20, 1914; *Variety*, June 26, 1914; *Kinematograph and Lantern Weekly*, November 26, 1914, quoted in Philip S. Foner, "Upton Sinclair's 'The Jungle': The Movie," Dieter Herms, ed., *Upton Sinclair: Literature and Reform* (Frankfurt am Main and New York, 1990), 155. For other reviews and descriptions, see ibid., 150–56; *NY Call*, May 31 and June 28, 1914; Brownlow, *Behind the Mask*, 472–74; Sloan, *Loud Silents*, 37–38.

31. For reviews of *Why?*, see *MPW*, May 31 and June 14, 28, 1913; *Moving Picture Stories*, June 13, 1913; producer synopsis, *Why?*, Copyright Records, LC.

32. *New York Dramatic Mirror*, February 10, 1915; also see *MPW*, February 6, 1915; Brownlow, *Behind the Mask*, 434–35. For reviews of *The Eternal City*, *The Rights of Man*, and *Martin Eden*, see *NY Call*, April 11, 1915; *MPW*, January 9 and October 30, 1915; *Variety*, January 1 and October 29, 1915.

33. "The Blacklist," producer's synopsis, Copyright Records, LC. The *New York Dramatic Mirror* called *The Blacklist* "a socialistic drama," but Upton Sinclair believed a film that solved class struggles by having its heroine marry the mine owner was far from socialistic. *New York Dramatic Mirror*, February 27, 1916; for Sinclair's review see *Screenland*, June 1930, 381. For further reviews, see *MPW*, February 19, 1916; *Variety*, February 18, 1916; *LA Citizen*, March 24, 1916; *NY Call*, March 19, 1918; Brownlow, *Behind the Mask*, 483–86.

34. *New York Dramatic Mirror*, August 12, 1914. For *The Bruiser*, see *MPW*, March 25, 1916. Negative depictions of scabs can also be found in *The Better Man* (1914) and *The Price of Power* (1916). For examples of other left-liberal films, see *The Sons of Toil* (1915), and *The Fourth Estate* (1916).

35. For *The Long Strike*, see *MPW*, December 23, 1911.

36. Karl Brown, *Adventures with D. W. Griffith* (New York, 1976), 122. For films with similar messages, see *Lily of the Valley* (1914), *Facing the Gatling Gun* (1914), and *The Man with the Iron Heart* (1915).

37. Quotes are from the film's intertitles.

38. *The Better Man*, producer synopsis, Copyright Records, LC; *MPW*, May 15, 1909.

39. For descriptions of these films, see *MPW*, August 26, 1916; October 31, November 21, 1914; *Dawn of Freedom*, producer synopsis, Copyright Records, LC.

40. For an overview of Populists, the producer ideology, and their critique of society see, Lawrence Goodwyn, *Democratic Promise: The Populist Moment in America* (New York, 1976); Robert C. McMath, Jr., *American Populism: A Social History 1877–1898* (New York, 1993); Michael Kazin, *The Populist Persuasion: An American History* (New York, 1995); Leon Fink, *Workingmen's Democracy: The Knights of Labor and American Politics* (Urbana, 1983). For a discussion of populist films, see Raymond Durgnat, "Genre: Populism and Social Realism," *Film Comment*, 11 (July–August 1975), 20–29, 63; Raymond Durgnat and Scott Simmon, *King Vidor, American* (Berkeley, 1988); Brownlow, *Behind the Mask*, 432–33; Brandon, "Populist Film," Brandon Coll.

41. Raymond Durgnat characterizes populist movies as ones "whose protagonists are ordinary people, and whose fair share of extraordinary or wish fulfillment passions are related to ordinary life." Wes Gehring, who writes about populist comedies, defines their politics as reflecting the "basic belief that the superior and majority will of the common man is forever threatened by a usurping, sophisticated, evil few." Durgnat, "Genre," 23; Wes D. Gehring, "Populist Comedy," in Gehring, *Handbook of American Film Genres*, 125.

42. For examples of other populist films, see *The Miner's Daughter* (1909), *Gold Is Not All* (1910), *By Man's Law* (Biograph 1913), *The Snare of Fate* (1913), *Money* (1915, Nordisk version), and *Two News Items* (1916). In this last film and in *By Man's Law*, the Rockefeller-like villain raises audience tempers by getting away with his crimes. I wish to thank Marcus Reddiker for his helpful suggestions about the nature of populist film.

43. Joseph Boskin, *Humor and Social Change in Twentieth-Century America* (Boston, 1979), 28. There were, of course, exceptions to this general rule. *The Incendiary Foreman* (Pathé 1908) was an anti-authoritarian melodrama, and *The Subpoena Server* (1906) was a populist comedy that showed John D. Rockefeller being stripped of his economic power. *The Coal Trust* and *Witness Mockefeller* were probably made before 1917. The social meaning of humor is also discussed in Henry Jenkins, *What Made Pistachio Nuts? Early Sound Comedy and the Vaudeville Aesthetic* (New York, 1992); Mary Douglas, *Implicit Meanings: Essays in Anthropology* (London, 1975).

44. *Motion Picture Classic*, November 1918, quoted in Koszarski, *Hollywood Directors*, 58; Paul Harrison, "Sennett Waxes Witty," quoted in May, *Screening out the Past*, 104. Sennett's life and films are described in Mack Sennett, as told to Cameron Shipp, *King of Comedy* (New York, 1954); Terry Brewer and Kalton C. Lahue, *Kops and Custards: The Legend of the Keystone Films* (Norman, Okla., 1968); Kalton C. Lahue, *Mack Sennett's Keystone* (South Brunswick, N.J., 1971).

45. James Combs, *American Political Movies: An Annotated Filmography of Feature Films* (New York, 1990), 3; Samuel Goldwyn, *Behind the Screen* (New York, 1923), 161. Chaplin's life, films, and politics are explored in Sklar, *Movie-Made America*, 107–16; Charles Musser, "Work, Ideology, and Chaplin's Tramp," in Robert Sklar and Charles Musser, eds., *Resisting Images: Essays on Cinema and History* (Philadelphia, 1990), 36–67; David Robinson, *Chaplin: His Life and Art* (New York, 1985); Charles J. Maland, *Chaplin and American Culture* (Princeton, 1989).

46. Films produced by reform and religious organizations are discussed in Steven J. Ross, "The Unknown Hollywood," *History Today*, 40 (April 1990), 40–46; Sloan, *Loud Silents*; Brownlow, *Behind the Mask*. For the rise of advertising and mass marketing, see Stuart Ewen, *Captains of Consciousness: Advertising and the Social Roots of the Consumer Culture* (New York, 1976); Roland Marchand, *Advertising the American Dream: Making Way for Modernity, 1920–1940* (Berkeley, 1985); Jackson Lears, *Fables of Abundance: A Cultural History of Advertising in America* (New York, 1994). The emergence of a new public sphere in Europe and the United States is discussed in Jürgen Habermas, *The Structural Transformation of the Public Sphere: An Inquiry into a Category of Bourgeois Society*, translated by Thomas Burger (Cambridge, Mass., 1989); Craig Calhoun, ed., *Habermas and the Public Sphere* (Cambridge, Mass., 1992).

47. *MPW*, August 19, 1911; Chicago *Party Builder*, November 1, 1913.

48. *MPW*, June 29 and December 28, 1912. In 1910, a Cleveland labor newspaper accused the NAM of being behind the spate of anti-union films flooding the screen. *Cleveland Citizen*, December 10, 1910. For Ivy Lee's work on behalf of Rockefeller, see *NY Call*, June 13, 1915, magazine, 1, 8–9, 14.

49. Quotations are from the film's intertitles. The movie was scripted by Progressive writer James Oppenheim.

50. For events surrounding the Triangle fire and union struggles within the garment industry, see Leon Stein, *The Triangle Fire* (Philadelphia, 1962).

51. Sloan, *Loud Silents*, 4. Films that defended railroad interests included *Steve Hill's Awakening* (1914), *The Price of Carelessness* (1915), and *The House That Jack Built* (1917). For a more detailed analysis of the ways in which businesses made and used movies, see Steven J. Ross, "Cinema and Class Conflict: Labor, Capital, the State, and American Silent Film," in Sklar and Musser, *Resisting Images*, 68–107; Daniel J. Perkins, "Sponsored Business Films: An Overview 1895–1955," *Film Reader*, 6 (1985), 125–32.

52. Diane Waldman, "'Toward a Harmony of Interests': Rockefeller, the YMCA and the Company Movie Theater," *Wide Angle*, 8 (May 1986), 42; Clifford M. Kuhn, Harlon E. Joye, and E. Bernard West, *Living Atlanta: An Oral History of the City 1914–1948*, (Athens, Ga., 1990), 14. The use of movies in industrial recreation programs is described in Bureau of Labor Statistics, "Welfare Work for Employees in Industrial Establishments in the U.S.," *Bulletin of the United States Bureau of Labor Statistics*, no. 250 (Washington, D.C., 1919), 82–85; Leonard J. Diehl and Floyd Eastwood, *Industrial Recreation, Its Development and Present Status* (Lafayette, Ind., 1940), 7–14; Stuart D. Brandes, *American Welfare Capitalism, 1880–1940* (Chicago, 1976); David Alan Corbin, *Life, Work, and Rebellion in the Coal Fields: The Southern West Virginia Miners, 1880–1922* (Urbana, 1981), 126; Ross, "Cinema and Class Conflict."

53. *The Miner's Lesson* was produced in cooperation with the Anthracite Coal Operators and *Sanitation in Mining Villages* with the New Jersey Zinc Company. The Bureau of the Mines was part of the Department of the Interior. For descriptions of early federal film activity, see Richard Dyer MacCann, *The People's Films: A Political History of U.S. Government Motion Pictures* (New York, 1973), 43–55; Raymond Evans, "The U.S.D.A. Motion Picture Service, 1908–1943," *Business Screen Magazine*, 5 (1943), 19–21, 32–33; "Films by American Governments," *Films*, 1 (Summer

1940), 5–33; Frederick S. Harrod, "Managing the Medium: The Navy and Motion Pictures before World War I," *The Velvet Light Trap*, 31 (Spring 1993), 48–58; Charles Musser, *The Emergence of Cinema: The American Screen to 1907* (New York, 1990), 359; and Records of the Departments of the Interior (RG 48) and Labor (RG 174), NA. For an overview of the scope of federal filmmaking and a list of surviving films, see "Motion Pictures in the National Archives," unpublished typescript finding aid (45 pages) in the Motion Picture Room, NA.

54. Quotations are from the film's intertitles.

55. Committee of Safety (U.S. Steel), *Bulletin*, December 1918, 5–6, quoted in Gerd Korman, *Industrialization, Immigrants, and Americanizers: The View from Milwaukee* (Madison, 1967), 159. Korman provides an excellent summary of state and corporate attitudes toward Americanization. Government views on the subject can also be found in the Bureau of Immigration film, *The Americanization of Stefan Skoles* (1916). *NY Call*, July 20 and August 27, 1916.

Chapter 4
Making a Pleasure of Agitation

1. *NY Call*, May 15, 1911. For accounts of the Westmoreland strike, see ibid., July 11, 1911, and July 17, 1912; for movie reviews, see *Film Index*, April 15, 1911; *MPW*, April 22, 1911.

2. *LA Citizen*, September 15, 1911; [Girard, Ka.] *Appeal to Reason*, October 7, 1911; Philip Foner, "A Martyr to His Cause; The Scenario of the First Labor Film in the United States," *Labor History*, 24 (Winter 1983), 103–11.

3. *Cleveland Citizen*, September 14 and October 26, 1907.

4. *LA Citizen*, July 14, 1911. Information about Wolfe's life and politics are drawn from the following sources: ibid., March 31 and June 9, 1911; *California Social Democrat*, September 30, 1911, May 17 and June 7, 1913; *Appeal to Reason*, September 2, 1911; Chicago *Party Builder*, November 1, 1913; Grace Heilman Stimson, *Rise of the Labor Movement in Los Angeles* (Berkeley, 1955), 324, 362; Paul Greenstein, Nigey Lennon, and Lionel Rolfe, *Bread and Hyacinths: The Rise and Fall of Utopian Los Angeles* (Los Angeles, 1992), 47, 62–66, 85–86, 91; Geoffrey Cowan, *The People v. Clarence Darrow: The Bribery Trial of America's Greatest Lawyer* (New York, 1993), xxiv, 192, 373; William Deverell, "The Neglected Twin: California Democrats and the Progressive Bandwagon," in William Deverell and Tom Sitton, eds., *California Progressivism Revisited* (Berkeley, 1994), 88–89.

5. *LA Citizen*, July 7, 1914. Wolfe was apparently quite a good editor; after his departure, the paper's circulation fell from 25,000 to 8,000.

6. *LA Citizen*, June 9, 1911. In addition to working as a publicist and running Darrow's "clipping bureau" during the trial, Wolfe wrote articles and gave numerous speeches defending the brothers. The two men became lifelong friends. Frank E. Wolfe, *Capitalism's Conspiracy in California: Parallel of the Kidnaping of Labor Leaders Colorado—California* (Los Angeles, 1911); Cowan, *People v. Darrow*, xxiv, 373.

7. Frank E. Wolfe, "The Movie Revolution," *Western Comrade*, 1 (July 1913), 125. The trial's impact on Socialist party fortunes is discussed in James P. Kraft, "The Fall of Job Harriman's Socialist Party: Violence, Gender, and Politics in Los Angeles, 1911," *Southern California Quarterly*, 70 (Spring 1988), 43–68.

8. *Western Comrade*, October 1913; Chicago *Party Builder*, November 1, 1913.

9. The uses of leisure by nineteenth- and early twentieth-century labor organizations are discussed in Roy Rosenzweig, *Eight Hours for What We Will: Workers and Leisure in an Industrial City, 1870–1920* (Cambridge and New York, 1983); Francis G. Couvares, *The Remaking of Pittsburgh: Class and Culture in an Industrializing City, 1877–1919* (Albany, 1984); Steven J. Ross, *Workers on the Edge: Work, Leisure, and Politics in Industrializing Cincinnati, 1788–1890* (New York, 1985); Richard Oestreicher, *Solidarity and Fragmentation: Working People and Class Consciousness in Detroit, 1875–1900* (Urbana, Ill., 1986). For a sampling of articles stressing the political importance of leisure, see *Ladies Garment Worker*, October 1910; *Appeal to Reason*, September 23, 1911; *LA Citizen*, April 7, 1916; for descriptions of leisure activities, see *LA Citizen*, March 8, 1907, and December 22, 1911; *Milwaukee Social Democratic Herald*, June 26, 1909; *NY Call*, March 11 and December 30, 1914, January 14, 1915.

10. *NY Call*, July 10, 1911. The battle between the bridge workers' union and the anti-union National Erectors' Association is discussed in Philip Taft, *The A.F. of L. in the Time of Gompers* (New York, 1957), 275–76.

11. Union ranks skyrocketed from 447,000 in 1897 to 2.1 million in 1904 and 3.5 million in 1917. Socialist party membership rose from about 10,000 members in 1900 to 118,000 in 1912. The Industrial Workers of the World made equally impressive gains, rising from approximately 14,000 in 1904–1905 (when it was founded) to 40,000 in 1916 and 100,000 in 1917. Nevertheless, Nick Salvatore estimates that the collective membership of the AFL, IWW, and Socialist party was less than 8 percent of the total labor force in 1910. Nick Salvatore, "Response to Sean Wilentz," *International Labor and Working Class History*, 26 (Fall 1984), 27. By 1907, NAM was using its $1.5 million war chest to fund a massive publicity campaign against organized labor. Philip S. Foner, *History of the Labor Movement in the United States*, vol. 3 (New York, 1964), 49–55. Membership statistics are taken from *Historical Statistics*, 1: 177; James Weinstein, *The Decline of Socialism in America: 1912–1925* (New Brunswick, N.J., 1987), 27; Melvyn Dubofsky, *We Shall Be All: A History of the IWW* (New York, 1969), 263, 349.

12. *The Nation*, 97 (August 28, 1913), 193; *NY Call*, May 15, 1911.

13. *Chicago Socialist*, August 30, 1910 (also see *LA Citizen*, September 2, 1910); *Report of the Proceedings of the 30th Annual Convention of the American Federation of Labor . . . for 1910*, 228. For movie industry responses to these charges, see *Film Index*, September 10, 1910; *Motion Picture News*, October 8, 1910.

14. *NY Call*, July 10 and 13, 1911, June 25, 1914, January 17, 1916; *Los Angeles Labor Press*, March 10, 1916; *AFL Proceedings 1915*, 309; *AFL Proceedings 1916*, 114, 278, 302; Samuel Gompers to James L. Pauley, February 4, 1917, Fred J. Doward to Gompers, January 21, 1917, Subject Correspondence (AFL), Box 15, NBRMP.

15. *NY Call*, March 10, 1912.

16. *NY Call*, December 28, 1908; *LA Citizen*, March 11, 1910. For the uses of theater and the arts as cultural weapons, see Leslie Fishbein, "The Paterson Pageant (1913): The Birth of Docudrama as a Weapon in the Class Struggle," *Journal of Regional Cultures*, 4–5 (Winter/Spring 1984–1985), 95–129; Raphael Samuels, Ewan MacColl, and Stuart Cosgrove, eds., *Theatres of the Left 1880–1935: Workers' Theatre Movements in Britain and America* (London, 1985); Harry Goldman and Mel Gordon,

"Workers' Theatre in America: A Survey," *Journal of American Culture*, 6 (Spring 1978), 169–81; Salvatore Salerno, *Red November Black November: Culture and Community in the Industrial Workers of the World* (Albany, 1969); John Graham, ed., *"Yours for the Revolution": The Appeal to Reason, 1895–1922* (Lincoln, Neb., 1990); Rebecca Zurier, *Art for "The Masses": A Radical Magazine and Its Graphics, 1911–1917* (Philadelphia, 1988); *Cleveland Citizen*, August 31, 1907; *NY Call*, July 30 and November 25, 1908; November 2, 1910; January 14 and May 11, 1911; June 8, 1912; June 8, 1913; April 12, 1914; *LA Citizen*, November 25, 1910, and September 15, 1911; *California Social Democrat*, January 13, 1912.

17. *NY Call*, August 17, 1912, and June 8, 1914.

18. *California Social Democrat*, September 19, 1911.

19. *Appeal to Reason*, September 23, 1911.

20. Unfortunately, none of the prewar worker films is known to have survived. However, I have compiled enough information about the three productions covered here that I break with my general rule and use the present tense in describing their plots.

21. For more detailed accounts of the bombing and subsequent trial, see Morrow Mayo, *Los Angeles* (New York, 1933), 155–88; Taft, *The AFL*, 275–87; Cowan, *People v. Clarence Darrow*, 69–269. Darrow had successfully defended WFM leaders William "Big Bill" Haywood, Charles Moyer, and George Pettibone in the murder trial of former Utah Governor Frank Steuneberg.

22. *AFL Weekly Newsletter*, #25, September 1911; *Milwaukee Social Democratic Herald*, October 14 and November 11, 1911. Information concerning production costs can be found in Executive Council Minutes, October 16, 1911, and January 8–13, 1912, reel 4, AFL Records.

23. For analyses of the ways in which George radicalized seemingly conservative values, see Steven J. Ross, "The Culture of Political Economy: Henry George and the American Working Class," *Southern California Quarterly*, 65 (Summer 1983), 145–66; David Scobey, "Boycotting the Politics Factory: Labor Radicalism and the New York City Mayoral Election of 1884," *Radical History Review*, 28–30 (September 1984), 280–325.

24. Quotations and scene descriptions are from the film's scenario, reprinted in Foner, "Martyr to His Cause," 107–11; also see *NY Call*, September 25, 1911.

25. *Milwaukee Social Democratic Herald*, October 14, 1911. The labor official was William Short of Washington. *NY Call*, August 27, 1911. The making and reception of the film are discussed ibid., October 21, November 4 and 11, 1911; Foner, "Martyr to His Cause," 103–11; Executive Council Minutes, October 16, 1911, and January 8–13, 1912, reel 4, AFL Records; *Cleveland Citizen*, September 9, October 21, and November 4, 18, 1911; *NY Call*, September 25, 1911; Washington, D.C., *AFL News Letter*, 20, 23, 24, 25 (September), and 30 (October) 1911; *Electrical Worker*, 12 (September 1911, October 1911).

26. Los Angeles *Western Comrade*, July 1913; *NY Call*, October 12, 1913.

27. Walter Millsap, "Llano Cooperative Colony," 20, transcript, U.C.L.A. Oral History Project, 1969, UCLA. Wolfe employed actors from the Kinemacolor Company and other studios. I was unable to find any information concerning the film's financing or production costs other than Wolfe's claim that the film was produced with the cooperation of the Los Angeles Socialist party.

28. My descriptions of the film are based upon reviews, photographs, and articles in the Los Angeles *Western Comrade*, July, August, and October, 1913; *California Social Democrat*, May 31, October 18, 1913; *Los Angeles Record*, October 13, 20, 25, 31, 1913; *LA Citizen*, September 19, October 10, 17, 24, 1913; *NY Call*, September 19, 28, and October 2, 5, 1913; *Cleveland Citizen*, May 31, 1913; *MPW*, September 13, 20, 1913; *Motography*, November 15, 1913; Chicago *Party Builder*, November 1, 1913, and March 14, 21, 1914; Chicago *15th Ward Optimist*, March 8, 1914.

29. For a brief account of Emma Wolfe and women like her, see Sherry Katz, "Socialist Women and Progressive Reform," in Deverell and Sitton, eds., *California Progressivism Revisited*, 117–43.

30. *LA Citizen*, October 10, 1913. The acting of these labor "stars" was apparently so good that the film's professional actors broke out in spontaneous applause after several moving speeches. *NY Call*, September 28, 1913. For audience reception see *California Social Democrat*, October 18, 1913; *LA Citizen*, September 19 and October 24, 1913; *Los Angeles Express*, October 20, 1913; *NY Call*, September 28, 1913; Chicago *Party Builder*, November 1, 1913, and March 14, 1914.

31. Chicago *Party Builder*, March 21, 1914; *NY Call*, October 5, 1913. *Dusk* ran for over five months in its first eastern tour. Wolfe's efforts to distribute the film are described in *NY Call*, September 28 and October 5, 12, 1913; *Los Angeles Record* October 15, 1913; *LA Citizen*, October 10, 31, 1913; *California Social Democrat*, October 18, 25, 1913; Chicago *Party Builder*, November 1, 1913, January 24, and March 21, 1914; *MPW*, September 20, 1913; Frank E. Wolfe to Jack London, December 8, 1913, Jack London Papers, Huntington Library, San Marino, Ca.

32. The movie was apparently shot in a rented studio space in New York City. Descriptions of the film, as well as Weiss's background, are based on a copy of the original scenario, Copyright Records, LC; *NY Call*, November 22, 1914, January 5, 1915; *New York Times*, December 26, 1941. For a history of the *Jewish Daily Forward*, see J. C. Rich, *The Jewish Daily Forward* (New York, 1967).

33. All quotations are taken from Weiss's script.

34. Robert Lang, *American Film Melodrama: Griffith, Vidor, Minnelli* (Princeton, 1989), 30, 31. For an analysis of the ways in which nineteenth-century dime novels resolved the seeming tensions between individualism and mutualism, see Michael Denning, *Mechanic Accents: Dime Novels and Working-Class Culture in America* (London and New York, 1987); for discussions of melodrama, ideology, and cinema, see the sources cited in Chapter 2, note 31.

35. Working-class challenges to dominant notions of gender identity in nineteenth- and early twentieth-century America are discussed in Denning, *Mechanic Accents*, 167–200; Christine Stansell, *City of Women: Sex and Class in New York, 1789–1860* (New York, 1986); Mary H. Blewett, *Men, Women, and Work: Class, Gender, and Protest in the New England Shoe Industry, 1780–1910* (Urbana, Ill., 1988); David Montgomery, *Workers' Control in America: Studies in the History of Work, Technology, and Labor Struggles* (Cambridge and New York, 1979); Kathy Peiss, *Cheap Amusements: Working Women and Leisure in Turn-of-the-Century New York* (Philadelphia, 1986). The ways in which early filmmakers confronted middle-class gender constructions are discussed in Lary May, *Screening out the Past: The Birth of Mass Culture and the Motion Picture Industry* (New York, 1980); Miriam Hansen,

Babel & Babylon: Spectatorship in American Silent Film (Cambridge, Mass., 1991); Lang, *American Film Melodrama.*

36. Excluded from white films, blacks also struggled to create an independent cinema; *Variety,* April 10, 1914; Henry T. Sampson, *Blacks in Black and White: A Source Book on Black Films* (Metuchen, N.J., 1977). Women's organizations also made films dealing with political and social issues ignored by the studios. Kay Sloan, *The Loud Silents: Origins of the Social Problem Film* (Urbana, Ill., 1988); Kevin Brownlow, *Behind the Mask of Innocence* (New York, 1990).

37. *Film Index,* May 27, 1911; *NY Call,* May 27, 1912. For descriptions of early actualities and slide shows, see *Cleveland Citizen,* September 14, 1907; *Film Index,* July 25, 1908; *The Nickelodeon,* March 9, 1909; *LA Citizen,* December 1 and 8, 1911; Sloan, *Loud Silents,* 61–62.

38. *NY Call,* July 20, 1913; *LA Citizen,* September 22, 1911; *NY Call,* July 20, 1913. For film efforts in San Francisco, see *MPW,* September 24, 1910; for Los Angeles and New York, see *NY Call,* August 17, 26, 28, 1912; July 26 and August 13, 1913; *California Social Democrat,* September 9 and 16, 1911; *LA Citizen,* September 15 and 22, 1911; for Chicago, see *Chicago Daily Socialist,* June 8, 1912, and *Chicago Evening World,* August 15, 1912. For the rise of commercial newsreels, see Koszarski, *An Evening's Entertainment: The Age of the Silent Feature Picture, 1915–1928* (New York, 1990), 167–70.

39. *NY Call,* April 5, 4, 1916; Harry Preston quoted in Gary M. Fink, "Labor Espionage: The Fulton Bag and Cotton Mill Strike of 1914–1915," *Labor's Heritage,* 1 (April 1989), 14; also see Gary M. Fink, *The Fulton Bag and Cotton Mills Strike of 1914–1915: Espionage, Labor Conflict, and New South Industrial Relations* (Ithaca, 1993), 91–116. The Atlanta films were shown in downtown movie theaters. I wish to thank Cliff Kuhn for sending me information about the cinematic activities of Atlanta workers.

40. *NY Call,* November 17, 1913.

41. *LA Citizen,* September 8, 1916; *Chicago American Socialist,* August 26 and September 30, 1916; for other campaign films see *Chicago Daily Socialist,* June 8, 1912; *Chicago Evening World,* August 15, 1912; *NY Call,* October 15, 1916.

42. Chicago *Party Builder,* May 30, 1914; also see ibid., June 20, 1914; Chicago *American Socialist,* November 7, 1914.

43. *NY Call,* August 13, and July 20, 1913.

44. *NY Call,* April 19, 1914, and January 8, 1911; *Cleveland Citizen,* November 8, 1913. In addition to the aforementioned sources, information concerning the making and uses of films by European workers prior to the 1920s can be found in Stephen G. Jones, *The British Labour Movement and Film, 1918–1939* (London, 1987); and the sources cited in the Preface note 4. For Hopp's involvement in the Madison Square Garden project and his subsequent endeavors, see *New York Times,* April 27 and September 8, 1915.

45. *NY Call,* July 10, 1911. The General Film Company, an offshoot of the Movie Trust, controlled fifty-seven of the nation's fifty-eight principal exchanges in 1912. For an overview of the early distribution system, see William Marston Seabury, *The Public and the Motion Picture Industry* (New York, 1926), 8–21; Howard T. Lewis, *The Motion Picture Industry* (New York, 1933), 3–27; Suzanne Mary Donahue, *American Film Distribution: The Changing Market Place* (Ann Arbor, 1987), 3–18.

46. Under the practice of "roadshowing," a producer "would either rent his film on a percentage basis or he would take over the operation of the theater for a limited time period." Reform and business organizations that made films in cooperation with Trust members had a much easier task, for their movies were included in studio packages sent to exhibitors. Donahue, *American Film Distribution*, 12. The distribution efforts of the AFL and Wolfe are described ibid., notes 25 and 31. For Sinclair's difficulties, see Upton Sinclair to W. H. Wayland, February 2, 1916; Paul Castle to Upton Sinclair, September 3, 1916, file J216, Brandon Coll.

47. *Chicago Daily Socialist*, December 13, 1909; *LA Citizen*, November 10, 1911.

48. *LA Citizen*, September 8, 1911; *Appeal to Reason*, October 7, 1911. For more information on the theater, its films, and its speakers, see *LA Citizen*, September 15 and 22, November 10, 1911; *California Social Democrat*, September 9, 11, 16, and December 2, 1911; *Cleveland Citizen*, September 16 and 30, 1911; *Appeal to Reason*, October 28, 1911. Workers in Leeds, England, opened a movie theater in 1913 in order "to bar pictures hostile to the working people and to have a means of spreading the principles of solidarity among the masses." *Cleveland Citizen*, November 8, 1913.

49. *NY Call*, August 28, 1912; also see August 17 and 26, 1912. For similar exhibition efforts by other workers, see Alvin Huff to Upton Sinclair, November 1, 1915, and Sinclair to Wayland, February 2, 1916; *Film Index*, May 27, 1911; Sloan, *Loud Silents*, 61–62.

50. *NY Call*, January 5, 1915; "Executive Council Minutes," January 21, 1913, reel 4, AFL Records; *NY Call*, July 11, 1915. The titles of films shown by Pittsburgh Socialists can be found ibid., November 28, 1914, and January 5, 1915.

51. Los Angeles *Western Comrade*, October–November 1914. The varied uses of films are described in *Film Index*, May 27, 1911; *NY Call*, May 27, 1912, July 20, 1913; February 22, July 11, August 25, 29, and September 5, 1915; *Chicago Daily Socialist*, January 22, 1912; *Variety*, March 7, 1913; Sinclair to Wayland, February 2, 1916.

52. Chicago *Party Builder*, March 14, 1914; *LA Citizen*, September 19, 1913; Chicago *Party Builder*, March 21, 1914; Sinclair to Wayland, February 2, 1916.

53. *NY Call*, July 3, 1914; *Los Angeles Record*, June 30, 1914. For audience reactions see *AFL Newsletter*, 30, October 28, 1911; *MPW*, May 13, 1913; *Appeal to Reason*, June 13, 1914; *Chicago American Socialist*, September 30, 1916; *California Social Democrat*, October 18, 25, 1913; *LA Citizen*, October 24, 1913; Chicago *Party Builder*, March 14, 1914.

54. Griffith maintained the only fully unionized studio in Los Angeles at the time of the filming. His actions there, according to the carpenters, helped unionize studios in Chicago and New York. *LA Citizen*, November 17, 24, 1916, and January 19, 1917. On September 8, 1918, Griffith was made an honorary member of Hollywood Local 33 of the International Alliance of Theatrical and Stage Employees. "Minutes of the Meetings of Local 33, IATSE," February 2, 1915, and September 8, 1918, Local 33 Headquarters, Burbank, Ca.

55. Sinclair to Wayland, February 2, 1916.

56. P. H. Reesburg to Upton Sinclair, January 18, 1915, quoted in Brandon, "Populist Film," chapter 1, 30, file C34, Brandon Coll.; Millsap, "Llano del Rio," 20–21, UCLA; *NY Call*, May 27, 1912.

57. R. J. Caldwell to National Board of Censorship, December 7, 1916, Box 105 (Supreme Test), NBRMP. The complaining Caldwell had his films confused; he wrote the NBRMP about *The Supreme Test*, but the scenes he described came from *The Blacklist*.

58. Chicago statute quoted in Edward de Grazia and Roger K. Newman, *Banned Films: Movies, Censors, and the First Amendment* (New York and London, 1982), 8. Censorship of early motion pictures is discussed ibid.; "An Unamerican Innovation," *The Independent*, 86 (May 22, 1916), 265; Ellis Paxson Oberholtzer, *The Morals of the Movie* (Philadelphia, 1922); "The Motion Picture in Its Economic and Social Aspects," special issue of *Annals of the American Academy of Political and Social Science*, 78 (November 1926), 146–86; Robert Fischer, "Film Censorship and Progressive Reform: The National Board of Censorship of Motion Pictures, 1909–1922," *Journal of Popular Film*, 4 (1975), 143–50; Kathleen D. McCarthy, "Nickel Vice and Virtue: Movie Censorship in Chicago, 1907–1915," *Journal of Popular Film*, 5:1 (1976), 37–55; Morris L. Ernst and Pare Lorentz, *Censored: The Private Life of the Movie* (New York, 1930); Lamar T. Beman, ed., *Censorship of the Theater and Moving Pictures* (New York, 1931); Francis G. Couvares, ed., *Movie Censorship and American Culture* (Washington, D. C., 1996).

59. The NBRMP was a reform body that sought to avoid mandatory censorship by working with producers. *The Nation*, August 28, 1913; W. D. McGuire to Samuel Gompers, February 5, 1917, Subjects Correspondence (AFL), Box 15, NBRMP; "Definition of Censorship Prepared by the National Board of Review of Motion Pictures. 1913," 2, Subject Papers, Box 166, NBRMP; W. D. McGuire to Thomas Ince, January 3, 1917, Company Correspondence, Box 4, NBRMP; *NY Call*, July 12, 1914.

60. Los Angles *Western Comrade*, December 1913; *NY Call*, September 28, 1913; Chicago *Party Builder*, February 21, 1914; censorship efforts in Chicago are described ibid., March 7, 1914. For the AFL's difficulties with the NBRMP, see "Executive Council Minutes," January 8–13, 1912 (see entries for September 30 and October 3, 1911), reel 4; Samuel Gompers to Walter Storey, October 13, 1911, reel 74, AFL Records.

61. W. D. McGuire to Samuel Gompers, February 3, 1917, Subjects Correspondence (AFL), Box 15, NBRMP; Sinclair to Wayland, February 2, 1916, file J216, Brandon Coll. *The Jungle* was also censored in Waltham, Massachusetts. *NY Call*, June 15, 1913.

62. *MPW*, January 10, 1914; *Chicago Daily Socialist*, June 13, 1912. For *The Mirror of Death*, see *Variety*, March 13, 1914.

63. Gompers quoted in letter from J. W. Binder to W. D. McGuire, January 29, 1917, Subjects Correspondence (AFL), Box 15, NBRMP; *AFL Newsletter*, April 1, 1916. For examples of socialist and AFL opposition to censorship, see *NY Call*, June 15 and July 12, 1914, and January 17, 1916; *Los Angeles Labor Press*, March 10, 1916; Samuel Gompers to [Governor] Charles S. Whitman, April 24, 1916, AFL Convention Records, reel 31; Samuel Gompers to James L. Pauley, February 4, 1917, Box 15, NBRMP; *AFL Proceedings 1916*, 114, 278, 302.

64. *AFL Proceedings 1916*, 114; Chicago *Party Builder*, March 26, 1913; *AFL Proceedings 1916*, 302.

65. Chicago *Party Builder*, March 21, 1914; Sinclair to Wayland, February 2, 1916; Gompers to McGuire, February 5, 1917. For a history of Llano del Rio and

Wolfe's plans for erecting a movie studio, see *NY Call*, February 21, 1915; Millsap, "Llano Cooperative Colony," 20–21; Llano del Rio Cooperative Colony, *The Gateway to Freedom* (Llano del Rio, n.d.); Greenstein, Lennon, and Rolfe, *Bread and Hyacinths*. For further exchanges between Gompers and Ince, see W. D. McGuire to Thomas Ince, January 3, 1917, Box 4, and McGuire to Gompers, February 3, 1917, Box 15, NBRMP.

66. Chicago *Party Builder*, March 14, 1914; Sinclair to Weyland, February 2, 1916; E. W. Perrin, quoted in Chicago *Party Builder*, March 26, 1913.

Chapter 5
When Russia Invaded America

1. Quotes are taken from intertitles in *Dangerous Hours* (Ince 1920), *Life's Greatest Problem* (Blackton 1918), and "Extracts from H. C. Witmer's story, 'Everybody's Business,'" 2, enclosed in letter from H. J. Shephard to W. D. McGuire, January 21, 1920, Box 104, NBRMP.

2. M.I. 4–5, The Military Intelligence Branch, "Report on the Committee On Public Information," 13, May 1918, Records of CPI, RG 63, Creel Correspondence, Box 5, folder 1-A1.

3. Lewis Jacobs, *The Rise of the American Film* (New York, 1968), 395. For similar views, see Richard Koszarski, *An Evening's Entertainment: The Age of the Silent Feature Picture, 1915–1928* (New York, 1990), 187; Lary May, *Screening out the Past: The Birth of Mass Culture and the Motion Picture Industry* (New York, 1980). Garth Jowett sees the shift away from serious social commentary coming as early as 1914. Garth Jowett, *Film the Democratic Art: A Social History of American Film* (Boston, 1976), 68–69, 186–87.

4. I was able to determine the political sympathies of 154 (90 percent) of the 171 films. Of these 154 labor-capital films, 27 were released between April and December 31, 1917; 37 in 1918; 46 in 1919; 33 in 1920; 14 in 1921; and 14 in 1922. For the general methods used in compiling this list, see Chapter 3 notes 3, 4.

5. Of the 205 labor-capital films whose politics I could determine, 131 (64 percent) were conservative, 46 (22 percent) liberal, 12 (6 percent) anti-authoritarian, 10 (5 percent) populist, and 6 (3 percent) radical. The 6 radical movies were made by worker filmmakers. My analysis of postwar films is informed by my viewing of 85 silent films made between April 1917 and the end of 1931; 44 of these films were released between April 1917 and the end of 1922.

6. Military death figures are taken from Paul Fussell, *The Great War and Modern Memory* (New York, 1975), 18. Production figures are taken from Jacobs, *Rise of American Film*, 159, 287. American efforts to capture the European film market are described in Thomas H. Guback, *The International Film Industry* (Bloomington, 1969).

7. The Senate Finance Committee estimated that Americans spent between $750 million and $1 billion on movies in 1921. The movie industry employed 250,000 people that year and its investments totaled $250 million. *Los Angeles Times*, December 28, 1921.

8. The rise of the studio system and the transformation of the movie industry during the war and postwar years are discussed in hundreds of books and articles.

Among the best older works are Terry Ramsaye, *A Million and One Nights* (New York, 1926); Benjamin B. Hampton, *A History of the Movies* (New York, 1931); Howard T. Lewis, *The Motion Picture Industry* (New York, 1933); Mae Huettig, *Economic Control of the Motion Picture Industry* (Philadelphia, 1944); Jacobs, *Rise of American Film*. The most useful recent works include Tino Balio, ed., *The American Film Industry* (Madison, 1976); David Bordwell, Janet Staiger, and Kristin Thompson, *The Classical Hollywood Cinema: Film Style and Mode of Production to 1960* (New York, 1985); Douglas Gomery, *The Hollywood Studio System* (New York, 1986); Thomas Schatz, *The Genius of the System: Hollywood Filmmaking in the Studio Era* (New York, 1988); Ethan Mordden, *The Hollywood Studios: House Style in the Golden Age of the Movies* (New York, 1988); Koszarski, *Evening's Entertainment*.

9. Gomery, *Hollywood Studio System*, 27.

10. For biographical material on Zukor and other movie moguls of the time, see Adolph Zukor, *The Public Is Never Wrong* (New York, 1953); Adolph Zukor, "Origin and Growth of the Industry," in Joseph Patrick Kennedy, ed., *The Story of the Films* (Chicago and New York, 1927), 55–76; Philip French, *The Movie Moguls: An Informal History of the Hollywood Tycoons* (London, 1969); Richard Dyer MacCann, *The First Tycoons* (Metuchen, N.J., 1987); Neal Gabler, *An Empire of Their Own: How the Jews Invented Hollywood* (New York, 1988).

11. Quoted in Gertrude Jobes, *Motion Picture Empire* (Hamden, Conn., 1966), 220. The *New York Times* described block booking as the policy of "leasing films in a block or group and compelling the picture house which shows the films to take all pictures in the group or block, or none at all, without regard to the character of the pictures or the wishes of the picture house." *New York Times*, July 10, 1927. Block-booking practices and the efforts of chains to standardize moviegoing experiences are discussed ibid.; James I. Deutsch, "The Rise and Fall of the House of Ushers: Teenage Ticket-Takers in the Twenties Theaters," *Journal of Popular Culture*, 13 (Spring 1980), 604–6; Douglas Gomery, "The Movies Become Big Business: Publix Theaters and the American Chain-Store Strategy," *Cinema Journal*, 18 (Spring 1979), 26–40; Lizabeth Cohen, *Making a New Deal: Industrial Workers in Chicago, 1919–1939* (New York, 1990), 125; Douglas Gomery, *Shared Pleasures: A History of Movie Presentation in the United States* (Madison, 1992).

12. *Film Daily Yearbook of Motion Pictures* (1927), 738, quoted in Koszarski, *Evening's Entertainment*, 69.

13. The rise of the star system and skyrocketing costs of production are described in Catherine E. Kerr, "Incorporating the Star: The Intersection of Business and Aesthetic Strategies in Early American Film," *Business History Review*, 64 (Autumn 1990), 383–410; George Mitchell, "The Consolidation of the American Film Industry, 1915–1920," in Ron Burnett, ed., *Explorations in Film Theory* (Bloomington, 1991), 254–72; and sources in note 8 above. For a contemporary view of changing industrial conditions, see New York State, *Report of the Joint Legislative Committee to Investigate the Moving Picture Industry* (Albany, 1917).

14. The rise and evolution of the director-unit system and the central producer system are described in W. E. Wing, "Tom Ince, of Inceville," *New York Dramatic Mirror*, December 24, 1913; Thomas Elsaesser, ed., *Early Cinema: Space, Frame, Narrative* (London, 1990); Charles Musser, "Pre-Classical Cinema: Its Changing

Modes of Film Production," in Richard Abel, *Silent Film* (New Brunswick, N.J., 1996), 85–108; Bordwell et al., *Classical Hollywood*. Koszarski argues that the central producer system was not widely used until 1916; *Evening's Entertainment*, 108–10.

15. Jacobs, *Rise of American Film*, 296; King Vidor, *A Tree Is a Tree: An Autobiography* (Hollywood, 1981), 70; Jan-Christopher Horak, *Dream Merchants: Making and Selling Films in Hollywood's Golden Age* (Rochester, 1989), 12.

16. In 1922, 84 percent of all American films were made in Hollywood, 12 percent in New York, and 4 percent in all other areas. Statistics taken from *New York Times*, November 11, 1920; Bordwell et al., *Classical Hollywood*, 123; Koszarski, *Evening's Entertainment*, 104–6. Selig is often credited for shooting the first film in Los Angeles in 1907, but Charles Musser notes that Biograph did it a year earlier. Musser, *Emergence of Cinema*, 455.

17. Robert Sklar, *Movie-Made America: A Cultural History of American Movies* (New York, 1994), 68. The rise of Hollywood and debates surrounding the industry's move west are described ibid.; Kevin Brownlow, *The Parade's Gone By* (Berkeley, 1968), 30–40; Koszarski, *Evening's Entertainment*; May, *Screening out the Past*; Ramsaye, *Million and One Nights*, 532–41.

18. Jacobs, *Rise of American Film*, 161. For descriptions and photographs of Universal and other new Hollywood studios, see Kevin Brownlow, *Hollywood: The Pioneers* (New York 1979), 90–107; Schatz, *Hollywood Studio System*, 6–20.

19. The evolution of "Poverty Row" is described in Paul Seale, "'A Host of Others': Toward a Nonlinear History of Poverty Row and the Coming of Sound," *Wide Angle*, 72 (January 1991), 72–103.

20. See the sources in note 8 above.

21. *NY Call*, October 17, 1919. For an overview of industry financing during this period, see A. H. Giannini, "Financing the Production and Distribution of Motion Pictures," *Annals of the American Academy of Political and Social Science*, 128 (November 1926), 46–49; Janet Wasko, *Movies and Money: Financing the American Film Industry* (Norwood, N.J., 1982).

22. Cecil B. DeMille, *The Autobiography of Cecil B. DeMille*, edited by Donald Hayne (Englewood Cliffs, N.J., 1959), 288–89.

23. Creel quoted in Jowett, *Film*, 66. The workings of the CPI are described in [George Creel], *Complete Report of the Chairman of the Committee on Public Information 1917, 1918, 1919* (Washington, D.C., 1920). For Creel's early movie experiences, see Robert Sobel, *The Manipulators: America in the Media Age* (New York, 1976), 91–92; Ramsaye, *Million and One Nights*, 611. For a more thorough view of the man, see George Creel, *Rebel at Large* (New York, 1947).

24. The June letter to the NAMPI, which carried Wilson's signature but was drafted by George Creel, is quoted in Craig W. Campbell, *Reel America and World War I: A Comprehensive Filmography and History of Motion Pictures in the United States, 1914–1920* (Jefferson, N.C., 1985), 67; also see "Working Agreement between the Committee on Public Information and the Export Division of the National Association of the Motion Picture Industry," July 12, 1918, Records of CPI, RG 63, Creel Correspondence, 1-A1, Box 2, folder 66; *New York Times*, July 29, 1917. Representatives from government departments and film companies met weekly as part of the Committee on Motion Picture Activities, and continued to do so until the end

of the war. Morton Leopold to Joseph Cotter, November 7, 1918, Records of the Office of the Secretary of the Interior, RG 48, Box 304, NA.

25. *Pershing's Crusaders* and *America's Answer* had over 4,000 screenings. The CPI planned to distribute films to "2280 colored theaters for colored people in the United States." C. S. Hart Memorandum, March 28, 1918, Records of CPI, RG 63, 10A–A1, Box 130. The work of the CPI and its Division of Films is discussed in Rufus Steele, "Progress Report of the Department of Scenarios and Outside Production," August 10, 1918, Records of CPI, RG 63, Box 41; [Creel], *Report of CPI*; James R. Mock and Cedric Larson, *Words That Won The War: The Story of the Committee on Public Information, 1917–1919* (Princeton, 1939); Stephen Vaughn, *Holding Fast the Inner Lines: Democracy, Nationalism, and the Committee on Public Information* (Chapel Hill, 1980); Robert Wood, ed., *Film and Propaganda in America: A Documentary History. Volume I: World War I* (Westport, Conn., 1990); Sobel, *Manipulators*; Campbell, *Reel America*.

26. [Creel], *Report of CPI*, 7, 103. Several federal officials denounced film companies for making excessive profits; see Leopold to Cotter, November 7, 1918, Records of Secretary of Interior, RG 48, Box 304, NA; [Carl Byoir] to George Creel, August 20, 1918, Records of CPI, RG 63, Box 19. For movie industry relations with the CPI and federal agencies, see sources in previous note and correspondence in Records of CPI, RG 63; *Variety* August 31, 1917; *New York Times* July 29, 1917, and July 7, August 26, 1918; Michael T. Isenberg, *War on Film: The American Cinema and World War I, 1914–1941* (Rutherford, N.J., 1981).

27. [Creel], *Report of CPI*, 104. The CPI was granted its authority under the Trading with the Enemies Act of July 1918.

28. Quotations taken from "Films Rejected for Export," Records of CPI, RG 63, 30-B3. A list of films and the reasons for their rejection can be found ibid.; [Creel], *Report of CPI*, 103–5. CPI officials granted export licenses for 6,200 reels of film. There are no figures for the number of films that were banned. Creel and Frank Wolfe apparently became friends during the war. Frank Wolfe to Chester Wright, February 24, 1918, RG 63, Creel Correspondence, 1–A1, Box 15, folder 3; *LA Citizen*, March 5, 1920. For the work of the Alliance, see Frank L. Grubbs, *The Struggle for Labor Loyalty: Gompers, the A.F. of L., and the Pacifists, 1917–1920* (Durham, N.C., 1968).

29. War Industries Board agreement quoted in *New York Times*, August 26, 1919; "Working Agreement between the Committee on Public Information and the Export Division of the National Association of the Motion Picture Industry," July 12, 1918, RG 63, Creel Correspondence, 1–A1, Box 2, folder 66. Creel lobbied government officials on behalf of the movie industry. *Motion Picture News*, June 22, 1918; Wood, *Film and Propaganda*, 201.

30. *NY Call*, July 11, 1918. Government authorities had already placed the nation's railroads under federal control and banned allegedly unpatriotic radical publications from the mail. Federal use of its wartime powers over industry is discussed in Alexander M. Bing, *War-Time Strikes and Their Adjustment* (New York, 1921); Melvyn Dubofsky, *The State and Labor in Modern America* (Chapel Hill, 1994), 61–81; for the banning of radical books and periodicals, see James R. Mock, *Censorship 1917* (Princeton, 1941); H. C. Peterson and Gilbert C. Fite, *Opponents of War 1917–1918* (Madison, 1957), 94–101.

31. The Goldstein case and wartime censorship of domestic films are discussed in Kevin Brownlow, *The War, the West, and the Wilderness* (New York, 1978); Mock and Larson, *Words That Won the War,* 143–47, 172–189; Campbell, *Reel America,* 50–52, 73; Mock, *Censorship,* 172–89. For *Dusk,* see *Los Angeles Record,* September 8, 1922.

32. Mock and Larson, *Words That Won the War,* 157.

33. The creation and activities of the Joint Committee are discussed in *Variety,* November 29, 1918; *New York Times,* January 5, 1919; Secretary of Labor William B. Wilson to Franklin Lane, January 13, 1919, and C. H. Moore to Mr. Cotter, February 27, 1919, Department of Interior, RG 48, Box 304, NA. The CPI was officially dissolved in June 1919.

34. For an overview of labor activity during this period, see Foster Rhea Dulles and Melvyn Dubofsky, *Labor in America* (Arlington Heights, 1993); David Montgomery, *The Fall of the House of Labor: The Workplace, the State, and American Labor Activism, 1865–1925* (Cambridge and New York, 1987); James R. Green, *The World of the Worker: Labor in Twentieth-Century America* (New York, 1980); Melvyn Dubofsky, *We Shall Be All: A History of the Industrial Workers of the World* (New York, 1969). For an analysis of wages and inflation, see Frank Stricker, "The Wages of Inflation: Workers' Earnings in the World War One Era," *Mid-America,* 63 (April-July 1981), 93–105.

35. The best study of the Red scare is Robert K. Murray, *Red Scare: A Study in National Hysteria, 1919–1929* (Minneapolis, 1955). For a brief history of the Third International (also known as Comintern), see Tom Bottomore, ed., *A Dictionary of Marxist Thought* (Cambridge, Mass., 1983), 236–38.

36. *Open Shop Review,* quoted in Murray, *Red Scare,* 93; other quotes ibid., 92.

37. Laurence Todd quoted in *Journal of the Electrical Worker,* 19 (February 1920), 366; Lester Cole, *Hollywood Red* (Palo Alto, 1981), 78.

38. David Niles to Roger Babson, December 13, 1918, Records of the Department of Labor, RG 174, Box 137, folder 129/10-A, NA. The anti-radical activities of the government are described in Julian F. Jaffe, *The Crusade against Radicalism: New York during the Red Scare, 1914–1922* (Port Washington, N.Y., 1972); Paul L. Murphy, *World War I and the Origin of Civil Liberties in the United States* (New York, 1985); Frank Donner, *Protectors of Privilege: Red Squads and Police Repression in Urban America* (Berkeley, 1990); James Weinstein, *The Decline of Socialism in America* (New York, 1967); Murray, *Red Scare;* Dubofsky, *We Shall Be All.*

39. Niles to Babson, December 13, 1918; also see Roger Babson to W. B. Wilson, December 14, 1918, ibid.

40. Niles' letter is reprinted in *Variety,* November 29, 1918. For scenarios and films sent to Niles' office, see David Niles to William Parsons, March 5, 1919, RG 174, Box 137, folder 129–C; David Niles to Hugh Kerwin, March 12, 1919, RG 174, Box 25, folder 16/24; for objections to Niles's views about "labor unrest," see W. D. McGuire to Frank Morrison, February 14, 1919, Subjects Correspondence (AFL), Box 15, NBRMP. Niles subsequently served as administrative assistant to Presidents Roosevelt and Truman. For biographical information, see *New York Times,* September 29, 1952; Karl Brown, *Adventures with D. W. Griffith* (New York, 1976), see photograph between pages 156 and 157.

41. R. M. Whitney, *Reds in America* (New York, 1924), 141, 150; William C. deMille, *Hollywood Saga* (New York, 1939), 196. The government also investigated its own filmmakers. In 1918, secret agents from the Military Intelligence Branch of the War Department were assigned to investigate charges that the CPI's Film Section was being run by socialist and Bolshevik sympathizers. M.I. 4–5, The Military Intelligence Branch, "Report on the Committee On Public Information," May 1918, RG 63, Creel Correspondence, 1-A1, Box 5, NA.

42. *Los Angeles Times*, January 3, 1920; "The Immigrant and the 'Movies': A New Kind of Education," *Touchstone*, 7 (July 1920), 328. For Lane's contact with Congress, see *New York Times*, December 18, 1919, and January 12, 1920; *Wid's Yearbook 1920–1921* (n.d.), 383. Americanization campaigns and crackdowns against foreign radicalism are discussed in John Higham, *Strangers in the Land: Patterns of American Nativism, 1860–1925* (New York, 1965); Gerd Korman, *Industrialization, Immigrants, and Americanizers* (Madison, 1967); Jennifer Daryl Slack, "Media and the Americanization of Workers: The Americanization Bulletin, 1918–1919," in Vincent Mosco and Janet Wasko, eds., *The Critical Communications Review. Volume I: Labor, the Working Class, and the Media* (Norwood, N.J., 1983), 23–44; and sources in note 38 above.

43. "Look through Lincoln's Eyes," letter circulated by the Americanism Committee, c. January 1920, Box 164, NBRMP. For correspondence regarding film scenarios, see Franklin K. Lane to George Kleine, May 19, 1920, and W. A. Ryan "To the Producer," May 19, 1920, Box 1, George Kleine Collection, Library of Congress, Washington, D.C.; W. A. Ryan to David Horsley, June 15, 1920, Horsley Papers, folder 28.

44. Quotes are from the film's intertitles. Other committee releases included *Democracy, The Vision Restored* (1920), *One Law for All* (1920), and *Stranger's Beware* (1920). Reviews and labor reactions to these films can be found in *Educational Film Magazine*, 3 (February 1920), 9 and 3 (March 1920), 20; *NY Call*, November 4, 1920, and March 5, 1921; Campbell, *Reel America*, 135; Samuel Gompers to W. D. McGuire, October 18, 1920, Box 15, NBRMP. Americanism films were distributed by the National Association of the Motion Picture Industry, whose members made up 95 percent of the nation's producers and distributors.

45. Americanism Committee, "Through Lincoln's Eyes," Box 164, NBRMP; *American Economic League Bulletin*, quoted in *NY Call*, March 5, 1921; ibid., November 4, 1920; Gompers to McGuire, October 18, 1920.

46. W. J. Reynolds to Rolin Film Corporation, August 31, 1918, Roach Papers, folder 3:1920. The two best sources for labor-capital relations in Hollywood during this era are the MPPA records kept in the Roach collection, and the Minute Books of IATSE Local 33 (which begin in January 1915) kept at union headquarters in Burbank, Ca. I thank Nick Long for allowing me access to IATSE records. For general histories of movie industry labor relations during this era, see Marion Dixon, "The History of the Los Angeles Central Labor Council," M.A. thesis, University of California, Berkeley, 1929; Michael Nielsen, "Toward a Workers' History of the U.S. Film Industry," in Mosco and Wasko, eds., *Critical Communications Review*, 48–59; and sources in Chapter 3 note 12. For the activities of MPPA spies see W. J. Reynolds to Hal Roach, February 13, 1919, MPPA: file 2; W. J. Reynolds to Hal Roach, January

19 and March 5, 1920, and W. J. Reynolds to W. H. Doane, September 13, 1920, MPPA: file 3, Roach Papers.

47. *LA Citizen*, May 17, 1918; "Minutes of the Meetings of Local 33, IATSE," July 24, 1921, Local 33 Headquarters, Burbank, Ca. D. W. Griffith was also a keen supporter of the studio unions and honorary member of Local 33. For the union leanings of Griffith, Hart, Pickford, and Fairbanks see "Minutes of Local 33," July 14 and September 8, 1918; *LA Citizen*, February 10, 1922.

48. "Minutes of Local 33," July 28, 1918. For membership statistics, see *Combined Convention Proceedings National Alliance of Theatrical Stage Employees and Moving Picture Operators of the United States and Canada: A Record of All Conventions Held Since the Inception of the Organization, July 1893* (New York, 1926) (hereafter *IATSE Convention Proceedings*), 695; "Financial Reports for 1919," found after entry for October 26, 1918, in "Minutes of Local 33." Stephenson was the local's most powerful figure until November 1919, when he was forced to quit under mysterious circumstances. My guess is that there was a secret deal between producers and IATSE's international officers; ibid., November 23, 1919. For Stephenson's appointment as the local's business agent, see *IATSE Convention Proceedings*, 600, 607, 695; "Minutes of Local 33," January 1, 26, 1918.

49. "Minutes of Local 33," July 14 and 28, 1918. For MPPA views on IATSE strikes, see W. J. Reynolds to Hal Roach, September 23, 1918, MPPA: file 1, and "Memorandum of Wage Scale and Working Conditions Effective September 15, 1919 and to Remain in Force and Effect until September 15, 1920," in MPPA: file 2, Roach Papers. For industry strike activities during this era, see sources in note 46 above.

50. *Los Angeles Times. The Forty Year War for a Free City: A History of the Open Shop Movement in Los Angeles* (Los Angeles, 1929), 25; *Journal of Electrical Workers*, 19 (November 1919), 206.

51. W. J. Reynolds to Warren Doane, August 1, 1921, MPPA: folder 4, Roach Papers; "Minutes of Local 33," September 28, 1919. The eleven studios initiating the wage cut were Famous Players-Lasky, Goldwyn, Roach, Fox, Universal, Metro, Realart, Brunton, Christie, Ince, and Buster Keaton. Information concerning the conflict is drawn from the "Minutes of Local 33"; Louis B. Perry and Richard Perry, *A History of the Los Angeles Labor Movement* (Berkeley, 1963), 323–24; Murray Ross, *Stars and Strikes: Unionization of Hollywood* (New York, 1941), 7–8; and daily labor columns in the *LA Citizen*, *NY Call*, and *Seattle Union Record*.

52. *NY Call*, December 11, 1921; *LA Citizen*, March 10, 1922, September 16, 1921.

53. *LA Citizen*, September 2, 1921. Once again, it seems quite possible that IATSE leaders were bribed by producers. For details of this very suspicious turn of events, see "Minutes of Local 33," July 31, August 3, 9, 14, 17, 24, 28, 1921; [IATSE] *General Bulletin #53*, August 2, 1921, and #72, December 13, 1921; "Minutes of the AFL Executive Council," November 17, 1921, 32–33, reel 7, AFL Records; *IATSE Convention Proceedings*, 804. Membership in Local 33 plummeted from 1,557 in September 1920 to 415 in September 1925.

54. There were 274 labor-capital films released between 1905 and April 6, 1917, and 171 released between April 7, 1917, and 1922. The percentages in this paragraph are based on films whose politics I could determine (i.e., 244 films for the

prewar era and 154 for 1917–1922). Conservative films of this era also included productions that portrayed American wage earners as the dupes of Bolsheviks or presented the Soviet Union and Communist ideology in the worst possible light. The following sources were especially valuable in compiling my list of labor-capital films during this era: Russell Campbell, "Bolsheviks and Nihilists: Revolutionary Russia in American Silent Film," *The Silent Picture*, 19 (1974), 4–36; and the sources cited in Chapter 2 note 22.

55. Walter K. Hill, review of "Its 'Everybody's Business' Now," *MPW*, August 9, 1919; copy of investment offering reprinted in *NY Call*, June 29, 1919; deMille, *Hollywood Saga*, 134.

56. *NY Call*, May 2, 1920. For Wall Street's involvement with the daily workings of film production, see Jesse Lasky with Don Weldon, *I Blow My Own Horn* (London, 1957), 144–46; Sobel, *Manipulators*, 109.

57. The American Plan is discussed in Selig Perlman and Philip Taft, *History of Labor in the United States*, 4 vols. (New York, 1937), 4: 489–514; Allen Wakstein, "The National Association of Manufacturers and Labor Relations in the 1920s," *Labor History*, 10 (Spring 1969), 163–76. For declining union membership, see *Historical Statistics*, 1: 177.

58. *NY Call*, May 2, 1920.

59. "Through Lincoln's Eyes," circular letter from William Ryan, c. 1920, Subjects Papers (Anti-Communism), Box 164, NBRMP; review of *The Great Shadow*, *Variety*, May 21, 1920. The shooting script of *Dangerous Hours* calls for the director to create an "atmosphere of horror" in the scene recreating the revolution. *The New Moon* (1919), *Common Property* (1919), and *The World and the Woman* (1919) exploited the alleged nationalization of women policy. For an account of the "nationalization yarn," see *NY Call*, August 26, 1919.

60. "Extracts from H. C. Witwer's story 'Everybody's Business,'" 2, enclosed in letter from H. J. Shephard to W. D. McGuire, January 21, 1920, Box 104, NBRMP. For *The Penalty*, see Kevin Brownlow, *Behind the Mask of Innocence* (New York, 1990), 195–200.

61. Quote is from intertitle in *Dangerous Hours*. Other films portraying the corruption of union officials include *Golden Goal* (1918), *False Gods* (Rothapfel 1919), *A Man's Fight* (1919), *The Other Man's Wife* (1919), *The Red Peril* (1919), and *Unchartered Channels* (1920).

62. Shooting script for "Americanism" (original title of *Dangerous Hours*), 2, Box 3 (Don Byrne folder), Thomas Ince Collection, Special Collections, Library of Congress, Washington, D.C. For examples of liberal films that avoided dealing with the Red menace, see *Dolly's Vacation* (1918), *Brothers Divided* (1919), *Democracy, the Vision Restored* (1920), *The Dwelling Place of Light* (1920), and *The Whistle* (Famous Players-Lasky 1921).

63. *NY Call*, November 4, 1920.

64. When Ole Hanson came to Los Angeles to speak about "Americanization" in January 1920, MPPA secretary Reynolds suggested that studios post notices urging their employees to attend. W. J. Reynolds to Hal Roach, January 16, 1920, MPPA: file 3, Roach Papers. The Seattle strike is analyzed in History Committee of the General Strike Committee, *The Seattle General Strike* (Seattle, 1919); Robert Friedheim, *The Seattle General Strike* (Seattle, 1964).

65. *The Face at Your Window* (1920) also presented a reactionary version of the Centralia massacre. For descriptions of IWW western organizing activities and the steel strike of 1919, see Dubofsky, *We Shall Be All*, 359–60; Perlman and Taft, *History of Labor*, 427–32, 461–68; Murray, *Red Scare*, 135–52, 166–89.

66. Intertitle from *Bolshevism on Trial*; reviewer quote in *Educational Film Magazine*, 1 (June 1919), 29.

67. *NY Call*, April 25, 1919; *Variety*, August 15, 1919. The controversy surrounding *Bolshevism* is described in *NY Call*, April 19, 1919. For the *Volcano*, see J. Hoberman, *The Bridge of Light: Yiddish Film between Two Worlds* (New York, 1991), 53; *Variety*, August 15, 1919. For government endorsements of anti-Red films, see Mathias Radin to Department of Labor, October 16, 1919, RG 174, Box 25, 16/24A, NA; Campbell, *Reel America*, 133–34.

68. Membership statistics are taken from Weinstein, *Decline of Socialism*, 27, 235; Murray, *Red Scare*, 50–51, 87–88; Dubofsky, *We Shall Be All*, 349, 473. The nation's adult population (over 18 years) in 1920 was 66,839,000.

69. *Seattle Union Record*, January 30, 1920; Frank Morrison to Universal Film Manufacturing Company, November 15, 1920, and P. H. Peterson to Samuel Gompers, November 12, 1920, AFL Convention 1920, reel 30, AFL Records.

Chapter 6
Struggles for the Screen

1. *Seattle Union Record*, December 19, 1919. The scenes described in the opening paragraph are taken, respectively, from the four films mentioned here.

2. Ibid., January 9, 1920.

3. Ibid., February 22, 1923.

4. Ibid., July 22, 1920; Robert A. Bowen to J. E. Hoover, January 7, 1921, RG 65, reel 926 (BS 212657), ICF.

5. *NY Call*, September 9, 1919.

6. Chicago *Daily Worker*, September 10, 1924.

7. *Variety*, November 21, 1919; *NY Call*, August 15, 1920; *Chicago New Majority*, January 8, 1921.

8. "Report of Agent 106," May 17, 1919, Box 1, folder 3, Beck Papers; *Seattle Union Record*, January 30, 1920.

9. "Minutes of the Seattle Central Labor Council," May 26, 1920, 106, Box 8, Records of the Seattle Central Labor Council, UW; for California endorsements, see *LA Citizen*, September 19, 1919.

10. *United Mine Workers' Journal*, 30 (April 15, 1919), 6; J. R. Dennison, of Motion Picture Theater Owners' Association, quoted in Chicago *Daily Worker*, September 10, 1925; *United Mine Workers' Journal* 30 (April 15, 1919), 6. In 1920, a peak year for organized labor, union members represented less than 13 percent of the total labor force. *Historical Statistics*, 1: 131, 177. The changing class composition of movie audiences is discussed in Chapter 7 below.

11. *NY Call*, May 9, 31, 1920. The rise and popularity of newsreels are discussed in Raymond Fielding, *The American Newsreel 1911–1967* (Norman, Okla., 1972); Richard Koszarski, *An Evening's Entertainment: The Age of the Silent Feature Picture, 1915–1928* (New York, 1990), 167–70.

12. Chicago *Daily Worker*, January 16, 1924; *NY Call*, May 31, 1920; *Chicago New Majority*, January 27, 1923.

13. *AFL Proceedings 1920*, 466; R. H. Cochrane to Frank Morrison, December 9, 1920; AFL Convention 1920, reel 30. Correspondence between Morrison and movie companies can be found in the same location on the microfilm; "Minutes of Meetings," August 28, 1923, 10, AFL Executive Council Reports, reel 7, AFL Records. For AFL meetings with NAMPI officials, see F. H. Elliott to Peter Brady, September 17, 1920, and Brady to Frank Morrison, September 20, 1920, AFL Convention 1920, reel 30, AFL Records.

14. *Seattle Union Record*, July 22, 1920; *Chicago New Majority*, January 8, 1921.

15. I use the terms "labor film company" and "worker filmmaker" interchangeably to describe companies owned and films made by workers, labor unions, or members of radical, worker-oriented organizations like the Socialist and Communist parties. For the rising costs of moviemaking in the early 1920s, see Janet Wasko, *Movies and Money: Financing the American Film Industry* (Norwood, N.J., 1982), 21; *AFL Proceedings 1922*, 139.

16. David Horsley, "The Power of Public Opinion," February 18, 1919, Horsley Papers. The first correspondence regarding the company's formation appeared in July 1918. Upton Sinclair to George Williams, July 26, 1918, file J215, Brandon Coll. Horsley's early life and conversion to socialism are described in David Horsley to Upton Sinclair, March 21, 1919, Upton Sinclair file, Horsley Papers; Anthony Slide, *The American Film Industry* (Westport, Conn., 1986), 59–60, 87–88; Terry Ramsaye, *A Million and One Nights* (New York, 1926), 584; Eileen Bowser, *The Transformation of Cinema* (New York, 1990), 76, 221, 223.

17. Ben M. Lyon to the President of the Brotherhood of Railway Trainmen, November 22, 1918, file J215, Brandon Coll.; circular letter, Ben Lyon to Railroad Locals, September 26, 1918; circular letter, Ben Lyon to Railroad Lodges, July 19, 1919, in file with letter, Ben M. Lyon to A. B. Garrettson, July 26, 1919, folder 25, Horsley Papers. Horsley was given 18,000 shares of MMPC stock in exchange for his studio. The structure of the company and its initial stock distribution scheme are laid out in "Incorporation Records of the Motive Motion Picture Corporation" (dated January 17, 1919), folder 28, Horsley Papers. For debates over railroad ownership, see Alexander Bing, *War-Time Strikes and Their Adjustment* (New York, 1921), 82–95.

18. MMPC advertisement in *Wid's Yearbook 1918*, n.p.; *LA Citizen*, February 14, 1919. Sinclair was to receive $1,000 and 1,000 shares of stock for his work. Upton Sinclair to George Williams, July 26, 1918, file J215, Brandon Coll. For Ford's background, see Slide, *American Film Industry*, 135; Bowser, *Transformation of Cinema*, 146, 156, 241–42, 248.

19. *LA Citizen*, March 7, 1919; *AFL Proceedings 1919*, 341.

20. Ben Lyon to David Horsley, July 2, 1919, folder 25, Horsley Papers.

21. David Horsley to Ben Lyon, August 4, 1919, and Ben Lyon to David Horsley, September 4, 1919, folder 25, Horsley Papers.

22. David Horsley to Ben Lyon, August 27, 1919, folder 25, Horsley Papers.

23. "Minutes of Special Meeting of the Board of Directors of MMPC," December 13, 1919, folder 28; on the death of the MMPC, see David Horsley to Upton Sinclair, March 11, 1920, Sinclair folder, Horsley Papers.

24. *NY Call*, May 28, 1920; *Seattle Union Record*, January 6, 1920, and December 19, 1919. The organization was also called the Federated Film Corporation.

25. "Report of Agent #172," April 2, 1920, Box 2, folder 6, Roy John Kinnear Papers, UW; *Seattle Union Record*, November 12, 1919. A list of the FFC's Board of Directors and Advisory Board can be found in *Seattle Union Record*, December 19, 1919, and April 7, 1920. For a history of Seattle's cooperative enterprises, see Dana Frank, *Purchasing Power: Consumer Organizing, Gender, and the Seattle Labor Movement, 1919–1929* (Cambridge and New York, 1994).

26. Instead of being paid a salary, Nelson was given $40,000 in FFC stock. *Seattle Union Record*, November 26, 1919. For biographical information on Nelson, see *Variety*, November 7 and 14, 1914; *Seattle Union Record*, December 19, 1919, December 1, 1921, and December 11, 1922; "Report of F. L. Turner," June 11, 1918, and "Report by E. Kosterlitzky," April 9 and 15, 1918, reel 512 (OG 125,871), ICF; Slide, *American Film Industry*, 315–16; J. Arthur Nelson, *The Photoplay: How to Write, How to Sell* (Los Angeles, 1913). On the FFC's search for a managing director, see "Minutes of AFL Executive Council," February 26, 1921, 20, AFL Executive Council Reports, reel 6, AFL Records.

27. *Seattle Union Record*, March 25, 1920, January 10, 1920.

28. *Seattle Union Record*, December 19, 1919. The FFC's largest stockholder was the Boilermakers' Union, which bought $10,000 in stock in January 1920. Fundraising efforts and exhibition deals are described in *Seattle Union Record*, January 15 and 26; May 24 and 28; July 17, 1920; "Report of Agent 17," June 2 and 19, 1920, Box 2, folders 7, 8, Beck Papers.

29. *Presenting the Motion Picture* (New York, 1920), LFS pamphlet included in correspondence of Robert C. Deming to W. P. Hazen, November 3, 1920, RG 65, reel 926 (BS 202600–197), ICF. The company was initially capitalized at $50,000 and planned to increase its stock to $250,000. New York *The Liberator*, 3 (July 1920), see advertisement on back cover.

30. *NY Call*, March 3, 1917. For biographical information on Cannon, see *NY Call*, February 9, 1913; July 3, 1916; March 31, 1917; May 14, July 5, and August 22, 1920; Chicago *American Socialist*, July 29, 1916; *New York Times*, January 5, 1952; "Report of Agent J. G. Tucker," July 10, 1920, RG 65, reel 616 (208369), ICF; Solon De Leon, ed., *The American Labor Who's Who* (New York, 1925), 36–37; Elizabeth Dilling, *The Red Network, A "Who's Who" and Handbook of Radicalism for Patriots* (Kenilworth, Ill., and Chicago, 1934), 270; Vernon H. Jensen, *Heritage of Conflict: Labor Relations in the Nonferrous Metals Industry up to 1930* (Ithaca, 1950), 190–91, 357–79, 391–93; Emma Angevine, *In League with the Future* (Chicago, 1959), 10–11; Gary Fink, *Biographical Dictionary of American Labor Leaders* (Westport, Conn., 1974), 143.

31. *Presenting the Motion Picture*. For Laura Cannon's experiences with film, see *LA Citizen*, September 22, 1911.

32. Circular letter "Dear Sirs and Brothers," from Joseph D. Cannon, October 19, 1920, copy contained in "Report of G. J. Starr," January 8, 1921, RG 65, reel 926 (BS 212657), ICF; also see circular letter "To Labor Unions and Members," from Joseph D. Cannon, July 7, 1920, included in correspondence of Robert C. Deming to W. P. Hazen, November 3, 1920, RG 65, reel 926 (BS 202600–197), ICF.

33. *NY Call*, August 10 and October 8, 1920. For descriptions of initial news-

reels, see ibid., July 17, 20, 21; August 29, 30; and September 3, 1920; *Seattle Union Record*, September 27, 1920. Cannon finished third in the election with 159,804 votes, 6 percent of the total.

34. *NY Call*, March 3, 1918. For Slayton's background, see ibid., January 17 and December 16, 1909; March 24 and October 15, 1910; January 20, 1919, and June 1, 1921; Chicago *American Socialist*, January 15 and July 29, 1916. Slayton's publications included *Props to Capitalism* (n.p., n.d.), *Criminology, Crimes and Criminals, and the United States Constitution, A Class Document* (c. 1910), *An Answer to the Roman Catholic Church's Attack on Socialism* (n.p., n.d.).

35. On the LFS' securing rights to Sinclair's productions, see *NY Call*, May 28, 1922, and correspondence between Upton Sinclair and Joseph Cannon in file J215, Brandon Coll. Cannon's efforts to court Sinclair were probably aided by Laura Cannon's long-time friendship with the writer, whom she first met during protests over the Ludlow Massacre in 1914. Upton Sinclair, *The Autobiography of Upton Sinclair* (London, 1963), 210–11.

36. Chicago *Daily Worker*, February 7, 1925; transcript of William Kruse interview with Russell Merritt and Vance Keply, January 18, 1975, Genoa City, Wisconsin, 20, 4, file I189, Brandon Coll. The IWA maintained branches in a number of countries. In the Soviet Union it was known as Mezhrabpom, in Germany the International Arbeiter Hilfe; its American name would later be changed to the Workers' International Relief. For further biographical information about Kruse, see transcript of William F. Kruse interview with Tom Brandon, May 20, 1975, Indianapolis, and Bill Kruse to Thomas Brandon, July 5, 1978, I189, Brandon Coll.; Chicago *American Socialist*, November 27 and December 25, 1915; January 22, March 18, and December 2, 1916; New York *The Worker*, November 24 and December 22, 1923; Rohama Lee, "The First Fifty Years Were the Hardest," *Film News*, 28 (1971), 6–9; Theodore Draper, *The Roots of American Communism* (New York, 1957), 330–31, 450 note 28; Bernard K. Johnpoll and Harvey Klehr, eds., *Biographical Dictionary of the American Left* (New York and Westport, Conn., 1986), 234.

37. Chicago *Daily Worker*, October 6, 1924; Kruse interview with Brandon, 3. For Kruse's own account of his filmmaking ventures see William F. Kruse to Steven Hill, July 15, 1974, and Bill Kruse to Thomas Brandon, July 5 and 6, 1978, Brandon Coll.; Vance Kepley, Jr., "Early Soviet-American Relations through Documentary Films: The Career of William F. Kruse," unpublished paper, file I189, Brandon Coll.; and sources in previous note.

38. *AFL Proceedings 1921*, 335. For information on other labor production companies created during this period, see Seymour Hastings to Frank Morrison, June 23, 1919, and Carl Stearns Clancy to Frank Morrison, July 29, 1919, AFL Convention 1919, reel 29; P. H. Peterson to Samuel Gompers, November 20, 1920, and A. J. Harriman to Samuel Gompers, November 24, 1920, AFL Convention 1920, reel 30; Ben Lyon to David Horsley, July 9 and 17, 1919, folder 25, Horsley Papers.

39. *Seattle Union Record*, December 11, 1922.

40. Information about the actors and production personnel involved in both films can be found in *Seattle Union Record*, November 17, 20, 23, 24, and December 20, 1920; *NY Call*, March 3, May 27, and June 2, 1921. *Filmerama: Twenty Years of Silents*, compiled by John Stewart, 2 vols. (Metuchen, N.J., 1974, 1977); Kemp R. Niver, *Early Motion Pictures: The Paper Print Collection in the Library of Congress*

(Washington, D.C., 1985), 281–82. The guest appearance by the Czar's dog is described in *NY Call*, July 3, 1922.

41. *NY Call*, March 3, 1921. I break my general rule here: although there are no surviving copies of *The New Disciple* or *The Contrast*, there is so much surviving material about the films—including stills in labor newspapers—that I use the present tense to describe them.

42. Intertitle quoted in *NY Call*, December 19, 1921. For reviews, photographs, and descriptions of the film, see *Seattle Union Record*, May 4, 6, 7, 9–12, 1921; *NY Call*, September 25 and December 17, 19, 23, 25, 1921; July 1, 2, 1922; *Wid's*, December 25, 1921; *Variety*, December 23, 1921; *MPW*, December 31, 1921; *LA Citizen*, March 10, September 1, and December 29, 1922; February 2, 9, 16, 23, 1923; *Photoplay*, March 1922, 116; *Chicago New Majority*, January 12, March 15, 1924; *Chicago Daily Worker*, March 18, 1924; Sacramento, *California Labor Chronicle*, October 2, 1925. For Seattle's farmer-labor cooperatives see Frank, *Purchasing Power*. I want to thank George Potamianos for the Sacramento reference.

43. *AFL Weekly News*, September 10, 1921. For Hollywood depictions of coal mine conflicts, see *Fanatics* (1917), *Courage of the Commonplace* (Edison 1917), *The Stranger's Banquet* (1922), and *Little Church around the Corner* (Warner Brothers 1923). For an analysis of the coal wars, see Henry M. Robinson and Rembrandt Pearle, *Award and Recommendations of the United States Bituminous Coal Commission* (Washington, D.C., 1920); Howard B. Lee, *Bloodletting in Appalachia* (Morgantown, W. Va., 1969); David Alan Corbin, *Life, Work, and Rebellion in the Coal Fields: The Southern West Virginia Miners, 1880–1922* (Urbana, 1981); Lon Savage, *Thunder in the Mountains: The West Virginia Mine War, 1920–21* (Pittsburgh, 1990).

44. Intertitle quoted in "Report of Agent H. J. Lennon," March 17, 1921, RG 65, reel 926 (BS 202600–197), ICF. For reviews and background information, see ibid.; *New York Evening Call*, March 19 and July 11, 1918, January 20, 1919; *NY Call*, March 3, May 27, June 2 and 4, September 25, 1921; *Chicago New Majority*, February 25, April 4 and 22, 1922; *Variety*, February 24, 1922; *Seattle Union Record*, March 10, 1922; R. M. Whitney, *Reds in America* (New York, 1924), 146–48.

45. *Journal of Electrical Workers*, 24 (October 1925), 783; *Chicago Federation News*, December 26, 1925. Rothacker had done work for Mary Pickford and Douglas Fairbanks.

46. Quotes are from film's intertitles; last quote is from *Chicago Federation News*, December 26, 1925. A restored version of parts of reel 1 and 3 can be seen at the UCLA Film and Television Archive. For reviews and reactions see *Chicago Federation News*, October 17 and December 12, 19, 26, 1925; January 9, 1926; *LA Citizen*, August 14 and November 20, 27, 1925; *Seattle Union Record*, January 9 and 11, 1926; John J. Manning, "Labor's Reward," *American Federationist*, 32 (November 1925), 1,056–58; John J. Manning, "Organization—Education," *American Federationist*, 32 (December 1925), 1,167–68; *AFL News*, November 21 and 28, December 12, 1925; January 16 and 30, February 5 and 20, March 6, 13, 20, 1926; and sources in previous note.

47. Quote is taken from film's intertitles. For descriptions of the strike and the events that led to it, see Albert Weisbrod, *Passaic: The Story of a Struggle against Starvation Wages and for the Right to Organize* (Chicago, 1926); Mary Heaton Vorse, *The Passaic Textile Strike 1926–1927* (Passaic, N.J., 1927); Paul Murphy, with Kermit

Hall and David Klaassen, *The Passaic Textile Strike of 1926* (Belmont, Ca., 1974); Martha Stone Asher, "Recollections of the Passaic Textile Strike of 1926," *Labor's Heritage*, 2 (April 1990), 4–23.

48. Chicago *Daily Worker*, May 10, 1927. A copy of the film can be found at MOMA. Sam Brody and Lester Balog, two of the cameramen on the film, went on to found the Workers' Film and Photo League in 1931. For reviews and descriptions, see Chicago *Daily Worker*, September 18, 23, 25, and October 18, 1926; *LA Citizen*, July 16, November 26, and December 17, 31, 1926; *Chicago Federation News*, October 2 and 23, 1926; New York *Daily Worker*, May 10, 1927; Kevin Brownlow, *Behind the Mask of Innocence* (New York, 1990), 498–508; Leslie Fishbein, "The Patterson Pageant (1913): The Birth of Docudrama as a Weapon in the Class Struggle," *Journal of Regional Cultures*, 4–5 (Fall 1984-Summer 1985), 116–21; Russell Campbell, *The Cinema Strikes Back: Radical Filmmaking in the United States 1930–1942* (Ann Arbor, 1982), 34–35; Steve Krinsky, "The Passaic Textile Strike and the Power of the Media," *Labor's Heritage*, 2 (April 1990), 20–21; Brandon, "Populist Film," 31–56, file D43, Brandon Coll.

49. *NY Call*, June 13, 1920; *Seattle Union Record*, November 12, 1920; Chicago *Daily Worker*, March 18, 1925; *NY Call*, June 15 and 19, 1920. In addition to these regular services, striking Kansas miners made newsreels documenting their struggles with mine owners in 1921; *NY Call*, July 29 and September 5, 17, 1921. For descriptions of LFS and FFC newsreels, see *NY Call*, August 10, 12, 21, 23, 29, 30, September 3, and October 8, 14, 19, 1920; *Seattle Union Record*, April 30, May 7, and November 12, 13, 22, 1920; and September 21, 1922; *Chicago New Majority*, August 19, 1922; "Minutes of the Seattle Central Labor Council," September 20 and October 25, 1922, Records of the Seattle CLC, Box 8, UW.

50. The importance of first-run houses and the increased monopolization of theaters in the early 1920s are discussed in William Marston Seabury, *The Public and the Motion Picture Industry* (New York, 1926); Douglas Gomery, *Shared Pleasures: A History of Movie Presentation in the United States* (Madison, 1992), 34–56; Koszarski, *An Evening's Entertainment*, 69–80.

51. *LA Citizen*, January 12, 1923; *NY Call*, May 27, 1921. For FFC distribution deals, see *Seattle Union Record*, May 24, 1920, December 1, 1921, December 16, 1922; "Report of Agent 17," June 2 and 19, 1920, Box 2, folder 7, 8, Beck Papers. Cannon was approached by a French firm that wanted the European rights to *The Contrast* and *The Jungle*. Joseph Cannon to Upton Sinclair, March 22, 1921, file J217, Brandon Coll.

52. Joseph Cannon to Upton Sinclair, April 8, 1921, file J217, Brandon Coll. For distribution networks, see *NY Call*, February 20, 1922; *LA Citizen*, February 16, 23, 1923; *AFL Proceedings 1925*, 36–38; *AFL Proceedings 1926*, 159–67; Sacramento *California Labor Chronicle*, November 27, 1925.

53. *Chicago New Majority*, January 12, 1924; William Green, "Planning Meeting for Union Label Campaign," May 6, 1925, AFL Convention 1924, reel 32.

54. *NY Call*, June 18, 1922; *Seattle Union Record*, January 8, 1926; *AFL News*, March 6, 1926.

55. R. M. McCaleb (Eccles, W. Va.) to National Board of Review of Motion Pictures, February 3, 1921, Subjects Correspondence (Charles Stelze), Box 43, NBRMP; *NY Call*, June 3, 1921. For worker-owned movie theaters in various cities, see *Seattle*

Union Record, July 22, August 11, September 17, 1920, and January 22, 24, February 4, 1921; *NY Call*, July 29, 1921; *Chicago New Majority*, December 10, 1921; *LA Citizen*, April 7 and July 21, 1922.

56. *Seattle Union Record*, December 16, 1922; *AFL Proceedings 1926*, 39, 159.

57. *World Almanac* quoted in Seabury, *Public and Motion Picture Industry*, 286; William F. Kruse, "Workers' Conquest of Films," *Workers Monthly*, 3 (September 1925), 503. *Labor's Reward*, for example, was still being shown as late as 1929. *Chicago Federation News*, February 16, 1929.

58. *NY Call*, May 2, 1922. *From Dusk to Dawn* was shown at the Barn Theater in downtown Los Angeles. *Los Angeles Record*, September 8, 1922. For revisions to *The Jungle*, see *NY Call*, January 26, 1922; Joseph Cannon to Upton Sinclair, September 20 and November 11, 1920, August 29, 1921, January 21 and September 21, 1922, file J217, Brandon Coll.

59. *Chicago New Majority*, March 1, 1924; *NY Call*, September 25, 1921; Chicago *Daily Worker*, March 18, 1924.

60. New York reviews reprinted in *Seattle Union Record*, December 14, 1922, and December 23, 1921; *Photoplay*, March 22, 1922; *Variety*, December 23, 1921; *MPW*, December 31, 1921.

61. *Seattle Union Record*, May 12, 1921.

62. Joseph Cannon to Upton Sinclair, March 22, 1921, file J217, Brandon Coll.

63. *Chicago New Majority*, March 1, 1924; *NY Call*, June 29, 1922; Long Beach, Ca., *International Oil Worker*, December 3, 1925; Ella Reeve Bloor, *We Are Many* (New York, 1940), 201–2.

64. *NY Call*, June 9, 1922. For the Frankfurt School and its successors, see Appendix II. For an analysis of class-conscious films made in a Communist society, see Denise J. Youngblood, *Movies for the Masses: Popular Cinema and Soviet Society in the 1920s* (New York, 1992).

65. The LFS held a "Labor Film Cycle" on New York's Lower East Side, and the IWA held "Worker Film Festivals" in Detroit and Chicago. *NY Call*, June 4, 14, 1922; Chicago *Daily Worker*, October 25 and December 2, 1924. For examples of screenings by working-class ethnic associations, see Chicago *Daily Worker*, October 9 and 25, November 14 and 17, December 2, 1924; July 18 and December 26, 1925; January 28, 1927; New York *Daily Worker*, October 11, 1928; Chicago *Federation News*, December 26, 1925. For the uses of film by women, see the *Chicago Federation News*, January 9, 1926, September 15, 1928; *Chicago New Majority*, January 28, 1922; "Minutes of the Seattle Central Labor Council," November 17, 1926, Box 8, Records of Seattle CLC, UW; Whitney, *Reds in America*, 98.

66. "Report of Agent H. J. Lennon," March 17, 1921, reel 926, BS 202600–197, ICF. The *Labor Film Magazine* is discussed in Robert A. Bowen to J. E. Hoover, January 7, 1921, RG 65, reel 926 (BS 212657), ICF, and Whitney, *Reds*, 148. Hoover, who passed on information about the labor film movement to Military Intelligence, kept files on John Arthur Nelson, Joseph Cannon, William Kruse, John Slayton, and Upton Sinclair. Agents were also sent to interview *Contrast* director Guy Hedlund. For a sampling of reports, see "Report of Robert S. Judge," March 1, 1918, RG 65, reel 590 (OG 186545); "Report of F. L. Turner," June 11, 1918, reel 512 (OG 125871); Robert C. Deming to W. P. Hazen, November 3, 1920, reel 926 (BS 202600–197); J. G. Tucker, "Weekly Report of Radical Activities in Greater New

York," July 10, 1920, reel 616 (BS 208639), and November 6, 1920, reel 924 (BS 202600–33); Hoover to Brigadier General A. E. Nolan, December 8, 1920, and January 10, 1921, reel 926 (202600–197–4); "Special Report of J. F. Loren," June 16, 1921, reel 941 (BS 202600–209); "Report of G. J. Starr," January 8, 1921, reel 926 (BS 212657), all ICF.

67. *NY Call*, April 25, 1921. Correspondence between the Department of Agriculture and the LFS are reprinted in *NY Call*, January 26, 1922. For examples of Seattle labor spy reports see "Report of Agent 106," November 21, 1919, folder 18; January 14, folder 20; and April 30, 1920, folder 24, all in Box 1, Beck Papers; "Report of Agent 17," March 25, folder 4; June 6, 1920, folder 7, both in Box 2, Beck Papers; "Report of Agent #172," April 20, 1920, Box 1, folder 6, Kinnear Papers, UW.

68. Morris L. Ernst and Pare Lorentz, *Censored: The Private Life of the Movie* (New York, 1930), 42; New York Motion Picture Commission, *Annual Report for the Moving Picture Commission for the Year 1922* (Albany, 1922), 10; W. D. McGuire to Samuel Gompers, March 1, 1922; W. D. McGuire to AFL, September 24, 1921, Subjects Correspondence (AFL), Box 15, NBRMP; *AFL News*, March 13, 1926.

69. Deputy Commissioner, New York State Motion Picture Commission to International Workers' Aid, October 8, 1926, file M247, Brandon Coll.; Chicago *Daily Worker*, December 31, 1924.

Chapter 7
Fantasy and Politics

1. New York *Evening Graphic*, March 12, 1927, quoted in Ben M. Hall, *The Best Remaining Seats: The Golden Age of the Movie Palace* (New York, 1975, reprinted 1988), 6. Descriptions of the Roxy and its opening-night festivities are taken from *Best Remaining Seats* and *New York Times*, March 12, 1927. Dollar equivalences are taken from figures in John J. McCusker, *How Much Is That in Real Money? A Historical Price Index for Use as a Deflator of Money Values in the Economy of the United States* (Worcester, Mass., 1992), 330–32.

2. Quoted in Hall, *Best Remaining Seats*, 10.

3. *NY Call*, April 25, 1921.

4. Movie attendance figures for this period vary greatly. The Wall Street investment house of Halsey, Stuart, and Company reported that weekly attendance in 1926 was above 100 million. Chicago sociologist Ernest W. Burgess pegged the figure at 120 million for 1925. The U.S. Census placed weekly attendance at 57 million for 1927 and 90 million for 1930. Halsey, Stuart, and Co., "The Motion Picture Industry as a Basis for Bond Financing, May 27, 1927," in Tino Balio, ed., *The American Film Industry* (Madison, 1976), 183; Ernest W. Burgess, "Studies of Institutions," in T. V. Smith and Leonard D. White, eds., *Chicago: An Experiment in Social Science Research* (Chicago, 1929, reprinted 1968), 166; *Historical Statistics*, 1: 400.

5. J. Walter Thompson [Advertising] Company newsletter, no. 139 (1 July 1926), quoted in Lizabeth Cohen, *Making a New Deal: Industrial Workers in Chicago, 1919–1939* (Cambridge and New York, 1990), 100; Nathan Malyn, "Mass Psychology and Socialism," *NY Call*, November 12, 1922.

6. Lary May's pioneering study helped open up new ways of looking at the historical significance of silent film and its relationship to the social and cultural changes that swept American society between 1900 and 1930. Yet any pioneering study is bound to be open to reinterpretation. In May's case, his emphasis on the positive aspects of the intersection of movies and consumer culture led him to underplay the class tensions that marked the era, both on and off the screen. I see the rise of the Hollywood studio system and its cross-class fantasy films as shifting class relations in a far more conservative and, for working-class activists, problematic direction. Neither films nor movie palaces were "breaking down the class divisions of the past" quite as much as May suggests. Lary May, *Screening out the Past: The Birth of Mass Culture and the Motion Picture Industry* (New York, 1980), 166.

7. Jesse Frederick Steiner, *Americans at Play: Recent Trends in Recreation and Leisure Time Activities* (New York, 1933, reprinted 1970), 191–92; Cleveland Recreation Survey, *Commercial Recreation* (Cleveland, 1920), 11. For an overview of changing attitudes toward commercial recreation, see Frances Ivins Rich, *Wage-Earning Girls in Cincinnati* (1927), reprinted in *Working Girls of Cincinnati* (New York, 1974); L. H. Weir, *Recreation Survey of Buffalo* (Buffalo, 1925); William H. Jones, *Recreation and Amusement among Negroes in Washington, D.C.* (Washington, D.C., 1927, reprinted 1970); Arthur L. Beeley, *Boys and Girls in Salt Lake City: The Results of a Survey Made for the Rotary Club and the Business and Professional Women's Club of Salt Lake City* (Salt Lake City, 1929); Eugene T. Lies, *The Leisure of a People: Report of a Recreation Survey of Indianapolis* (Indianapolis, 1929); Charles B. Raitt, *A Survey of Recreation Facilities in Rochester, New York* (Rochester, 1929). For an excellent overview of American life in the 1920s, see Lynn Dumenil, *The Modern Temper: American Culture and Society in the 1920s* (New York, 1995).

8. Lies, *Leisure of a People*, 67.

9. Figures are taken from Robert H. Zieger, *American Workers, American Unions, 1920–1985* (Baltimore, 1986), 4; Stanley Lebregott, *The American Economy: Income, Wealth and Want* (Princeton, 1976), 272–88.

10. Robert S. and Helen Merrell Lynd, *Middletown: A Study in Modern American Culture* (New York, 1929), 80–81. Work-week figures are for manufacturing workers; *Historical Statistics*, 1: 170. For changing attitudes toward work, leisure, and consumption, see Daniel T. Rodgers, *The Work Ethic in Industrial America 1850–1920* (Chicago, 1974); Benjamin Kline Hunnicutt, *Work without End: Abandoning Shorter Hours for the Right to Work* (Philadelphia, 1988); David R. Roediger and Philip S. Foner, *Our Own Time: A History of American Labor and the Working Day* (London and New York, 1989); Gary Cross, *Time and Money: The Making of Consumer Culture* (London and New York, 1993); Daniel Horowitz, *The Morality of Spending: Attitudes toward the Consumer Society in America, 1875–1940* (Baltimore, 1985); Richard Wightman Fox and T. J. Jackson Lears, eds., *The Culture of Consumption: Critical Essays in American History 1880–1980* (New York, 1983).

11. Statistics are taken from Jurgen Kocka, *White Collar Workers in America 1890–1940: A Social-Political History in International Perspective*, translated by Maura Kealey (London and Beverly Hills, 1980), 19, 159, 291 note 45; *Historical Statistics*, 1: 139, 143. Imprecise occupational categories listed in census reports make it difficult to obtain accurate figures for white-collar workers. Kocka's book is

the most rigorous attempt at rearranging census categories in a meaningful manner. Skilled workers, who dominated the nation's manufactories in the nineteenth century, composed only 39 percent of the manual workforce in 1930. *Historical Statistics,* 1: 65.

12. *Historical Statistics,* 1: 129, 138–39; James R. Green, *World of the Worker: Labor in Twentieth-Century America* (New York, 1980), 105. The percentage of working women who were professionals rose from 9 percent in 1910 to 14 percent in 1930. Dumenil, *Modern Temper,* 116. For recent works describing the entry of women into the clerical and service sectors, see Elyce J. Rotella, *From Home to Office: U.S. Women at Work, 1870–1930* (Ann Arbor, 1981); Margery Davies, *Woman's Place Is at the Typewriter: Office Work and Office Workers, 1870–1930* (Philadelphia, 1982); Susan Porter Benson, *Counter Cultures: Saleswomen, Managers, and Customers in American Department Stories, 1880–1940* (Urbana, Ill., 1988); Lisa Fine, *The Souls of the Skyscraper: Female Clerical Workers in Chicago, 1870–1930* (Philadelphia, 1990); Ileen De Vault, *Sons and Daughters of Labor: Class and Clerical Work in Turn-of-the-Century Pittsburgh* (Ithaca, 1991); Sharon Strom Hartman, *Beyond the Typewriter: Gender, Class, and the Origins of Modern Office Work* (Urbana, Ill., 1992). For overviews of working women in the early twentieth century, see Alice Kessler-Harris, *Out to Work: A History of Wage-Earning Women in the United States* (New York, 1982); Leslie Woodcock Tentler, *Wage-Earning Women: Industrial Work and Family Life in the United States, 1900–1930* (New York, 1979).

13. *NY Call,* February 8, 1914; Horowitz, *Morality of Spending,* 69; Henry A. Deering, "The Middle Class," *NY Call,* October 10, 1920. Statistics on the numbers of self-employed are taken from C. Wright Mills, *White Collar: The American Middle Class* (New York, 1951), 63. The percentage of farmers who were tenants rather than owners rose from 26 percent in 1880 to 42 percent in 1930. Likewise, the percentage of production workers employed by corporations rose from 71 percent in 1889 to 90 percent in 1929. *Historical Statistics,* 1: 465, 2: 688. For sources analyzing class development and the changing language of class, see Chapter 1 note 10.

14. New York's Socialist party suggested that the middle class of 1920 "comprised between one-quarter and one-third of the country's population." *NY Call,* May 11, 1920. The rise of the new middle class and blurring of class lines are discussed ibid., October 14, 1911, December 24, 1912, October 31, 1916, September 29, 1918, August 15, 1919, and October 10, 1920; *New York Leader,* October 30, 1923; *LA Citizen,* April 21, 1911, November 14, 1913, and December 8, 1916; *California Social Democrat,* November 18, 1911, and May 24, 1913; *Seattle Union Record,* January 10, 1927; *Historical Statistics,* 1: 166–69; Stephen Thernstrom, *Poverty and Progress: Social Mobility in a Nineteenth-Century City* (Cambridge, Mass., 1964); Stephen Thernstrom, *The Other Bostonians: Poverty and Progress in the American Metropolis, 1800–1970* (Cambridge, Mass., 1973); Thomas Kessner, *The Golden Door: Italian and Jewish Immigrant Mobility in New York City 1880–1915* (New York, 1977); Frank Stricker, "Prosperity for Whom?—Another Look at Prosperity and the Working Classes in the 1920's," *Labor History,* 24 (Winter 1983), 5–33; and sources in the previous two notes.

15. *NY Call,* May 11, 1920.

16. Roland Marchand, *Advertising American Culture: Making Way for Modernity 1920–1940* (Berkeley, 1985), 218. The rise of a consumer society and advertisers'

efforts to link consumption and democracy are discussed ibid.; Andrew R. Heinze, *Adapting to Abundance: Jewish Immigrants, Mass Consumption, and the Search for American Identity* (New York, 1990); Jackson Lears, *Fables of Abundance: A Cultural History of Advertising in America* (New York, 1994); Stuart Ewen, *Captains of Consciousness: Advertising and the Social Roots of the Consumer Culture* (New York, 1976); Martha L. Olney, *Buy Now, Pay Later: Advertising, Credit, and Consumer Durables in the 1920s* (Chapel Hill, 1991); and the sources in note 10 above. Employer efforts to use company welfare programs to foster class loyalties are examined in Sanford M. Jacoby, *Employing Bureaucracy: Managers, Unions, and the Transformation of Work in American Industry, 1900–1945* (New York, 1985); Stuart D. Brandes, *American Welfare Capitalism, 1880–1940* (Chicago, 1976); Irving Bernstein, *The Lean Years: A History of the American Worker, 1920–1933* (Baltimore, 1966); and Dumenil, *Modern Temper*, 67–71.

17. Meeker quoted in Horowitz, *Morality of Spending*, 123; *New York Times*, September 6, 1927. Total union membership in the United States dropped from 5 million in 1920 to 3.5 million in 1929. *Historical Statistics*, 1: 177. The importance of leisure and consumption to the labor movement of the 1920s is explored in Cross, *Time and Money*; Roediger and Foner, *Our Own Time*, 209–42; Hunnicutt, *Work without End*, 76–84. For the impact of consumption and leisure on the language of Labor Day celebrations, see Michael Kazin and Steven J. Ross, "America's Labor Day: The Dilemma of a Workers' Celebration," *Journal of American History*, 78 (March 1992), 1,294–1,323. For overviews of organized labor during the 1920s, see Green, *World of the Worker*; Zieger, *American Workers*; Bernstein, *Lean Years*.

18. Brookings' Institute findings quoted in Zieger, *American Workers*, 7–8; Department of Commerce figures quoted in Paul A. Carter, *Another Part of the Twenties* (New York, 1977), 162. For an accessible overview of wage and salary data for this period, see Stricker, "Affluence for Whom?"; changing standards of living are also discussed in Gordon S. Watkins, *Labor Problems* (New York, 1929); Cohen, *Making a New Deal*; Zieger, *American Workers*. For working-class analyses of cost-of-living studies, see *NY Call*, January 21, 1917, May 7, 1920, April 6, 1921, and January 22, 1926; *Chicago New Majority*, January 28, 1922; *Journal of the Electrical Workers*, 28 (December 1929), 628, 663.

19. Lynds, *Middletown*, 82 note 18. Liz Cohen observes that in 1926, approximately $6 billion worth of retail goods were sold on installment—15 percent of all sales. Cohen, *Making a New Deal*, 103.

20. Box-office receipts are taken from *Historical Statistics*, 1: 400–1. Longtime movie reporter W. Stephen Bush estimated that women and girls composed 60 percent of the audience in 1920; other surveys suggested that men and women attended in relatively equal numbers throughout the decade; for survey results, see David Nasaw, *Going Out: The Rise and Decline of Public Amusement* (New York, 1993), 233. The number of female wage earners rose by 2.2 million during the 1920s; *Historical Statistics*, 1: 129.

21. The lives and careers of Abe Balaban and Sam Katz are discussed in Carrie Balaban, *Continuous Performance: The Story of A. J. Balaban* (New York, 1942); Samuel Katz, "Theatre Management," in Joseph P. Kennedy, ed., *The Story of the Films* (Chicago and New York, 1927, reprinted 1971), 263–84, 350–51; Arthur Mayer, *Merely Colossal: The Story of the Movies from the Long Chase to the Chaise*

Lounge (New York, 1953); Will Irwin, *The House That Shadows Built* (Garden City, N.Y., 1928); Benjamin Hampton, *A History of the Movies* (New York, 1931); Douglas Gomery, *Shared Pleasures: A History of Movie Presentation in the United States* (Madison, 1992); Christine Basque, "The Paradoxes of Paradise: Elements of Conflict in Chicago's Balaban and Katz Movie Palaces," *Marquee*, 27: 2 (1995), 4–11; Richard Koszarski, *An Evening's Entertainment: The Age of the Silent Feature Picture, 1915–1928* (New York, 1990); Hall, *Best Remaining Seats*.

22. Gomery, *Shared Pleasures*, 43.

23. Ibid., 44.

24. Balaban, *Continuous Performance*, 33.

25. Ibid., 159.

26. Gomery, *Shared Pleasures*, 43; also see *Chicago Federation News*, October 31, 1925.

27. *Chicago Herald-Examiner*, October 1917, quoted in Balaban, *Continuous Performance*, 51; second quote, ibid., 173; "The Reason Balaban and Katz Theatres Do Not Reserve Seats," *Balaban and Katz Magazine*, 1 (July 25, 1925), 10, quoted in Nasaw, *Going Out*, 232.

28. Mayer, *Merely Colossal*, 71. The rise and success of Publix are described in Douglas Gomery, "The Movies Become Big Business: Publix Theatres and the Chain Store Strategy," *Cinema Journal*, 18 (Spring 1979), 26–40; Howard Thompson Lewis, compiler, *Harvard Business Reports. Volume 8: Cases on the Motion Picture Industry* (New York, 1930), 514–24.

29. Goldwyn quoted in Hall, *Best Remaining Seats*, 15. Theater figures are taken from William Marston Seabury, *The Public and the Motion Picture Industry* (New York, 1926), 277; Koszarski, *Evening's Entertainment*, 9. For sources describing the campaign of theater acquisition see Chapter 5 notes 8, 21.

30. Lewis, *Cases on Motion Picture Industry*, 476; William A Johnson, "The Structure of the Motion Picture Industry," *Annals of the American Academy of Political and Social Science*, 128 (November 1926), 27. Theater construction costs are described in *New York Times*, November 14, 1926; Robert Kirk Headley, Jr., *Exit: A History of Movies in Baltimore* (University Park, Md., 1974); Hall, *Best Remaining Seats*; Koszarski, *Evening's Entertainment*.

31. Seabury, *Public and Motion Picture Industry*, 34.

32. Ernest W Burgess, "Urban Areas," in Smith and White, *Chicago*, 127. The importance of choosing the right location is discussed in many of the case studies contained in Lewis, *Cases on the Motion Picture Industry*.

33. Hall, *Best Remaining Seats*, 94. The rise and daily workings of palaces are described in Charlotte Herzog, "The Movie Palace and the Theatrical Sources of Its Architectural Style," *Cinema Journal*, 20 (Spring 1981), 15–37; Harold B. Franklin, *Motion Picture Theater Management* (New York, 1927); David Kneeler, *American Picture Palaces: The Architecture of Fantasy* (New York, 1981); Douglas Gomery, "The Picture Palace: Economic Sense or Hollywood Nonsense," in Paul Kerr, ed., *The Hollywood Film Industry* (London and New York, 1986), 204–19; Lary May, *Screening out the Past: The Birth of Mass Culture and the Motion Picture Industry* (New York, 1980); Lary May, "Designing Multi-Cultural America: Modern Movie Theaters and the Politics of Public Space 1920–1945," in James Combs, ed., *Movies and Politics: The Dynamic Relationship* (New York and London, 1993), 183–235; Dennis Sharp,

The Picture Palace (New York, 1969); Ben Rosenberg, "An Usher's Life—Part I," *Marquee*, 27: 2 (1995), 18–26; Katz, "Theatre Management"; Gomery, *Shared Pleasures*; Hall, *Best Remaining Seats*; Headley, *Exit*; Nasaw, *Going Out*. For descriptions of movie theaters in smaller urban areas, see Gregory A. Waller, *Main Street Amusements: Movies and Commercial Entertainment in a Southern City, 1896–1930* (Washington, D.C., 1995), 193–248; Kathryn Helgesen Fuller, " 'You Can Have the Strand in Your Own Town': The Marginalization of Small Town Film Exhibition in the Silent Film Era," *Film History*, 6 (Summer 1994), 166–77.

34. Harold Rambusch, quoted in Hall, *Best Remaining Seats*, 93.

35. Eric Clarke, quoted in Koszarski, *Evening's Entertainment*, 54; *Los Angeles Times*, July 31, 1921. Survey results cited in Koszarski, *Evening's Entertainment*, 30–31. The leading attractions according to Fresno patrons were: music (28 percent), courtesy (19 percent), seat comfort (18 percent), beauty (15 percent), pictures (10 percent), lighting (5 percent), and prestige (5 percent). The priorities of the Hepner results were: music (43 percent), comfort (24 percent), pictures (17 percent), prestige (6 percent), beauty (4 percent), lighting (3 percent), courtesy (3 percent).

36. Cole, *Hollywood Red*, 86; Hall, *Best Remaining Seats*, 210; *Seattle Union Record*, January 22, 1927; *Chicago Federation News*, July 23, 1927.

37. *Chicago Federation News*, October 10, 1925. The importance of orchestra leaders is discussed in Balaban, *Continuous Performance*; Hall, *Best Remaining Seats*; Hugo Riesenfeld, "Music and Motion Pictures," *Annals of the American Academy of Political and Social Science*, 128 (November 1926), 58–62. Employment statistics for musicians are taken from James P. Kraft, "Stage to Studio: American Musicians and Sound Technology," Ph. D. dissertation, University of Southern California, 1990, 39–40, 60. For an overview of movie theater music and musicians during this era, see James P. Kraft, *Stage to Studio: Musicians and the Sound Revolution, 1890–1950* (Baltimore, 1996).

38. The practice of holding films off the market after each successive run is described in Lewis, *Cases on the Motion Picture Industry*, 561–71. For studio ownership of theaters, see ibid.; Gomery, *Shared Pleasures*.

39. Fox quoted in May, *Screening out the Past*, 152–53; *NY Call*, May 18, 1918.

40. For photographs illustrating the racial composition of palace personnel, see Hall, *Best Remaining Seats*, 47, 162–69. The trials and tribulations of ushers and palace workers are described in James I. Deutsch, "The Rise and Fall of the House of Ushers: Teenage Ticket Takers in the Twenties Theaters," *Journal of Popular Culture*, 13 (Spring 1980), 602–8; Rosenberg, "An Usher's Life," 18–26; Basque, "Paradoxes of Paradise," 7; Cole, *Hollywood Red*, 86–87.

41. The moviegoing habits of various peoples of color are discussed in Commonwealth of Pennsylvania, Department of Welfare, *Negro Survey of Pennsylvania* (Harrisburg, 1927); William Y. Bell, Jr., "Commercial Recreation Facilities among Negroes in the Hill District of Pittsburgh," M.A. thesis, University of Pittsburgh, 1938; Mary Carbine, " 'The Finest Outside the Loop': Motion Picture Exhibition in Chicago's Black Metropolis, 1905–1928," *Camera Obscura*, 23 (May 1990), 8–41; Jeff Kisseloff, *You Must Remember This: An Oral History of Manhattan from the 1890s to World War II* (New York, 1989), 276; Jones, *Recreation among the Negroes in Washington*; Junko Ogihara, "The Exhibition of Films for Japanese Americans

in Los Angeles during the Silent Film Era," *Film History*, 4: 2 (1990), 81–87; Commission of Immigration and Housing of California, *A Community Survey Made in Los Angeles City* (San Francisco, c. 1917–1918); Cohen, *Making a New Deal*, 123–24; Waller, *Main Street Amusements*, 240–47; Gomery, *Shared Pleasures*, 155–63.

42. Mayer, *Merely Colossal*, 70–71; Lloyd Lewis, "The Deluxe Picture Palace," *New Republic* 58 (March 27, 1929), 175.

43. Author interviews with Ted Ellsworth, April 26, 1989, Los Angeles; Bill Edwards, May 31, 1989, Sherman Oaks, Ca.; and Harry Eston, June 27, 1989, Los Angeles. Burgess, "Studies of Institutions," 169. Making special trips to downtown palaces was popular with working-class movie fans from Worcester, Massachusetts, to the Los Angeles blue-collar community of South Gate. Roy Rosenzweig, *Eight Hours for What We Will: Workers and Leisure in an Industrial City, 1870–1930* (Cambridge and New York, 1983), 220–23; Becky Marianna Nicolaides, "In Search of the Good Life: Community and Politics in Working-Class Los Angeles, 1920–1955," Ph.D. dissertation, Columbia University, 1993, 208, 212–23.

44. *NY Call*, August 8, 1918. For similar complaints by working-class and middle-class writers alike, see *Educational Film Magazine*, 3 (May 1920), 12; *LA Citizen*, December 2, 1921; *Seattle Union Record*, June 26, 1924; Beeley, *Boys and Girls in Salt Lake City*, 25; Koszarski, *Evening's Entertainment*, 12, 43–45. Lizabeth Cohen's tendency to romanticize neighborhood theaters and downplay the appeal of palaces among working-class moviegoers is the one flaw in her otherwise brilliant analysis of working-class encounters with mass culture in Chicago. Working-class movie fans like Edwards and Ellsworth (quoted in the previous paragraph) may have attended local theaters during the week, but they definitely preferred the palaces on the weekends—the time when most working adults went to the movies. Moreover, contrary to Cohen's suggestion, working-class patrons, as Gardy's quote indicates, probably welcomed the attention of ushers. Cohen, *Making a New Deal*, especially 120–31.

45. Rosenzweig, *Eight Hours*, 217–18; Bell, "Commercial Recreation Facilities among Negroes," 47. Similar arguments about the continuing vitality of neighborhood theaters can be found in Robert Slayton, *Back of the Yards: The Making of a Local Democracy* (Chicago, 1986); Cohen, *Making a New Deal*.

46. For free summer visits, see *NY Call*, July 2, 1920; for Loew, see ibid., October 4, 1919; for socialist and union meetings, ibid., January 6 and 18, 1919, May 31 and July 1, 1920; *Seattle Union Record*, August 21, 1925; New York *Daily Worker*, January 9, 1930.

47. Arkansas theater manager quoted in Peter Stead, *Film and the Working Class: The Feature Film in British and American Society* (London and New York, 1989), 38–39; Halsey, Stuart and Co., "Motion Picture Industry," 184; Lies, *Leisure of a People*, 92–95; Lorentz quoted in Stead, *Film and the Working Class*, 38; also see Beeley, *Boys and Girls in Salt Lake City*, 145–50.

48. *Seattle Union Record*, April 6, 1920, and November 12, 1921; Rosenzweig, *Eight Hours*, 213. For Los Angeles and South Gate, see Nicolaides, "In Search of the Good Life," 208. The popularity of movies among the working class and middle class is also discussed in Chicago *Daily Worker*, October 29, 1924; Rosenzweig, *Eight Hours*, 208–21; Cohen, *Making a New Deal*, 120–21; Nasaw, *Going Out*, 232–34; May, *Screening out the Past*, 164.

49. Seabury, *Public and Motion Picture Industry*, 53; Sidney R. Kent, "Distributing the Product," in Kennedy, *Story of Films*, 218. Palace profits are also detailed in Hampton, *History of the Movies*, 333–34.

50. Even fine scholars such as Lawrence Levine tend to overstate audience impact on setting the agenda of American filmmaking. As Robin Kelley notes, offering opinions about films "is not the same as having a direct voice in cultural production from inception to completion." Audiences were "largely relegated to the receiving end, and, in that capacity, they made choices under circumstances not of their own choosing." Robin D. G. Kelley, "Notes on Deconstructing the Folk,'" *American Historical Review*, 97 (December 1992), 1,404, 1,408; also see Levine, "The Folklore of Industrial Society: Popular Culture and Its Audiences," and responses to his article ibid., 1,369–1,430. For debates concerning the power of audiences, see Preface notes 7, 8.

51. John Drinkwater, *The Life and Adventures of Carl Laemmle* (New York, 1931), 235.

52. Will Hays, "Supervision from Within," in Kennedy, *Story of Films*, 38. The idea that producers were actively shaping, not just reflecting, audience tastes is also raised in Paul Rotha, *The Film till Now: A Survey of the Cinema* (New York, 1930), 70; George Mitchell, "The Consolidation of the American Film Industry 1915–1920," in Ron Burnett, ed., *Explorations in Film Theory: Selected Essays from "Cine-Tracts"* (Bloomington, 1991), 266–71.

53. Hampton, *History of the Movies*, 221.

54. Kevin Brownlow, *Behind the Mask of Innocence* (New York, 1990), 290; William C. de Mille, *Hollywood Saga* (New York, 1939), 239–40.

55. Chicago *Daily Worker*, March 18, 1925. For *Whistle*, see *NY Call*, August 5, 1921; for newsreel censorship see "In re: Censorship of News Weeklies by State Board of Censorship of Pennsylvania," c. March 1921, and W. D. McGuire to Samuel Gompers, July 12, 1922, both in Subject Correspondence (AFL), Box 15, NBRMP; General Solicitation Letter by W. D. McGuire, March 16, 1921, and Charles Stelze to Dr. Herbert Gates, March 17, 1921, in Subjects Correspondence (Stelze), Box 43, NBRMP; Chicago *Daily Worker*, April 1, 1924. Of the 579 features reviewed by censors in 1928, only 42 passed untouched. Morris L. Ernst and Pare Lorentz, *Censored: The Private Life of the Movie* (New York, 1930), 84. The spread of censorship boards in the postwar era is discussed ibid.; Ford H. MacGregor, "Official Censorship Legislation," *Annals of the American Academy of Political and Social Science*, 128 (November 1926), 163–74; Brownlow, *Behind the Mask*, 7–12.

56. Drinkwater, *Life of Laemmle*, 225; Jack L. Warner with Dean Jennings, *My First Hundred Years in Hollywood* (New York, 1965), 125. Production costs are taken from Hampton, *History of the Movies*, 205, 308–21; *New York Times*, December 13, 1925. The cost of a typical Paramount release rose from $10-$30,000 in 1914 to $150-$500,000 in 1924. Hampton, *History of the Movies*, 313; for "orgy of extravagance," see ibid., 338.

57. Hays quoted in Anthony Slide, *The American Film Industry* (Westport, Conn., 1986), 219; Brownlow, *Behind the Mask*, 17; Jesse L. Lasky with Don Weldon, *I Blow My Own Horn* (London, 1957), 144. The impact of censorship, the Arbuckle and Taylor scandals, and the influence of Will Hays are discussed ibid., 153–58; Hays, "Supervision from Within," 46–50; Seabury, *Public and Motion Picture Industry*,

143–59; C. B. DeMille, *Autobiography*, 237–42; Robert Sklar, *Movie-Made America: A Cultural History of American Movies* (New York, 1994), 78–85, 131–34; Garth Jowett, *Film the Democratic Art* (Boston, 1976), 154–84; Nancy J. Rosenbloom, "Between Reform and Regulation: The Struggle over Film Censorship in Progressive Era America," *Film History* 1: 4 (1987), 319–22; Hampton, *History of the Movies*, 281–303. For details of Wall Street involvement with studios, see *New York Times*, July 24, 1921; *Film Year Book 1925*.

58. These percentages are based on the number of films (excluding worker-made films) whose politics I could determine (45 of the 48 films released between 1923 and 1929, and 33 of the 35 films released between 1924 and 1929). Only 16 percent of the films produced between 1923 and 1929 maintained a liberal perspective, 11 percent an anti-authoritarian point of view, and a mere 2 percent espoused a populist vision. No radical films were made by studios. Simultaneously, Socialist party membership dropped from 100,000 in 1917 to 8,000 dues-paying loyalists in 1928. The Industrial Workers of the World and the various American Communist parties, both of which claimed over 100,000 members between 1917 and 1919, experienced equally devastating losses in the 1920s. The number of strikes and lockouts also dropped from 3,411 in 1920 to 921 in 1929. Strike and lockout figures are taken from *Historical Statistics*, 1: 177, 179; membership figures for radical organizations can be found in Mari Jo Buhle, Paul Buhle, and Dan Georgakas, eds., *Encyclopedia of the American Left* (New York, 1990), 720; and sources mentioned in Chapter 5 note 68. In compiling my list of labor-capital films, I followed the same procedure as described in Chapter 3 notes 3, 4. In placing films into political categories, I relied heavily on the comments of reviews contained in labor and radical periodicals.

59. Koszarski, *Evening's Entertainment*, 184. For discussions of society melodramas and the changing class images of 1920s films, see ibid., 179–80, 184, 295; David Robinson, *Hollywood in the Twenties* (London and New York, 1968); Lewis Jacobs, *The Rise of the American Film: A Critical History* (New York, 1968); Sumiko Higashi, *Virgins, Vamps, and Flappers: The American Silent Movie Heroine* (Montreal, 1978); Sumiko Higashi, *Cecil B. DeMille and American Culture: The Silent Era* (Berkeley, 1994); Stead, *Film and the Working Class*, 22–45; Rosenzweig, *Eight Hours*, 216–17; May, *Screening out the Past*; Brownlow, *Behind the Mask*.

60. Rosenzweig, *Eight Hours*, 217. According to the census, the total number of professionals, white-collar workers, and service workers rose from 13.8 million in 1920 to 17 million in 1930; the number of manual workers rose from 17 million to 19.3 million. *Historical Statistics*, 1: 139.

61. Between 1920 and 1930, the number of working women and men rose, respectively, by 26 and 15 percent. Statistics computed from figures in *Historical Statistics*, 1: 129. For a brief discussion of films about women office workers, see Fine, *Souls of Skyscrapers*, 140–45.

62. I computed the figures for society films by looking at the genre classification for all 6,606 films listed in volume one of the *American Film Institute Catalog . . . 1921–1930*. The figure of 308 includes films classified as "society dramas," "society melodramas," "society comedies," and "society comedy-dramas." It does not include "society crook" films or sound films. If we add in the dramas, melodramas, and comedies dealing with cross-class love not included under "society" films the total number of cross-class fantasies was undoubtedly over 400 films, or roughly 7 per-

cent of all features made between 1921 and 1929. Since the AFI greatly underesti-
mates the number of labor-capital films, I use my own numbers. Despite the many
studies of society films, there is still need for a systematic analysis of class relations
in films of the postwar era. Kenneth W. Munden, ed., *The American Film Institute
Catalog of Motion Pictures Produced in the United States. Feature Films 1921–1930*, 2
vols. (New York and London, 1971). For another set of figures for the major genres
of the era, see May, *Screening out the Past*, 257.

63. Welford Beaton, *Film Spectator*, May 26, 1928, quoted in Stead, *Film and the
Working Class*, 38.

64. Quotes taken from film's intertitle.

65. Jacobs, *Rise of American Film*, 407.

66. My arguments in this section differ from those of Lary May's in two key
respects: first, I suggest that he overemphasizes the ability of movies and movie
palaces to break down class divisions in any lasting fashion; and second, the fact that
audiences liked films about sex, jazz, consumerism, and the fast life does not mean
that they no longer wanted to see serious films about class conflict. May implies that
the disappearance of the latter was due primarily to changing audience tastes. Yet he
overlooks the internal economic pressures that affected studio decisions about what
films to make. Making politically charged films about class conflict, as I argue, simply proved too risky for the bottom line of studio executives. May, *Screening out the
Past*, 147–236.

67. Arthur Knight, *The Liveliest Art* (New York, 1957), 118. For analyses of
DeMille's life, movies, and times, see Higashi, *DeMille and American Culture*; Cecil B.
DeMille, "Building a Photoplay," in Kennedy, *Story of Films*, 123–50, 352–53;
Charles Higham, *Cecil B. DeMille* (New York, 1973); Edward Wagenknecht, *The
Movies in the Age of Innocence* (Norman, Okla., 1962); DeMille, *Autobiography*; de
Mille, *Hollywood Saga*; May, *Screening out the Past*, 205–6.

68. Brownlow, *Behind the Mask*, 459; DeMille, *Autobiography*, 169.

69. All quotations are from film's intertitles.

70. *Daytime Wives* (1923) and *Poor Men's Wives* (1923) offer two examples of
workers as industrious salt-of-the earth types. For films dealing with the problems
of the idle rich, see *The Idle Rich* (1923), *The Making of a Man* (1922), *Fools and
Riches* (1923), and *The Triumph* (Famous Players-Lasky, 1924).

71. *Variety*, January 5, 1923.

72. *NY Call*, June 27, 1921. The portrayal of women during this era is discussed
in Mary Ryan, "The Projection of a New Womanhood: The Movie Moderns in the
1920s," in Jean E. Friedman and William G. Shade, eds., *Our American Sisters* (Boston, 1976), 366–83; Marjorie Rosen, *Popcorn Venus: Women, Movies and the American Dream* (New York, 1974), 75–135; Higashi, *Virgins, Vamps, and Flappers*.

73. *Seattle Union Record*, July 12, 1924. *Smouldering Fires* (Universal 1925) offers
an especially interesting look at the plight of women who preferred running a
"man's" business to starting a family.

74. *Chicago New Majority*, May 12, 1923; for another positive review of this film,
see *NY Call*, April 2, 1923. After reading nearly a dozen different labor newspapers,
it is clear to me that Lloyd and Chaplin were undoubtedly the two most popular
actors in the labor and radical press. Reviews of their films were usually accompanied with remarks about how much the audience loved their characters. For a biting

satire of the crass materialism of the nouveau riche, see *Beggar on Horseback* (Famous Players-Lasky 1925).

75. Sklar, *Movie-Made America*, 117–19; also see review of *The Balloonatic* in *Chicago New Majority*, April 2, 1923.

76. From review of *Poor Men's Wives*, see *Chicago New Majority*, April 2, 1923.

77. *Chicago New Majority*, September 9, April 8, December 2, 1922, and May 12, 1923. For examples of other critical reviews of cross-class fantasy films, see review of *Poor Men's Wives* in *NY Call*, January 29, 1923 and *Chicago New Majority*, April 2, 1923; *Brass* in *Chicago New Majority*, June 2, 1923; for a positive review of *Humoresque*, see *NY Call*, July 1, 1920.

78. *NY Call*, June 25, 1923; results of *Saturday Evening Post* survey are reprinted in Lewis, *Cases on the Motion Picture Industry*, 134–36. For a survey of rural tastes, see Harold Ellis Jones and Herbert S. Conrad, "Rural Preferences in Motion Pictures," *Journal of Social Psychology*, 1 (August 1930), 421; also see Benjamin DeCasseres, "Movies That People Want," *New York Times*, September 3, 1922. In all fairness, it should be noted that the Lynds found that "sensational society films" were very popular among the residents of Muncie. Lynd and Lynd, *Middletown*, 263–69. For other surveys of adult audience tastes, see Rev. J. J. Phelan, *Motion Pictures in a Typical City* (Toledo, Ohio, 1919); Garth J. Jowett, "Giving Them What They Want: Movie Audience Research before 1950," in Bruce A. Austin, ed., *Current Research in Film: Audiences, Economics, and Law* (Norwood, N.J., 1985), 19–35; Koszarski, *Evening's Entertainment*, 29–34.

79. *NY Call*, January 26, 1923.

80. *Seattle Union Record*, August 5, 19, 1919; January 22, 1921; and July 9, 1920. Two-thirds of SUTC stock was reserved for union members. Initial stock sales are reported ibid., August 13, 1919. For information about Ault, Rust, and Seattle labor capitalism, see Dana Frank, *Purchasing Power: Consumer Organizing, Gender, and the Seattle Labor Movement, 1919–1929* (Cambridge and New York, 1994), 76, 154, 155; Jonathan Dembo, *Unions and Politics in Washington State 1995–1935* (New York, 1983). The best source of information concerning SUTC and the films shown in its theaters is the *Seattle Union Record*.

81. *Seattle Union Record*, May 1, 1920. For dividends, see ibid., January 22, 1921. The Class A also hosted the Seattle premier of the FFC's *The New Disciple* and the New York Labor Film Service's newsreel series. For descriptions of various political events within the theater, see ibid., October 18–20; November 2, 17, 19, 22, 1920, and May 5, 1921. Pro-labor films screened in the first several months included *Nurse Marjorie* (Realart 1920), *Suds* (1920), *The Birth of Democracy* (1920), and *The Woman God Sent* (1920). Older labor-capital films included *The Jungle* (1914), *The Absentee* (1915), *The Profiteer* (1919), and D. W. Griffith's *The Mother and the Law* (Griffith 1919).

82. The SUTC bought the Colonial, Star, Joy, and Florence. Apparently the SUTC had invested in the FFC, and the latter's failure to pay dividends hurt the exhibition firm. Information concerning the expansion and collapse of the SUTC can be found ibid., November 12, and 1921, July 1, 1922. Also see John Danz to Seattle Union Theater Company, December 28, 1921, Part 2, Box 4, folder 3; E. B. Ault to Roger Baldwin, August 29, 1922, Part 1, Box 4, folder 17; A. W. Blumenthal to E. B. Ault, September 17, 1922, Part 1, Box 2, folder 7; E. B. Ault to A. W. Blumenthal, October

17, 1922, and E. B. Ault to A. W. Blumenthal, March 21, 1923, Part 1, Box 4, folder 18, all in the E. B. Ault Papers, UW. Jonathan Dembo, "John Danz and the Seattle Amusement Trades Strike, 1921–1935," *Pacific Northwest Quarterly*, 71 (October 1980), 172–82; and see "Agent 106," August 24, 1919, and September 1 and 10, 1919, Box 1, folder 13, Beck Papers.

83. *Chicago Federation News*, July 25, 1925. For examples of opening-night coverage, see ibid., February 27 and March 6, 1926; *NY Call*, October 25, 1919; *Seattle Union Record*, December 31, 1927; *Milwaukee Leader*, April 28, 1928.

84. Cross-class fantasies and labor-capital films, when combined, equaled about 10 percent of the total films produced during the decade. Yet, to reiterate a critical point made in Chapter 3, the total number of these films or their relative percentage to all films is less important than what audiences saw when they watched films about class relations. And what audiences saw in the 1920s was far more conservative than what they saw in the 1905–1917 era.

Chapter 8
Lights Out

1. Murphy quoted in "Beginnings—The Quest for Independent Movie Product," *Journal of Electrical Workers*, 27 (February 1928), 59.

2. *NY Call*, May 28, 1922; *Seattle Union Record*, September 21, 1922. For Cannon's plans to produce Sinclair's screenplays, see Joseph D. Cannon to Upton Sinclair, June 18, 1922, file J217, Brandon Coll. For negotiations with Hauptmann and the Interchurch World Movement, see *NY Call*, June 28, 1920; Cannon to Sinclair, August 23, 1920, file J217, Brandon Coll.

3. Production costs are taken from figures cited in a Congressional report, *New York Times*, December 13, 1925. Dollar equivalences are taken from tables in John J. McCusker, *How Much Is That in Real Money? A Historical Price Index for Use as a Deflator of Money Values in the Economy of the United States* (Worcester, Mass., 1992), 330–32.

4. Joseph Cannon to Upton Sinclair, January 15, 1923, file J217, Brandon Coll. For further information on distribution deals, see Cannon to Sinclair, March 22, 1921, and January 21, 1922, ibid.; *NY Call*, February 18, 1922; *Seattle Union Record*, May 28, 1920. For a description of sales operations at Famous Players-Lasky, see *New York Times*, September 19, 1921; Sidney R. Kent, "Distributing the Product," in Joseph P. Kennedy, ed., *The Story of the Films* (Chicago and New York, 1927, reprinted 1971), 203–32.

5. Joseph Cannon to Upton Sinclair, May 10, 1922, file J217, Brandon Coll. For Cannon's financial problems and problems with *The Jungle* print, see Cannon to Sinclair, May 10 and September 21, 1922; Sinclair to Cannon, August 7, 1922, file J217, Brandon Coll.

6. Joseph Cannon to Upton Sinclair, August 4, 1921, file J217, Brandon Coll.

7. W. D. McGuire to AFL, September 24, 1921; McGuire to Samuel Gompers, March 1, 1922, both in Subjects Correspondence (AFL), Box 15, NBRMP. *Variety*, February 24, 1922, and September 20, 1923. Also see [Kansas] State Moving Picture Censorship Commission. *Complete List of Motion Pictures Presented to the Kansas*

State Board of Review for Action. July 1 to September 30, 1921. Report no. 17 (Topeka, 1922), 2.

8. Joseph Cannon to Upton Sinclair, January 21, 1922, file J217, Brandon Coll.; Dr. Attilio H. Giannini, "Financial Aspects," in Kennedy, *Story of Films*, 90.

9. Joseph Cannon to Upton Sinclair, August 15, 1921, file J217, Brandon Coll.

10. Cannon circular letter, "To Labor Unions and Members," July 7, 1920, included in materials sent by Robert Deming to W. P. Hazen, November 3, 1920, RG 65, reel 926 (BS 202600–197), ICF.

11. Joseph Cannon to Upton Sinclair, September 21, 1922, file J217, Brandon Coll.; William F. Kruse, "Workers' Conquest of the Films," *Workers Monthly*, 4 (September 1925), 503. For Sinclair's final dealings with the LFS, see Upton Sinclair to Mr. Dakers, September 10, 1924, file J217, Brandon Coll.

12. When asked to arrange a screening in April 1924, Seattle unionists refused on the grounds that they had already sponsored two showings. "Minutes of the Seattle Central Labor Council," April 9, 1924, Box 8, Records of the Seattle CLC, UW. For exhibition runs in 1924, see *Chicago New Majority*, January 12 and March 1, 1924; Sacramento, *California Labor Chronicle*, October 2, 1925.

13. E. B. Ault to A. W. Blumenthal, October 17, 1922, Pt. 1, Box 4, folder 18, E. B. Ault Papers, UW. The failure of these and other labor-owned enterprises in Seattle are discussed in Dana Frank, *Purchasing Power: Consumer Organizing, Gender, and the Seattle Labor Movement, 1919–1929* (Cambridge and New York, 1994). Dollar equivalences are from McClusker, *How Much Is That in Real Money?*, 330, 332.

14. *Chicago New Majority*, June 20, 1925; also see *Seattle Union Record*, May 19, 1925.

15. *Seattle Union Record*, September 3, 1925. In March 1922, Nelson opened a new distribution company, the Federation Services, with offices in New York. It is unclear whether this was part of the FFC or a separate company that Nelson used to skim profits away from the labor-film company. *Chicago New Majority*, March 25 and August 19, 1922. For Nelson's prior arrest, see Anthony Slide, *The American Film Industry: A Historical Dictionary* (New York and Westport, Conn., 1986), 316; "Report of E. Kosterlitzy, April 9, 15, 1918," Los Angeles, RG 65, reel 512 (OG 125,871), ICF.

16. Kruse, "Workers' Conquest of Films," 526; Chicago *Daily Worker*, May 20, 1925. IWA Relief funds went to Russian famine victims during the early 1920s and to American strikers in the latter part of the decade.

17. David A. Cook, *A History of Narrative Film* (New York, 1990), 143. For the rise of documentary filmmaking in the United States, Europe, and the Soviet Union, see Erik Barnouw, *Documentary: A History of the Non-Fiction Film* (New York, 1974); Jay Leyda, *Kino: A History of the Russian and Soviet Film* (Princeton, 1983); Paul Rotha in collaboration with Sinclair Road and Richard Griffith, *Documentary Film* (London, 1936). The importance of newsreels and nonfiction films to left-wing activists is discussed in Jonathan Buchsbaum, *Cinema Engagé: Film in the Popular Front* (Urbana, 1988).

18. Interview with William Kruse, conducted by Russell Merritt and Vance Kepley, January 18, 1975, Genoa City, Wisc., 33, file 1189, Brandon Coll.; Chicago

Daily Worker, February 7, 1925. Most sources suggest that the term "documentaire" was first used in the January 1924 issue of the French publication *Cineopse*, and first applied to an individual by John Grierson in his 1926 review of Flaherty's *Moana*. Kruse based his claim to be the first documentarian on a comment made in 1923 by the National Board of Review of Motion Pictures in which they hailed *Russia through the Shadows* as "a living document of the screen." Kruse interview with Merritt and Kepley, 33, file 1189, Brandon Coll. For a complete listing of Kruse's films, see Chicago *Daily Worker*, October 6, November 17, and December 5, 1924; William F. Kruse, "The Proletarian Film in America," *International Press Correspondence*, 6 (February 11, 1926), 184.

19. Chicago *Daily Worker*, October 10, 1925. For Kruse's efforts to distribute Russian films, see William Kruse to Vance Kepley, Jr., April 24, 1975, file 1189, Brandon Papers; Kruse, "Proletarian Film." For an overview of the IWA's international filmmaking activities, see Vance Kepley, Jr., "The Workers' International Relief and the Cinema of the Left 1921–1935," *Cinema Journal*, 23 (Fall 1983), 7–23; Russell Campbell, *Cinema Strikes Back: Radical Filmmaking in the United States 1930–1942* (Ann Arbor: UMI Research Press, 1982); Jonathan Buchsbaum, "Left Political Filmmaking in the West: The Interwar Years," in Robert Sklar and Charles Musser, eds., *Resisting Images: Essays on Cinema and History* (Philadelphia, 1990), 126–48.

20. Kruse, "Proletarian Film," 184; Chicago *Daily Worker*, December 23, 1924. For examples of IWA film packages and the theaters sponsoring them, see ibid., December 2, 12, 23, 26, 1924; January 5, February 2, 14, March 19, May 11, and June 6, 1925.

21. Advertisement in *Workers Monthly*, 4 (November 1924), 48; Chicago *Daily Worker*, January 21, 1925. For examples of IWA sponsors and venues, see ibid., February 27, March 6, May 11 and 30, 1925; New York *The Worker*, November 24, December 22 and 29, 1923, March 2, 1924; New York *Daily Worker*, March 22 and May 20, 1927.

22. Kruse, "Workers' Conquest of Films," 503. For attendance figures and fund-raising activities, see ibid.; "Making Thousands of New Friends," *Soviet Russia Pictorial* (November 1923), 248; Chicago *Daily Worker*, October 24 and 30, 1924.

23. Kruse, "Workers' Conquest of Film," 526. Kruse is vague about the exact dates of his Russian trip. He left for the Soviet Union sometime between July 1925 and May 1926, when he filed an article from Moscow; see *International Press Correspondence*, 6 (May 13, 1926), 666. Kruse was expelled for supporting Jay Lovestone in his fight against Stalin over the party's future direction. Details of Kruse's trip and subsequent expulsion can be found in interview with Kruse by Merritt and Kepley, January 18, 1975; U.S. House of Representatives, *Investigation of Communist Propaganda. Hearings before a Special Committee to Investigate Communist Activities in the United States* (Washington, D.C., 1930–1931), P. 4, vol. 2, p. 63; Bernard K. Johnpoll and Harvey Klehr, eds., *Biographical Dictionary of the American Left* (New York and Westport, Conn., 1986), 234, 253–54; Daniel Bell, *Marxian Socialism in the United States* (Princeton, 1967), 132–33.

24. King Vidor, *A Tree is a Tree: An Autobiography* (Hollywood, 1981), 153. Wagenknecht's life and career as a Communist organizer are described in Johnpoll and Klehr, *Biographical Dictionary*, 399–400; Solon De Leon, ed., *The American Labor Who's Who* (New York, 1925), 237.

25. Charles Stelze to Dr. Herbert W. Gates, March 17, 1921 (Stelze), Box 43, NBRMP; Chicago *Daily Worker*, April 14, 1924. For more examples of class-based censorship, see "In re: Censorship of News Weeklies by State Board of Censorship of Pennsylvania," c. March 1921; and W. D. McGuire to Samuel Gompers, July 12, 1922, Subject Correspondence (AFL), both in Box 15, NBRMP. The popularity of newsreels is explored in Raymond Fielding, *American Newsreel 1911–1967* (Norman, Okla., 1972); Richard Koszarski, *An Evening's Entertainment: The Age of the Silent Feature Picture* (New York, 1990), 167–69; *New York Times*, July 31, 1927. For newsreels made by workers here and abroad, see Bert Hogenkamp, "Worker's Newsreels in the 1920s and 1930s," *Our History*, pamphlet 68 (London, 1977).

26. For an excellent discussion of the historical links between social realism and documentary film, see Campbell, *Cinema Strikes Back*, 1–28. *The Passaic Textile Strike* is discussed in Chapter 6 above.

27. New York *Daily Worker*, August 13, 1928.

28. Quotations and descriptions of the film are taken from New York *Daily Worker*, August 13 and July 21, 27, 1928; and February 26, 1929. For the strike itself, see Irving Bernstein, *The Lean Years: A History of the American Worker 1920–1933* (Boston, 1960); Vera Weisbrod, *A Radical Life* (Bloomington, 1977), 153–72. I found no evidence to indicate that IWA filmmakers self-consciously adopted the styles of the Russians. Eisenstein's films, for example, were not widely distributed in this country until late in 1926. For Soviet filmmaking during this period, see Denise Youngblood, *Soviet Cinema in the Silent Era 1918–1935* (Austin, 1991); Leyda, *Kino*.

29. *Chicago Federation News*, September 2, 1929. For more information about the film, see New York *Daily Worker*, June 25, July 11, 20, August 19, and November 5, 1929; David Platt, "A Postscript on Sam Brody," in Platt, ed., *Celluloid Power: Social Film Criticism from The Birth of a Nation to Judgment at Nuremberg* (Metuchen, N.J., 1992), 160–62; Campbell, *Cinema Strikes Back*, 18. For accounts of the strike, see William J. Dunne, *Gastonia: Citadel of the Class Struggle in the New South* (New York, 1929); Liston Pope, *Millhands and Preachers: A Study of Gastonia* (New Haven, 1942); Mary Heaton Vorse, *Strike* (Urbana, 1991); John A. Salmond, *Gastonia 1929: The Story of the Loray Mill Strike* (Chapel Hill, 1995); Weisbrod, *Radical Life*, 173–79.

30. For IWA/WIR film activities in the late 1920s and early 1930s, see U.S. House of Representatives, *Investigation of Communist Propaganda*, Pt. 4, vol. 2, pp. 11, 173–74; Pt. 5, vol. 1, pp. 3, 46, 77; vol. 2, pp. 49, 371; vol. 3, p. 49, vol. 4, pp. 19, 21–22, 595–99, 613, 618–20; William Alexander, *Film on the Left: American Documentary Film from 1931 to 1942* (Princeton, 1981); Campbell, *Cinema Strikes Back*; Kepley, "Workers' International Relief."

31. R. W. Whitney, *Reds in America* (New York, 1924), 152; *Chicago New Majority*, March 17, 1923; Chicago *Daily Worker*, March 18, 1925; New York *Daily Worker*, February 26, 1929. IWA/WIR productions were also cut or banned by officials in Seattle, Cleveland, Denver, Portland, New York, Kansas City, Mo., and numerous other cities. See Kruse, "Conquest of Films," 503, 525–26; Kruse, "Proletarian Film," 184.

32. Chicago *Daily Worker*, June 23, 1924; U.S. House of Representatives, *Investigation of Communist Propaganda*, Pt. 5, vol. 4, p. 22.

33. Chicago *Daily Worker*, April 30, 1924. The YMCA alone showed movies to 7.5 million people in 1928. "Y.M.C.A. Motion Picture Bureau," Howard Thompson Lewis, *Harvard Business Reports. Volume 8. Cases on the Motion Picture Industry* (New York, 1930), 172–81. Additional information on audience size and the variety of nontheatrical venues can be found in *Seattle Union Record*, December 6, 1923, and November 10, 1926; *NY Call*, September 8, 1922; Frank W. Collier, "The Motion Picture in Industry," *American Industries*, 21 (February 1921), 28; Daniel J. Perkins, "Sponsored Business Films: An Overview 1895–1955," *Film Reader*, 6 (1985), 128; Malcolm M. Willey and Stuart A. Rice, *Communication Agencies and Social Life* (New York, 1933), 184–85; Edward Stevenson, *Motion Pictures in Advertising and Selling* (New York, 1929), 9–10; Lewis, *Cases on the Motion Picture Industry*, 160; Earle W. Hammons, "Short Reels and Educational Subjects," in Kennedy, *Story of Films*, 151–74. Production and projector costs are described ibid.; Arthur H. Loucks, "Industrial Pictures Coming Back," *American Industries*, 24 (September 1923), 12; advertisement for the Atlas Machine Company in *American Industries*, 24 (September 1923), 39; Herbert E. Farmer, "A Survey of the Distribution of Non-Theatrical Motion Pictures," M.A. Thesis, University of Southern California, 1955, 13–16.

34. James E. Lough, "The Screen the Best Friend of Americanism," *Educational Film Magazine*, 4 (October 1920), 9; "Memorandum: Programs for Northern Pacific Railway Company," January 22, 1920, file T401, Brandon Coll. The cinematic activities of Ford are described in Mayfield Bray, *Guide to the Ford Film Collection in the National Archives* (Washington, D.C., 1970). For corporate uses of nontheatricals during this era, see Steven J. Ross, "Cinema and Class Conflict: Labor, Capital, the State, and American Silent Film," in Sklar and Musser, *Resisting Images*, 85–89; Raymond Cavanaugh, "Industrial Uses of the Motion Picture," *American Industries*, 20 (May 1920), 29; John Kelley, "Five Ways Every Factory Can Use Films," *Moving Picture Age*, 4 (January 1921), 11–12; Walter Rohde, "Elevating Morale with Moving Pictures," ibid., 4 (February 1921), 29; Harlow P. Robert, "How Our Company Uses Motion Pictures," ibid., 4 (March 1921), 17–18.

35. For synopses of films made in cooperation with corporations, see "List of Motion Pictures, U.S. Bureau of Mines. May 1921," Records of the Department of the Interior, RG 48, Box 304, NA; U.S. Employment Service, Dept. of Labor, *Industrial Films. A Source of Occupational Information* (Washington, D.C., 1946). By 1929, the Bureau had produced over fifty films in cooperation with industrial corporations. Lewis, *Case Studies of the Motion Picture Industry*, 169. Whereas films made by the Bureau of Mines were markedly favorable to capitalists, those produced by the Women's Bureau of the Department of Labor offered sympathetic depictions of the conditions and needs of women wage earners. For a discussion of these films, see U. S. Department of Labor, Women's Bureau, *2nd Annual Report of the Director of the Women's Bureau for the Fiscal Year Ended June 30, 1920* (Washington, D.C., 1920), 12, and subsequent annual reports through 1920; Ross, "Cinema and Class Conflict," 87. For a list of surviving government films, see "Motion Pictures in the National Archives," typescript finding aid, Motion Picture Room, NA.

36. Sir Gilbert Parker, quoted in *NY Call*, November 28, 1920. In 1929, over 120 industrial corporations supplied the YMCA with films. Lewis, *Cases on the Motion Picture Industry*, 176. For an overview of company recreational programs using films, see "Health and Recreation Activities in Industrial Establishments, 1926,"

Bulletin of the U.S. Bureau of Labor Statistics, no. 458 (Fall 1928); 34–41; Charles B. Raitt, *A Survey of Recreation Facilities in Rochester, New York* (Rochester, 1929), 363–75; Jackson Anderson, *Industrial Recreation: A Guide to Its Organization and Administration* (New York, 1955), 53–61; Diane Waldman. "'Toward Harmony of Interests': Rockefeller, the YMCA and the Company Movie Theater," *Wide Angle*, 8: 1 (1986), 45–48.

37. Julius Frankenberg to the Secretary of the Interior, February 2, 1923, Department of the Interior Records, RG 48, Box 304, NA; Chicago *Daily Worker*, October 6, 1924. The first advertisement for the Motion Picture Bureau appeared in the September 1922 issue of NAM's monthly periodical, *American Industries*, p. 49. The Bureau set up distribution networks in twelve areas around the nation; see ibid., 23 (July 1923), 44. For other organizations involved in distributing business films, see Frances Holley to Albert B. Fall, May 7, 1921, and W. D. Heydecker to U.S. Department of the Interior, November 23, 1922, Department of the Interior Records, RG 48, Box 304, NA; George Zehrung, "Bettering the Industrial Film," *American Industries*, 23 (April 1923), 31; *Educational Film Magazine*, 4 (August 1920), 9; Ford Motor Company to People's Institute, March 16, 1922, Box 4, NBRMP; Leslie Sprague [Community Motion Picture Bureau], *Motion Pictures in Community Service* (n.p., c. 1919–1920), and Leslie Sprague, *Motion Pictures in the Mill* (n.p., c. 1919–1920), pamphlets in Box 2, NBRMP. For the appearance of nontheatricals at the Rialto and Roxy, see *NY Call*, July 3 and August 10, 1920; Perkins, "Sponsored Business Films," 128–29.

38. First two quotes from *Seattle Union Record*, September 28, 1925; *Boston Globe* review reprinted ibid., November 13, 1925. The film was also referred to as *Am I My Brother's Keeper?* and *My Brother's Keeper*. For further information, see ibid., November 2, 14, 17, 18, 19, 1925; "Minutes of Seattle CLC," October 21, 28 and November 4, 28, 1925, Box 8, Records of Seattle CLC, UW.

39. New York *Daily Worker*, September 14, 1927. For descriptions of the strike, see Selig Perlman and Philip Taft, *History of Labor in the United States, 1896–1932* (New York, 1935), 604–5; Bernstein, *Lean Years*, 12–13. For examples of other strikes filmed by local workers, see Chicago *Daily Worker*, November 17, 1924, and March 14, 1929.

40. "Union Label and Organizing Campaign Meeting, Washington, D.C., May 6, 1925," reel 32, AFL Convention 1924; *NY Call*, July 1, 1920. For postal workers and cigarmakers, see *NY Call*, June 29, 1920; "Union Label Meeting, May 6, 1925," reel 32, AFL Convention 1924. For the use of movies by labor and the left, see *NY Call*, April 4, 1922; *LA Citizen*, April 14, 1922, and May 13, 1927; *Chicago New Majority*, March 24 and December 1, 1923; *Chicago Federation News*, July 2 and August 6, 1927; Chicago *Daily Worker*, March 18, 1924, and July 18, 1925; New York *Daily Worker*, June 2, 1927, August 7, 1928, and December 10, 1929; *Seattle Union Record*, November 5, 1927, and February 11, 1928.

41. *Seattle Union Record*, February 22, 1922.

42. Hatfield's murder and events surrounding the coal strikes and lockouts are described in Howard B. Lee, *Bloodletting in Appalachia* (Morgantown, W. Va., 1969), 57. Lee provides no further information about the film or the production company that made it. He does note that several years later, "when the public had lost all interest in the picture, the film was expressed to the theater owner from Cincinnati,

Ohio, by an unknown party." ibid., 58. Also see Lon Savage, *Thunder in the Mountains: The West Virginia Mine War, 1920–21* (Pittsburgh, 1990).

43. [William Short] President, Washington State Federation of Labor, to "WHOM ITMAY CONCERN," May 2, 1923, Box 34, Washington State Federation of Labor Papers, UW; *Chicago New Majority*, June 23, 1923.

44. In June 1924, a UMW representative asked the Chicago Federation of Labor for financial help to produce their film; he came away with a scant $100. No further mention of the UMW film appeared in the country's major labor newspapers. *Chicago New Majority*, June 21, 1924. For the making of *Matewan*, see John Sayles, *Thinking in Pictures: The Making of the Movie Matewan* (Boston, 1987). I want to thank John Sayles for helping me track down references to *Smilin' Sid*.

45. Kevin Brownlow pointed out to me that Thomas Ince made films for around $10,000 and wound up grossing $100,000; personal communication, March 25, 1996. Most contemporaneous sources, however, suggest that a modest but well-made feature was more likely to cost $40,000 to $60,000. Dollar equivalences are taken from 1919 and 1990 figures in McCusker, *How Much Is That in Real Money?*, 330, 332. Rising production costs and the problems of financing films are discussed in Jesse L. Lasky, "Production Problems," in Kennedy, *Story of Films*, 99–122; Janet Wasko, *Movies and Money: Financing the American Film Industry* (Norwood., N.J., 1982); Upton Sinclair, *Upton Sinclair Presents William Fox* (Los Angeles, 1933).

46. Ben Lyon to Upton Sinclair, September 28, 1918, file J215, Brandon Coll.; *AFL Proceedings 1919*. 341. Horsley was made an honorary member of the MPPU in July 1919. Lyon to Horsley, July 21, 1919, folder 25, Horsley Papers.

47. *AFL Proceedings 1919*, 200; Carl Stearns Clancy to Frank Morrison, July 29, 1919, reel 29, AFL Convention 1919; P. H. Peterson to Samuel Gompers, November 12, 1920, and A. J. Harriman to Gompers, November 24, 1920, reel 30, AFL Convention 1920; "Minutes of Meetings," February 22, 26, 1921, 5–6, 20–21, reel 6, AFL Executive Council Records, AFL Records. Clancy's project received the full backing of the MPPU, and the FFC came with letters of support from city and state labor federations.

48. *AFL Proceedings 1910*, 338; *AFL Proceedings 1916*, 302; "Minutes of Meetings," February 28, 1921, reel 6, AFL Executive Council Records, AFL Records. For labor film-company appeals to the AFL and subsequent replies, see Frank Morrison to Carl Stearns Clancy, July 19, 1919, reel 29, AFL Convention 1919; W. G. Lee to Samuel Gompers, June 7, 1919; Samuel Gompers to P. H. Peterson, March 5, 1921; J. Arthur Nelson to Samuel Gompers, February 25, 1921; Gompers to Nelson, March 13, 1921, all on reel 30, AFL Convention 1920; and sources in previous note.

49. Carl Clancy to Frank Morrison, July 29, 1919, reel 29, AFL Convention 1919; P. H. Peterson to Samuel Gompers, November 12, 1920, reel 30, AFL Convention 1920. On the important role the AFL could have played in facilitating distribution and exhibition, see Seymour Hastings to David Horsley, May 2, 1919, folder 28, and David Horsley to Ben Lyon, June 30, 1919, folder 25, Horsley Papers; *LA Citizen*, March 16, 1923.

50. "AFL Report on Joseph Cannon," included in Report of Agent G. J. Starr, January 8, 1921, reel 926, ICF. For coal miners and the LFS, see William Diamond to Samuel Gompers, February 26, 1921, Gompers to Diamond, March 3, 1921, both on reel 30, AFL Convention 1921. For descriptions of Cannon's and Duncan's oppo-

sition to Gompers, see *NY Call*, June 15, July 13, 1919, and June 16, 1920; Philip Taft, *The A.F. of L. in the Times of Gompers* (New York, 1957), 446–51. For Gompers' clash with the Seattle CLC, see ibid., 455–57; Frank, *Purchasing Power*, 163–90. Avis Harriman's chances of receiving help from the AFL were undoubtedly hurt by the leftist sympathies of the Vallejo Central Labor Council, which supported their Seattle brethren in their subsequent clash with the AFL. *Seattle Union Record*, November 15, 1923.

51. *United Mine Workers' Journal*, 30 (April 15, 1919), 6; 34 (October 1, 1923), 12; and 34 (September 15, 1923), 12; *Proceedings of the 22nd Annual Convention. California State Federation of Labor. San Jose, October 3–7, 1921* (San Francisco, 1921), 74. Scharrenberg was secretary-treasurer of the California Federation of Labor. For an overview of the tensions between the UMW and communist miners and the problems of boring from within, see Alan Singer, "Communists and Coal Miners: Rank-and-File Organizing in the United Mine Workers of America during the 1920s," *Science and Society*, 55 (Summer 1991), 132–57; Perlman and Taft, *History of Labor*, 538–61.

52. *AFL Proceedings 1921*, 335. A year earlier, James Duncan offered a similar motion calling on labor "to interest itself in the use of the film to exploit its own educational work." No action was taken on his proposal. *AFL Proceedings 1920*, 467.

53. *AFL Proceedings 1922*, 139. The Executive Council estimated that the average cost of a film that "could compete with the pictures now in the market, would range between $60,000 and $75,000" ($469,000 to $586,000 in 1990 dollars); ibid.

54. *Journal of Electrical Workers*, 26 (November 1927), 587; 27 (February 1928), 61. The call for a theater chain was first sounded by the journal's editors in September 1927 and then picked up by Local #40. See ibid., 26 (September 1927), 463. William Kruse proposed a similar plan in October 1924, but his idea was ignored by AFL leaders. Chicago *Daily Worker*, October 29, 1924.

55. *Journal of Electrical Workers*, 27 (February 1928), 109, 61.

56. Koszarski, *Evening's Entertainment*, 83; *Journal of Electrical Workers*, 27 (February 1928), 61, 60. For examples of successful movie theaters run by workers, many of them out of labor temple auditoriums, see John Daniels, *America via the Neighborhoods* (New York, 1920), 330; *United Mine Workers' Journal*, 31 (March 15, 1920), 14, (April 1, 1920), 17; and sources in Chapter 6 note 55.

57. *Journal of Electrical Workers*, 27 (February 1928), 109; Beaton quoted ibid., 59; *Chicago Federation News*, March 17, 1928. For a sampling of responses, see *Journal of Electrical Workers*, 27 (March 1928), 129, (May 1928), 252, and (September 1928), 475; New York *Daily Worker*, February 15, 1928.

58. Author interview with David Beck, July 20, 1988, Seattle, Wa. For Beck's career, see Jonathan Dembo, *Unions and Politics in Washington State 1885–1935* (New York, 1983); John D. McCallum, *Dave Beck* (Mercer Island, Wa., 1978).

59. *Industrial Worker*, December 23, 1922.

60. *AFL Proceedings 1922*, 140; *Journal of Electrical Workers* 27 (May 1928), 261. Reports of central labor council meetings printed in labor newspapers are filled with admonitions to union families who patronized blacklisted movie houses.

61. Garsson quoted in Chicago *Daily Worker*, November 14, 1925; *New York Times*, December 13, 1925. The FTC charges are cited ibid., April 28 and June 21, 1928; Benjamin Hampton, *A History of the Movies* (New York, 1931), 364–68. For

the consolidation of the studio system during these years, see Lewis, *Cases on Motion Picture Industry*; Kennedy, *Story of Films*; and sources cited in Chapter 5 note 8.

62. Upton Sinclair to Maxine Alton, November 17, 1922, file J215, Brandon Coll.; Pickford quoted in Lewis, *Cases on Motion Picture Industry*, 248.

63. Chicago *Daily Worker*, April 14, 1924; New York Motion Picture Commission, *Annual Report of the Moving Picture Commission for the Year 1922* (Albany, 1922), 10; *Jungle* intertitles quoted in a typescript report by MDF, "The Jungle," Motion Picture Commission of the State of New York, c. October 1927, file M247, Brandon Coll.; quotes from the 1932 New York censors' report are cited in Harry Alan Potamkin, "Who Owns the Movie?" *Workers Theatre*, 1 (April 1932), 21. The film was retitled *Volga to Gastonia*.

64. Figures are from Hampton, *History of Movies*, 383. By 1930, all Chicago theaters with seating capacities greater than 1,500 were wired for sound; fewer than a quarter of those seating less than 350 had done so. Cohen, *Making a New Deal*, 128. On the money needed for sound wiring, see J. Douglas Gomery, "The Coming of the Talkies: Invention, Innovation, and Diffusion," in Balio, *American Film Industry*, 193–211; Harry Warner, "Future Developments," in Kennedy, *Story of Films*, 330–31. Chicago comment on silent films mentioned in Cohen, *Making a New Deal*, 127.

65. In 1925, AFL convention delegates called upon the Executive Council to open a national radio station to bring the AFL's message to the masses. *AFL Proceedings 1925*, 316; *AFL Proceedings 1926*, 59–61, 247–48; *AFL Proceedings 1927*, 74–75, 169–70, 319, 379. The efforts of unionists and socialists to use radio are discussed in Nathan Godfried, "The Origins of Labor Radio: WCFL, the 'Voice of Labor,' 1925–1928," *Historical Journal of Film, Radio and Television*, 7 (1987), 143–159; Robert W. McChesney, "Labor and the Marketplace of Ideas: WCFL and the Battle for Labor Radio Broadcasting, 1927–1934," *Journalism Monographs*, no. 134 (August 1992); Sara U. Douglas, *Labor's New Voice: Unions and the Mass Media* (Norwood, N.J., 1986); Cohen, *Making a New Deal*, 136–42; "Radio Broadcasting," reel 33, AFL Convention 1925; *LA Citizen*, August 21, 1925, July 23, 1926, and April 15, 1927; *Seattle Union Record*, August 29 and December 14, 1925, March 5 and October 27, 1927; *Chicago Federation News*, January 9, 1926. For a superb account of the struggles for control of radio, see Robert W. McChesney, *Telecommunications, Mass Media, and Democracy: The Battle for Control of U. S. Broadcasting, 1928–1935* (New York, 1993).

66. Biographical information was compiled from sources cited in Chapter 6 note 30.

67. *Los Angeles Examiner*, May 18, 1928. For coverage of the case and trial, see Ibid., June 11, 28, 30, 1928.

68. Rohama Lee, "The First 50 Years Were the Hardest," *Film News*, 28 (September 1971), 6–9; Kruse interview with Merritt and Kepley, January 18, 1975.

69. For an overview of Sinclair's life, see Leon Harris, *Upton Sinclair: American Rebel* (New York, 1975); on the thwarted film partnership with Eisenstein, see Ronald Gottesman and Harry Geduld, *Eisenstein and Sinclair: The Making and Unmaking of 'Que Viva Mexico'* (Bloomington, 1979); for Sinclair's account of the phony newsreel campaign, see William J. Perlman, ed., *The Movies on Trial* (1936), 189–95.

70. *Los Angeles Examiner*, March 15, 1929, July 8, 1932, and February 24, 1933; *New York Times*, February 24, 1933; *Variety*, February 28, 1933.

71. For Clancy's various screen credits, see Kenneth W. Munden, ed., *American Film Institute Catalog of Motion Pictures Produced in the United States. Feature Films 1921–1930*, 2 vols. (New York and London, 1971), 1: 7, 330, 536, 728; New York *Daily Worker*, May 26, 1928.

Epilogue
The Movies Talk But What Do They Say?

1. For analyses of *Hoffa* and its historical inaccuracies, see Sean Wilentz, "Tales of Hoffa," *New Republic*, 208 (February 1, 1993), 53; Murray Kempton, "The Jumper: *Hoffa*," *New York Review of Books*, 40 (February 11, 1993), 31; Bryant Simon, "*Hoffa*," *American Historical Review*, 98 (October 1993), 1,184–86.

2. The *Fortune* February 1940 survey results are cited in Arthur Marwick, *Class: Image and Reality in Britain, France, and the USA Since 1930* (New York, 1980), 105–7; Harold L. Wilenski, "Class, Class Consciousness, and American Workers," in William Haber, ed., *Labor in a Changing America* (New York, 1966), 17; Linda Dittmar, "All That Hollywood Allows: Film and the Working Class," *Radical Teacher*, 46 (Spring 1995), 39; Barbara Ehrenreich, *Fear of Falling: The Inner Life of the Middle Class* (New York, 1989), 4. For surveys dealing with American perceptions of class, see Richard Centers, *The Psychology of Social Class* (Princeton, 1949); Joseph A. Kahl, *The American Class Structure* (New York, 1957); Richard F. Hamilton, *Class and Politics in the United States* (New York, 1972); Reeve Vanneman and Lynn Weber Cannon, *The American Perception of Class* (Philadelphia, 1987).

3. John Howard Lawson, *Film in the Battle of Ideas* (New York, 1953), 98; Ken Margolies, "Silver Screen Tarnishes Unions: How Hollywood Movies Have Given Workers a Black Eye," *Screen Actor*, 23 (Summer 1981), 43; Schrank quoted in Barbara Isenberg, "Unions Are Looking for the TV Label," *Los Angeles Times*, November 9, 1980, Calendar Section.

4. For a detailed analysis of the depiction of working people in television and news, see International Association of Machinists and Aerospace Workers, *IAM Television Entertainment Report, Part II: Conclusions and National Summary of Occupational Frequency in Network Primetime Entertainment for February 1980* (Washington, D.C., 1980), and *Network News and Documentary Report: A Member Survey and Analysis* (Washington, D.C., 1980). For two overviews of media treatment of workers and labor unions, see Sara U. Douglas, *Labor's New Voice: Unions and the Mass Media* (Norwood, N.J., 1986); William J. Puette, *Through Jaundiced Eyes: How the Media View Organized Labor* (Ithaca, 1992).

5. My discussion of labor-capital films of the sound era is based on my viewing of forty-five films and extensive reading of secondary sources. The following are especially useful for describing mainstream cinematic depictions of workers, unions, and radicals: Peter Stead, *Film and the Working Class: The Feature Film in British and American Society* (London, 1989); Tom Zaniello, *Working Stiffs, Union Maids, Reds, and Riffraff: An Organized Guide to Films about Labor* (Ithaca, 1996); David E. James and Rick Berg, eds., *The Hidden Foundation: Cinema and the Question of Class* (Minneapolis, 1996); Tino Balio, *Grand Design: Hollywood as a Modern Business Enterprise, 1930–1939* (New York, 1993); Peter Roffman and Jim Purdy, *The Hollywood Social Problem Film: Madness, Despair, and Politics from the Depression to*

the Fifties (Bloomington, 1981); Harry Alan Potamkin, *The Compound Cinema: The Film Writings of Harry Alan Potamkin* (New York, 1977); Michael Rogin, *Ronald Reagan, the Movie and Other Episodes in Political Demonology* (Berkeley, 1987); Stanley Aronowitz, *False Promises: The Shaping of American Class Consciousness* (New York, 1973); George Lipsitz, *Rainbow at Midnight: Labor and Culture in the 1940s* (Urbana, 1994); Peter Biskind, *Seeing Is Believing: How Hollywood Taught Us to Stop Worrying and Love the Fifties* (New York, 1983); Michael Ryan and Douglas Kellner, *Camera Politica: The Politics and Ideology of Contemporary Hollywood Film* (Bloomington, 1990); David Manning White and Richard Averson, *The Celluloid Weapon: Social Comment in the American Film* (Boston, 1972); Lewis Jacobs, *The Rise of the American Film: A Critical History* (New York, 1968); Terry Christensen, *Reel Politics: American Political Movies from Birth of a Nation to Platoon* (New York, 1987); James Combs, *American Political Movies: An Annotated Filmography of Feature Films* (New York and London, 1990); Brian Neve, *Film and Politics in America: A Social Tradition* (London and New York, 1992); Robert Sklar, *Movie-Made America: A Cultural History of American Movies* (New York, 1994); David Platt, ed., *Celluloid Power: Social Film Criticism from "The Birth of a Nation" to "Judgment at Nuremberg"* (Metuchen, N.J., 1992); Peter Roffman and Jim Purdy, "The Worker and Hollywood," *Cineaste*, 9: 1 (1978), 8–13; Lynn Garafola, "Hollywood and the Myth of the Working Class," *Radical America*, 14 (January/February 1980), 7–15; Al Auster et al., "Hollywood and the Working Class: A Discussion," *Socialist Review*, 9 (July/August 1979), 109–21; Francis R. Walsh, "The Films We Never Saw: American Movies View Organized Labor, 1934–1954," *Labor History*, 27 (Fall 1986), 564–80; Douglas, *Labor's New Voice*; Puette, *Through Jaundiced Eyes*; Marwick, *Class*; Dittmar, "All That Hollywood Allows"; Margolies, "Silver Screen Tarnishes Unions."

6. Report of a Special Task Force to the Secretary of Health, Education and Welfare, *Work in America*, 34.

7. For films featuring radical agitators stirring up trouble among workers, see *Red Dust* (MGM 1932), *The Power and the Glory* (1933), *Riffraff* (MGM 1935). Red agents were also shown causing trouble among student activists during the Popular Front campaigns of the 1930s; see *Red Salute* (1935), *Fighting Youth* (1935), and *Soak the Rich* (1936).

8. Prologue quoted in Puette, *Through Jaundiced Eyes*, 23. For analyses of more recent images of union corruption and labor's links to organized crime, see Frank Stricker, "Hollywood Meets the Unions," *New Labor Review*, 2 (Fall 1978), 111–18; Al Auster and Leonard Quart, "The Working Class Goes Hollywood: 'F.I.S.T.' and 'Blue Collar,'" *Cineaste*, 9: 1 (1978), 4–7; Gay P. Zieger and Robert H. Zieger, "Unions on the Silver Screen: A Review Essay of F.I.S.T., Blue Collar, and Norma Rae," *Labor History*, 23 (Winter 1982), 67–78; and the sources in note 5 above.

9. Frank Stricker, "Repressing the Working Class: Individualism and the Masses in Frank Capra's Films," *Labor History*, 31 (Fall 1990), 455.

10. Clayton R. Koppes and Gregory D. Black, *Hollywood Goes to War: How Politics, Profits, and Propaganda Shaped World War II Movies* (New York, 1987), 4.

11. Stead, *Film and the Working Class*, 77. For discussions of censorship from the 1930s to the 1950s, see Raymond Moley, *The Hays Office* (New York, 1945); Leonard J. Leff and Jerold L. Simmons, *The Dame in the Kimono: Hollywood, Censorship, and the Production Code from the 1920s to the 1960s* (New York, 1990);

Gregory D. Black, *Hollywood Censored: Morality Codes, Catholics, and the Movies* (New York, 1994); Francis G. Couvares, ed., *Movie Censorship and American Culture* (Washington, D.C., 1996); Frank Walsh, *Sin and Censorship: The Catholic Church and the Motion Picture Industry* (New Haven, 1996); Richard Maltby, *Harmless Entertainment: Hollywood and the Ideology of Consensus* (Metuchen, N.J. 1983); Sklar, *Movie-Made America*.

12. Undated script, *Black Hell*, Special Collections, USC, quoted in Walsh, "Films We Never Saw," 566. Walsh shows how studios were repeatedly forced to tone down pro-labor films to the point where their class politics either disappeared or were transformed into far more conservative messages than were originally intended by the screenwriter.

13. Robert Lord to Hall Wallis, May 2, 1934; Joseph I. Breen to Jack L. Warner, September 2, 1934; Wallis, "Inter-Office Memo," September 13, 1934, all quoted in Walsh, "Films We Never Saw," 566–67. For further information about Judge Musmanno, the original screenplay, and the subsequent changes, see Jacob Lawrence, *Actor: The Life and Times of Paul Muni* (New York, 1974), 184, 200–5.

14. *New York Times*, April 6, 1935; Lawrence, *Actor*, 205.

15. Auster and Quart, "Working Class Goes to Hollywood," 4. Exhibition revenue figures are taken from Mae Hettig, *Economic Control of the Motion Picture Industry* (Philadelphia, 1944), 61, 69. Despite its reputation as the "workingman's studio" of the 1930s, Warner Brothers, argues Tino Balio, "typically sidestepped [contentious] issues by narrowing the focus of the exposé to a specific case or by resolving problems at the personal level of the protagonist rather than at the societal level." The studio produced topical films about working-class life largely as a cost-saving venture rather than out of a commitment to popular causes. Balio, *Grand Design*, 281.

16. Lester Cole, *Hollywood Red: The Autobiography of Lester Cole* (Palo Alto, 1981), 424. The organizing efforts of screenwriters and actors are described ibid.; John Howard Lawson, *Film: The Creative Process* (New York, 1964); Murray Ross, *Stars and Strikes: Unionization of Hollywood* (New York, 1941); David F. Prindle, *The Politics of Glamour: Ideology and Democracy in the Screen Actors Guild* (Madison, 1988); Danae Clark, *Negotiating Hollywood: The Cultural Politics of Actors' Labor* (Minneapolis, 1995); Lary May, "Movie Star Politics: The Screen Actors' Guild, Cultural Conversion, and the Hollywood Red Scare," in Lary May, ed., *Recasting America: Culture and Politics in the Age of the Cold War* (Chicago, 1989), 125–53; Marjorie Penn Lasky, "Off Camera: A History of the Screen Actors Guild during the Era of the Studio System," Ph.D. dissertation, University of California, Davis, 1992.

17. For accounts of the mob's penetration of IATSE, its dealings with movie industry leaders, and worker efforts to oppose their arrangements, see George H. Dunne, *Hollywood Labor Dispute: A Study in Immorality* (Los Angeles, 1950); Mike Nielsen and Gene Mailes, *Hollywood's Other Blacklist: Union Struggles in the Studio System* (London, 1995); Robert Joseph, "Re: Unions in Hollywood," *Films*, 11 (Summer 1940), 34–50; Denise Hartsough, "Crime Pays: The Studios' Labor Deals in the 1930s," *Velvet Light Trap*, 23 (Spring 1989), 49–63; Larry Ceplair, "A Communist Labor Organizer in Hollywood: Jeff Kibre Challenges the IATSE, 1937–1939," ibid., 64–74; Ida Jeter, "The Collapse of the Federated Motion Picture Crafts: A Case Study of Class Collaboration in the Motion Picture Industry," *Journal of the University Film*

Association, 31 (Spring 1979), 37–45; Michael C. Nielsen, "Motion Picture Craft Workers and Craft Unions in Hollywood: The Studio Era, 1912–1948," Ph.D. dissertation, University of Illinois, 1985; Laurie Pintar, "Off Screen Realities: A History of Labor Activism in Hollywood, 1933–1942," Ph.D. dissertation, University of Southern California, 1995; Ross, *Stars and Strikes*; Cole, *Hollywood Red*.

18. Albert Warner quoted in Steven Vaughn, *Ronald Reagan in Hollywood: Movies and Politics* (Cambridge and New York, 1994), 135; Judge Kern quoted in Dunne, *Hollywood Labor Dispute*, 7.

19. James R. Silke, *Here's Looking at You Kid: Fifty Years of Fighting, Working, and Dreaming at Warner Brothers* (Boston, 1976), 299. For a general history of strikes and studio labor relations in the 1930s and 1940s, see Louis B. Perry and Richard S. Perry, *A History of the Los Angeles Labor Movement, 1911–1941* (Berkeley and Los Angeles, 1963); and sources in note 17. For Reagan's role, see Vaughn, *Ronald Reagan in Hollywood*, 133–44.

20. Auster and Quart, "Working Class Goes to Hollywood," 6; Puette, *Through Jaundiced Eyes*, 29. For other films that stress mob-union ties, see *Inside Detroit* (1956), *Slaughter on Tenth Avenue* (1957), *The Garment Jungle* (1957), *Never Steal Anything Small* (1959), and *Blue Collar* (1978).

21. Thomas cited in Lawson, *Film in the Battle of Ideas*, 12. For government efforts to influence depictions of class relations during World War II, see Koppes and Black, *Hollywood Goes to War*.

22. Biskind, *Seeing Is Believing*, 25, 173; the figure for anti-communist films comes from ibid., 162. For a superb discussion of Communism and Cold War films, see Rogin, *Ronald Reagan, the Movie*, 236–71. For overviews of the Red Scare's impact on the movie industry, see John Cogley, *Report on Blacklisting: I. Movies* (n.p., 1956); Larry Ceplair and Steven Englund, *The Inquisition in Hollywood: Politics in the Film Community, 1930–1960* (Berkeley, 1983); Thom Anderson, "Red Hollywood," in Suzanne Ferguson and Barbara Groseclose, eds., *Literature and the Visual Arts in Contemporary Society* (Columbus, Ohio, 1986), 141–96.

23. Elvis quoted in Margolies, "Silver Screen Tarnishes Unions," 51. Dramas and comedies that disparage unions include *Teachers* (1984), *The River* (1984), *My Favorite Year* (1982), and *Armed and Dangerous* (1986). For a sampling of movies dealing with labor unions from the 1930s to the present, see Richard P. Krafsur, ed., *American Film Institute Catalog of Motion Pictures Produced in the United States, Feature Films, 1961–1970*, 2 vols. (New York, 1976); and sources in notes 5 and 8.

24. Mills, "The Unions and the Mobs," 97; *Los Angeles Times*, June 2, 1996, M5.

25. Jacobs, *Rise of American Film*, 518. For radical filmmaking in the 1930s and 1940s, see "Class-Struggle through the Camera," *Workers' Theater*, 1 (February 1932), 29–31; *Filmfront*, reprint edition edited and annotated by Anthony Slide (Metuchen, N.J., 1986); Herbert Cline, ed., *New Theatre and Film* (San Diego, 1985); "NATIVE LAND: An Interview with Leo Hurwitz," *Cineaste*, 6: 3 (1974), 2–7; Mari Jo Buhle, Paul Buhle, and Dan Georgakas, *Encyclopedia of the American Left*, (New York, 1990), 630–33; and sources in Preface, note 2.

26. Most of the films mentioned here can be found in the AFL-CIO Film Collection housed in the Motion Picture Room, NA. The filmmaking activities of labor unions are described in Albert Hemsing, "Labor and the Film," in Cecile Starr, ed., *Ideas on Film: A Handbook for the 16mm Film User* (New York, 1951), 35–38; special

issue on "American Labor Films," *Film Library Quarterly*, 12: 213 (1979); Douglas, *Labor's New Voice*; Buhle et al., *Encyclopedia of the American Left*, 798–801. For union forays into television, see Jack Howard, "Labor Day: San Francisco,'" *The Quarterly of Film, Radio and Television*, 10 (Fall 1955), 42–43; AFL-CIO, *Film for Labor*, publication 22 (Washington, D.C., 1979); Fred Glass, "Labor and New Media Technology: A Union of Necessity," *Labor Studies Journal*, 9 (Fall 1984), 131–50; Glass, "A Locally Based Labor Media Strategy," ibid., 14 (Winter 1989), 3–17; Puette, *Through Jaundiced Eyes*; Douglas, *Labor's New Voice*.

27. *Salt of the Earth* was completed in 1953 but not released until 1954.

28. Biberman's company was known as the Independent Productions Corporation.

29. Quotations are taken from the film.

30. Jackson's diatribe is quoted in Stead, *Film and the Working Class*, 168. *Salt of the Earth* remained popular on college campuses, art circuit theaters, and abroad (it won the International Grand Prix for the best film shown in France in 1955). For favorable reporting about the film, see *Hollywood Review*, March-April 1953 through November-December 1954. The best accounts of the difficulties in making and exhibiting the film can be found in Herbert Biberman, *Salt of the Earth: The Story of a Film* (Boston, 1965); Deborah Silverton Rosenfelt and Michael Wilson, *Salt of the Earth* (Old Westbury, N.Y, 1978).

31. John Sayles, *Thinking in Pictures: The Making of the Movie Matewan* (Boston, 1987), 39. Sayles' book contains a complete copy of the shooting script.

32. Puette, *Through Jaundiced Eyes*, 30.

33. Auster and Quart, "Working Class Goes to Hollywood," 7. For left filmmaking since the 1960s, see Peter Stevens, ed., *Jump Cut: Hollywood, Politics and Counter Cinema* (New York, 1985); Bill Nichols, *Newsreel: Documentary Filmmaking on the American Left* (New York, 1980); Michael Renov, "Newsreel: Old and New—Toward an Historical Profile," *Film Quarterly*, 41 (Fall 1987), 20–33; Eric Breitbart, "Point of Production: Films about Work and Workers," *Cineaste*, 7: 2 (1976), 26–29; "Radical American Film? A Questionnaire," *Cineaste*, 4: 1 (1973), 14–21; Dan Georgakas, "The Wobblies: The Making of a Historical Documentary," *Cineaste*, 10 (Spring 1980), 14–19, 58.

34. *U.S. News and World Report*, March 30, 1981, 39; *Newsweek*, July 8, 1996, 44. The U.S. Labor Department reported that the median weekly wage of full-time union workers rose $21 in 1987 as opposed to a $17 increase for non-union workers. *Los Angeles Times*, January 23, 1988.

35. Patrick Murphy quoted in *Journal of Electrical Workers and Operators*, 27 (February 1928), 60.

36. When we add in labor organizations that do not belong to the AFL-CIO, the total number of American unionists in 1996 is nearly 17 million. Making feature films is not beyond the financial reach of the AFL-CIO. It spent nearly "$35 million to elect a Democratic Congress and to re-elect Bill Clinton" in 1996. James Weinstein, "Conventional Wisdom," *In These Times*, 20 (June 24, 1996), 27.

Index